LEGAL CHALLENGES IN THE GLOBAL FINANCIAL CRISIS

The global financial and economic crisis which started in 2008 has had devastating effects around the globe. It has caused a rethinking in different areas of law, and posed new challenges to regulators and private actors alike. One of the emerging issues is the apparent eclipse of boundaries between different legal disciplines: financial and corporate lawyers have to learn how public law instruments can complement their traditional governance tools; conversely, public lawyers have had to come to understand the specificities of the financial markets they intend to regulate.

While commentary on financial regulation and the global financial crisis abounds, it tends to remain within disciplinary boundaries. This volume not only brings together scholarship from different areas of law (constitutional and administrative law, EU law, financial law and regulation), but also from a variety of backgrounds (academia, practice, policy making) and a number of different jurisdictions.

The volume illustrates how interdisciplinary scholarship belongs at the centre of any discussion of the economic crisis, and indeed regulation theory more generally. This is a timely exploration of cutting-edge issues of financial regulation.

Volume 18 Studies of the Oxford Institute of European and Comparative Law

Studies of the Oxford Institute of European and Comparative Law

Editor
Professor Stefan Vogenauer

Board of Advisory Editors
Professor Mark Freedland, FBA
Professor Stephen Weatherill
Professor Derrick Wyatt, QC

Recent titles in this Series

Legal Challenges in the Global Financial Crisis

Bail-outs, the Euro and Regulation

Edited by

Wolf-Georg Ringe

and

Peter M Huber

·HART·
PUBLISHING
OXFORD AND PORTLAND, OREGON
2014

Published in the United Kingdom by Hart Publishing Ltd
16C Worcester Place, Oxford, OX1 2JW
Telephone: +44 (0)1865 517530
Fax: +44 (0)1865 510710
E-mail: mail@hartpub.co.uk
Website: http://www.hartpub.co.uk

Published in North America (US and Canada) by
Hart Publishing
c/o International Specialized Book Services
920 NE 58th Avenue, Suite 300
Portland, OR 97213-3786
USA
Tel: +1 503 287 3093 or toll-free: (1) 800 944 6190
Fax: +1 503 280 8832
E-mail: orders@isbs.com
Website: http://www.isbs.com

Hart Publishing is an imprint of Bloomsbury Publishing plc

British Library Cataloguing in Publication Data
Data Available

ISBN: 978-1-84946-439-0

Typeset by Hope Services, Abingdon
Printed and bound in Great Britain by
TJ International Ltd, Padstow, Cornwall

CONTENTS

LIST OF CONTRIBUTORS

Thomas Ackermann holds the Chair of Civil Law and European and International Business Law at LMU. He studied Law at the Universities of Bonn and Cambridge, obtaining his doctorate in Bonn in 1997 with a thesis on the 'rule of reason' in European anti-trust law. In 2004, he completed his dissertation in Bonn on the protection of the reliance interest, a fundamental topic in the law of obligations. In the same year, he was appointed to the Chair of German, European and International Civil and Business Law at the University of Erlangen-Nürnberg. His research interests cover the legal constitution of markets, with particular reference to the areas of contract law and competition law. His work has a special focus on the European dimension of these subjects. Thomas Ackermann is a member of the Editorial Board of the 'Common Market Law Review', the leading international peer-review journal in the area of European Union law. He is a member of the Munich Risk and Insurance Center and of the Faculty of the International Max Planck School for Competition and Innovation as well as head of the Munich University Summer Training Programme in German and European Law.

Pavlos Eleftheriadis, BA (Athens), LLM, PhD (Cambridge), MA, is a University Lecturer in the Faculty of Law and Fellow and Tutor in Law at Mansfield College. He is also a barrister in England and Wales. He joined Oxford in 2003 from the London School of Economics. He was a Visiting Professor at Columbia University in 2001 and was awarded the Bodossaki Prize for Law in 2005. He teaches and publishes in the areas of philosophy of law, European Union law and constitutional law.

Christos Hadjiemmanuil is a Professor of International and European Monetary and Financial Institutions at the University of Piraeus and a Visiting Professor at the Department of Law of the London School of Economics. He is a member of the Athens Bar Association.

Born in 1964, he studied law at Athens University (LLB) and University College London (LLM and PhD). His first academic appointment was at the Centre for Commercial Law Studies (CCLS) of Queen Mary, University of London. From 1997 to 2007 he was Lecturer, Senior Lecturer and then Reader in Law with the LSE Department of Law. A specialist in European and international financial law and regulation, he has acted as a consultant to the International Monetary Fund (IMF), where he advised in the Global Bank Insolvency Initiative. He has also served as member of the Advisory Board of the UNDP's Regional for Public Administration Reform (RCPAR) for Eastern Europe and the CIS. He has held a number of visiting academic and consultancy positions and is a member of the Monetary Law Committee of the International Law Association (MOCOMILA).

From May 2004 until September 2007, he served as President and CEO of Hellenic Olympic Properties, the special-purpose company responsible for post-Olympic management of the Athens 2004 Olympic facilities. From September 2007 until December 2009, he was Chairman and CEO of OPAP SA, one of Greece's largest public corporations. He has been President, and is now a member of the Governing Board of the Athens-based Center for Political Research, Greece's oldest nongovernmental think-tank.

Alexander Hellgardt studied Law and Philosophy at Eberhard-Karls-University Tübingen (First State Exam, 2002; BA, 2003), the University of Hamburg (PhD, 2008) and Harvard University (LLM, 2009) and completed his practical legal training in Hamburg (Second State Exam, 2008). He worked as a research associate with Professor Klaus J Hopt at the Max Planck Institute for Comparative and International Private Law in Hamburg (2003–08). Since 2009 he has been a senior research fellow with Professor Wolfgang Schön at the Max Planck Institute for Tax Law and Public Finance and Lecturer in Law at Ludwig-Maximilians-University in Munich. He was an academic visitor to the Oxford Faculty of Law and the Oxford University Centre for Business Taxation in 2012. His research interests encompass capital market law, company law and the theory of private law.

Peter M Huber is Professor of Public Law and Legal Philosophy at the Faculty of Law of the University of Munich, where he is also Director of the Research Centre for the Law of European Integration. From 2009 to 2010 he served as Minister of the Interior of the Free State of Thuringia. Since November 2011 he has been a Justice of the Federal Constitutional Court of Germany (Second Senate). He is the author of several books and over 300 articles on constitutional and administrative law, European Union law and human rights, including (with A von Bogdandy and others (eds)) *Handbuch Ius Publicum Europaeum* vol 1, 2007; vol 2, 2008; vol 3, 2010; vol 4, 2011; more volumes projected.

Gregor Kirchhof, born 1971, studied law in Freiburg, London and Munich (First and Second State Examinations in Law, Munich, 1998 and 2000). He completed his legal traineeship with Landgericht München 1 and was research assistant to Professor Dr Udo Di Fabio, former judge of the Federal Constitutional Court, at the University of Munich from 2001 to 2002. He was senior research assistant to Professor Di Fabio at the University of Bonn from 2003 to 2008. He studied at the University of Notre Dame, USA (LLM), London Law Program; Fachanwalt für Steuerrecht, Munich (qualifying examination to practise as a specialist tax lawyer) and attained his Doctorate and Habilitation in Law from the University of Bonn (2005 and 2009). Gregor was Acting Professor at the Universities of Hannover, Munich and Augsburg (2009–11); Professor at the University of Munich (2011–12) and has held the Chair of Public Law, Finance Law and Tax Law at the University of Augsburg since 2012.

John McEldowney is Professor of Law at the University of Warwick and currently Chair of the Study of Parliament Group. He has published widely in the fields of public law including legal history and environmental law. He has held a number of visiting positions and in 2001 he was elected the New Zealand Law Foundation Distinguished Visiting Fellow. He has given evidence to many select committees and his recent publications include: 'Managing financial risk: the precautionary principle and protecting the public interest in the UK' in John Raymond LaBrosse, Rodrigo Olivares–Caminal and Dalvinder Singh (eds), *Managing Risk in the Financial System* (London, Edward Elgar, 2011) 449–72 and J and S McEldowney, 'Science and Environmental Law: Collaboration Across the Double Helix' (2011) 13(3) *Environmental Law Review* 169–98. In 2000 he was the World Bank Visiting Fellow in the Supreme Court in Venezuela. In 2004 he was awarded a medal of honour from the University of Lille.

Christoph Ohler currently holds the Chair of Public Law, European Law, International Law and International Economic Law at the Friedrich-Schiller-University in Jena, Germany. Prior to joining academia he worked as a lawyer for an international law firm in Frankfurt/Main in the field of structured finance and banking supervision. Since 2009 he has been the spokesperson for a graduate pro-gramme on financial stability funded by the Deutsche Bundesbank. His areas of research comprise financial regulation, EMU and the constitutional processes of the EU.

Conor Quigley QC is a barrister and a research fellow at the Institute of European and Comparative Law at Oxford University. He specialises in European and com-petition law. He has appeared in many leading cases in the UK in the High Court, Court of Appeal, House of Lords, Supreme Court and in the European Union General Court and the Court of Justice. He has been involved in investigations and complaints before the European Commission and the Office of Fair Trading. Clients include public and private companies, private individuals and UK public authorities. He is identified in both Legal 500 and Chambers & Partners Directory as a leading silk in EU, competition and public procurement law.

Wolf-Georg Ringe is Professor of International Commercial Law at Copenhagen Business School and a Departmental Lecturer at the University of Oxford. He is an associate member of the Oxford-Man Institute of Quantitative Finance and a research fellow at the Oxford Institute of European and Comparative Law. He has held visiting positions at Columbia Law School, New York, Essec Business School, Paris, and at IDC Herzliyah, Israel. As part of a European-wide consortium, he regularly advises the European Parliament on issues of European company law. His current research interests are in the general area of law and finance, corporate insolvency law, (comparative) corporate governance, financial regulation and the conflict of laws.

Gustaf Sjöberg is Associate Professor of Private Law at Stockholm Centre for Commercial Law, Faculty of Law, Stockholm University. He is a member of the Board of the Swedish Financial Supervisory Agency and a member of the

Government Inquiry, the Financial Crisis Committee and an Expert in the Government Inquiry on Life Insurance.

After training to become an Associate Judge of Appeal, he went on to serve in the government offices mainly working with financial legislation. He serves regularly on different Government Inquiries in the financial field including central banking.

Rudolf Streinz studied Law, Political Science and History at Ludwig-Maximilians-University in Munich. He attained his First and Second Legal State Examinations in Bavaria; a Doctorate (Dr iur) at Ludwig-Maximilian-University; and Habilitation (Dr iur habil) in Public Law (Constitutional and Administrative Law), Public International Law, European Community Law at Passau University. Rudolf held the Chair of Public Law, Public International Law and European Community Law and was Director of the Institute of German and European Food Law in the Faculty of Law and Economics of Bayreuth University from 1989 to 2003. He has also held the Chair of Public Law and European Community Law in the Faculty of Law of Ludwig-Maximilians-University, Munich since 2003 and from 2005 to 2007 he was the Dean of the Faculty of Law. His main areas of research are European Union law, German public law, public international law, German and European food law and sports law. He is the author of around 400 publications, including *Europarecht*, 9th edn (Heidelberg, CF Müller, 2012); *EUV/AEUV-Kommentar* (*TEU/TFEU-Commentary*), 2nd edn (Munich, CH Beck, 2012 (ed)). His publications in English include 'European Integration through Constitutional Law' in H Blanke and S Mangiameli (ed), *Governing Europe under a Constitution. The Hard Road from the European Treaties to a European Constitutional Treaty* (Berlin/Heidelberg, Springer, 2006) 122; 'Risk decisions in cases of persisting scientific uncertainty: the precautionary principle in European food law' in G Woodman and D Klippel (eds), *Risk and the Law* (Oxford/New York, Routledge/Cavendish, 2009) 53–74.

Dr John Vella is a Senior Research Fellow at the Oxford University Centre for Business Taxation and a member of the Faculty of Law at the University of Oxford. John studied Law at the University of Malta (BA and LLD) and at the University of Cambridge (LLM and PhD). Prior to his current post he was Norton Rose Career Development Fellow in Company Law at the Faculty of Law at Oxford. John has been a Program Affiliate Scholar at New York University and has acted as a co-arbitrator in a tax dispute before the ICC International Court of Arbitration. In November 2011 he gave evidence twice before the House of Lords EU Sub-Committee A on Financial Transaction Taxes (November 2011 and March 2013) and before the Parliamentary Commission on Banking Standards, on the role of tax in relation to banking standards and culture (January 2013). His main research interests are in the taxation and regulation of the financial sector, corporate and international taxation, and tax administration.

Paul Yowell has been Fellow and Tutor in Law at Oriel College, Oxford since 2012. Prior to that he was Lecturer in Law at New College, and a postdoctoral fellow with the Oxford Law Faculty for the AHRC project Parliaments and Human Rights. His main areas of research are in constitutional and legal theory, comparative constitutional law, and human rights. At Oxford he teaches Constitutional Law, EU Law, Jurisprudence and Human Rights.

Franz-Christoph Zeitler was Vice President of the Deutsche Bundesbank from 2005 until he retired in May 2011; he was Deputy of the President of the Deutsche Bundesbank to the ECB-Council meetings and co-head of the German delegation to the Basel III-negotiations. He has worked with the Deutsche Bundesbank from 1995, first as President of the Land Central Bank of Bavaria, then from 2002 as Member of the Board in Frankfurt. From 1990 until 1995 he was State Secretary to the Minister of Finance following a professional career in the Ministry of Finance of Bavaria from 1975 to 1990. He has been Honorary Professor of Public Law at the University of Augsburg since 2001 and currently works as a lawyer. He has contributed to several textbooks, mainly in the areas of monetary policy, European law, tax law and accounting, and constitutional law.

TABLE OF CASES

TABLE OF LEGISLATION

EU Secondary Legislation

International Treaties

National Legislation

Austria

1

Introduction

WOLF-GEORG RINGE AND PETER M HUBER

I. Law and the Financial Crisis

The financial crisis dominates the academic discourse. This is not only true for economists, but also for political scientists, historians, psychologists, sociologists, and, of course, for lawyers. The global financial crisis which began in 2007 and has been constantly morphing into various shapes was – and is still – one of those epochal events that we see 'once in a generation'. Apart from its devastating economic consequences, the crisis has forced us to rethink some of the fundamental assumptions about our society and our market economy.

Lawyers from practice and academia are equally faced with enormous challenges. The financial system has to be rebuilt and strengthened, the economic survival of our countries has to be secured, and the fulfilment of the European project has to be ensured. Multiple interests have to be taken into account – the citizens who fear that they may be punished for the mistakes of others; the governments and the international community, who have to overcome reticence towards closer co-operation and protectionism; the banks, who are blamed for some of the excesses of the crisis. Lawyers from all fields are working on improving and overhauling our organisational framework to adapt to these challenges.

One of the problems that lawyers are facing – and probably not only them – is that we are all somewhat limited within our particular fields of specialisation. Law is traditionally a primarily national affair; our man-made discipline ends at the national border. Lawyers from the United States respond differently to the problem of a bail-out programme than a German or British lawyer would. Also, different disciplines within the law often prevent scholars from gaining an overall perspective. Lawyers are specialised in constitutional law, administrative law, financial regulation, European Union law, taxation law, and many more. Each of these sub-disciplines considers the current challenges from within its own discourse and by using its own familiar tools, techniques and language. Yet these artificial limitations obscure the view to understanding the financial crisis as a holistic affair which requires all our joint efforts in coordinated attention.

The present volume addresses this gap in bridge-building to a certain extent by bringing together scholars and practitioners from different disciplines of the law and from different countries. The contributions are the fruit of a conference held in Oxford in March 2012 and organised primarily by the Faculty of Law of the University of Oxford and the Ludwig-Maximilians-Universität München. In this way, participants are drawn from the two countries represented by these universities. But, more than that, the conference, and this volume, is a joint venture between different legal disciplines: predominantly constitutional law, financial markets regulation and European law. During the course of this project, we have sometimes been told that the second aspect is an even more remarkable achievement than the first one. In fact, we find ourselves now at the beginning of a new tendency to converge. One of the emerging issues from the crisis is the apparent eclipse of boundaries between different legal disciplines: financial and corporate lawyers have to learn how public law instruments can complement their traditional governance tools; conversely, public lawyers must understand the specificities of financial markets they intend to regulate.

II. Legal Issues Arising from the Financial Crisis

The financial crisis had many faces. It exposed supervision shortcomings of the financial sector in many countries, including EU Member States. Even more worryingly for the EU's financial services market, cross-border supervision was shown to be weak. Bail-outs for banks and countries had to be arranged and executed, and bank resolution regimes were devised.

By applying principles of State aid law, the European Commission was able to steer the different rescue measures to some extent. While ultimately approving State aid payments to financial institutions, the Commission has often required banks or insurers which received a large amount of aid to agree to a significant restructuring plan.

The more recent events known as the sovereign debt crisis have caused concerns about the solidity of various peripheral EU Member States, threatening the stability of the Euro. We can also observe a shift of power back to nation states, which are ultimately in charge of coordinating rescue measures for weak states. Closer integration is envisaged for the Eurozone countries alone, which might potentially open up new conflicts between these Member States and those which are not part of the Eurozone. Legal problems have included the creation of the European Financial Stability Facility (EFSF) and the European Stability Mechanism (ESM). National parliaments feel side-lined in the decision-making process, deploring the loss of their budgetary rights.

The present volume features six main contributions, touching on three legal fields relevant for the crisis. Each of the six essays is accompanied by a response text from a discussant. The constitutional law dimension is represented by the following contributions: Peter M Huber discusses the constitutional dimension of bail-out decisions (chapter two), emphasising the role of democracy and the rule of law in responding to the financial crisis. The German Constitutional Court has repeatedly defined the limits to bail-out measures and other crisis reactions on the European Union, measured against the German *Grundgesetz*, and in particular against its understanding of democracy.[1] These reflections prompt Pavlos Eleftheriadis to ask whether an entity like the EU – and the Eurozone within it – can indeed become democratic (chapter three). He distinguishes between two approaches to democracy, first as collective self-government or, second, as a set of egalitarian institutions, and argues that the German Constitutional Court supports the first theory and for that reason is very cautious about the idea of bringing democracy to the EU. Gregor Kirchhof then explores one of the potential solutions to overcoming the sovereign debt crisis, the so called debt brake (chapter four). The debt brake is an instrument establishing legal rules to limit public borrowing: politicians are essentially trying to control themselves by subjecting themselves to legal scrutiny. John McEldowney in his chapter offers a British perspective on this predominantly German-led project, and introduces us to a distinctly different understanding of budgetary control (chapter five).

Part II then moves on to the European stage. Paul Yowell puts the spotlight on the European Central Bank (ECB), the institution pivotal to dealing with the sovereign debt crisis (chapter six). His argument is that the ECB is mired in a dilemma: its legal mandate does not allow for the bold role it takes on or which some politicians and economists say it should take on. Yowell concludes that legal certainty and predictability as well as the rule of law are intrinsic values in themselves and should take precedence over arbitrary arguments of functionality. This claim is further developed by Christoph Ohler in his assessment that Europe is caught in a governance crisis which exhibits signs of both an economic and a constitutional crisis (chapter seven). The European Treaty framework is certainly not very flexible in allowing for fast and efficient solutions to respond to the problems brought about by the financial crisis. Conor Quigley then explores to what extent European State aid rules have performed during the crisis (chapter eight). The EU State aid system, unique to the specific EU setting, was seen as a key disadvantage of the European landscape in comparison to international competitors like the United States where the state is unfettered in its decisions to support the private sector as it likes. Some commentators, however, consider the State aid rules as the only real instrument the European Commission possessed during the crisis – admitting that the rules were not cut out for a crisis of this dimension. Thomas Ackermann observes two developments: first, he believes that the weakening or bending of State aid rules will only be of a temporary nature. By contrast, he sees the position of the European Commission structurally strengthened beyond the current crisis (chapter nine).

---

[1] See the decision by the German Constitutional Court of 12 September 2012, available in English at http://www.bundesverfassungsgericht.de/entscheidungen/rs20120912_2bvr139012en.html.

Financial markets were seen by many as the original creator of all evil. Alexander Hellgardt explores the different techniques that lawmakers have in sanctioning misbehaviour in financial markets, drawing inter alia from classic liability standards, taxation law, and even criminal sanctions (chapter ten). His trans-disciplinary account is a helpful classification of the menu of choices that regulators have, and the comparative overall costs and benefits of individual choices are not always taken into account. In his response, John Vella picks and elaborates on one of them – taxation (chapter eleven). Before the crisis, taxation law had never been really seen as a tool of financial regulation. Now that its corrective potential has been better understood in financial markets, the corrective role risks being exploited, or even misused, to 'sell' the introduction of a populist tax to the voter. Finally, Gustaf Sjöberg complements the picture by studying 'resolution' of banks as a novel tool to deal with the situation of failing banks (chapter twelve). Whereas traditional insolvency law will work perfectly well in the situation of smaller, local banks, it has proved unsuitable for dealing with global, systemically important financial institutions (G-SIFIs). Sjöberg's hope is that the introduction of a credible resolution mechanism will have anticipatory effects on the governance of solvent banks. Christos Hadjiemmanuil is more sceptical in his assessment of these regulatory tools, arguing that there will always be the risk of political forbearance or, in effect, de facto pressure to bail out (rather than wind down) an essential bank (chapter thirteen).

III. Law Versus Politics, or the Limits of Regulation

All contributions exhibit a golden thread. One of the key questions is to what extent legal rules are at all suitable for dealing with these enormous economic and sovereign problems of such extent. Put differently, the financial crisis has dramatically demonstrated the limits of legal rules. Countries are bailed out despite strong constitutional concerns. The ECB is forced to bow to economic pressure despite observing its strict legal mandate. Sovereign countries contractually promise to limit their own possibility to raise debt and subject themselves to external court control to that end, although we expect that this will be a political test rather than the strict legal standard. And finally, bank resolution attempts above all to introduce a 'credible' legal framework for dealing with large banks, knowing that many legal rules only exist in the books and fail to be applied in practice. The final two chapters of the volume draw these issues together in exploring, more generally, the limits of legal regulation. Rudolf Streinz (chapter fourteen) and Franz-Christoph Zeitler (chapter fifteen) demonstrate that sometimes, employing the law can be a futile attempt to resolve what are, in fact, political problems. The best historical example is the Maastricht Treaty and its convergence criteria for the common currency: as soon as they were violated by certain Member States, the text of the legal treaty was not worth the paper it was written on. If this happens repeatedly, the credibility of our entire legal system will be affected.

Drawing these issues together, we see an extensive array of legal problems that the financial crisis has created. Lawyers in all different fields are working on improving the current framework, to make it better, safer and more coherent. The good news is that lawyers from different jurisdictions and different disciplines are co-operating and are willing to learn from each other. And not just lawyers: interdisciplinary research and study has received a significant boost in recent years. However, all our attempts to regulate must be seen in context and it is clear that law cannot replace the political determination to solve these problems in a sustainable way.

Part I

The Constitution

2

The Rescue of the Euro and its Constitutionality

PETER M HUBER[1]

I. Introduction

On 12 September 2012 the Federal Constitutional Court (FCC) decided on several constitutional complaints and applications demanding a temporary injunction against the Federal law approving the Treaty on the European Stability Mechanism (TESM), the Federal laws implementing that Treaty into the national legal order and the Federal law approving the Treaty on the so called Fiscal Compact (TFCP). These demands had been put forward by the largest number of plaintiffs in the 62 year-old history of the FCC – 76 MPs, several professors of economics, the parliamentary group of the Left and more than 41,000 citizens.

The decision of 12 September was the fourth significant decision of the FCC dealing with the sovereign debt crisis since 2011, and it won't be the last. The first judgment of 7 September 2011 dealt with the guarantees for Greece and the European Financial Stabilisation Facility (EFSF), the second (28 February 2012) with parliamentary control over State guarantees or aids in Europe and the third with the right of Parliament to be informed on European issues such as the ESM and the Euro Plus Compact (EPP) as early and as comprehensively as possible.

There have been other court decisions on the EFSF and the ESM too: from the Constitutional Courts of Slovenia and Estonia, the French Conseil Constitutionnel and the Supreme Court of Ireland, which had handed over its famous *Pringle* case to the ECJ by way of a preliminary ruling.[2]

But Karlsruhe's involvement in the rescue of the Euro seems to be deeper and more persistent. This might be because Germany is the biggest country by population and economic power, or because it would have to bear the greatest burden. These may be reasons, but they don't fully explain the situation.

---

[1] I am most grateful to Wienke Werner who has done a great job translating this chapter.
[2] Case C-370/12 *Thomas Pringle v Governement of Ireland, Ireland and The Attorney General*, nyr.

The real reason seems to me that law and the courts play a greater role in the political life of Germany than they do in most other European states. This has to do with our history. Social psychologists maintain that all of us carry with us the historical experiences of our forefathers for the last 400 or 500 years. We are shaped by this even if we are not aware of it. If that's true, it may be important that political issues in Germany have been dealt with by laws and decided by courts since the fourteenth century, that already in the Holy Roman Empire there had been two 'Supreme Courts' – the Reichskammergericht in Wetzlar and the Reichshofrat in Vienna, which were supposed to settle conflicts between the Emperor and the princes, independent cities and other entities of the Empire. The federal structure was complicated and conflicts couldn't be simply settled by the order of the Emperor. Against this background Immanuel Kant could state in his book *Zum Ewigen Frieden* (*Eternal Peace*) that politics must always be bound by law but not law by politics.[3] That's pretty German, and if we go on to the nineteenth century, we find again a very specific concept of the rule of law, the Rechtsstaat. As the revolution of 1848–49 failed, the bourgeoisie and the monarchy agreed on a compromise: monarchical supremacy was upheld but bound to laws that had to be passed by Parliament, where representatives of the bourgeoisie assembled. Infringements of life, liberty and property needed to be sanctioned by law and the courts had to make sure that state actions did not go beyond those powers. Although the Empire after 1871 was no democracy, our great-grandfathers enjoyed similar living conditions under the protection of the Rechtsstaat as their contemporaries in London, Paris or New York. However the theoretical or conceptual basis was quite different. This path dependency continued after the Second World War, when German courts and academics tried to optimize the Rechtsstaat on the basis of the Basic Law (Grundgesetz), the new constitution which came into force in 1949.

II. The Role of the FCC in the German Political Order

Bearing this in mind, it might become a little bit clearer why courts and legal issues play such an enormous role in the political life of Germany. It is not entirely a joke when justices of the FCC, who wear robes of a bright red silk, are called 'cardinals'. There is also a grain of truth in it. This may be good or bad – but it is simply the way it is.

Against this background it is no surprise that almost every major political debate in Germany is only settled once the FCC has given its final opinion. Whether our army can be sent abroad,[4] whether the fundamental right of asylum

---

[3] Immanuel Kant, *Über ein vermeintes Recht aus Menschenliebe zu lügen*, 1793 (Akademieausgabe, vol VIII, 1923 423 ff.: 'Das Recht muss nie der Politik, wohl aber die Politik jederzeit dem Recht angepasst werden'.

[4] BVerfGE 90, 286ff – *Out of area*.

can be amended,[5] how tax revenues are to be distributed between the federation and the states,[6] how the war against terrorism can be fought, whether homosexual marriages are allowed, and almost every step in the process of European integration had to be finally settled by the FCC.

III. From *Solange I* to the *ESM* Judgment

1. EU and Member States

The *Solange I* and *II* decisions, the *Maastricht* judgment (12 October 1993),[7] the Banana-market decision (2000), the decision on the European arrest warrant (2005), the *Lisbon* judgment (30 June 2009),[8] the judgment on State guarantees for Greece and the EFSF (7 September 2011),[9] the decision on the special committee dealing with EFSF measures (28 February 2012), the decision on Parliament's right to be informed in European affairs (19 June 2012) and the judgment on the pleas for a temporary injunction against the TESM and the TFCP (12 September 2012) are the main landmarks on this way.

The FCC had started to deal with European integration as early as the 1970s. There may have been a change in tone over the past 40 years, however, the cornerstones of the Court's approach have remained unchanged. At the base of this long line of case law is the view that the EU is an association of sovereign states (Staatenverbund) in which the Member States are 'masters of the treaties' and cannot be deprived of their role except by an act of the constituent power – in Germany by a referendum according to Article 146 of the Basic Law.

2. National Legislation as the Basis of European Integration

EU law has to be applied in the respective Member States because and insofar as national parliaments have approved it by ratification (Rechtsanwendungsbefehl). The Federal Act Approving the EEC Treaty and its subsequent amendments are the basis of Germany's membership of the EU, and the conceptual basis of the precedence EU law takes over national law. If EU membership is based on national legislation, it seems to be inevitable that especially national constitutional law may also set limits to European integration. In the end there are two limits to European integration derived from national constitutional law: (a) the national

---

[5] BVerfGE 94, 49ff – *Sichere Drittstaaten*; 94, 115ff – *Sichere Herkunftsstaaten*; 94, 166ff – *Flughafenverfahren*.
[6] BVerfGE 1, 117, 119 – *FAG I*; 72, 330, 383 – *FAG II*; 86, 148, 214 – *FAG III*; 101, 158, 214 – *FAG IV*.
[7] BVerfGE 89, 155ff – *Maastricht*.
[8] BVerfGE 123, 267ff – *Lissabon*.
[9] BVerfGE 129, 124ff – *Griechenland-Hilfe und Euro-Rettungsschirm*.

or constitutional identity on the one hand and (b) the programme of integration on the other (b). They both limit the precedence of (c) EU law.

a) Constitutional Identity as a Limit to Integration

The constitutional identity of the Federal Republic of Germany, which according to Article 23 (1) third sentence of the Basic Law is not open to integration is determined by and only by the so called eternity clause of Article 79 (3) of the Basic Law.

But this is not a specifically German characteristic; the majority of national constitutions contain express or implicit (elaborated by jurisprudence) provisions on the limits of integration. Where those limits lie precisely, however, has not been properly determined by any Member State up to the present day.[10] In Greece, human rights and the foundations of democratic government are not open to integration (Article 28(2), (3) of the Greek constitution), as well as the protected principles of the parliamentary republic, human dignity, equal access to public office, the right to freely develop one's personality listed in Article 110(1) of the constitution and the separation of powers guaranteed in Article 26.[11] For Denmark, it is the requirement of national sovereignty,[12] in the United Kingdom it is the sovereignty of Parliament,[13] in Italy and France[14] the republican form of government, and in Austria the fundamental principles (Baugesetze) of the federal constitution as shaped by the Federal Constitutional Act concerning the accession to the EU 1994.[15] The Swedish Instrument of Government names the 'basic principles of the form of the government' as a limit to integration (chapter 10 § 5), among which the academic commentary primarily counts the Freedom of the Press Act, transparency and access to documents,[16] whereas the Tribunal

---

[10] PM Huber, 'Offene Staatlichkeit: Vergleich' in A v Bogdandy, P Cruz Villalón and PH Huber (eds), *Handbuch Ius Publicum Europaeum*, vol II (Heidelberg, CF Mueller, 2008) § 26 para 83; in favour of a restrictive interpretation: KP Sommermann, 'Offene Staatlichkeit: Deutschland' ibid. § 14 para 25.

[11] For problems of interpretation see J Iliopoulos-Strangas, 'Offene Staatlichkeit: Griechenland' in v Bogdandy, Cruz Villalón and Huber, *Handbuch Ius Publicum Europaeum* (n 10) § 16 paras 41ff.

[12] Supreme Court (*Højesteret*) [1999] EuGRZ 49, 52 para 9.8; F Thomas, 'Das Maastricht-Urteil des dänischen Obersten Gerichtshofs vom 6. April 1998' [1998] ZaöRV 879, 898.

[13] P Birkinshaw and E Künnecke, 'Offene Staatlichkeit: Großbritannien' in v Bogdandy, Cruz Villalón and Huber, *Handbuch Ius Publicum Europaeum* (n 10) § 17 para 41.

[14] Article 89 French Constitution; JG Flauss, 'Rapport français' in J Schwarze (ed), *Die Entstehung einer europäischen Verfassungsordnung* (Baden-Baden, Nomos, 2000) 25, 79: 'la principe de la souveraineté du peuple français ou/et le principe démocratique ne pourraient être abrogés que par le corps électoral agissant non pas dans le cadre d'un acte de révision constitutionnelle, mais au moyen d'un acte constituant nullifiant la constitution préexistante'.

[15] C Grabenwarter, 'Offene Staatlichkeit: Österreich' in v Bogdandy, Cruz Villalón and Huber, *Handbuch Ius Publicum Europaeum* (n 10) § 20 paras 34, 55; T Öhlinger, 'Verfassungsrechtliche Aspekte des Vertrages von Amsterdam in Österreich' in W Hummer (ed), *Die Europäische Union nach dem Vertrag von Amsterdam* (Wien, Manz, 1998) 297, 300f.

[16] J Nergelius, 'Offene Staatlichkeit: Schweden' in v Bogdandy, Cruz Villalón and Huber, *Handbuch Ius Publicum Europaeum* (n 10) § 22 paras 19, 34.

Constitucional in Spain identified a 'core' of 'values and principles' not open to integration, but left its concrete outlines undefined.[17]

In Germany, the FCC has continuously emphasised in a long line of case law[18] that there are limits to the constitutional empowerment for European integration. It has stated with regard to Article 24(1) of the Basic Law, which was originally the relevant prescription for the transfer of powers, that that provision does not grant the power to transfer sovereign rights to inter-state institutions to the point where the identity of the constitutional order is abandoned by modifying the basic principles of the constitution.[19] When amending the constitution in 1992, the legislator codified this judicature in Article 23(2) third sentence of the Basic Law and established that 'the establishment of the European Union as well as changes in its treaty foundations . . . that amend or supplement this Basic Law or make such amendments or supplements possible, . . . shall be subject to paragraphs (2) and (3) of Article 79'.[20] Insofar, 'the division of the federation into Länder (states), their participation in the legislative process, or the principles laid down in Articles 1 and 20' are off limits even for legislation concerning European integration. In other words, the limits the lawmaker has to abide by when amending the constitution apply to the advancement of European integration as well.

In the *Lisbon* judgment, the FCC attempted to clarify this further and stated that the Basic Law also guarantees the sovereign statehood of the Federal Republic of Germany.[21] Consequently, Parliament, Federal Council, and the Government, the so called 'pouvoirs constitutes', do not possess the power to abolish the sovereign nation state over the heads of the German people; this would require an act of the constituent power, the pouvoir constituant (Articles 79(3) and 146 of the Basic Law).[22] It further stated that, in spite of all the misinterpretations of the term 'multi-level-constitutionalism', the European Union remains an association of sovereign states based on public international law. In the future, it will therefore continue to be steered by the Member States, who, as earlier judgments put it, are and will continue to be the 'Masters of the Treaties'[23], and that the principle of democracy (Article 20(1) and (2) of the Basic Law) entails a special responsibility for Parliament when it comes to integration; it demands that national parliaments

---

[17] STC 64/1991; DTC 1/2004; A López Castillo, 'Offene Staatlichkeit: Spanien' in v Bogdandy, Cruz Villalón and Huber, *Handbuch Ius Publicum Europaeum* (n 10) § 24 paras 21, 63ff.

[18] BVerfGE 37, 271ff – *Solange I*; 73, 339ff – *Solange II*; 75, 223ff – 6. *MwStRiL*; 80, 74ff – e. A. *Fernsehrichtlinie*; 89, 155ff – *Maastricht*; 123, 267ff – *Lissabon*.

[19] BVerfGE 73, 339, 375ff – *Solange II*.

[20] For a more flexible approach to these limits, see J Schwarze, 'Ist das Grundgesetz ein Hindernis auf dem Weg nach Europa?' [1999] *Juristenzeitung* 637, 640.

[21] BVerfGE 123, 267, 346ff – *Lissabon*; see also PM Huber, *Maastricht – ein Staatsstreich?* (Stuttgart, Richard Boorberg, 1993) 22ff.

[22] BVerfGE 123, 267, 348ff – *Lissabon*; see also PM Huber, 'Bundesverfassungsgericht und Europäischer Gerichtshof als Hüter der gemeinschaftsrechtlichen Kompetenzordnung' [1991] *Archiv des öffentlichen Rechts* 210, 250; PM Huber, in M Sachs (ed), *Grundgesetz*, 1st edn (Munich, CH Beck, 1996) Article 146 para 19; H Dreier, in H Dreier (ed), *Grundgesetz*, vol III, 1st edn (Tübingen, Mohr Siebeck, 2000) Article 146 para 16.

[23] BVerfGE 75 *MwStRiL*, 223, 242 – 6. ; 89, 155, 190 – *Maastricht*; PM Huber, *Recht der Europäischen Integration*, 2 nd edn (Munich, Vahlen, 2002) § 5 paras 13ff.

have to take an active part in European matters. These requirements, laid down in Article 23(2) to (6) of the Basic Law resemble what Article 12 of the Treaty on European Union (TEU) and the Protocols on the Role of National Parliaments in the EU and on the Application of the Principles of Subsidiarity and Proportionality require from an EU perspective.[24]

As far as the distribution of competences between the EU and the Member States is concerned, this means that the latter have to retain the right to unilaterally withdraw from the Union, which is now expressly established in Article 50 TEU, that the EU cannot be granted the Kompetenz-Kompetenz, but rather that the allocation of competences is to be based on the principle of conferral[25] and that the 'majority of functions and powers' must remain with the Member States.[26] The *Lisbon* judgment tried to substantiate this – admittedly intangible – phrase by listing examples of areas of policy – citizenship, the civil and the military monopoly on the use of force, revenue and expenditure including external financing and all elements of the welfare state that are decisive for the realisation of fundamental rights.

Because of the ongoing Euro crisis the Court has had the opportunity to further shape the budgetary dimension of the constitutional identity. In its decisions concerning the aid measures for Greece and the Euro rescue package,[27] as well as the ESM,[28] it has identified the budget autonomy of the German Parliament as a fundamental part of the constitutional identity and declared the Bundestag's overall fiscal autonomy to be inalienable. It stated verbatim:

> Against this background, the German Bundestag must not transfer its budget autonomy to other participants by granting indefinite authorisations concerning fiscal policy. In particular, it may not – not even by statute – subject itself to mechanisms of financial importance which – be it because of the general concept or the result of an overall evaluation of individual measures – could lead to incalculable burdens on the budget (expenditure or loss of revenue) without the essential prior approval. Prohibiting the Bundestag from relinquishing its budget autonomy in this way is not an inadmissible restriction of the legislator's budgetary competence, but is in fact aimed at its protection.[29]

In order to give a full picture, however, it should be mentioned that so far, no (constitutional or supreme) court has risked an actual clash between the precedence of EU law and the minimum requirements of national constitutional law. The FCC,[30] the Conseil Constitutionnel, the House of Lords,[31] the Italian Corte Costituzionale, the Danish Højesteret as well as other Member States courts have avoided a conflict with the ECJ for the most part – be it through interpreting

---

[24] See on this BVerfGE 131, 152, 198 – *Informationsrechte.*
[25] See BVerfGE 75, 223, 242 – *6. MwStRiL.*
[26] BVerfGE 89, 155, 186 – *Maastricht.*
[27] BVerfGE 129, 124, 179ff – *Griechenlandhilfe und Euro-Rettungsschirm.*
[28] BVerfG, [2012] NJW 3145ff – *ESM-Vertrag, Fiskalpakt.*
[29] BVerfGE 129, 124, 179ff – *Griechenlandhilfe und Euro-Rettungsschirm.*
[30] Most recently, BVerfGE 102, 147ff – *Bananenmarkt.*
[31] *R v Secretary of State for Transport ex parte Factortame* [1991] AC 603, [1991] 3 All ER 769.

national constitutional law in conformity with EU law or by interpreting EU law in the light of the national constitution. As the *Solange* line of judgments[32] or the 'cammino communitario' of the Corte Costituzionale show, the courts have undergone a learning process which has led them eventually to lower the constitutional courts vis a vis EU law. The precedence of EU law is thus ensured, and conflicts with the ECJ are limited to truly exceptional cases.

On the other hand, the Treaties have expressly established an obligation to respect the Member States' national identity (Article 4(2) and (3) TEU), which the ECJ takes into account (albeit not too enthusiastically).[33]

b) The Principle of Conferral and the Ultra Vires Problem

If national legislation is the basis of EU law, the EU can only possess such competences that have been conferred upon it by the Member States (principle of conferral). Activities of the EU and its organs are therefore democratically legitimate only insofar as they keep within the scope of the programme of integration approved by national parliaments – as far as Germany is concerned by Bundestag and Bundesrat.

The limit of competences conferred on EU institutions, that is, the scope of the programme of integration, is inevitably a recurring source of conflict. This becomes an explosive constitutional law issue especially when the ECJ, who possesses inter alia the competence to adjudicate on whether the EU institutions keep within their competences (Article 19(1) second sentence TEU), approves acts that exceed the conferred competences and thus acts ultra vires itself.

This was enunciated explicitly for the first time in the *Maastricht* judgment[34] and has since been confirmed in the *Lisbon* judgment[35] and outlined in more detail in the *Honeywell* ruling.[36] It has gained a large following among other Member States' constitutional or supreme courts. In 2012 the Czech Constitutional Court, for the first time, even considered an ECJ judgment to be ultra vires.[37]

Although this case has remained an exception so far – the FCC has rejected ultra vires claims by the majority[38] with regard to the ECJ's *Mangold* line of cases in 2010 – this does not mean that the Court's reserve control is ineffective. The mere fact that the majority of national (constitutional) courts claims to apply the standards of national law to determine whether the ECJ had acted ultra vires has

---

[32] BVerfGE 37, 271, 280 – *Solange I*; BVerfGE 52, 187ff – *Vielleicht*; BVerfGE 73, 339ff – *Solange II*.

[33] Case C-36/02 *Omega Spielhallen- und Automatenaufstellungs-GmbH v Oberbürgermeisterin der Bundesstadt Bonn* [2004] ECR I-9609 para 39; Case C-208/09 *Sayn-Wittgenstein v Landeshauptmann von Wien* [2010] ECR I-13693 paras 25ff, 92ff; for further references, see PM Huber, in R Streinz (ed), *EUV/AEUV*, 2nd edn (Munich, CH Beck, 2011) Article 19 EUV para 65.

[34] BVerfGE 89, 155, 188, 195, 210 – *Maastricht*.

[35] BVerfGE 123, 267, 398ff – *Lissabon*.

[36] BVerfGE 126, 286ff – *Honeywell*; on this, see A Proelß, 'Zur verfassungsgerichtlichen Kontrolle der Kompetenzmäßigkeit von Maßnahmen der Europäischen Union: Der "ausbrechende Rechtsakt" in der Praxis des BVerfG' [2011] *Europarecht* 241.

[37] Czech Constitutional Court, Pl. ÚS 5/12 – *Slovak Pensions*.

[38] BVerfGE 126, 286, 308ff; see Dissenting Opinion of *Landau* at 318ff.

been incentive enough for the ECJ to avoid such conflicts. It has thus – with a somewhat clumsy reasoning – upheld the Irish constitution's prohibition of abortion, and only classified the prohibition of women's armed military service, which was included in the German Basic Law until 2000 (Article 12a(4) third sentence), as an infringement of Directive 76/207/EEC after the Advocate General realised that this prohibition is not a provision in the sense of Article 79(3) of the Basic Law. The *Omega* case may be another example.[39] It will however be interesting to see how matters develop after the *Akerberg/Franson* judgment of 26 February 2013.[40]

c) The Precedence of EU Law

Having shown that there are two limits to European integration derived from national constitutional law – the national or constitutional identity on the one hand and the programme of integration on the other – it must be acknowledged that this has practical consequences since the FCC and other national courts safeguard these limits.

The programme of integration grants EU law precedence[41] over national law as far as it reaches, and in principle this applies also to national constitutions. On the other hand, there cannot be precedence of EU measures or democratic legitimation beyond the competences conferred within the integration programme. This is the conceptual basis of the precedence in all Member States – although they differ in their concrete design.[42]

Therefore, the ECJ's case law concerning supremacy of EU law over national constitutional law has generally not been met with approval. The FCC with its *Solange* and *Maastricht* doctrine and the Italian Corte Costituzionale with its 'controlimiti' doctrine[43] are in this respect on a level with the Conseil Constitutionnel,[44] the Greek Council of State, the House of Lords (Supreme Court),[45] the Polish Constitutional Court[46] and the majority of the other Member States' constitutional and supreme courts.[47]

---

[39] Case C-36/02 *Omega Spielhallen- und Automatenaufstellungs-GmbH v Oberbürgermeisterin der Bundesstadt Bonn* [2004] ECR I-9609 para 39.

[40] Case C-617/10 *Åklagaren v Hans Åkerberg Fransson*, nyr.

[41] Case 6/64 *Costa/ENEL* [1964] ECR 1251, 1269; Case 11/70 *Internationale Handelsgesellschaft* [1970] ECR 1125 para 3; Case 106/77 *Simmenthal* [1978] ECR 629 paras 17ff.

[42] See Huber, 'Offene Staatlichkeit: Vergleich' (n 10) § 26 para 34.

[43] C Panara, 'Offene Staatlichkeit: Italien' in v Bogdandy, Cruz Villalón and Huber *Handbuch Ius Publicum Europaeum* (n 10) § 18 paras 20ff, 34, with reference to the decisions of *Frontini*, *Granital* and *Fragd v Amministrazione delle Finanze No 232*.

[44] C Haguenau-Moizard, 'Offene Staatlichkeit: Frankreich' in v Bogdandy, Cruz Villalón and Huber, *Handbuch Ius Publicum Europaeum* (n 10) § 15 para 28.

[45] Birkinshaw and Künnecke, 'Offene Staatlichkeit: Großbritannien' (n 13) § 17 para 17.

[46] Polish Constitutional Court, K 18/04 [2006] 41 *Europarecht* 236; S Biernat, 'Offene Staatlichkeit; Polen' in v Bogdandy, Cruz Villalón and Huber, *Handbuch Ius Publicum Europaeum* (n 10) § 21 para 45.

[47] FC Mayer, 'Europäische Verfassungsgerichtsbarkeit' in A v Bogdandy and J Bast (eds), *Europäisches Verfassungsrecht. Theoretische und dogmatische Grundzüge*, 2nd edn (Berlin/Heidelberg, Springer, 2009) 559, 578ff; Sommermann 'Offen Staatlichkeit: Deutschland' (n 10) § 14 para 61.

IV. The Detection of the Democratic Principle

Until the 1990s the main constitutional concern in Germany was that European integration would endanger the level of protection the fundamental rights guarantee as they are laid down in the Basic Law. This has become a lesser concern in the past 20 years whereas the democratic issue has turned out to be the key question of European integration.

1. Basics

Behind this line of adjudication is again a uniquely German concept of democracy whose origins can be traced back to the *KPD* judgment of 1954,[48] but which did not emerge clearly until after reunification. The other Member States' democratic principles if they are theoretically recognised at all, are less intense and doctrinally elaborated.[49] Europe's 'most democratic' state, Switzerland, does not even recognise any *principle* of democracy.[50] Democracy does not extend past the application of the procedures provided for the forming of the political will.

The German concept substantially amounts to the proposition that the principle of democracy and the sovereignty of the people (Article 20(1) and (2) of the Basic Law) are based on the individual right to political self-determination, which itself is based on human dignity (Article 1(1) of the Basic Law) and, as with all fundamental rights, has a tendency to strive for an expansion of the range of opportunities that it involves.[51] Therefore, democracy in Germany is not merely an abstract principle that is given effect to by elections of some kind; it means taking the individual seriously as a voter and as a citizen, in fact aiming to free him from being a subject who is controlled and patronized by the state, the European Union or other political institutions. It is aimed at optimizing the possibilities for political participation and at maintaining the political value of the right to vote in national elections (as elections to the European Parliament do not amount to a comparable level of participation for the individual).

2. Practical Consequences

Democratic legitimation – seen from the point of view of the Basic Law – is realised primarily through decisions of Parliament (Wesentlichkeitsdoktrin) and

---

[48] BVerfGE 5, 85, 204f – *KPD-Urteil.*

[49] Huber (n 33) Article 10 EUV paras 9ff.

[50] KP Sommermann, 'Demokratiekonzepte im Vergleich' in H Bauer, PM Huber and KP Sommermann (eds), *Demokratie in Europa* (Tübingen, Mohr Siebeck, 2005) 191ff.

[51] Seminally BVerfGE 107, 59, 91f – *Wasserverbände NRW*; 123, 267, 342ff – *Lissabon*; PM Huber, 'Demokratie in Europa – Zusammenfassung und Ausblick' in Bauer, Huber and Sommermann, Demokratie in Europa (n 50) 491, 495f; S Unger, *Das Verfassungsprinzip der Demokratie* (Tübingen, Mohr Siebeck, 2008).

through the involvement of the Bundestag in the decision-making process of the EU. The national Parliament is considered the centre of democracy and an essential part of our constitutional identity.[52] If the Bundestag therefore loses competences, the right to vote guaranteed in Article 38(1) sentence 1 of the Basic Law loses substance. The capacity of the individual to political self-determination is diminished and he or she must therefore be entitled to make a constitutional complaint arguing that the treaty or the measure at stake would go too far and violate the constitutional identity of the Basic Law. This concept of democracy, laid down in Article 20(1) and (2) of the Basic Law, is part of the constitutional identity and therefore unalienable for the ordinary legislator as well as for the constitution amending legislator or the legislator in European affairs.

V. Euro Crisis – Jurisprudence

1. Decision of 7 September 2011

In a more specific way the democratic principle as it is laid down in Article 20(1) and (2) of the Basic Law entails the requirement that the Bundestag remains the place where decisions on the amount of loans and guaranties which Germany may give to other countries, their duration and their conditions, have to be made in order to allow for public debate and accountability.

The Federal Constitutional Court's judgment concerning the aid measures for Greece and Germany's participation in the EFSF[53] (7 September 2011) is the most important case so far in which these questions have arisen in practice. The FCC has not only made clear that the limits to integration cannot be skirted by switching to treaties of international public law, but has stated moreover, that is the individual's right that such limits are obeyed. This continued expansion of the position is defended against scholarly criticism as follows:

> The citizen's right to democracy which is ultimately based on human dignity ... would be ineffective if the parliament relinquished core parts of political self-determination and thus permanently deprived the citizen of the possibility of democratic participation. The Basic Law has declared the connection between the right to vote and the government in Article 79 (3) and Article 20 (1) and (2) Basic Law to be inviolable. . . . The legislator has made clear when revising Article 23 Basic Law that the obligation to develop the European Union is tied to the adherence to structural requirements of constitutional law (Article 23 (1) first sentence Basic Law) and that Article 79 (3) has set an absolute limit in order to protect the constitutional identity (Article 23 (1) third sentence) which is transgressed not just when there is an impending seizure of power by totalitarian forces. The citizen must have a recourse of constitutional law against a

---

[52] See Huber 'Offene Staatlichkeit: Vergleich' in v Bogdandy, Cruz, Villalón and Huber, *Handbuch Ius Publicum Europaeum* (n 10) § 26 paras 83ff.

[53] BVerfGE 129, 124ff – *Griechenlandhilfe und Euro-Rettungsschirm*.

transfer of competences by the parliament that is in breach of Article 79 (3) Basic Law. The Basic Law does not provide for a more extensive right to complain. Article 38 (1) Basic Law becomes important in situations in which there is a danger of the competences of the present or future Bundestag being undermined in a way that would make the realisation of the citizen's political will legally or practically impossible. The applicant is only entitled to make an application if he can substantiate that his right to elect the Bundestag may be devalued. There may be a right to lodge a constitutional complaint via Article 38 (1) Basic Law as well, if, what is alleged in this case, the authorisations to give guarantees, can have a substantial detrimental effect on budget autonomy, either by their nature or by their amount.[54]

At the centre of this decision, which is primarily based on Article 20(1) and (2) as well as Article 79(3) of the Basic Law, is the proposition that the Bundestag must not transfer its budget autonomy to other entities or subject itself to mechanisms of financial importance which, 'be it because of the general concept or the result of an overall evaluation of individual measures, could lead to incalculable burdens on the budget (expenditure or loss of revenue) without the essential prior approval'.[55] Against this background, the Court has stated that the legislature is prohibited from establishing permanent mechanisms under the law of international agreements which result in an assumption of liability for other states' voluntary decisions, especially if they have consequences whose impact is difficult to calculate. Sufficient parliamentary influence must also be ensured with regard to the manner in which the funds that are made available are dealt with.[56] With regard to the possibility of having to make payments in a guarantee situation, the legislature has a considerable margin of appreciation. The FCC has to respect this as well as the legislature's assessment of the future sustainability of the federal budget and of the economic performance of the Federal Republic of Germany.[57]

The Senate could uphold the statutes in question – the Monetary Union and Financial Stability[58] Act and the EFSF Act[59] – mostly because the possible liabilities arising from those Acts were sufficiently definite – because of a limit regarding the sum, a time limit, strict conditions and the requirement of unanimity.[60] Against this background, it did not require Parliament to decide on EFSF issues in plenary session but accepted that the law has put the budget commission of the Bundestag in charge of the control of the execution of the EFSF Act. However, that approval of the budget committee had to be obtained *prior* to giving guarantees which could only be ensured by interpreting § 1(4) first sentence of the EFSF Act in conformity with the constitution and by pushing the boundaries of interpretation.[61]

---

[54] BVerfGE 129, 124, 169f – *Griechenlandhilfe und Euro-Rettungsschirm.*
[55] BVerfGE 129, 124, 179f – *Griechenlandhilfe und Euro-Rettungsschirm.*
[56] BVerfGE 129, 124, 180f – *Griechenlandhilfe und Euro-Rettungsschirm,* with reference to BVerfGE 123, 267, 356ff – *Lissabon.*
[57] BVerfGE 129, 124, 180f – *Griechenlandhilfe und Euro-Rettungsschirm.*
[58] BGBl. I 2010, 537.
[59] BGBl. I 2010, 627.
[60] BVerfGE 129, 124, 184ff – *Griechenlandhilfe und Euro-Rettungsschirm.*
[61] BVerfGE 129, 124, 186 – *Griechenlandhilfe und Euro-Rettungsschirm.*

2. Decision of 28 February 2012

After the FCC had allowed the transfer of responsibility for details of State guarantees and aids from the parliamentary plenum to the budget committee, the legislature planned to give the parliamentary supervision of the sovereign debt crisis
as a whole to a special committee of nine elected Members of Parliament.

This has prompted the FCC to issue a temporary injunction against the entering into force of the amendment of § 3(3) StabMechG[62] and has led to a crucial
decision regarding the internal organisation of the Bundestag.[63] At the core of this
decision is the principle that the Bundestag complies with its function as a body of
representation in its entirety, that is, by participation of all its members, and not
by single Members of Parliament, a group of members, or the majority of
Parliament. This holds true especially when it comes to the budget:

> The German Bundestag's right to decide on the budget and its overall budgetary
> responsibility are, in principle, exercised through deliberation and decision-making in
> the plenary sitting . . ., through deciding on the Budget Act, statutes with financial
> importance or any other constitutive decision of the plenum. . . . Every Member of
> Parliament has the right to assess the draft budget of the federal government and the
> proposed amendments (Article 38 (1) in conjunction with Article 77 (1) first sentence
> and Article 110 (2) first sentence Basic Law). A Member of Parliament shall be able to
> present his views on how the budgetary funds should be spent und thereby influence
> the decision on a budget. . . . Moreover, the members of the German Bundestag have
> the right and the obligation to comply with their function to control fundamental deci-
> sions on budgetary politics[64]

However, this is not an absolute guarantee. A restriction of the Member of
Parliament's equal participation (Article 38(1) sentence 2 of the Basic Law) can be
justified by other legal interests of constitutional rank, as the Parliament's ability
to function. This amounts to a gradual guideline which is based on the idea of
essentiality and directed by the principle of proportionality – in the words of the
FCC:

> If Members of Parliament are excluded from participating in Parliamentary decision-
> making by a transfer of decision-making competences to an executive committee, this
> is admissible only in order to protect other legal interests of constitutional rank and
> only if the principle of proportionality is strictly observed. The competence to internal
> organization does not permit to completely deprive a Member of Parliament of his
> rights.[65]

---

[62] BVerfGE 129, 284ff – *e. A. EFSF.*
[63] BVerfGE 130, 318ff – *Sondergremium.*
[64] BVerfGE 130, 318, 345 – *Sondergremium.*
[65] BVerfGE 130, 318, 350.

3. Decision of 19 June 2012

a) *The Case*

In its judgment handed down on 19 June 2012, the FCC considered well-founded the applications made by the Alliance 90/The Greens parliamentary group which asserted that the Bundestag's right to be informed by the Federal Government had been infringed in connection with the European Stability Mechanism (ESM) and the Euro Plus Pact (EPP).

According to Article 23(2) sentence 2 of the Basic Law, the Federal Government shall keep the Bundestag informed, comprehensively and at the earliest possible time 'of matters concerning the European Union'. The first application was aimed at the ESM. The applicant applied for a declaration that the Federal Government had infringed the Bundestag's rights under Article 23(2) of the Basic Law by omitting to inform immediately before and after the European Council of 4 February 2011 comprehensively, at the earliest possible time and continuously, about the configuration of the ESM, and in particular that it had omitted to send the Draft Treaty establishing the ESM to the Bundestag on 6 April 2011 at the latest.

The second application concerned the EPP, which was presented to the public for the first time at the European Council of 4 February 2011. This agreement is intended to reduce the risk of currency crises in the Euro area. In this context, the parliamentary group applied for a declaration that the Federal Government had infringed the Bundestag's rights under Article 23(2) of the Basic Law by omitting to inform the Bundestag before the European Council of 4 February 2011 about the Federal Chancellor's initiative for enhanced economic coordination.

Against this backdrop, the FCC had to clarify whether the rights of participation and the rights to be informed under Article 23(2) of the Basic Law also apply to intergovernmental instruments of the nature described which are dealt with by the Federal Government in the context of European integration and which are related to the European Union. The Senate ruled that the Federal Government had infringed the Bundestag's right to be informed under Article 23(2) sentence 2 of the Basic Law with regard both to the ESM and to the agreement on the EPP.

b) *Standard of Review*

Article 23 of the Basic Law confers on the Bundestag far-reaching rights of participation and rights to be informed in matters concerning the European Union. The strong involvement of Parliament in the process of European integration serves as compensation for the competence shifts in favour of governments that result from Europeanization. The Federal Government's duty, to keep the Bundestag informed comprehensively and at the earliest possible time is intended to make it possible for Parliament to exercise its right to participate in matters concerning the European Union. The information must make it possible to influence the Government's opinion-forming timeously and effectively; information must be provided in such a way that Parliament's role is not reduced to merely exercising indirect influence. Apart from this, the interpretation and application of Article 23(2) must take into account that the provision also serves to publicise parliamentary work, a requirement which is derived from the democratic princi- ple laid down in Article 20(2) of the Basic Law. The more complex the matter, the deeper it intervenes in the legislative's area of competences and the closer it gets to formal decision making or to a formal agreement, the more comprehensive the required information has to be.

The term 'at the earliest possible time' in Article 23(2) sentence 2 means that the Bundestag must receive the Federal Government's information at the latest at a point in time that enables it to deal with the matter in a substantiated manner and to prepare a statement before the Federal Government makes declarations which have an effect on third parties, in particular binding declarations concern- ing legislative acts of the European Union and intergovernmental agreements. Boundaries of the duty to inform result from the principle of the separation of powers. As long as the Federal Government's internal formation of opinion has not come to an end, Parliament has no right to be informed. If, however, the Federal Government's opinion-forming has reached a point at which it can com- municate interim or partial results to the public or would like to set out on a process of joint action with third parties with a position of its own, a project no longer falls within the core area of the Federal Government's own executive responsibility that is shielded from the Bundestag.

c) Subsumption

With regard to the establishment of the ESM the Government had infringed the Bundestag's rights to be informed under Article 23(2) sentence 2 of the Basic Law.

The establishment and configuration of the ESM constituted a matter concern- ing the European Union because from an overall perspective, the characteristics which define it show substantial connections with the integration programme of the European Treaties. The fact of its being intertwined with supranational ele- ments and its hybrid nature mean that it has to be considered a matter concerning the European Union. The establishment of the ESM is to be safeguarded by amending the Treaty on the Functioning of the European Union (TFEU), fur- thermore, the treaty to be concluded for its establishment assigns to the institu- tions of the EU, in particular to the European Commission and the ECJ, new responsibilities concerning the identification, realisation and monitoring of the financing programme for Member States in need of assistance. The role of the ESM is to complement and safeguard the economic and monetary policy, which has been assigned to the EU as an exclusive responsibility.

The Federal Government infringed the rights of the Bundestag under Article 23(2) sentence 2 of the Basic Law by omitting to submit a text of the European Commission on the establishment of the ESM, which was available to the Federal Government on 21 February 2011 at the latest, and the Draft Treaty Establishing the European Stability Mechanism (ESM) of 6 April 2011. Oral and written information, in particular the Draft Treaty Establishing the European Stability Mechanism, which had already been discussed in the extended Eurogroup on 17 or 18 May 2011, was sent too late and therefore did not compensate for the infringement. The duty to inform could not be exercised 'in an overall package' with regard to processes of the nature existing in this case. It was not sufficient for the Federal Government to supply the Bundestag with the text of a treaty when deliberations had already been concluded, or after the treaty has been adopted, these had to be submitted to it at the earliest possible time.

The Federal Government also infringed the Bundestag's rights under Article 23(2) sentence 2 by not informing it comprehensively and at the earliest possible time about the EPP.

4. Decision of 12 September 2012

On 12 September 2012 the FCC pronounced its judgment regarding several applications for a temporary injunction. The main objective of the applications was to prohibit the Federal President from signing the statutes approving the Treaty establishing the European Stability Mechanism (TESM) and the Treaty on Stability, Coordination and Governance in the Economic and Monetary Union (TFCP) passed by the Bundestag and the Bundesrat on 29 June 2012 until the decision in the principal proceedings. The Second Senate of the FCC refused the applications with two provisos. The TESM could only be ratified if it was ensured at the same time under international law that:

1. the limitation of liability set out under Article 8 (5) sentence 1 of the ESM Treaty (TESM) limits the amount of all payment obligations arising to the Federal Republic of Germany from this Treaty to its share in the authorized capital stock of the ESM (EUR 190 024 800 000) and that no provision of this Treaty may be interpreted in a way that establishes higher payment obligations for the Federal Republic of Germany without the agreement of the German representative,
2. the provisions of the ESM Treaty concerning the inviolability of the documents of the ESM (Article 32 (5), Article 34 and Article 35 (1) TESM) and the professional secrecy of all persons working for the ESM (Article 34 TESM) do not stand in the way of the comprehensive information of the Bundestag and of the Bundesrat.

The Federal Republic of Germany was obliged to inform the other members of the ESM that it does not wish to be bound by the TESM as a whole if the reservations made by it should prove to be ineffective.

a) Extent of Review/Admissibility of the Main Action

Diverging from the usual extent of review in temporary injunction proceedings, the Senate did not restrict its review to a mere weighing of the consequences. Instead, it performed a summary review of the challenged Acts of assent and of the accompanying laws to assess whether the violations of the rights asserted by the applicants could indeed be proven. This was necessary because with the ratification of the treaties, Germany would make commitments under international law whose cancellation would not be easy in the event that violations of the constitution should be found in the principal proceedings. The principal proceedings were held admissible to the extent that the applicants, relying on Article 38 of the Basic Law, asserted a violation of the overall budgetary responsibility of the Bundestag, which is entrenched in constitutional law through the principle of democracy (Article 20(1) and 2, Article 79(3) of the Basic Law).

b) Standard of Review

As the Senate had already held in its decision regarding the aid for Greece and the EFSF of 7 September 2011, Article 38 of the Basic Law in conjunction with the principle of democracy (Article 20(1) and (2), Article 79(3)) demands that decisions on public revenue and public expenditure must remain with the Bundestag. As elected representatives of the people, Members of Parliament must retain control of fundamental budgetary decisions even in a system of intergovernmental governance. In this respect, the Bundestag is not allowed to establish mechanisms of considerable financial importance which may result in incalculable burdens with budget significance being incurred without its mandatory approval. On the contrary, the Bundestag must individually approve every large-scale federal aid measure on the international or European Union level that results in expenditure. Sufficient parliamentary influence must also be ensured on the manner of dealing with the funds provided.

c) Subsumption

Measured against these standards, the applications proved to be largely unfounded.

The Act of approval of the insertion of Article 136(3) TFEU did not impair the principle of democracy. It was provided for by the European Council decision of 25 March 2011 and contains the authorisation to establish a permanent mechanism for mutual aid between the Member States of the Euro currency area. Unlike the ECJ, the FCC was convinced that the establishment of the ESM changes the design of the economic and monetary union in a way that moves away from the principle of the independence of national budgets which has characterised the monetary union so far. This may be wise or not. It is important however, that it does not result in a loss of national budget autonomy because through the challenged Act of assent, the Bundestag does not transfer budget competences to bodies of the EU or to institutions created in connection with the EU.

The approval of the TESM essentially takes account of the requirements set out under constitutional law with regard to the safeguarding of the overall budgetary responsibility of the German Bundestag.

However, the FCC thought it necessary to ensure that the framework of the ratification procedure under international law provides that the TESM may only be interpreted or applied in such a way that the liability of the Federal Republic of Germany cannot be increased beyond its share in the authorised capital stock of the ESM of €190 billion without the approval of the Bundestag and that the passing on of information to the Bundestag and the Bundesrat according to the constitutional requirements is ensured. Admittedly, it can be assumed that the express limitation of the liability of the ESM Members to their respective portions of the authorised capital stock, which is provided for in Article 8(5) sentence 1 TESM, limits the Federal Republic of Germany's budget commitments undertaken in connection with the activities of the ESM to €190 024 800 000. However, it cannot be ruled out that the TESM will be interpreted so that in the case of a revised increased capital call, the ESM Members cannot rely on the liability ceiling.

Such a reservation in the ratification procedure was also required with regard to the provisions of the TESM on the inviolability of the documents (Article 32(5), Article 35(1) TESM) and on the professional confidentiality of the legal representatives of the ESM and of all persons working for the ESM (Article 34 TESM). Also in this respect one could argue that these provisions are above all intended to prevent a flow of information to unauthorised third parties but not to national parliaments that must bear political responsibility for the commitments based on the TESM vis-a-vis their citizens throughout any further treaty implementation. However, again the provisions do not explicitly address the provision of information to the national parliaments by the ESM and constitutional law (bearing in mind that parliaments' rights of participation and their right to be informed is quite different in the Member States). It therefore is not unconceivable that those prescriptions could have stopped the Bundestag from monitoring the ESM.

On the other hand, the amount of the payment obligations of a total nominal value of €190 024 800 000 did not exceed the limit of the burden on the budget to such an extent that the budget autonomy would no longer be valid. This even applies if Germany's overall commitment undertaken with regard to the stabilisation of the Eurozone of approximately €310 billion is taken into consideration. As had already been pointed out in the decision of 7 September 2011, the legislature has a broad scope of discretion in this respect, which entails the assessment of the future soundness of the Federal budget and the economic performance capacity of the Federal Republic of Germany.

VI. Future Cases

Whilst the applicants objected to Euro rescue measures taken by the European Central Bank (ECB), in particular to the acquisition of government bonds on the secondary market, arguing that the measures go beyond the framework of authorisation established by the programme of integration laid down in the TFEU, they did not ask for a temporary injunction. To what extent the decision taken by the Governing Council of the ECB on 6 September 2012 on a programme concerning the purchase of government bonds of financially weak Member States complies with these legal requirements was therefore not a matter for decision in the proceedings for the issue of temporary injunctions. Their constitutional complaints and application will consequently have to be reviewed in the principal proceedings.

So, the next step will be the principal proceeding in the *ESM* case and the question whether the ECB's policy to buy government bonds of distinguished members of the Eurozone under specific conditions is in accordance with the TFEU and its constitutional foundations.

VII. Outlook

The strong emphasis on the principle of democracy that has just been outlined and its particular requirements for political decision making are not just a consequence of the jurist's love for designing elaborate concepts. It is supported by the experience-based finding that the application of the principle of majority and the willingness to be subject to a majority vote involve historical, cultural, economic and political preconditions that require a certain degree of social cohesion and matching interests.

The extent to which this applies to the European Union or the Eurozone is an open question which cannot be answered generally, but depends on the individual areas of policy. Subjecting nations to majority decisions on an EU level can in any case only make sense if they, or rather the individuals in those nations, have a realistic chance of being in the majority and if a Europeanisation of the area at stake entails lasting benefits that add to their status quo. Against this background, the simple call for 'more Europe' is overly simplistic at best.

As expectations all over Europe are quite different, it is necessary to stick to the rule of law and the principle of democracy even during the ongoing crisis. This means that treaties and constitutions must be observed. The requirements of the rule of law and democracy may slow down responses to the financial markets' actual or perceived demands. This means, as the president of the International Monetary Fund (IMF), Christine Lagarde, Mario Monti and Wolfgang Schäuble have stated in several interviews, that democracy and the rule of law may prove to be an impediment to overcoming the crisis. Yet, this is a price we must be willing to pay for the sake of our own and our children's freedom and self-determination.

3

Democracy in the Eurozone

PAVLOS ELEFTHERIADIS

Professor Huber's discussion of the German case law gives us a very valuable account of the questions surrounding the constitutionality of the rescue of the Euro. The Federal Constitutional Court (FCC) in Germany is a pioneer in examining the European Union from the point of view of domestic constitutional law. Its thorough discussions of the nature of the European Union and its institutions are carefully studied and frequently followed by other courts. The recent judgments on the Eurozone will be no exception. Nevertheless, in my view one key element of the Court's approach on the Eurozone is very seriously flawed and should quickly be abandoned. My disagreement with the Court's reasoning touches on issues of general principle, the idea of democracy and its relevance to the institutions of monetary union. I will therefore present my arguments starting from some of the most abstract theoretical questions.

I. The Problem

Until very recently the Euro largely escaped the notice of constitutional lawyers. Some of the best books on European constitutional law make little or no mention of monetary union.[1] This omission was understandable. Monetary union was supposed to be a specialised technical subject. The European Central Bank (ECB) was given complete independence from political institutions in order to set monetary policy without interference by finance ministers or parliaments.[2] Its

---

[1] eg there are no chapters on European Monetary Union in the otherwise comprehensive and excellent books by A von Bogdandy and J Bast (eds), *Principles of European Constitutional Law*, 2nd edn (Oxford, Hart Publishing, 2009), A Rosas and L Armati, *EU Constitutional Law* (Oxford, Hart Publishing, 2010) or in R Schütze, *European Constitutional Law* (Cambridge, Cambridge University Press, 2012).

[2] See eg Article 282(3) TFEU: 'The European Central Bank shall have legal personality. It alone may authorise the issue of the euro. It shall be independent in the exercise of its powers and in the management of its finances. Union institutions, bodies, offices and agencies and the governments of the Member States shall respect that independence'.

independence is protected by treaties and protocols that are beyond the reach of ordinary legislation and are the result of unanimous support by the governments of the Member States.[3] Physically as well, the Bank is located in Frankfurt, a safe distance away from the seats of power.

The era of quiet obscurity is now surely over. Politics in Europe has been transformed by the financial crisis. The risk of financial meltdown because of the interdependence of sovereigns and banks now dominates political and institutional debate. The policies of the ECB are high on the political agenda. The emergency response by way of the European Financial Stabilisation Facility (EFSF) and the European Stability Mechanism (ESM) have had great constitutional implications. The decision of the Council of the European Union not to enforce the Stability and Growth Pact against France and Germany during the first breach of its rules in 2004 is now seen in a very different light as the origin of the Euro's current troubles, because it invited other states to consider these duties with greater flexibility – with disastrous results.[4]

Constitutional lawyers and courts are now looking very closely at the monetary union. There are cases regarding the Eurozone emergency measures in European and national courts.[5] The emergency actions that had to be decided by way of intergovernmental agreements and pledges of support for the countries in distress are the subject of scrutiny.[6] The crisis has forced us to think anew about the relations between democracy and monetary union in Europe.

In a unique statement entitled 'Towards a Genuine Economic and Monetary Union' the President of the European Council joined by the President of the European Parliament, the Commission and the Central Bank declared on 5 December 2012 that monetary union required serious reform, which included strengthening its democratic credentials. The statement included a brief section entitled 'democratic legitimacy and accountability' where, without giving much detail, it is proposed that the institutions of the Euro require democratic legitimacy:

> The creation of a new fiscal capacity for the EMU should also lead to adequate arrangements ensuring its full democratic legitimacy and accountability. The details of such arrangements would largely depend on its specific features, including its funding

[3] According to Article 130 TFEU and Article 7 of the Statute of the ESCB and the ECB 'neither the ECB, nor a national central bank, nor any member of their decision-making bodies can may seek or take instructions from Union institutions or bodies, from any government of a Member State, or from any other body'.

[4] For an excellent account of this episode see F Snyder, 'EMU-Integration and Differentiation: Metaphor for European Union' in P Craig and G de Burca (eds), *The Evolution of EU Law*, 2nd edn (Oxford, Oxford University Press 2011) 687, 705–09. The Court of Justice annulled the Council's decision to hold the excessive deficit procedure in abeyance in Case C-27/04 *Commission v Council* [2004] ECR I-6649.

[5] See eg Case C-370/12 *Thomas Pringle v Ireland*, 27 November 2012 (Court of Justice, Full Court) nyr and Case T-590/10 *Thesing and Bloomberg Finance LP v European Central Bank*, 29 November 2012 (General Court) nyr. The German cases are cited by Peter Huber, 'The Rescue of the Euro and Its Constitutionality', ch 2 in this volume.

[6] See eg de Gregorio Merino, 'Legal Developments in the Economic and Monetary Union during the debt crisis: The mechanisms of financial assistance' (2012) 49 *CM LR* 1613.

sources, its decision-making processes and the scope of its activities . . . Ultimately, these far-reaching changes undertaken by the European Union in general and the Economic and Monetary Union in particular require a shared sense of purpose amongst Member States, a high degree of social cohesion, a strong participation of the European and national parliaments and a renewed dialogue with social partners. The openness and transparency of the process as well as the outcome are crucial to move towards a genuine Economic and Monetary Union.[7]

Democracy, or 'full democratic accountability', is on the agenda. But what do these ideas mean? Here we face some important difficulties.

First, the very premise of European Monetary Union is that monetary policy should not be the subject of political contest. Instead, the founding premise is that its institutions ought to work independently from politics seeking to meet policy targets set out in advance. How then can 'European and national parliaments' participate? Second, it is by no means clear what 'democratic legitimacy' means in the context of the European Union. Democracy is a virtue of states, not necessarily of international entities. One of the most distinguished and sophisticated scholars of democracy, Robert Dahl, has persuasively argued that a democracy exists when a political association provides equal participation in decisions about its policies. Respect for democracy requires, for Dahl, a number of substantive or qualitative standards, which he lists as: 'effective participation', 'voting equality', 'enlightened understanding', 'control of the agenda', and 'inclusion of adults'.[8] Democracy is not just a decision procedure.

Dahl argues that international entities in general and the European Union in particular cannot meet these standards. They cannot offer the same opportunities for political participation, influence and control offered by the domestic political context.[9] Other distinguished scholars have come to the same conclusion by a different route. Sabel and Cohen argue, for example, that the international domain is not to be assessed with the conventional tools of democracy but could instead be seen as a 'deliberative polyarchy'.[10] After a thorough analysis Ruth Grant and Robert Keohane take the view that 'there is no simple analogy that can be made between domestic democratic politics and global politics'.[11] Even those who argue for the creation of a supranational democracy in a federal European Union agree too, at least implicitly, with the premise that the EU cannot be a democracy, until it sufficiently resembles a state. Jürgen Habermas' latest book proposes supranational democracy only after we somehow create a 'cosmopolitan community'.[12]

---

[7] Four Presidents Report, 'Towards a Genuine Economic and Monetary Union', 5 December 2012, 17.

[8] RA Dahl, *On Democracy* (New Haven & London, Yale University Press, 2000) 37–38.

[9] ibid 115.

[10] J Cohen and C Sabel, 'Global Democracy?' (2006) 37 *New York University Journal of International Law and Policy* 763–97, 779ff.

[11] RW Grant and RO Keohane, 'Accountability and Abuses in World Politics' 99 *American Political Science Review* (2005) 29–43, 34.

[12] J Habermas, *The Crisis of the European Union: A Response* (Cambridge, Polity, 2012).

Such theoretical views create a problem for the plan outlined by the Four Presidents. How can we expect that the European Union can be more democratic, without at the same time promoting a full political union that would make the European Union resemble a domestic constitutional order? And to the extent that the proposed 'democratic accountability' fails to meet the tests of domestic democracy, it will always seem an evasion, a false façade hiding Europe's real domination by the states' executives. This is then the theoretical and policy challenge that we now face: can the European Union be truly democratic and if so, what are the implications for monetary union? This issue of principle lies underneath the difficult dilemmas posed by the nascent project of banking and political union. In this chapter I offer some preliminary thoughts in this direction.[13]

II. Democracy

Democracy is a controversial idea. Historical experience provides us with multiple examples of democratic government. It is not always apparent what they have in common. Presidential systems, as those established in France and the United States, put a great deal of executive and legislative power into the hands of a directly elected President and to that extent differ greatly from parliamentary systems, like those in the United Kingdom, Germany or Greece, which make the executive continuously depend on the composition of Parliament. Nevertheless, in spite of their great differences all such systems are broadly taken to meet the general standards of democratic government. This is a commonplace both of constitutional theory and of international institutions such as the Council of Europe. Some of these constitutional models provide for a dedicated Constitutional Court (Germany, Italy) and others do not (eg United Kingdom, Greece). A common theme in all is the emphasis on representative government and not direct majoritarian decision-making.

Historians give varied accounts of its development over the centuries since the Greek city-states.[14] Philosophers disagree about its core meaning.[15] The European Convention on Human Rights does not list an independent principle of democracy although it mentions democracy as an essential component of the protection of rights in the preamble. It also organises the limitations of rights on the grounds that they may be necessary in a 'democratic society'. Article 3 of the First Protocol, which was agreed after the Convention, tersely states that 'The High

---

[13] One additional difficulty is that the banking and political union that is currently being planned by the European Union is still under construction. It would be pointless to seek to track this moving target. It will therefore be prudent, in more ways than one, to paint with a broad brush.

[14] See eg J Dunn (ed), *Democracy: The Unfinished Journey, 508 BC to AD 1993* (Oxford, Oxford University Press, 1993).

[15] See eg R Harrison, *Democracy* (London, Routledge, 1995); H Richardson, *Democratic Autonomy: Public Reasoning about the Ends of Policy* (Oxford, Oxford University Press, 2003).

Contracting Parties undertake to hold free elections at reasonable intervals by secret ballot, under conditions which will ensure the free expression of the opinion of the people in the choice of the legislature'. The Protocol does not specify what institutions are required for an effective democracy. As a legal and philosophical principle, democracy therefore remains open-ended.

I believe that much of the present puzzles about democracy in the European Union are the result of this ambiguity. In particular, some of our disagreements stem from a failure to distinguish between three competing theories of democracy. The first theory believes democracy to be an ideal of collective empowerment. The second considers it to be a principle of a fair procedure. The third argues for democracy as a substantive ideal of equality. Most accounts of democracy borrow freely from and combine the three theories I distinguish here. For example, collective self-government may be seen as a component of equality or fairness, and a fair procedure may be grounded in substantive equality. But the theories are competing in that they offer rival grounds for democracy. They suggest three inconsistent general arguments, with significant consequences for practice. Or so I will seek to argue in this chapter. I start therefore by outlining the three central theories of democracy.

1. The Collective Theory

The theory of democracy as collective empowerment believes in the self-government of a sovereign people. The theory starts from common assumptions about the paramount value of popular sovereignty and builds on them a structure of collective will formation. In its purest form this theory was expressed by the German constitutional lawyer Carl Schmitt for whom democracy was the method for giving voice to the people's will. I will quote it at length because it informs much of modern constitutional theory in Europe:

> The people are *anterior* to and *above* the constitution. Under democracy, the people are the subject of the constitution-making power. The democratic understanding sees every constitution, even the *Rechtstaat* component, as resting on the concrete political decision of the people capable of political action. Every democratic constitution presupposes such a people capable of action.[16]

Schmitt goes on to argue for the unusual position that democracy is beyond constitutionalism. He asserts that: 'under the democratic theory of the people's constitution-making power, the people stand as the bearer of the constitution-making power outside of and above any constitutional norm'.[17] This position

---

[16] C Schmitt, *Constitutional Theory*, trans. by Jeffrey Seitzer (Durham, NC, Duke University Press, 2008) 268. For constitutional theory that is influenced by Schmitt's view of 'popular sovereignty' see eg M Loughlin and N Walker, 'Introduction' in Loughlin and Walker (eds), *The Paradox of Constitutionalism* (Oxford, Oxford University Press, 2007) 1. I discuss some of the problems of this view in P Eleftheriadis, 'Law and Sovereignty' (2010) 29 *Law and Philosophy* 535.

[17] Schmitt, *Constitutional Theory* 271.

Pavlos Eleftheriadis

made Schmitt, surprisingly perhaps, critical of the modern methods of voting by secret ballots because he took democracy to be 'the rule of public opinion' which went well beyond any formal manifestation, by way of election or any other procedure.[18] As a result he supported a vague collectivism. It is perhaps not surprising that Schmitt ended up a theoretical supporter of totalitarianism in Germany during the Nazi era.[19] I will return to Schmitt later, because more than a kernel of his theory appears in the German Constitutional Court's reasoning in cases regarding the European Union.[20]

Other theorists of democracy have used a far less radical account of collective empowerment, according to which the self-expression of the public is not the only guiding principle of democracy. John Dewey wrote a well-known essay on the idea of the public advocating democratic experimentalism but warned that the 'the wrong place to look [for the public] is in the realm of alleged causal agency, of authorship, of forces which are supposed to produce a state by an intrinsic *vis genetrix* [originating power]'.[21] Popular sovereignty is for modern theories an institutional ideal, not a causal phenomenon. Jürgen Habermas has written that 'the source of all legitimacy lies in the democratic law-making process, and this in turn calls on the principle of popular sovereignty'.[22] In the United States similar ideas were already present with the founders. Alexander Hamilton wrote that: 'The fabric of American empire ought to rest on the solid basis of *the consent of the people*. The streams of national power ought to flow immediately from that pure, original fountain of all legitimate authority'.[23] Bruce Ackerman's account of 'higher law-making' in American constitutionalism echoes a similar ideal of collective self-government.[24] Unlike Schmitt, however, in all these cases public consent or participation is part of a solid institutional framework that respects the rule of law.

Most political philosophers consider the collective context of democracy a means to other ends. The best known defender of the ethical dimensions of nationality, the Oxford philosopher David Miller, argues, for example, that national self-determination is not a collective end but just the best means for achieving equality and social justice for every individual member of a political community. For Miller, nations provide the trust and deliberative context that can make democracy succeed.[25] Miller writes that deliberation requires trust among those doing the deliberating so that any compromise does not seem just

---

[18] ibid 275.

[19] For Schmitt's defence of Hitler see M Lilla, *The Reckless Mind: Intellectuals in Politics* (New York, New York Review Books, 2001) 47–76.

[20] See eg JHH Weiler, 'Does Europe Need a Constitution? Demos, Telos and the German Maastricht Decision (1995) 1 *European Law Journal* 219–58.

[21] J Dewey, 'The Public and its Problems' in J Dewey, *The Later Works 1925–1953*, edited by Jo Ann Boydston, vol 2 (Carbondale, Southern Illinois University Press,1984; originally published 1927) 289.

[22] J Habermas, *Between Facts and Norms*, trans. by W Rehg (Cambridge, Polity Press, 1996) 89.

[23] J Madison, A Hamilton and J Jay, *The Federalist Papers*, edited by I Kramnick (London, Penguin, 1987) No XXII, 184.

[24] B Ackerman, *We the People: Foundations* (Cambridge, Mass., Harvard University Press, 1991).

[25] D Miller, *On Nationality* (Oxford, Oxford University Press, 1995) 81–118.

'a sign of weakness'.[26] This and other similar approaches to the relevance of nationality and identification with a group see collective self-government as one of the necessary means of democracy, not its essence.[27]

It is therefore safe to say that the collective view of democracy as articulated by Schmitt remains a minority position in philosophy. Most theories of democracy are rights-based or egalitarian. Such theories are divided into procedural and substantive.

2. Democracy as Egalitarian Procedure

The procedural egalitarian view concentrates on the value of a fair procedure for participation in deliberation and decision-making. Some of the variations of this view are more strongly procedural whereas others concentrate on the right to vote as an aspect of equal standing.[28] In the best known defence of this view Jeremy Waldron has argued that the individual right to participate entails that majoritarian procedures of deliberation and decision-making should be available on all important political decisions, including matters of constitutional significance. For Waldron, the point of democracy is that the possibility of successful self-government requires accommodating our disagreements about how to go about governing ourselves and everything else in a just way. We must offer grounds to each other for tolerating the fact that our views lose out. Belief in equal rights requires that we adopt procedures for settling political disagreements which do not themselves specify what the outcome is to be.[29]

Waldron's views are seen in competition with the rival constitutional conception of democracy, which identifies democracy with an argument for substantive rights encompassing not just procedures but also outcomes. The best known account of this view is that offered by Ronald Dworkin.

3. Democracy as Substantive Equality

For Dworkin, democracy is continuous with our deeper moral duties to treat each other with equal concern and respect. Democracy entails the protection of rights even when this goes against the wishes of the majority. He contrasts this view to

---

[26] ibid 97.

[27] Henry Richardson also writes that 'civic integrity and civic magnanimity are virtues that are practically necessary for [policy] discussion to progress towards a mutual acceptance of conclusions about what we ought to do and hence are necessary to motivate involvement in public discussion'; HS Richardson, *Democratic Autonomy: Public Reasoning about the Ends of Policy* (Oxford, Oxford University Press, 2002) 188.

[28] For this terminology see the excellent essay by R Bellamy, 'Introduction' in Bellamy (ed), *Constitutionalism and Democracy* (Aldershot, Ashgate, 2006).

[29] J Waldron, *Law and Disagreement* (Oxford, Oxford University Press, 1999). See also R Bellamy, *Political Constitutionalism: A Republican Defence of the Constitutionality of Democracy* (Cambridge, Cambridge University Press, 2007).

the 'majoritarian' conception of democracy, a term by which he seems to include both the collective conception I presented at (1) and the procedural view I outlined in (2). The constitutional conception of democracy by contrast speaks of equality as the defining value of democracy. For this view political equality is not a matter of the shares of political power that each one of us has, because that depends on contingent matters of how we divide on particular issues. That some of us, for example communists in the United States, have no share in power because they are so few does not mean that that the system that makes them powerless is undemocratic.

For Dworkin, democracy 'confirms in the most dramatic way the equal concern and respect that the community together, as the custodian of coercive power, has for each of its members'.[30] Dworkin notes that this defence of democracy is far more consistent with the constitutional practice of institutions of representative government in the world today, which does not guarantee the results required by the majoritarian conception of democracy. Our practice does not follow the open-ended procedural theories, he argues, but secures outcomes that respect equal rights for all.[31]

The three views, the collective view of democracy, the procedural egalitarian and the substantive egalitarian theories, are the leading theories of democracy today. This is not the place for me to argue for the merits of one or the other.[32] My task here is simpler. I wish to argue that our puzzles about democracy in the European Union have their origin in precisely the disagreements between these three philosophical views about democracy. Our disagreements over the best conception of democracy, cause our disagreements about democracy and its place in the European Union.

III. Democracy and the European Union

It is often said that the EU suffers from a 'democratic deficit'. The most well developed defence of this position was offered by the Oxford political theorist Larry Siedentop, who argued more than 10 years ago that the preconditions for a genuine democracy – the kinds of things that Tocqueville observed in the United States – are lacking in Europe. Siedentop included among them a common political tradition, a common language, some identification with other communities and mutual trust.[33]

---

[30] R Dworkin, *Justice for Hedgehogs* (Cambridge, Mass, Harvard University Press, 2011) 390.

[31] A powerful argument for the same view is also made by Elizabeth Anderson, for whom: 'democratic equality regards two people as equal when each accepts the obligation to justify their actions by principles acceptable to the other, and in which they take mutual consultation, reciprocation, and recognition for granted'; see Elizabeth Anderson, 'What is the Point of Equality' (1999) 109 *Ethics* 287–337, 313.

[32] I have offered a defence of a substantive egalitarian theory of rights in P Eleftheriadis, *Legal Rights* (Oxford, Oxford University Press, 2008).

[33] L Siedentop, *Democracy in Europe* (London, Penguin, 2000).

He considered that all of these were absent from the European Union. He concluded that the federalist project of 'ever closer union' must be held up, at least until the conditions of democracy were closer to being met. In effect Siedentop argued that without a 'demos', that is, a group of people joined by common traditions and bonds of trust, there would be no place for 'democracy'. This view is echoed in broader arguments about international institutions. In a thorough analysis of mechanisms of accountability in international law, Grant and Keohane concluded that the attempts to conceive of an analogy with domestic democracy in a global domain 'founder on the absence of a coherent and well-defined global public'.[34]

A direct response to Siedentop's argument came from Andrew Moravcsik. Although Moravcsik did not challenge the factual assumptions Siedentop made about trust, common traditions and identities, he considered that he had drawn the wrong conclusions. Moravcsik argued that the European Union is not for that reason undemocratic, since it does not seek to replicate the functions of a state. If it is not a state, then the principles of democracy do not apply to it in the same way.[35] But this does not mean that no ideas of democratic accountability apply to it at all. There may well be other tests of democratic accountability, appropriate for non-states, which, for Moravcsik, once carefully identified, could be seen to be mostly satisfied by the present European institutions, whose political power and influence were in any event greatly exaggerated.[36]

The debate between Siedentop and his critics showed that the debate on democracy and the European Union was really about two different issues. The first issue is the success of domestic democracy, namely whether the relationship of the European Union with the Member States and the power it has given to the domestic executives has undermined democracy inside the Member States. The second issue is about a possible European democracy and more particularly about the question if and by what way the institutional architecture of the European Union could on its own satisfy some relevant tests of democratic government. Siedentop ruled this option out. He assumed that democracy is only a domestic ideal. Moravcsik, however, argued that some version of democratic accountability may be open to international institutions.

It seems that the Four Presidents in their December document agree with Moravcsik on the viability of European democracy. They envisage a new set of institutions of 'democratic accountability' at the European level as a means of bringing about legitimacy to the Eurozone's mechanisms of governance. They seem to argue that there is no need for full federal union for these institutions to become democratically successful.[37] By contrast, most sceptics argue that the

---

[34] Grant and Keohane, 'Accountability and Abuses in World Politics' (n 11) 33.

[35] A Moravcsik, 'In Defence of the "Democratic Deficit": Reassessing the Legitimacy of the European Union' (2002) 40 *Journal of Common Market Studies* 603–34.

[36] See also A Follesdal and S Hix, 'Why there is a Democratic Deficit in the EU: A Response to Majone and Moravcsik' (2006) 44 *Journal of Common Market Studies* 533–62.

[37] A third question concerns the *process* by which powers may be removed from the Member States and handed over to collective institutions and whether the processes that have been adopted have satisfied the tests of democracy. I will have very little to say about the last issue. It is something that depends

European Union invariably undermines domestic democracy.[38] In order to assess these views we shall need to look at domestic and European democracy separately.

IV. Domestic Democracy

The first theory of democracy, the view of democracy as primarily collective self-government is very likely to consider that the European Union does not suffer from a democratic deficit. It does not require self-government in the way that a nation state does. If democracy expresses the collective will of its people, then insufficient democracy will only occur at the level where some collective will exists but fails to find appropriate expression. The problem does not arise where there is no such will. Given that Europe does not have an appropriate collective entity, a 'people' of its own, then it cannot fail to be democratic. The only democratic deficit could lie in the way the EU relates to real democracies, that is, the Member States. The democratic deficit could then be in the loss of democracy observed at the national level, which results from the transfer of powers from national capitals to Brussels.

This is the position, I believe, that is articulated in the complex and careful judgments issued by the German Constitutional Court and which Professor Huber has so effectively summarised for us. As I read them, at the heart of these judgments lies a distinct theory of democracy which corresponds closely to the collective theory as I identified it above.

In its judgment on the Lisbon Treaty the Court outlined a very general view of the EU as an international union of self-governing states. The fact that they were nation states was intimately related to their democratic nature. The Court said 'The citizens' right to determine, in equality and freedom, public authority with regard to persons and subject-matters through elections and other votes is the fundamental element of the principle of democracy'.[39] The argument is based on Article 20(2) of the German Constitution, which states that 'all state authority is derived from the people' and 'shall be exercised by the people through elections and other votes and through specific legislative, executive, and judicial bodies'. In the Court's view an excessive transfer of powers to the European Union would be

on the procedures follow in each Member State. There could be indeed undemocratic ways of entering into an EU Treaty (say, by deception or by executive order) that would constitute a violation of democratic procedure. But I will assume here that the processes of decision making in all the Member States generally meet the tests of democracy.

[38] See eg N Malcolm, 'The Case Against "Europe"' (1995) 74, No 2 *Foreign Affairs* 52–68.

[39] *Re the Lisbon Treaty*, 2 BvE 2/08 et al, Federal Constitutional Court, 30 June 2009, available at www.bverfg.de. For commentaries see FC Mayer, 'Rashomon in Karlsruhe: A reflection on democracy and identity in the European Union' (2011) 9 *International Journal of Constitutional Law* 757, as well as D Halberstam and C Möllers, 'The German Constitutional Court says: "Ja zu Deutschland" (2009) 10 *German Law Journal* 1241 and C Tomuschat, 'The Ruling of the German Constitutional Court on the Treaty of Lisbon' (2009) 10 *German Law Journal* 1259.

unacceptable if it weakened the ability of the German people to decide their own affairs. The Court said:

> The Basic Law does not grant the bodies acting on behalf of Germany powers to abandon the right to self-determination of the German people in the form of Germany's sovereignty under international law by joining a federal state. Due to the irrevocable transfer of sovereignty to a new subject of legitimisation that goes with it, this step is reserved to the directly declared will of the German people alone.[40]

That a loss of all significant powers would be detrimental to democracy is, of course, a commonplace. But it is a view that is not particularly tied to democracy. A dictatorship would suffer too. The point is rather that a political community must have power to determine its own affairs. So the point that the Court made above could be accepted by any theory of democracy.

In fact, we are a very long way from such an undemocratic transfer of essential powers. The FCC has not suggested that the Maastricht or Lisbon Treaties amounted to such a transfer. The fundamental constitutional documents of the EU are still treaties of public international law, which are made by the Member States, so that the states remain in control of everything that happens in the European Union. Moreover, the most powerful legal institution in the EU, the Court of Justice, does not have a right to hear appeals from the Member States' courts. So it is not in any sense a supreme court of the Union as a whole.[41] In fact the Lisbon Treaty itself has inserted a new provision in Article 4(2) of the Treaty on the European Union according to which: 'The Union shall respect the equality of Member States before the Treaties as well as their national identities, inherent in their fundamental structures, political and constitutional, inclusive of regional and local self-government'. And if there was any doubt it goes on specifying that the Union 'shall respect their essential State functions, including ensuring the territorial integrity of the State, maintaining law and order and safeguarding national security'.

The Court has made a further point, however. In its Maastricht judgment the Court said that democracy requires a strong and cohesive *people*, so as to be able to successfully express itself. The Court said:

> If the peoples of the individual States provide democratic legitimation through the agency of their national parliaments (as at present) limits are then set by virtue of the democratic principle to the extension of the European Communities' functions and powers. Each of the peoples of the individual States is the starting point for a state power relating to that people. The States need sufficiently important spheres of activity of their own in which the people of each can develop and articulate itself in a process of political will-formation which it legitimates and controls, in order thus to give legal

---

[40] *Re the Lisbon Treaty* (n 39) para 228 (from the English translation provided on the Court's website).

[41] For a thorough and persuasive analysis of the European Union as an international legal 'experiment' see B de Witte, 'The European Union as an International Legal Experiment' in G de Burca and JHH Weiler (eds), *The Worlds of European Constitutionalism* (Cambridge, Cambridge University Press, 2012) 19–56. I defend a similar view in P Eleftheriadis, 'The Idea of a European Constitution' (2007) 27 *OJLS* 1; P Eleftheriadis, 'Pluralism and Integrity' (2010) 23 *Ratio Juris* 365.

expression to what binds the people together (to a greater or lesser degree of homogeneity) spiritually, socially and politically.[42]

So the right to political participation is directed to a collective 'will-formation', which gives expression to 'what binds the people together'. This is the core, as I see it, of a collective theory of democracy. The Court sees democracy as a process of collective self-determination, not merely a process of the aggregation of individual civil and political rights.[43] It follows from this type of reasoning that the EU cannot, strictly speaking, become democratic, since there is no independent people whose will could possibly be expressed through European Union institutions. Democracy is only to be achieved through domestic institutions, which represent the Member States in the EU: 'If such a community power is to rest on the political will-formation which is supplied by the people of each individual State, and is to that extent democratic, that presupposes that the power is exercised by a body made up of representatives sent by the Member States' governments, which in their turn are subject to democratic control'.[44]

The same theory was used by the German Constitutional Court in its Lisbon Treaty judgment. The Court repeated that there is a natural limit to what could potentially be moved to the Union at all. The limit is constitutional and not just procedural. Any such transfer by whatever means would be unconstitutional or undemocratic, even if the majority had voted for it. The Court said that the principle of democracy, which is protected by the 'eternity' clause of Article 79 of the German constitution, imposed limits on European integration. It ruled that the principle of democracy requires that an infringement of the 'constitutional identity codified in Article 79(3) of the Basic Law is at the same time an infringement of the constituent power of the people'.[45] It follows that there is no institution in Germany that could legally amend the constitutional identity of Germany. Technically, any such attempt would be undemocratic. In effect, the Court has established the principle of collective self-government as the highest principle of the German constitution.

The Court applied this view of democracy to the European Union and concluded that it could not be properly democratic: 'Also in their elaboration by the Treaty of Lisbon, no independent people's sovereignty of the citizens of the Union in their entirety results from the competences of the European Union'. [46] In effect, because there is no single European people, there can be no European democracy.

---

[42] *Manfred Brunner and Others v The European Union Treaty*, 2 BvR 2134/92 & 2159/92, Federal Constitutional Court, 12 October 1993, [1994] 1 CMLR 57, 88.

[43] I therefore differ from Professor Huber in my reading of the cases, because for him the principle of democracy 'means taking the individual seriously as a voter and as a citizen'. In my view, the collective element is the more important one in the Court's case law. This is perhaps also implicitly acknowledged by Professor Huber because he argues that the principle of democracy seeks to maintain the 'political value of the right to vote in national elections'. It is obvious that a single vote always has insignificant 'political value'. No election in a large country has ever been won by a single vote.

[44] *Brunner* (n 42) para 46, p 88.

[45] *Re The Lisbon Treaty* (n 39) para 218.

[46] Lisbon judgment (n 39), para 281.

It follows also that the constitution sets out the division of labour between domestic constitutional arrangement and the Union. Violation of these limits would be a violation of democracy as self-government.

Partly in response to these famous judgments the German philosopher Jürgen Habermas has offered a sophisticated rival view. At its heart is a proposal that a cosmopolitan people can be constructed in Europe. Habermas argues that the crisis of legitimacy of the EU can be answered by promoting transnational democracy by way of creating a 'cosmopolitan community' of European citizens, which will soon become the appropriate domain of self-government.[47] Habermas argues that 'a transfer of sovereign rights does not diminish the scope of civic autonomy only on the condition that the citizens of the one affected state co-operate with the citizens of the other affected states in making supranational law in accordance with a democratic procedure'.[48] In other words, the institutions of democracy can be replicated at the EU level once the mutual understanding and solidarity among European citizens reaches a required degree of completeness. Yet, Habermas seems to share the Court's analysis about the nature of democracy, namely the view that democracy requires a strong and cohesive people to exist. Their disagreement lies in their account of the prospects of bringing about such a people in Europe.

Here we come to our first important conclusion. The collective theory is more sceptical of the prospects of European democracy. It sees democracy in the Union and its Member States as a more or less zero sum game. Either we have self-government for a national people, or self-government for the European people.

This is not the case for the egalitarian theories. If we take democracy to be a principle of individual entitlements and not that of a collective, then it is far less significant if powers are shared with other states. What matters is how power affects the standing of individuals, not where it lies exactly. International law, for example, provides known mechanisms by which power can be shared on the basis of reciprocity. States that enter into such treaty arrangements with others gain influence over the policies of their partners, by giving up the same influence over their own. Joining the World Trade Organisation (WTO), for example, allows Member States to co-ordinate their trade policies in a reciprocal way and rules out arbitrary or protectionist measures. Of course, the actions of the WTO do not express the collective will of any single nation. But they are decisions that are public, legally limited and can be held accountable to the peoples of different nations at the same time. It follows that if directed to appropriate subject matters and if done by states that respect democracy internally, then multilateral coordination may enhance democracy.

This is an argument made with great clarity by Robert O Keohane, Stephen Macedo and Andrew Moravcsik in a thoughtful essay, which is very important for the theory of the European Union.[49] The key to their argument is a definition of

---

[47] J Habermas, *The Crisis of the European Union: A Response* (Cambridge, Polity, 2012) 53.

[48] ibid 19.

[49] RO Keohane, S Macedo, and A Moravcsik, 'Democracy-Enhancing Multilateralism' (2009) 63 *International Organization* 1.

democracy that plays down the collective element. They contrast majoritarian to constitutional democracy and emphasise that modern democracies are mostly already insulated against direct majoritarian control. Constitutional constraints are aimed to prevent majority rule form turning into faction or majority tyranny. In practice constitutional systems reject the majoritarian argument. Keohane, Macedo and Moravcsik argue that government becomes *more* and not less democratic when nations ensure that minority or unpopular interests are fairly attended to and the equal rights of everyone protected.[50]

Multilateralism enhances democracy when, for example, it assists domestic institutions in the protection of human rights (as in the case of the European Convention of Human Rights), whenever it contributes to the better understanding of policy issues (as in the case of the OECD), or whenever it directs the public interest towards the public good and not toward the benefit of special interests that are well organised domestically but powerless internationally (as in the case of the EU). While they recognise that it would be undemocratic for an 'elite multilateral institution . . . to override repeated demonstrations of informed rights-regarding, fairly represented popular will', they argue that the EU does not constitute such 'benign technocracy'.[51] They argue instead that 'properly authorized multilateral institutions, such as other commonplace constitutional institutions, may be justified in imposing checks, constraints and corrections on majorities that are not well-informed, rights-regarding, or fairly represented'.[52] They argue that the institutions of the European Union pass those tests for the most part.

This is, then, the first major finding of our analysis. Collective theories of democracy restrict the application of criteria of democracy to a single, cohesive people or public. For these theories the EU cannot be democratic until it becomes a new such people. This is the view defended by the German Constitutional Court. Egalitarian theories, by contrast, take democracy to be a matter of the protection of individual rights which can be done both domestically and internationally. For the egalitarian theories of democracy it follows that democracy can be enhanced by participation in appropriate supranational organisations.[53]

V. Debt and Democracy

How does domestic democracy deal with the emergency measures taken in the Eurozone? This is the question that the German Constitutional Court was called

---

[50] ibid 5–6.
[51] ibid 15.
[52] ibid.
[53] I do not discuss here the theories that deny the singleness of demos but allow for the collective understanding of democracy as 'demoicracy'. See eg K Nicolaidis, 'European Demoicracy and its Crisis' (2013) 51 *Journal of Common Market Studies* 351 and F Cheneval and F Schimmelpfennig, 'The Case for Demoicracy in the EU' (2013) 51 *Journal of Common Market Studies* 334.

upon to answer in a number of recent cases, which Professor Huber helpfully refers to. Its first case, in 2011, was about the rescue of Greece, Ireland and Portugal.[54] The second case was about the permanent European Stability Mechanism and was decided in 2012.[55] In the first case the Court examined the legality of Germany's participation in arrangements for loans to Greece and to the setting up of the European Financial Stability Facility, which assists Ireland and Portugal. Its decisions were based almost entirely on a theory of democracy as collective self-government.[56]

The Court rejected the more extravagant submissions of the applicants, for instance the claim that the bail-out violated the right to property or that it was against European Union law. But the Court dealt seriously with a claim that the bail-out violated the 'right to vote'. The Court restated the doctrine that as a matter of principle that any transfer of power from the German Parliament to the EU institutions might violate the right 'to vote' if that transfer took away significant powers form Germany. The Court used the expression 'the right to vote' to capture something wider than voting, namely the fact that the architecture of checks and balances set up by the German constitution as a whole might be undermined by a loss of influence.

According to the Court the German legislature must always effectively control the budget decisions both in a domestic and in international settings. This entails that the Government must obtain prior approval by the Parliament's Budget Committee before giving any new guarantees under the current terms of the EU bail-out. This is fully in line with conventional understandings of democratic deliberation. Nevertheless, a second and more important aspect of the ruling was that the Court set limits to what any political institution could do to address crises in the European Monetary Union. The Court concluded:

> It is not permitted to establish permanent mechanisms under an international treaty which would result in the Federation assuming any liability for other states' voluntary decisions, especially if this can have consequences whose impact is difficult to calculate. Every large scale aid measure of the Federation, which may be taken in a spirit of solidarity and involving public expenditure at international or EU level must be specifically approved by the *Bundestag*. Any such international agreement, which on the basis of its size can have structural consequences for the law of the budget, either through the provision of guarantees whose redemption may threaten the 'budgetary autonomy' of the Federation or through participation in a relevant financial insurance scheme, must be specifically approved by the Bundestag. It must also be guaranteed that that there should be parliamentary influence in the way the available funds are used.[57]

---

[54] *Re the Rescue of Greece and the Euro*, Federal Constitutional Court, 7 September 2011. The next few paragraphs are adapted from P Eleftheriadis, 'The Euro and the German Courts' (2012) 128 *LQR* 216.

[55] *Re the ESM Treaty*, Federal Constitutional Court, 19 June 2012.

[56] BVerfG, 2 BvR 987/10, 2 BvR 1485/10, 2 BvR 1099/10, Judgment of 9 September 2011, available on the Court's website. All references in brackets are to paragraphs of this judgment. Translation is my own.

[57] *Re the Rescue of Greece and the Euro* (n 54) para 128.

There are many ideas here, not always clearly distinguished. In effect the Court introduces four different tests. First, Parliament cannot formally transfer its own powers to control the budget to a permanent international mechanism. Second, when the Government wishes to participate in a 'large scale' rescue package, it must have the prior approval of the Bundestag. Third, for a rescue to be lawful it must be 'specifically approved' and on the condition that it allows for German parliamentary influence on the how the funds are spent. And, fourth, if a rescue package is too large it may end up undermining, through its structural 'consequences', the 'budgetary autonomy' of the Federation, irrespective of who decided it. It is not enough that it has been specifically approved by Parliament. The first test follows something that the Court had said before, most recently in its controversial Lisbon Treaty judgment of two years ago.[58] But the others are new. When these general tests were applied to the Euro bail-outs the Court concluded that the relevant agreements did not transfer any formal powers. Since the setting up of the rescue package had been done by means of two German statutes, the procedural aspects were also satisfied.

The Court then said something extraordinary. It found that the amount of the guarantees given, namely €170 billion in total, 'did not exceed' the limit of budget capacity in such a way as to threaten 'budgetary autonomy' or to render it empty of content. This was because 'there is no reason to assume an irreversible process with consequences for the *Bundestag's* "autonomy"'.[59] The point is extraordinary because it goes to the heart of the decisions made by Parliament and suggests that a higher commitment by Parliament might be unconstitutional. I will return to that point immediately below. In any event, the Court cleared the German Acts implementing these decisions. In its 2012 decision the Court repeated exactly the same doctrine, speaking again of the 'principle of budgetary autonomy', although it did not set an explicit limit this time to the guarantees that Germany could commit to its European partners.

It is uncontroversial that democracy requires Parliament to have an active role in the way public money is spent. Yet, two other aspects of the judgment are more striking. The first is the view that democracy may be violated when the amount of money pledged in support of the Euro is 'too high'. The second is that there may well be a principle of 'budgetary autonomy' which rules out certain policy choices, even if they are adopted by Parliament. This latter point was made explicitly, since the Court found that bail-out was within constitutional limits so that €170 billion in total, 'did not exceed' the limit of budget capacity in such a way as to threaten 'budgetary autonomy'. This part of the judgment is very hard to understand. It appears that the Court is telling Parliament that there are certain economic policies that are so risky as to be unconstitutional and 'undemocratic'. What is striking here is that the policy may be undemocratic even though it may have been taken by Parliament. So it is on a par in its significance with human rights violations.

---

[58] BVerfG, 2 BvE 2/08 et al, judgment of 30 June 2009.
[59] Re the Rescue of Greece and the Euro (n 54), para 136.

The point the Court makes is that no German institution could possibly assume any liability for the 'voluntary decisions' of other states, especially if this can have consequences whose impact is 'difficult to calculate.' But why is that? Is Germany not already involved in sharing risks inside the European Union's common market, the Schengen area of common borders and inside the Eurozone? Are these common risks from the free movement of persons, goods and capital unconstitutional in Germany because they expose German social and economic life to the consequences of the decisions of its partners on banking, trade, policing or immigration?[60] The German Parliament has repeatedly decided that this sharing of risks is for the benefit of Germany. Its repeated commitments to the European Union and the ratification of EU treaties suggest that participating in European integration is a firm policy choice. The Court suggested, however, that there is a constitutional limit as to what Parliament can decide within this policy of pooling risks through integration.

Other jurisdictions reach the directly opposite conclusion. They normally hold that economic policy belongs entirely to Parliament. If Parliament wants to share risks with other states as a matter of the best economic policy, there is no violation of the constitution. Democracy requires only that decisions are taken by states including the decision to share institutions and processes. When the English High Court was asked by journalist and politician William Rees Mogg to intervene in the ratification of the Maastricht Treaty in 1993 the Court said that it was very conscious of the need 'to confine judicial review within its proper sphere'. It could only examine the legal question raised by the claimant whether by entering into an international treaty the Crown had unlawfully sought to abandon 'prerogative powers'.[61] The Court quickly dismissed the claim saying that entering into the Maastricht Treaty was precisely the exercise of these prerogative powers and that a treaty by itself cannot, in any event, changes the domestic constitution. Similar answers were given by the same court when Stuart Wheeler, another Euro-sceptic campaigner, challenged the ratification of the Lisbon Treaty 15 years later.[62] Elected politicians were to have the first and last word on such matters. And in a case where the Court of Appeal was asked to review payments from the United Kingdom to the then EEC in order to finance a supplementary budget, the court dismissed the challenge and laid down a general principle: 'It therefore behoves the courts to be ever sensitive to the paramount need to refrain from trespassing upon the province of Parliament or, so far as this can be avoided, even appearing to do so.'[63]

How then does the German Court reach the directly opposite conclusion, namely that democracy requires Parliament not to pursue a particular economic

---

[60] A very powerful account of the way in which risks and benefits are shared in the EU and the moral duties that follow from it is offered by A Sangiovanni in 'Solidarity in the European Union' (2013) 33 *OJLS* 1–29.

[61] *Regina v Secretary of State for Foreign and Commonwealth Affairs, Ex parte Rees-Mogg* [1994] QB 552.

[62] *Wheeler v Prime Minister* [2008] EWHC 1409 (Admin).

[63] *Regina v Her Majesty's Treasury, Ex parte Smedley* [1985] QB 657, 666 (Sir John Donaldson, MR).

policy? The explanation is in the kind of democracy that the Court has in mind. For the Court, as we saw in the Maastricht and Lisbon judgments above, democracy means the collective ideal of self-government and requires independence from the will of others. This explains how the ground for the Court's judgment can be Article 38 of the German constitution, which establishes the right to vote. This provision says that Members of Parliament are to be elected and that everyone should have the right to vote and to stand for election. Although the provision is extremely simple, the Constitutional Court builds on it an elaborate argument. The right to vote is not seen by the Court as an individual political right to participate in political life. It is not a right to equal status.

What kind of right is violated by the economic policy of integration with others in the Eurozone? Like in Maastricht and Lisbon, voting is not actually affected. The decision at issue was for Germany and the other members of the Eurozone to guarantee the loans of highly indebted Member States through the EFSF or the ESM and on the condition that an IMF programme would be put in place. The risk that the Court has in mind was that the programme would fail, the debt might be restructured and that Germany would then be left with some losses. The key concept here is the will of the German people. The losses would not be a result of mistakes made by Germany, but of mistakes made by the borrowers. The Court assumes that as a matter of constitutional principle the people should be independent of the will of other nations. The point is, or appears to be, that Germany should not be trapped into a corner of indebtedness, like Ireland, Greece and Portugal, from which it is extremely difficult to escape.

I have strong reservations about the collective theory of democracy.[64] But I do not see how even this theory is engaged in the rescue of the Euro in the two cases that the Constitutional Court has deployed it. Guaranteeing the loans of other Member States may be a policy with inherent risk. But how can it undermine the power of Parliament to govern itself if it is a matter of Parliament's own decision to take those risks? The connection between the Euro rescue and autonomy is based on a simple confusion. The court mistakes the powers an agent may have over his or her own *decisions,* which is the heart of self-government for persons as well as states, with the control an agent may have over the *outcomes* of his decisions. When I decide to go into business with others our fate becomes common. The outcome of our venture now depends on our collective processes, not just on my own judgement. If my partners make bad decisions I too stand to lose. If I don't start a business with others, any gains or losses are my own doing alone. But voluntary co-operation of this kind does not signal any loss of self-government. I control my decisions, even though I am not in complete control of the outcome of co-operation. Even as a member of a collective project I remain free to vote and act inside the organisation as I see fit or even to exit, if my judgement says so. Companies are voluntary associations, but gains and losses are shared.

---

[64] I have expressed some of these reservations in P Eleftheriadis, 'The Moral Distinctiveness of the European Union' (2011) 9 *International Journal of Constitutional Law* 695.

The same applies to the European Union. Its members are masters of the treaties, even though they are not entirely masters of their fate. What happens to their economy and society depends to a large extent on decisions taken collectively in Brussels, where they may be outvoted by other states. The founding rationale of the EU is precisely for the Member States to open their borders to each other. Yet, the Member States still remain independent and self-governing, because they still have the power as sovereign states to exit the Union. So their continuing compliance and membership of the European Union is an act of self-government, not an act of submission.

The same applies to their financial relations, which is not a special case. As sovereign states, the Member States are free to engage with other sovereigns, borrow and lend, and ultimately join their monetary policies and central banks operations. But unlike private persons who are subject to a particular jurisdiction, they are also free to default on their loans, since there is no higher power in international law that can force them to pay. Their co-operation in all these structures of politics and economics is a matter of international legal co-operation of states, not a matter of the authority of a single jurisdiction. There is not such global jurisdiction over states. So the continuing participation of states in the world financial system under international law is the result of their continuing self-government, not its denial.

The German Court was therefore mistaken to say that self-government was at stake in agreeing the Eurozone rescue programmes. What was at stake was something equally important, namely the sharing of risks inside the common project of European Monetary Union. But this important issue is not a matter of constitutional law. It is a matter of economic policy. Such issues are properly left to democratically elected governments. So democracy in the Eurozone requires the opposite of what the Federal Constitutional Court said it does. It requires that independent peoples are free to choose economic policies through the deliberations of their parliaments, not the pronouncements of courts.

VI. Representation and Accountability

It is now time to look at the European side of the problem. The German Constitutional Court's sceptical view of the Eurozone rescue was based on a mistake. The Court identified power over decisions with power over outcomes. Its judgment sought to apply a collective theory of democracy, a theory which in any event sits uneasily with most of the philosophical discussion on the subject. Yet, it failed to apply even that theory well for the sharing of economic risks does not affect self-government as the power to make decisions. We must now turn to the egalitarian theories. For these theories, I remind you, democracy is an individual and not a collective entitlement. It signifies rights to a certain equal political procedure or participation as argued by Waldron or to a fuller range of substantive equality as argued by Dworkin. The great advantage of these theories is that they do not draw a stark distinction between domestic and international institutions. It is clear that international institutions can respect equality as well as or even better than domestic ones. What does this mean for the Eurozone?

I start with the premise, which I argued for above, that we cannot expect European institutions to imitate national democracy. They need to adjust democracy in ways appropriate for the international domain. I now assume, with the egalitarian theories, that democracy is not simply a procedural device, which could perhaps be readily transposed in some formal way to the European Union. Democracy, the egalitarian theories argue, requires a political community which is committed to deliberation and treats all its members, both in its procedures and in its outcomes, as worthy of equal respect. The European Union is not a political community in this sense. It is a union of peoples who themselves are organised in representative democracies and whose institutions enjoy legitimacy within the institutional architecture of the union itself. A union of peoples can promote democratic equality without at the same time aiming to become a democracy.

We must draw an important distinction in the institutions of democracy. We need to distinguish between mechanisms of representation and mechanisms of accountability. The first operate in advance of decision making, for example making sure that the exercise of decision-making power is allocated to those with the appropriate standing. Elections of Members of Parliament or of a president play that role in all Western democracies. The mechanisms of accountability, on the other hand, operate in a different way. They provide for techniques of retrospective evaluation after a decision has been reached. It is clear that because the process is known in advance, the prospect of such evaluation serves as a check on power as it is being exercised. In this way representation and accountability are two sides of the same coin. Decision makers are elected by people who care about their own interests. Those elected then act with a view to serving these interests and with a view to the assessment they will be subject to. In turn, the public mechanism of accountability will inform the process of election and the new round of representation.

The distinction between representation and accountability helps us understand the difference between procedural theories and substantive theories of democracy. Procedural theories put their emphasis on representation. It is important to them how the bodies that make decisions are constituted. They demand equality primarily in the procedures by which the decision-making body comes about. Substantive theories, by contrast, put the emphasis elsewhere. They consider equality in representation to be as important as equality in accountability. They impose additional egalitarian standards on the outcome of the decisions of parliaments and elected presidents. They need this as an ex post facto test of the democratic standing of any decision reached by the correct procedure and as a guarantee that the rights of minorities will not be violated. In a way, for substantive theories, procedure is not enough.

Looking at the institutions of democracy as they work in the modern state it is obvious that our systems do not choose between one and the other theory. In practice they combine both. The United Kingdom recognises very wide parliamentary sovereignty but at the same time accepts substantive tests via the Human Rights Act and a very robust system of legal accountability through judicial review. The United States gives power to the Supreme Court to hold laws unconstitutional, but at the same time permits elected bodies to amend the constitution if they muster enough parliamentary support. Democracy relies both on representation and on accountability. Representation and accountability work together, even though they do different jobs. In the best cases, they jointly ensure effective, transparent and legitimate government.[65]

How does a more sophisticated view of egalitarian democracy help us understand the European Union? I believe that the EU respects both representation and accountability, but it does so as an international organisation, a union of peoples, not as a federal state. The key here is to understand that the treaties assume that the task of representation is largely domestic. Representation in the EU is respected indirectly, first, in the way that governments are held to represent their peoples in the procedures of the Council, second in the amendment of the treaties and third in the process of appointing the Commission and the Court of Justice. It is respected, moreover, directly in the direct election of the European Parliament. It is obvious, however, that the European Parliament is not the main focus of representation. It does not enjoy full legislative powers like domestic parliaments, but shares its powers with the Commission and the Council. Moreover, it is not elected according to a test of population, but allows smaller states to be overrepresented. So representation in the EU is not neglected, but is adjusted for the case of a union of independent peoples.

In the Eurozone the situation is somewhat more complex. A great deal of legislative power belongs to the Commission, the Council and the Parliament, but most of the emergency measures were decided by the informal group of the Eurozone finance ministers, the 'Eurogroup'. The Member States are also powerful in the Governing Council of the recently created European Stability Mechanism. The ECB is obviously independent of all these other decision makers. Does the Eurozone respect the principle of representation when it acts in these complex ways? I believe that it does, partly. Both in EU policies as a whole and in the Eurozone in particular, representation is achieved through domestic institutions, a fact which the FCC has correctly observed in all of its decisions. The missing element from representation in the Eurozone is the role of national parliaments, and especially of the opposition to the government, which ought to have a way of questioning the decisions of the 27 governments as a whole.

The most distinctive way, however, in which the European Union respects democratic equality concerns accountability. I follow here Ruth Grant and Robert Keohane, for whom international institutions must respond to tests of accountability appropriate to their origins and functions, without seeking to imitate

[65] And it is perhaps important to note that 'direct democracy', ie democracy that is based on majority decision making wherever possible by all those affected by the decisions, requires neither representation nor accountability.

domestic democracy.[66] They define accountability as meaning that 'some actors have the right to hold other actors to a set of standards, to judge whether they have fulfilled their responsibilities in light of these standards, and to impose sanctions if they determine that these responsibilities have not been met'.[67] Grant and Keohane make the important point that accountability mechanisms can take different forms that, although not constituting principles of democracy, may be taken to be principles compatible with democratic accountability. These include less political forms such as 'reputational' and 'market' accountability. For the more political kinds of accountability, however, they distinguish between five types, namely 'hierarchical', 'supervisory', 'legal', 'fiscal' and 'peer' accountability. The first two do not apply to the EU. The last three, however, do.

Legal accountability means that 'agents abide by formal rules and procedures and be prepared to justify their actions in those terms, in courts or quasi-judicial arenas'.[68] There are numerous examples of this in the European Union. The most important, in my view, is that the Member States are subject directly to the supervision of the Court of Justice, either by way of actions by the Commission through preliminary references or by their own courts. This means that the Member States do not need to rely on sanctions or other measures of international law in their mutual relations. But the same accountability applies to EU institutions. Both the Council and the Commission can be brought before the Court of Justice. Important exclusive powers of the EU are open to judicial scrutiny before national and European courts. The powerful Directorate General of Competition, for example, publishes its own standards on its procedures[69] and is subject to judicial scrutiny which is judged to satisfy the standards of the European Convention of Human Rights.[70] The ECB is also subject to judicial supervision.[71] There are numerous other examples.

'Fiscal accountability' means 'mechanisms through which funding agencies can demand reports from, and ultimately sanction, agencies that are recipients of funding'.[72] There is a great deal of fiscal accountability, although it is not as powerful as it ought to be. For years, the Commission has been turning a blind eye to suspect practices. This attitude is now changing. Ideally, strong institutions of fiscal accountability will apply whenever the EU distributes funds directly to the Member States (eg 'cohesion funds') and also in the process of the 'programmes' of financial stability initiated for Greece, Ireland and Portugal in 2010. These

---

[66] R Grant and RO Keohane, 'Accountability and Abuses of Power in World Politics' (2005) 99 *American Political Science Review* 29–43.

[67] ibid 29.

[68] ibid 36.

[69] See eg European Commission, *Commission notice on best practices for the conduct of proceedings concerning Articles 101 and 102 TFEU* [2011] OJ C308/6.

[70] See Judgment of the European Court of Human Rights of 27 September 2011 in case *A Menarini Diagnostics SRL v Italy* (Application No 43509/08) paras 57–67 and Cases C-272/09 P *KME Germany AG and Others v Commission*, C-386/10 P *Chalkor AE Epexergasias Metallon v Commission* and C-389/10 P *KME Germany AG and Others v Commission*, judgments of 8 December 2011.

[71] See eg Case C-11/00 *Commission v European Central Bank* [2003] ECR I-7215.

[72] Grant and Keohane, 'Accountability' (n 66) 36.

schemes of assistance have come with very strong conditionality, monitored by the Commission, the ECB and the IMF.

Finally peer accountability 'arises as the result of mutual evaluation of organizations by their counterparts'.[73] It sits alongside what they call 'reputational' accountability. This is a complex set of ideas. Here we must take into account that the institutions and the leaders of the EU are constantly being evaluated in the public sphere by their counterparts in the Member States, courts, governments and the civil service. So peer accountability is the negotiating context for all the meetings of the Member States from the European Council down. We must bear in mind that the whole institutional apparatus of the European Union is entirely in the hands of the Member State governments and parliaments, which can amend every aspect of it by way of treaty amendment. There are, therefore, reputational costs for national leaders and parliaments, if they are seen to support failing policies or persons at the European level. This kind of accountability requires the highest possible transparency of the organisations being evaluated, but the EU, at least in principle, provides for it.

The Union has a comprehensive law of freedom of information, based on Article 15(1) of the Treaty on the Functioning of the European Union (TFEU), which states that in order to promote good governance and ensure the participation of civil society, the Union's institutions, bodies, offices and agencies are to conduct their work as openly as possible. Details of the right to access to documents are to be outlined in secondary legislation applicable to each institution. Interestingly, monetary union provides for some exceptions to these general rules. Article 15(3) TFEU provides that the Court of Justice, the ECB and the European Investment Bank are to be subject to such transparency rules only when 'exercising their administrative tasks'. This is a reflection of the effect that sensitive information may have on the markets. In fact, the secrecy of certain internal reports was recently successfully defended by the ECB in a case, where the General Court ruled that prohibition of access was allowed on the basis that disclosure might have 'affected the effective conduct of economic policy in Greece and the Union'.[74]

So all in all, the institutional framework of the European Union provides some important opportunities for both representation and accountability. Is this sufficient for democratic legitimacy of the EU and the Eurozone? Only a detailed assessment can provide a complete answer. Nevertheless, I hope that I have shown that an answer is possible. The tests we need to apply in order to answer the question are not the unreasonable ones of a collective view of democracy nor the unwarranted tests of a complete egalitarian democracy as they apply to the domestic case. The EU is a union of peoples and needs to be assessed both collectively as an international project and separately as a union of distinct democracies. Both assessments are best performed, in my view, with the tools of egalitarian democracy.

---

[73] ibid 37.
[74] See Case T-590/10 *Thesing and Bloomberg Finance LP v European Central Bank*, General Court 29 November 2012, para 63.

VII. Applications

What can we say about the institutions of the Eurozone? I will now try to bring the various strands of the argument together in a rough and ready review of the Eurozone and its institutions. I will say a few things about the ECB, the European Stability Mechanism and the Fiscal Compact. I will argue that when all is taken into account, they are on the way to meeting the tests of democratic accountability for a union of peoples.

The most independent institution in the EU is the ECB. But its status, for the time being, is not a threat to democracy. Its mandate was agreed unanimously by the various Member States. Those unwilling to participate in monetary union have opted not to. The operation of the ECB is controlled mainly by reputation and legal accountability. Its mandate is fixed in treaties and secondary legislation, whereas its operations are overseen by the Court of Justice. The ECB's stated mission of price stability is clear and is outlined in the TFEU and the Protocol On the Statute of the European System of Central Banks and the ECB, which were duly ratified by all Member States. It may be criticised on the basis of policy reasons, yet as long as the Bank stays within its mandate, there is no threat to representation or accountability.

Some acts of the Bank may threaten this assessment. The decision of its Governing Council of 6 September 2012 to proceed with 'Outright Monetary Transactions' (OMT) tests the limits of the Bank's mandate – and is now under challenge before the German Constitutional Court.[75] In its decision of September 2012 the Court said: 'an acquisition of government bonds on the secondary market by the European Central Bank aiming at financing the Members' budgets independently of the capital markets is prohibited as well, as it would circumvent the prohibition of monetary financing'.[76] The Court says that the Bank cannot circumvent Article 123 TFEU, which prohibits it from financing the Member States. I think the FCC is right to raise the issue, because the terms of reference of the ECB must be respected, not just for rule of law reasons but also for reasons of democratic accountability. The Bank must only do the job it has been given. Nevertheless, the best forum to decide this issue must be the Court of Justice of the European Union.

The European Stability Mechanism, by contrast, is a fully political because fully inter-governmental mechanism that now supplements the EMU as provided for by the treaties. The ESM is a new international organisation that is effectively in the hands of the Member States. It is only accountable in a fragmented way. Its decision makers decide for the Eurozone as a whole, but are accountable only before a part of it. So a German minister is accountable to German voters alone,

---

[75] See Editorial Comments, 'Debt and Democracy: "United States then, Europe now?"' (2012) 49 *CMLR* 1833, 1837.

[76] BVerfG, para 247 of the English translation.

even when they are taking a decision that affects profoundly the future of other nations. This inter-governmental arrangement meets the tests of representation only partially. It represents the voices of one party only, whereas the decisions it reaches affect everyone. For the same reason the ESM may fail the tests of account-ability. Perhaps an appropriate way to remedy this defect is to create a special Assembly or Chamber that collects elected representatives from the Eurozone countries, who would be able to question the members of the Eurogroup and then debate its decisions. Such a European Assembly could well be composed of mem-bers of national parliaments, so as to have not only government representatives but also representatives from the opposition in the affected countries.[77]

Finally, the Treaty on Stability, Coordination and Governance (TSCG) is an inter-governmental agreement which is technically not part of EU law. For that reason it seems to escape the institutional mechanisms described above. It has been signed by all the members of the EU except for the UK and the Czech Republic. The Treaty will only be binding for all Euro-area Member States, while other contracting parties will be bound once they adopt the Euro or earlier if they wish. The fiscal part of the Treaty is referred to as 'Fiscal Compact' and requires that parties achieve macroeconomic objectives clearly defined. The Treaty pro-vides for automatic penalties in case of failure to comply. It also requires that these budget rules shall be implemented in national law through provisions of 'binding force and permanent character, preferably constitutional'. It is obvious, however, that the Treaty is not entirely outside the scope of the EU. First, it pro-vides for some enforcement on the part of the Court of Justice, on the basis of state to state actions. But it also provides for some process of accountability. Article 13 of the Treaty provides for a new European Assembly of parliamentari-ans. It says that 'the European Parliament and the national Parliaments of the Contracting Parties will together determine the organisation and promotion of a conference of representatives of the relevant committees of the European Parliament and representatives of the relevant committees of national Parliaments in order to discuss budgetary policies and other issues covered by this Treaty'. This is clearly to be welcomed as an indication of the desire of the Member States to improve both representation and accountability in the Eurozone.

VIII. Conclusion

Democracy is a principle of equality. It finds its truest expression in institutions that are supported by a culture of trust and a tradition of public deliberation. But democracy is not just a principle for internal policies. It extends to the proper

---

[77] One detailed such proposal was presented by A Schäfer and F Schulz, 'A Conference of Parliaments for Europe: New Ways of Interparliamentary Cooperation' (Berlin, Friedrich-Ebert-Stiftung, International Policy Analysis, 2013) www.library.fes.de/pdf-files/id/ipa/09869.pdf.

terms of any state's relations with other states and other democracies. It requires states to engage with others in a way that recognises and actively respects their equal standing. In that sense an international organisation or union can be governed by exactly the same principles of democratic equality as any state. In this domain, however, the principle requires fair, open and collective institutions of decision making that complement national institutions and not compete with them.

The FCC's decisions on democracy and the European Union sought to express these insights through the device of a theory of democracy focused on the sovereign will of a people. This theory, in my view, leaves out some very important institutional elements of democracy. The preceding analysis suggests two crucial distinctions that we need to make. First, we must distinguish between egalitarian and collective views of democracy. The collective view of democracy is tempting because it simplifies the problem, but it is ultimately a flawed attempt at understanding democracy. Second, we must distinguish between institutions of representation and institutions of accountability. We must accept that democracy requires both and that institutions of accountability can and should be shared with other democracies, even though institutions of representation may not. Finally, any theory of democracy for the EU must distinguish between the legitimacy of state institutions before its own citizens and the legitimacy of the European architecture as a whole before all the citizens of Europe. A legitimate EU must respect both the equality of states as self-governing communities and the demand for accountability of all institutions to all citizens.

Looked at from this perspective the institutions of the European Union are not as illegitimate as they seem to many. That the European Parliament, for example, is not a proper representative institution for the European peoples is not a valid criticism. That the Court of Justice is not a supreme court with a right to hear appeals from all courts in Europe is not a valid criticism. An egalitarian conception of a democratic union of peoples allows both for deep integration of distinct areas of policy, such as trade, product safety, environmental policy, competition and monetary policy among others, and for the independence of the self-governing states that are its members. It is part of an ideal architecture of a union of peoples that the Member States must retain their sovereign power and democratic right to decide how exactly to participate. The same architecture provides for continuing mechanisms of representation and accountability.

If this is true, then improving the democratic accountability of current European institutions is both possible and necessary. When the Four Presidents of the European Union institutions proposed democratic accountability in their plan for a more complete monetary union, they were not making a mistake. The Union can become more democratic without seeking to become a democracy.

4

Debt Limits in Constitutional Law: The 'Debt Brake'

GREGOR KIRCHHOF

The historical development of public debt in post-war Germany reflects a paradigm shift that took place in the early 1970s. During the first 25 years following the war, explicit government debt rose to approximately €63 billion,[1] which by current standards is almost negligible. Yet today, 42 years later, explicit public debt exceeds €2,000 billion.[2] This figure also does not include the implicit governmental debt due to commitments for retirement benefits and future claims concerning the social security system.[3] It is estimated that these items exceed explicit debt by a factor that falls between two and four. Given the magnitude of this debt, it is surprising that public finances in Germany are regarded as sound.

During the early 1970s, incurring debt became a normal way of financing governmental expenditure.[4] However, given Germany's historical background, the opposite would have been expected. In the wake of the Second World War, Germany was after all faced with a unique situation because it was necessary to rebuild the country.[5] Thereafter, it was frequently argued that special circumstances warranted public borrowing in the interest of future generations.[6] At no period in the history of the Federal Republic was this argument more valid than

---

[1] Statistisches Bundesamt, *Finanzen und Steuern, Schulden der öffentlichen Haushalte, Fachserie 14, Reihe 5* (2011) 20, 25.

[2] Bundesministerium der Finanzen (BMF), *Monatsbericht*, September 2011, 110.

[3] Sachverständigenrat zur Begutachtung der gesamtwirtschaftlichen Entwicklung, *Staatsverschuldung wirksam begrenzen. Expertise im Auftrag des Bundesministers für Wirtschaft und Technologie* (Berlin, 2007) 24.

[4] E Dönnebrink, M Erhardt, F Höppner and M Sudhof, 'Entstehungsgeschichte und Entwicklung des BMF-Konzepts' in C Kastrop, G Meister-Scheufelen and M Sudhof (eds), *Die neuen Schuldenregeln im Grundgesetz. Zur Fortentwicklung der bundesstaatlichen Finanzbeziehungen* (Berlin, Wissenschafts-Verlag, 2010) 22, 25.

[5] cf Statistisches Bundesamt, *Statistisches Jahrbuch 2011*. For the Federal Republic of Germany, using 'international overviews' (237ff); HJ Brodesser, B Fehn, T Franosch and W Wirth, *Wiedergutmachung und Kriegsfolgenliquidation. Geschichte – Regelungen – Zahlungen* (Munich, CH Beck, 2000) 247ff.

[6] See for further discussion G Kirchhof, *Die Allgemeinheit des Gesetzes* (Mohr Siebeck, Tübingen, 2009) 574ff.

immediately after the war. From a legal point of view, the new paradigm had its origins in the reform of the so called 'debt brake' in the year 1969.[7]

This paradigm shift could also be taken as an example of what took place elsewhere. Public debt underwent a comparable development in several countries – except, among others, in the United Kingdom.[8] The Euro was introduced at a time when public debt was high. Thus, the risks of a common currency were known, but so were the benefits for the Common Market and freedom.[9] The myriad interlinkages and interdependencies between financial systems, which were brought even closer together by the introduction of the Euro, were not likely to have been so well known. Due to these interlinkages and the potential chain reactions that could be triggered in the event a country leaves the Eurozone, the Chancellor believes that there are no other options as regards rescue of the Euro: 'The dangers of uncontrolled insolvency on the part of Greece [a small Euro country] are', she added, 'incalculable. If the Euro fails, Europe fails.'[10] This presumption is at the very least questionable. Nevertheless, Mrs Merkel insists on this credo with a tenacity that is reminiscent of Cato the Elder. A recent study may help to make this more understandable. According to this study, Greece, Ireland, Portugal and Spain received so called target loans. If these countries leave the Eurozone, Germany will – this is the conclusion of the study – be left standing with a three digit billion amount of debts resulting from these loans alone.[11]

The stability of the Eurozone is weakened over the long term, rather than strengthened by such covert rescue packages. Consistent budgetary discipline on the part of the Euro countries is necessary to ensure stability.[12] Therefore, the planned Fiscal Compact that will compel the Member States to adopt national debt brakes will be a welcomed step in the right direction. A growth pact, as currently proposed,[13] will help as well, but only if it does not pave the way to unreasonable government debt. However, the planned Fiscal Compact would be in violation of European law.[14] Nevertheless, the Member Countries would still be well-advised to introduce clear debt ceilings on their own. The provisions of

---

[7] See below section I.

[8] cf C Cottarell and A Schaechter, 'Long-Term Trends in Public Finances in the G-7 Economies' (IMF Staff Position Note, IMF 2010) www.imf.org/external/pubs/ft/spn/2010/spn1013.pdf, 5ff.

[9] See BVerfGE 97, 350, 360f – *Euro*.

[10] Policy Statement by Chancellor Angela Merkel, 27 February 2012.

[11] HW Sinn and T Wollmershäuser, 'Target Loans. Current Account Balances and Capital Flows: The ECB's Resuce Facility' (2011) NBER Working Paper 17626, available at www.nber.org/papers/w17626, 5ff; cf J Weidmann, 'Was steckt hinter den Target2-Salden' *Frankfurter Allgemeine Zeitung* (13 March 2012) 11.

[12] cf N Heinen, 'Debt brakes for Euroland. Strengthening the stability pact with national debt rules' Deutsche Bank Research, EU Monitor 74 (12 July 2010) 1.

[13] G Westerwelle, 'A Growth Pact for Europe' *The Washington Post* (Washington DC, 30 May 2010) www.washingtonpost.com/opinions/a-growth-pact-for-europe/2012/05/23/gJQAFOr9kU_story.html. S Gabriel, FW Steinmeier and P Steinbrück, 'Der Weg aus der Krise – Wachstum und Beschäftigung in Europa' (15 May 2012) available at www.spd-berlin.de/w/files/spd-positionen/201205_spd_wachstumspakt.pdf.

[14] See below section II.

Germany's constitution could serve as an important example here,[15] for the debt crisis represents a threat to the rule of law and democracy.[16]

I. The Paradigm Shift in the 1970s

In the 1970s, borrowing became an accepted instrument for financing parts of the German budget – and there has been no change in that attitude ever since. This paradigm shift resulted from the reform of the German constitution, the Basic Law, in 1969.[17]

The original version of the Basic Law quite effectively limited public borrowing; deficit spending was permitted only in the case of exceptional need and then only for investment purposes.[18] These criteria were certainly broadly constructed, but the basic tenor was that borrowing should be limited to exceptional circumstances. This interpretation was however abandoned in 1969.[19]

The resignation of finance minister Alex Möller in May 1971 is indicative of a turning point. Möller refused to accept responsibility for national debts in the region of €8 billion, a figure that hardly seems alarming by today's standards. He resigned because he was concerned about the stability of the federal budget and did not want to go down in history as the 'inflation minister'.[20] No minister of finance has resigned since for similar reasons.[21]

The purpose of the 1969 reform was to facilitate an anticyclical economic policy in keeping with the teachings of Keynes.[22] These teachings were however disregarded because public debt was not reduced – even when the economic landscape was favourable.[23] Similar to Goethe's sorcerer's apprentice ('Der Zauberlehrling'), politics were not able to handle the spirits they summoned.

---

[15] See below section III.

[16] See below section IV.

[17] 20th Act modifying the Basic Law of 12 May 1969, BGBl. I, 357; cf Kirchhof, *Die Allgemeinheit des Gesetzes* (n 6) 574ff.

[18] BGBl. 1949, 1.

[19] Dönnebrink, Erhardt, Höppner and Sudhof, 'Entstehungsgeschichte und Entwicklung des BMF-Konzepts' (n 4) 22, 23ff.

[20] E Wolfrum, *Die geglückte Demokratie. Geschichte der Bundesrepublik Deutschland von ihren Anfängen bis zur Gegenwart* (Klett-Cotta, Stuttgart,, 2006) 322; A Möller, *Genosse Generaldirektor* (Munich, Droemer Knaur, 1978) 486: 'Ich will keine Störung und keine gesteigerte Komplikation, sondern versuchen, alle Fraktionen des Bundestages wieder zurückzuführen auf den Weg der finanzpolitischen Solidität. Das gilt auch für die Opposition, die Milliardenanträge gestellt hat. Ich wollte, daß Solidität und Stabilität als die beiden Grundforderungen deutscher Innenpolitik beachtet werden'. See also A Möller, *Tatort Politik* (München, Droemer Knaur, 1982) 366ff.

[21] Dönnebrink, Erhardt, Höppner and Sudhof, 'Entstehungsgeschichte und Entwicklung des BMF-Konzepts' (n 4) 25.

[22] BVerfGE 79, 311, 331 f – *Staatsverschuldung I*; dissenting vote of Judges Di Fabio and Mellinghoff, BVerfGE 119, 96, 155, 157 – *Staatsverschuldung II*.

[23] Dissenting vote of Judges Di Fabio and Mellinghoff, BVerfGE 119, 96, 155, 172 – *Staatsverschuldung II*: 'Dauerrechtsverletzung' (continuous infringement). Statistisches Bundesamt, *Finanzen und Steuern. Schulden der öffentlichen Haushalte, Fachserie 14, Reihe 5* (2011) 20, 25.

The revised Article 115 of the Basic Law limited public borrowing to the total of investment expenditure. Any further borrowing was not to exceed that required to prevent 'disturbance of the overall economic equilibrium'.[24] The legal notion of what constitutes a 'disturbance of the overall economic equilibrium' has never been properly defined.[25] Statutory law defines this equilibrium in terms of four partial goals:[26] 1) price stability, 2) high employment, 3) balanced foreign trade and 4) steady and adequate economic growth. This configuration of goals has been referred to as the 'magic square' because it would indeed take a feat of magic to achieve all four objectives simultaneously. But the square was defective from the very beginning as the goal of equitable distribution of income and wealth was not included for political reasons. Experts then soon added another seven sides: 1) a call for stable governmental financing, 2) protection of the environment, 3) humane working conditions, 4) social safety nets, 5) conservation of resources, 6) co-operation at the European and international levels and 7) global responsibility on the part of the industrialised countries. In this regard, the side of stable governmental financing is remarkable. The upshot would have been a magic 12-sided polygon, but one that would not have met with consensus.[27]

The Government used this imprecise legal concept to steadily increase the national debt. In every other year since 1969 there was the assumption that the overall economic equilibrium was disturbed.[28] These assumptions cannot possibly have been valid over a period of 40 years. The Government also avoided another constitutional issue as the Basic Law permits borrowing only insofar as it is necessary to restore economic equilibrium.

This experience should serve as a warning against the use of legal terms that do not set clearly defined limits to borrowing during the budget process. Any subsequent judicial controls are necessary to enforce the law, but will regularly be too late. Of course, it is always possible to declare a budget unconstitutional retrospectively, but the funds will have already been borrowed and spent.

---

[24] Article 115 of the Basic Law, 20th Act modifying the Basic Law of 12 May 1969, BGBl. I, 357: '(1) The borrowing of funds and the assumption of surety obligations, guarantees, or other commitments that may lead to expenditures in future fiscal years shall require authorization by a federal law specifying or permitting computation of the amounts involved. Revenue obtained by borrowing shall not exceed the total of investment expenditures provided for in the budget; exceptions shall be permissible only to avert a disturbance of the overall economic equilibrium. Details shall be regulated by a federal law.'

[25] Kirchhof, *Die Allgemeinheit des Gesetzes* (n 6) 579ff; cf BVerfGE 119, 96 – *Staatsverschuldung II*.

[26] § 1(2) Gesetz zur Förderung der Stabilität und des Wachstums der Wirtschaft (Act on the Advancement of Stability and of Economic Growth) of 8 June 1967, BGBl. I, 582.

[27] G Kirchhof, in H v Mangoldt, F Klein and C Starck, *Kommentar zum Grundgesetz*, 6th edn (München, Vahlen, 2010) Article 109 para 42; Kirchhof, *Die Allgemeinheit des Gesetzes* (n 6) 580ff.

[28] M Groneck and W Kitterer, *Schuldenverbot für die Bundesländer* (IFO-Schnelldienst, 2007) 12–13; cf H Beck and A Prinz, *Staatsverschuldung: Ursachen, Folgen, Auswege* (Munich, CH Beck, 2012) 94; see also Statistisches Bundesamt, *Finanzen und Steuern. Schulden der öffentlichen Haushalte, Fachserie 14, Reihe 5* (2011) 20, 25.

II. Current Reform Efforts at the European Level

European law does in fact set such clearly defined limits to national debt. It does not make use of vague legal terms, but rather figures. National deficits may not exceed 3 per cent and public debt is capped at 60 per cent of gross domestic product.[29] These quantitative requirements have, however, not been followed – and that is one reason why the Member States of the European Union, with the exception of the United Kingdom and the Czech Republic, agreed on what is referred to as the Fiscal Compact on 2 March 2012. The compact is intended to be ratified in the near future.[30] The parties to the Treaty agree to the principle – and that itself is an accomplishment – that the budget has to be balanced without borrowing funds.[31] However, this goal will be considered to have been achieved if the countries make timely progress in the direction of medium-term objectives that they proposed themselves. This involves the use of what is referred to as an 'adjustment path', which will be reviewed with the Commission in the context of overall assessment.[32] If a country deviates from its adjustment path, correction mechanisms, which will also be co-ordinated with the Commission, will be triggered automatically.[33] The countries must adopt all these rules in the form of binding – preferably constitutional – provisions of national law and the European Court of Justice will be responsible for enforcement.[34]

The obligation to balance the budget without borrowing is to be fulfilled with the help of an adjustment path that is itself vague. That makes it surprising that the Federal Ministry of Finance praises the new debt ceilings for being strict.[35] But the Treaty is correct to call for agreement on an adjustment path because it would preserve the budgetary independence of the national parliaments and permit the necessary transition from burgeoning debt to solid budgetary policy.

National debt brakes would especially represent a viable approach – and that is what makes it so regrettable that the Fiscal Compact is incompatible with European law. The Compact would give the Commission and the Court of Justice additional authority. It might constitute a special agreement about the jurisdiction of the Court.[36] Even in this case, because of the principle of conferral, giving the Commission additional authority would require the consent of all Member

---

[29] Article 126(2)2 TFEU; accompanying Protocol (No 12) on the Excessive Deficit Procedure, [2010] OJ C83/279.

[30] cf Article 14(2) of the Treaty on Stability Coordination and Governance in the Economic and Monetary Union, available at www.european-council.europa.eu/media/639235/st00tscg26_en12.pdf (Fiscal Compact).

[31] Fiscal Compact, Article 3(1)(a).

[32] ibid Article 3(1)(b), (c); Article 5.

[33] ibid Article 3(1)(e), (2); cf Article 4.

[34] ibid Article 3(2); Article 8.

[35] FAQ on the Fiscal Compact, see www.bundesfinanzministerium.de/Content/DE/FAQ/2012-08-17-fiskalvertrag-faq.html.

[36] Article 273 TFEU.

States of the European Union.[37] In the event that the United Kingdom and the Czech Republic should continue to withhold their consent, the Fiscal Compact cannot enter into force and effect. The European countries should nevertheless still adopt clear national debt brakes – the new German legislation could serve as an example.

III. The New German Debt Brake

German law concerning governmental debt was reformed again in 2009.[38] For the first time in German constitutional history, the Basic Law explicitly requires budgets to be balanced without borrowing of funds.[39]

---

[37] Article 5(1), (2) TEU; Article 23(1) of the Basic Law; A v Bogdandy and J Bast, in E Grabitz, M Hilf and M Nettesheim (eds), *Das Recht der Europäischen Union*, 46th edn (Munich, CH Beck, 2011) Article 5 TEU para 14: An extension of the Union's competences is only possible via a Treaty change, which guarantees participation and veto rights of each Member State. See PC Müller-Graff, 'Die rechtliche Neujustierung der Europäischen Wirtschafts- und Währungsunion' (2012) 176 *Zeitschrift für das Gesamte Handels- und Wirtschaftsrecht* 2, 12–13; D Thym, *Ungleichzeitigkeit und Europäisches Verfassungsrecht* (Nomos, Baden-Baden, 2004) 317: 'Hierauf aufbauend kann man die Organleihe der europäischen Institutionen durch folgende allgemeine Regeln beschränken: Die Übertragung eines funktionellen Ausschnitts des institutionellen Gefüges der Europäischen Union auf eine völkerrechtliche Kooperation einiger Mitgliedstaaten ist grundsätzlich zulässig, soweit das Primärrecht dies gestattet oder ein besonderer Vertrag aller Mitgliedstaaten dies vorsieht.' See also D Thym, 'Ein Bypass, kein Herzinfarkt', verfassungsblog.de, 13 December 2011: 'Ob neue Befugnisse der Kommission aufgrund des Fiskalpakts der Zustimmung aller Mitgliedstaaten bedürfen, ist nicht abschließend geklärt. Hierauf dürfte es im Ergebnis jedoch nicht ankommen, soweit die Schuldenbremse einzig im Rahmen bestehender Überwachungsverfahren beurteilt wird. Eben diese ermächtigen die Kommission bereits zur Aufsicht über nationale Sparbemühungen.'

[38] 57th Act modifying the Basic Law of 29 July 2009, BGBl. I, 2248.

[39] C Seiler, 'Konsolidierung der Staatsfinanzen mithilfe der neuen Schuldenregel' [2009] *Juristenzeitung* 721, 721f; G Kirchhof, *Die Allgemeinheit des Gesetzes* (Tübingen, Mohr Siebeck, 2009) 589.

Article 109(3) of the Basic Law reads:

The budgets of the Federation and the Länder shall in principle be balanced without revenue from credits. The Federation and Länder may introduce rules intended to take into account, symmetrically in times of upswing and downswing, the effects of market developments that deviate from normal conditions, as well as exceptions for natural disasters or unusual emergency situations beyond governmental control and substantially harmful to the state's financial capacity. For such exceptional regimes, a corresponding amortisation plan must be adopted. Details for the budget of the Federation shall be governed by Article 115 with the proviso that the first sentence shall be deemed to be satisfied if revenue from credits does not exceed 0.35 percent in relation to the nominal gross domestic product. The Länder themselves shall regulate details for the budgets within the framework of their constitutional powers, the proviso being that the first sentence shall only be deemed to be satisfied if no revenue from credits is admitted.

Article 115 of the Basic Law reads:

(1) The borrowing of funds and the assumption of surety obligations, guarantees, or other commitments that may lead to expenditures in future fiscal years shall require authorisation by a federal law specifying or permitting computation of the amounts involved.

(2) Revenues and expenditures shall in principle be balanced without revenue from credits. This principle shall be satisfied when revenue obtained by the borrowing of funds does not exceed 0.35 percent in relation to the nominal gross domestic product. In addition, when economic

According to the Law, borrowing of funds by the federal government may not exceed 0.35 per cent of the country's gross domestic product. That means the Basic Law starts out by prohibiting public borrowing, but then goes on to allow for an exception, the limit to which is expressed in quantitative terms. The budget – so goes the argument – needs room to breathe, but right now, however, the situation is such that excessive debt is threatening to suffocate the Government. The 0.35 per cent limit represents an exception to the prohibition of borrowing of funds. As a result, deficit spending is reserved for use only under special circumstances and with an explicit explanatory statement.[40] It is ironic that the 0.35 per cent figure is equivalent to the amount of national debts preceding the resignation of Alex Möller in 1971.[41]

The Basic Law permits two exceptions to the balanced budget rule. Both the federal government and the Länder may borrow funds in cases of exceptional occurrences and for economic reasons.[42] The Länder will have to achieve compliance with the newly set limits by the year 2020 and the federal government will have to comply by 2016.[43] Federal and state legislatures are already required to prepare budgets so that it will be possible to achieve this, but many of the Länder at least are currently in violation of this transitional requirement.

In the case of natural disasters or extraordinary events such as reunification, the country may borrow funds. But in that case, a corresponding amortisation plan must be adopted.[44] The Fiscal Compact also makes provision for such exceptional circumstances[45] – and that is as it should be. People who have been affected by a natural disaster ought to be helped even if it is necessary to borrow the means to do so.[46]

The Basic Law – again in this regard like the Fiscal Compact[47] – allows anti-cyclical measures to be taken to counteract the impact of economic upswings and

developments deviate from normal conditions, effects on the budget in periods of upswing and downswing must be taken into account symmetrically. Deviations of actual borrowing from the credit limits specified under the first to third sentences are to be recorded on a control account; debits exceeding the threshold of 1.5 percent in relation to the nominal gross domestic product are to be reduced in accordance with the economic cycle. The regulation of details, especially the adjustment of revenue and expenditures with regard to financial transactions and the procedure for the calculation of the yearly limit on net borrowing, taking into account the economic cycle on the basis of a procedure for adjusting the cycle together with the control and balancing of deviations of actual borrowing from the credit limit, requires a federal law. In cases of natural catastrophes or unusual emergency situations beyond governmental control and substantially harmful to the state's financial capacity, these credit limits may be exceeded on the basis of a decision by a majority of the Bundestag's Members. The decision has to be combined with an amortisation plan. Repayment of the credits borrowed under the sixth sentence must be accomplished within an appropriate period of time.

[40] Kirchhof, 'Kommentar zum Grundgesetz, (n 27) Article 109(3) paras 103ff.
[41] See above section I.
[42] Article 109(3)2 of the Basic Law.
[43] Article 143d(1) of the Basic Law.
[44] Article 109(3)2, 3 GG.
[45] Fiscal Compact, Article 3(1)(c), (3).
[46] Kirchhof, 'Kommentar zum Grundgesetz, (n 27) Article 109(3) paras 97ff.
[47] Fiscal Compact Article 3(1)(c), (3).

downswings.[48] Like the rule that dates from the year 1969, this is also rooted in the teachings of Keynes. It is questionable whether such teachings are to be invoked once again, given the existence of €2,000 billion in explicit government debts.[49] But the clear legal obligation to repay debt when the economy is thriving solves the problem arising from the fact that the teachings of Keynes were disregarded, that borrowing was not reduced when the economy was prospering.[50] Imitating the Swiss model, liabilities of the federal government are to be carried in a 'control account'.[51] In addition, an early warning system was created through the establishment of a new institution – the Stability Council.[52] The members of this council, in particular the ministers of finance of the federal government and the Länder, monitor the development of the budget to counter any crises that may result early on.[53] Thus, this system and the figures of the control account would be a reliable way to cap national debt.

However, statutory law seems to open the floodgates for new borrowing of funds. According to the Law, an exceptional situation would be considered to exist if the economy-wide production capacity rate is expected to be too low. As a result, concrete application of this possibility necessarily involves a forecast; productive capacity must be estimated for the gross domestic product targeted.[54] This is too vague to permit effective limitation of borrowing funds.[55] Change is called for here at the level of statutory law, rather than at the constitutional level. Whether or not the economic situation is to be considered exceptional should be determined on the basis of clear figures[56] stemming from the analysis of a longer series of budget years.[57] But even if the analysis shows that the economy is going through an unusual downswing – this does not automatically mean that funds may be borrowed. The Bundestag must show that anticyclical borrowing is required to restore economic stability.[58] Given the criticism of the teachings of Keynes,[59] this would also prove difficult.

After all, whether or not the new debt brake is successful will depend on the acceptance of a new paradigm – that borrowing must be limited to exceptional situations and specific reasons. If the legislative bodies are determined to violate

[48] Article 109(3)2 of the Basic Law.

[49] See above section I.

[50] Article 109(3)2 of the Basic Law; H Kube, in T Maunz, G Dürig and others (eds), *Grundgesetz* (Munich, CH Beck, October 2009) Article 115 paras 151–52.

[51] Article 115(2)4 of the Basic Law; Kirchhof, *Die Allgemeinheit des Gesetzes* (n 39) 595f.

[52] Article 109a of the Basic Law.

[53] Kirchhof, '*Kommentar zum Grundgesetz*, (n 27) Article 109a paras 1ff.

[54] § 5(2) Gesetz zur Ausführung von Artikel 115 des Grundgesetzes (Act on the execution of Article 115 Basic Law) of 10 August 2009, BGBl. I, 2702.

[55] Seiler, 'Konsolidierung der Staatsfinanzen mithilfe der neuen Schuldenregel' (n 39) 724; S Korioth, 'Das neue Staatsschuldenrecht – zur Zweiten Stufe der Föderalismusreform' [2009] *Juristenzeitung* 729, 732; Kube, 'Grundgesetz (n 50) Article 115 para 164; Kirchhof, (n 27) Article 109(3) paras 91–92.

[56] Kube, 'Grundgesetz (n 50) Article 115 paras 161ff.

[57] C Lenz and E Burgbacher, 'Die neue Schuldenbremse im Grundgesetz' [2009] *Neue Juristische Wochenschrift* 2561, 2563.

[58] Kirchhof, *Kommentar zum Grundgesetz*, (n 27) Article 109 paras 90ff.

[59] See for a summary Kube. 'Grundgesetz (n 50) Article 115 paras 153ff; Kirchhof, *Kommentar zum Grundgesetz*, (n 27) Article 109 paras 93, 95.

the law governing national deficits, this is likely to overburden the Federal Constitutional Court and erode the debt brake as well as the rule of law.

IV. Rule of Law and Democracy

According to Hegel, the Enlightenment was a glorious sunrise[60] that hailed legitimate public power: the rule of law and parliamentary democracy. The debt crisis represents a threat to these pillars of the modern state. If European law had been respected by the Member States, if the existing national debt limits had been complied with, there would hardly have been any debt crisis. Laws that are not obeyed lose their legitimacy and threaten the existence of the rule of law. Excessive public debt dilutes the authority of Parliament. This is obviously true in the case of Greece. But German democracy is also being eroded by national debt. In 2012, the federal government spent approximately €30 billion on interest repayments alone – which is 10 per cent of the whole budget. If this sum were available to further family, social, education or economic policy, society would benefit and the legislative power would be significantly strengthened. Interest expenses represent the second-largest item in the national budget after employment and social security. If the interest rate for 2010 had been 1 per cent higher, Germany's interest expense would have increased by approximately €17 billion.[61] This is indicative of the way politics depend on the financial economy and is therefore a further threat to democracy. The latitude of operation of the Bundestag is restricted even further by the costs of being in the Eurozone. High implicit national debt can be reduced only by reforming the social systems.[62] Reforms like the ones required here can be implemented at the political level only with great difficulty, but they are necessary if debt is to be distributed equitably over the generations. The path leading away from governmental debt will be long and steep. We will not be able to navigate this path without a paradigm shift: borrowing must be limited to exceptional situations and specific reasons.

The Fiscal Compact must not enter into force without the consent of all Member States of the European Union. Nevertheless, it could strengthen the rule of law and parliamentary democracy if it results in a trend towards effective national debt brakes throughout Europe and thereby triggers the required paradigm shift. After all, the crisis stresses an awareness of the Enlightenment, that recalls the famous etching of Francisco de Goya:[63] rule of law and parliamentary democracy have to be wide awake.

---

[60] GWF Hegel, *Vorlesungen über die Philosophie der Geschichte*, E Gans (ed), 3rd edn (Berlin, Duncker & Humblot, 1848) 535.

[61] Bund der Steuerzahler Deutschland e. V., *Zinsausgaben der öffentlichen Haushalte in Deutschland* (May 2011).

[62] Sachverständigenrat zur Begutachtung der gesamtwirtschaftlichen Entwicklung, *Staatsverschuldung wirksam begrenzen. Expertise im Auftrag des Bundesministers für Wirtschaft und Technologie* (2007) 24.

[63] Francisco de Goya, *The Sleep of Reason Produces Monsters*, 1797–99.

5

Debt Limits in German Constitutional Law – A UK Perspective

JOHN MCELDOWNEY

I. Introduction

Germany's so called 'debt brake' is a constitutional mechanism that seeks to ensure that fiscal policy is legally immune from direct political interference and acts as a constraint against bids for debt funded public spending. Eurozone countries have adopted a similar approach to Germany through the Fiscal Compact, a mechanism to constrain debt and borrowing. The Fiscal Compact was established for 26 out of the 27 EU Member States (with the exception of the UK) adopted through an inter-governmental (international agreement) outside the institutional framework of the EU. This was followed by the Treaty on Stability, Co-ordination and Governance in the Economic and Monetary Union (TSCG), signed by 25 Member States (the UK and the Czech Republic are the two exceptions). This chapter evaluates the German debt brake and the implications of the Fiscal Compact and the TSCG and takes account of Gregor Kirchof's valuable analysis of the German debt brake and its role in economic thinking.

The German debt brake can also be considered from a UK perspective. Although the UK is outside the Eurozone and the Fiscal Compact, it is the largest country whose exports and banks are closely tied to the Eurozone economy. The impact of the German debt brake and the Fiscal Compact on the UK are likely to be significant for the UK's economy and future growth. Instead of a legally enforceable debt brake, the UK first introduced a Fiscal Responsibility Act 2010, later, replaced by the Budget Responsibility and National Audit Act 2011, containing similar principles to the Fiscal Responsibility Act but with the innovation of an independent Office of Budget Responsibility (OBR) to monitor public spending and borrowing.

The UK's approach offers a less rigid alternative to the German debt brake that is capable of adapting to changing economic and fiscal conditions as well as any unexpected developments. In general the adoption of a less rigid form of debt brake that is less tied to legally enforceable rules under a Fiscal Responsibility law may offer a more workable alternative in the current economic climate. It may be argued that the weakness of the UK approach is its vulnerability to political change and direction. One benefit is that it cannot be directly enforced by the courts. The German debt brake and the Fiscal Compact certainly provide a strong constitutional and legal means of enforcing economic instruments with a heavy onus on the legal system and the judiciary. This might give preference to legal and constitutional doctrines over systems of political and parliamentary control. For example the German Constitutional Court has begun deliberations about Germany's contribution to the bail-out to help Greece and Ireland following the German Cabinet's approval of legislation to ratify the ESM Treaty and authorising Germany's contribution to the ESM. The ESM Treaty could not take effect on 1 July 2012 as originally planned.[1] The German Constitutional Court will conduct substantial hearings in 2013.[2]

II. The German 'Debt Brake'

Setting limits on public borrowing against the total of investment expenditures is contained in the newly revised Article 115 of the German Basic Law, fully operative in the fiscal year 2011. This is the first time the so called 'debt brake' has been adopted as a means of setting a stringent limit to govern sovereign debts. Before the adoption of the debt brake in Germany, there had been a 'golden rule' in a previous version of Article 115 that rather loosely set the limits of governmental borrowing to the level of net public investment. This limited net borrowing to net public investment meaning that borrowing was limited to the level of gross capital formation less depreciation and disinvestment. This approach gave rise to ambiguities in terms of what constituted 'investments' and for which there was no associated or direct net asset growth for the state. Many aspects of public spending contained elements of an investment including expenditure on research and development or education expenditure. Under various interpretations of Article 115, the Government was able to steadily increase the national debt based on a broad interpretation of Article 115 and use borrowing as a means of restoring economic equilibrium. This broad interpretation was favoured by the Government of the day. Borrowing was also supported by various statutory laws that set four broad goals: price stability, high employment, balanced foreign trade and steady and adequate economic growth. This was expanded to include broader social and environmental objectives and even stretched to global responsibility reaching into co-operation at European and international levels. Germany's experience of debt

---

[1] The ESM Treaty entered into force on 27 September 2012 for 16 signatories.
[2] House of Commons Library: *Germany and the Euro Rescue Agreements* SN/IA/6062 (16 July 2012).

financing had many positive aspects including the generation of its economy as well as the unification of the country. In such circumstances debt was regarded as justified. It was also underpinned by impressive growth in German economic output. The debt legacy left Germany to sustain debt at unprecedented levels that had to be reduced. The scale of borrowing in 2009 resulted in a debt to GDP ratio of 43.7 per cent for the federal government and 21.9 per cent for Germany's regional federal states. Overall the debt to GDP ratio was 73.2 per cent in 2009, a broader measure of debt including liquidity loans, holding arrangements and support to banks. The regular use of debt financing gave rise to a culture that considered debt as a 'normal' way of financing governmental expenditure. The legacy of debt financing that had begun in the 1970s, extended to the 1980s and '90s, and had been integrated into government thinking of that period. A close look at the original version of the Basic Law before 1969 reveals that it had been relatively effective in limiting public borrowing as deficit spending was rarely permitted and confined to the case of exceptional need and for investment purposes only.

The introduction of the debt brake is a useful mechanism to deter future government borrowing. It is also intended to address Germany's future demographic changes including potential increases in social security payments. Overall it is aimed at ensuring that public finances are sustainable in the long term and the debt to GDP ratio should be permanently reduced. The 2008 uncertainties raised by the financial crisis for banking financing and the instabilities in the Euro arising from inherent risks in the creation of a common currency have underlined the significance of the debt brake. It has helped to reinforce Germany's high reputation for prudence and good government, especially in the light of unification. Adopting a debt brake has arguably enhanced Germany's financial credibility and enhanced its reputation for balancing its budget. This provides an important bulwark against any economic downturn. Germany's other rationale for introducing the 'debt brake' arose, in part, from the requirements of the European Stability and Growth Pact. Germany's influence in the drawing up of the Fiscal Compact as part of a package of measures has driven forward the Eurozone members to adopt national debt brakes. In fact the German debt brake is tougher than that required by the Eurozone. National deficits may not exceed 3 per cent and public debt is capped at 60 per cent of GDP. This chapter addresses a number of questions. What lessons may be drawn from Germany's use of a debt brake? What is the UK's constitutional perspective and approach to debt limits? Is there a role for debt limits in addressing the current financial crisis? There is an active debate between economists as to the desirability of adopting debt brakes. It is seen by some as a means of constitutionally protecting electorates from prolific or self-serving politicians and assuring markets of financial responsibility. Others view debt brakes as too rigid and inappropriately adopting economic instruments into law in a form that is open to judicial interpretation. This may make it more difficult to respond to uncertain and unpredictable financial markets, that are often susceptible to fickle, eclectic and unforeseen events. Financial markets may act in an irrational way. This makes legality a difficult test of appropriateness.

III. Lessons from the Debt Brake in Germany

Article 110 of Germany's post-war constitution[3] stated that 'the budget shall be balanced with respect to revenue and expenditure'. Article 115 states that revenue obtained by borrowing shall not exceed the total of investment expenditures provided for in the budget'. Exceptions 'shall be permissible only to avert a disturbance of the overall economic equilibrium'. Although the exception was reasonably worded, it did not inhibit Germany from accumulating debts. Over many years this became common practice and in 1989 the reunification of Germany was accommodated through additional borrowing. It is estimated that German public debt increased from an equivalent of €623 billion in 1991 to €1.04 trillion in 1995, an increase of 67 per cent. The aftermath of the 2008 economic crisis questioned the wisdom of how Article 115 was interpreted. Germany reformed Article 115 of the Basic Law in 2009. The basic principle of having structurally balanced budgets at federal and Länder levels is to be found in Article 109 of the Basic Law. The reformed Article 115 brings into the Basic Law, for the first time, an explicit requirement that budgets should be balanced without borrowing federal funds. The principle of a balanced budget should be adhered to and the scope for borrowing is restricted. Funds by the Federal Government may not exceed 0.35 per cent of GDP annually and 0 per cent for the Länder. In essence this sets a fundamental prohibition on the Federation and the Länder balancing their budgets by borrowing, and the Länder are to comply by 2020. From 2016 the upper borrowing limit will be 0.34 per cent of GDP annually and this cannot be exceeded through any special funds or other means. In setting the upper limit the aim is not to borrow up to the limit but to use the upper limit as a means of operating a debt brake within a safety margin of the upper limit. Budget policy will also face the restriction that the previous practices of utilising one-off privatisation proceeds can no longer be used.

There is also a cyclical component in the debt brake. The aim is to address the long-term viability of public finances by taking account of a responsive approach to cyclical conditions as part of policy making. This is to avoid action used to stabilise the economy in phases of recession being used to continue borrowing when there is an upturn in the economy. There is a cyclical adjustment component to avoid this effect built into paragraph 5 of the reformed Article 115. Restrictions on borrowing are intended to be sustainable and the aim is to secure compliance with the rules when the budget is drawn up as well as when the budget is being executed. The means to achieve this end is through the operation of a control account with a duty to ensure that the budget is balanced within the medium term. The 0.35 per cent limit annually may represent an exception to the general rule against borrowing but it is to be limited. Implementing provisions are to be

[3] I am very grateful to Timothy Dodsworth LLB (Sheffield), LLM and LPC for help with some aspects of German law and practice.

found in ordinary legislation and this limits the obligation to reduce net borrowing in an upturn. It is difficult to set controls on legal obligations that are part of a statutory framework. According to the Federal Ministry of Finance this means reducing net borrowing to a lower threshold 1 per cent of GDP.

The debt brake also contains some exceptions in paragraph 2 of Article 115 that allow for debt borrowing for natural disasters or unusual emergency situations which are outside the control of the Government. The Federal Government and the Länder may borrow funds in cases that fall within the exception. It is intended that the exceptions should be limited and offer a more restrictive interpretation than the previous formulation of increasing net borrowing to avert 'a disturbance of the overall economic equilibrium'. Consequently normal cyclical variations are not grounds for justifying an exception. There is a further safety net to prevent government borrowing in breach of Article 115 through a re-interpretation of the exception. The Bundestag has to approve the operation of the exception as part of a so called 'amortisation plan', which provides for net borrowing above the standard limit to be reduced within a reasonable time frame. Finally, there is also the possibility under Article 109 of the Basic Law whereby there is a general rule that the Federal Government and the Länder may borrow funds in the case of exceptional circumstances and for economic reasons. This is a curious retention of the state of affairs existing before the revised Article 115. It may create opportunities to use statutory formulations of spending that meet economic necessity and boost spending when the economy requires, but is difficult to alter when the economy is unable to support such spending. As Gregor Kirchhof has shown there is the possibility that various statutory laws might operate to increase borrowing:

> However, statutory law seems to open the floodgates to new borrowing of funds. According to the law, an exceptional situation would be considered to exist if the economy-wide production capacity rate is expected to be too low. As a result, concrete application of this possibility necessarily involves a forecast; productive capacity must be estimated for the GDP targeted. This is too vague to permit effective limitation of borrowing funds.[4]

A newly established Stability Council was set up as a mechanism to check on borrowing as an 'early warning system'. The proof of the arrangements will only be demonstrated by their effectiveness. Undoubtedly the debt brake is intended to set serious restraints on the German Government's ability to borrow. In the light of the financial figures for the years 2009 and 2010, the new debt brake will have substantial impact on the scope for borrowing at federal and Lander levels. If long-term growth of 3 per cent GDP is secured, public debt would fall to below 50 per cent of GDP by 2040 and over the longer term to below 20 per cent. Critics of the debt brake point to transparency and accountability issues that arise from the Federal Government's operation of the debt brake. They point to the 2011 budget procedures not being published in detail until after the budget was passed. The

---

[4] See G Kirchof, 'Debt Limits in Constitutional Law: The "Debt Brake"', ch 4 in this volume.

example of the Swiss constitutional debt brake introduced in 2003 suggests that from 2003 to 2010 the debt ratio fell by 15 per cent, but this was mainly attributable to favourable economic trends. Similarly German success is not seen as being directly due to the debt brake but to rapid economic recovery in 2010 and 2011, accountable for GDP increases of 3.7 per cent and 3 per cent respectively.[5]

Critics of the German debt brake question whether the economic arguments justify the hype that the debt brake has enabled Germany to be more successful than its main rivals in balancing its budget.[6] They challenge assumptions that the Euro crisis is caused by unstable fiscal policy. Imbalances in foreign trade and individual Member States' problems may have been too easily discounted. There is the further assumption that financial markets are rational and respond to rational solutions. Still further there is an argument about the level at which the debt brake should be set. Setting at an artificial level may not be sufficiently well judged or appropriate. This benchmark is also important in terms of future investment in German debt.

The debt brake also ignores the operation of the Golden Rule – a prime economic tool that has been operational for over 60 years and for which there is considerable experience. The Golden Rule roughly permits new structural borrowing beyond the cycle equivalent to net public investment. This recognises the needs of future generations. Future prosperity and productivity are in part based on productive investments that are currently made. The past history of the Golden Rule suggests that when it is abused it leads to problems. Finding a suitable solution to the problem of abuse may mean adopting more stringent scrutiny and greater transparency in the way the Government calculates gross and net investment. Public investment is needed, excessive borrowing is not. Constitutional protection might be more appropriately calibrated to save this problem.

Operation of the debt brake coincides with a period when public budgets are under financed in structural terms as the strain of tax cuts has taken its effect. Closing the revenue gap leaves governments with serious challenges linking debt limits to stringent public spending cuts. The debt brake will inevitably lead indirectly to a legally enforced means of securing public spending cuts. This may damage the very policy making for which the debt brake is designed, namely a sustainable economy. The debt brake comes at a time of considerable economic instability which may not best suit its adoption. With the benefits of hindsight, it is difficult to have predicted at the time the scale and size of the instability in the Eurozone.

The design of the debt brake is also open to technical and operational questions about how it is monitored and implemented. This has given rise to serious ques-

---

[5] A Truger, 'The German Debt Brake – A shining Example for Europe?' *Social Europe Journal*, 28 March 2012, available at www.social-europe.eu/2012/03/the-german-debt-brake-a-shining-example-for-europe/.

[6] See A Truger, H Will and D Teichmann, *IMK Steuerschätzung 2011-2015. Kräftige Mehreinnahmen: kein Grund für finanzpolitischen Übermut*, IMK Report No 62, May 2011, available at www.boeckler.de/pdf/p_imk_report_62_2011.pdf.

tions from the 17 Länder as to how it should be implemented and their input into the process. There are potentially 17 different versions of the debt brake at local level. There are considerable questions about how this might all impact on future economic development.[7] Perhaps there ought to be some caution about adopting a 'one size fits all' strategy; an important consideration when adopting a debt brake strategy for other countries.

Doubts about the German debt brake amongst some economists raise questions about its effectiveness in view of the 17 Länder States and their budgetary autonomy. Whilst Länder autonomy is important, the control of debt is a key part of future federal fiscal strategy and perhaps a higher economic priority. This has given rise to friction between Länder and federal governments. The Federal Constitutional Court was asked to rule on the debt brake in a challenge undertaken by Schleswig-Holstein.[8] The Court upheld the debt brake and made clear that financial and economic issues fall within the competence of the Court. This is an important decision in terms of mapping out the role of the debt brake and its facility to be considered under the judicial functions of the Constitutional Court. The case is also indicative of the implications for enshrining economic rules within the constitution.

Critics see that Germany's problems over the debt brake with the Länder sends warning signs about similar stresses within the Eurozone and Member States.[9] This may not be an unreasonable point to make. The debt brake has been influential in German attitudes to Euro rescue agreements, including over the Greek debt. Germany's consistently tough approach to debt financing is also due to German reluctance to discourage indebtedness in Member States. Exporting the debt brake or similar fiscal rules into the Eurozone is seen as a major step in addressing the financial crisis. The acceptance within the Eurozone of a similar form of debt brake to that of Germany rests on the assumption that the German example of the debt brake is successful, but this assumption has yet to be fully tested. A cautious approach might have been to wait and see whether the German experience lives up to the high expectations placed upon it. The Treaty of Stability that was finalised on 30 January 2012 requires a balanced budget rule by the 25 Member States with the UK and the Czech Republic opting out. This is a European Union form of a golden rule that requires the Member States to enact balanced budgets by limiting their deficit to 0.5 per cent of GDP. The mode of

---

[7] A Truger and H Will (lately deceased), 'Open to manipulation and pro-cyclical: a detailed analysis of Germany's "debt brake"' Berlin School of Economic and Law, working paper, available at www. euroframe.org/fileadmin/user_upload/euroframe/docs/2012/EUROF12_Truger_Will.pdf.

[8] Federal Constitutional Court Press Release No 60/2011 (16 September 2011) 2 BvG 1/10 (19 August 2011). See the discussion in Responsive Public Management, 'Germany: What is the "Golden Rule"?' Public Management Monitoring News No 41, January 2012, available at www.institut.minefi. gouv.fr/sections/recherche_publications/gestion-publique-a-l_internati/responsive-public-management/rpm-n41---germany-_-what-is-t/downloadFile/attachedFile/Reactive_41AlllemagneENG. pdf?nocache=1328804511.88.

[9] See A Breidthardt and M Sobolewski, 'EU debt brake puts pressure on German states', Reuters UK, 2 March 2012, available at www.uk.reuters.com/article/2012/03/02/us-germany-debt-idUS-TRE8210Y920120302.

adoption into law will depend on the Member States' constitutional arrangements. The Irish Republic approved a constitutional amendment by referendum in June 2012.

There are doubts about whether the Treaty of Stability will be suitable for the economies of Member States that do not have Germany's potential for GDP growth. It is clear that the adoption of the German debt brake has been influential in German policy making. Since May 2010, and the creation of the European Financial Stability Facility (EFSF) under the Ecofin Council, bail-out mechanisms have been unpopular with public opinion in Germany. Euro-policies have also been unpopular within the CDU-led coalition. Publicly, many politicians have favoured exclusion of debt ridden Member States. Constitutional Court challenges came after the Bundestag approved legislation to approve the financial bail-out programme. A group of four professors sought a temporary injunction preventing the German President from signing the bill into law on the basis that German participation in the measure was unconstitutional. The Constitutional Court rejected the claim. A further claim was made challenging the bail-out arrangements as a misuse of Article 122 TFEU. The claim was made that the Greek 'bail-out' required observance of previous Constitutional Court rulings on the role of the German Parliament in matters of EU law.[10] The Court rejected an interim injunction[11] and held that the[12] EU's 2010 bail-out for Greece and subsequent aid through the rescue fund was legal. The Court also mentioned that the German Parliament should have a future role in the determination and debate on Eurozone bail-outs. These would need the approval of the Parliament's budget committee which fell short of full plenary approval. The Constitutional Court held that the finance committee, set up to fast-track decisions authorising the use of German funds for emergency Eurozone financial bail-out measures was in many ways unconstitutional. The Committee was designed to bypass the approval from the full membership of the Bundestag. The Constitutional Court stressed the importance of the role of the Bundestag, underpinned by the German constitution. The narrow composition of the finance committee was perhaps the main problem, perhaps a more representative body would have been adequate to meet the needs of the constitution. It is noticeable how the Constitutional Court is expected to have a role and takes that role seriously because of the nature of the German constitution. In respect of the Greek bail-out, the President of the Constitutional Court explained that the Court 'is not deciding on economic policy but on a question of law'.[13] The role of the Constitutional Court is challenging

---

[10] See T Jeck, 'Euro-Rettungsschirm bricht EU-Recht und deutsches Verfassungsrecht', CEP study of 5 July 2010, available at www.cep.eu/fileadmin/user_upload/Kurzanalysen/Euro-Rettungsschirm/CEP-Studie_Euro-Rettungsschirm.pdf.

[11] Constitutional Court Release: 55/2011 (7 September 2011).

[12] See generally V Miller, *Germany and the Euro Rescue Agreements*, House of Commons Library SN/IA/6062 (7 September 2011), available at www.mercury.ethz.ch/serviceengine/Files/ISN/151101/ipublicationdocument_singledocument/728568e5-c404-4289-a942-496578e355e4/en/SN06062.pdf.

[13] President Andreas Voßkuhle. See H Mahony, 'Germany's top court to decide on Greek bailout' EU Observer, 6 September 2011, available at www.euobserver.com/economic/113526.

and interesting as it sets unchartered constitutional legal principles in an era dominated by financial crisis.[14] Similar issues are likely to arise in the interpretation of the legality of Germany's role in bail-outs for Ireland and Portugal. The Constitutional Court sees its role as not focused on economic and political issues but confined to constitutional issues. The strict separation might appear an attractive way to determine the key issues, but it is doubtful if future developments would make such a strict distinction between constitutional challenge, and economic and political factors, achievable. The German Court has also emphasised the fundamental point that the executive should be respectful of the legislature's role in the scrutiny of taxpayers' money. The United Kingdom's Supreme Court does not have the same constitutional role and has a much more limited scrutiny of financial matters, which is largely a parliamentary matter.[15]

IV. The Fiscal Compact and the Eurozone

The Eurozone countries[16] agreed to the Fiscal Compact in December 2011 which was implemented throughout all the Eurozone States. It was adopted through an inter-governmental (international agreement) outside the institutional framework of the EU. The Treaty on Stability, Co-ordination and Governance in the Economic and Monetary Union (TSCG) was signed by 25 Member States (the UK and the Czech Republic were exceptions). The main parts of the Fiscal Compact are as follows: Eurozone States will introduce into their law or constitutions the requirement that the annual structural deficit should not exceed 0.5 per cent of nominal GDP. Member States that breach a 3 per cent deficit limit are liable to automatic sanctions at the EU level. This is subject to a blocking qualified majority in the Council. The role of the European Commission has been greatly enhanced allowing the Commission oversight of national budgets and commentary on their adequacy. Additional sums were agreed to enhance the European Stability Mechanism (ESM) and additional sums of €200 billion made payable to the International Monetary Fund (IMF). It was also agreed to consider the introduction of Eurobonds in the future.

The TSCG took matters to the stage of creating a treaty, Article 1(1) of the Treaty is aimed 'to strengthen the economic pillar of the Economic and Monetary Union by advancing a set of rules intended to foster budgetary discipline through a fiscal compact to strengthen the coordination of economic policies and to improve the governance of the euro area'. The intention is to achieve objectives

---

[14] See D Hipp, 'German Constitutional Court at Risk of Losing Power' *Der Spiegel* 29 November 2011, www.spiegel.de/international/europe/struggle-over-the-euro-german-constitutional-court-at-risk-of-losing-power-a-800465.html.

[15] R Pennington-Benton, 'Germany: Constitutional Court steps into eurozone funding crisis, striking down attempt to side-line Federal Parliament' [2012] *Public Law* 576.

[16] Miller, *Germany and the Euro Rescue Agreements* (n 12).

for sustainable growth, employment, competitiveness and social cohesion. The main element of the TSCG is to take forward the Fiscal Compact. Articles 3 and 4 are crucial. These are that government budgets shall be balanced or in surplus. The annual structural deficit shall not exceed 0.55 per cent of GDP unless government debt is very low, in which case the structural deficit can be up to 1 per cent. There will be an automatic correction mechanism, triggered if the State deviates from a country-specific medium-term objective, and there is an adjustment path towards that objective; if the ratio of government debt to GDP exceeds 60 per cent, The outcome is that there may be differences between the actual ratio and 60 per cent and if so such differences should be reduced by an average of one twentieth per year.

Article 3(2) is significant as it provides a clear obligation on Member States to put into law the balanced budget rule. The Article has a clear expectation that States are expected to operate '. . . provisions of binding force and permanent character, preferably constitutional, or otherwise guaranteed to be fully respected and adhered to' and also to transpose the automatic correction mechanism specified in Article 3. Article 8 makes clear that the Court of Justice has a role in ensuring the observance of the TSCG. Many UK commentators have expressed criticism of the TSCG, in similar terms to many of the reservations made about the German debt brake.

Particular concern has focused on Article 3(1) whereby the debt rules are expected to take effect. Simon Hix has raised serious doubts about the operation of budgetary discipline – a key element in the implementation of budgetary discipline is based on national electorates and Parliamentary processes. Paul Craig observes how the terms of Article 3(2) make the debt rules take effect in national law – even if they are not found in statute or constitutional law. Craig's interpretation is far reaching in the application of legally enforceable rules. There are related questions about the necessity for the TSCG.

V. What is the UK's Constitutional Perspective and Approach to Debt Limits?

The UK's approach to debt is very different from that of Germany. At the constitutional level the most striking differences are that the UK does not have a written constitution and there is a unitary rather than a federal state with devolved government to London, Wales, Scotland and Northern Ireland. There is only one sovereign United Kingdom Parliament. In common with Australia, the UK adopted a Fiscal Responsibility Law aimed at providing clear information on past, expected and likely fiscal developments. The main objectives of the Fiscal Responsibility Law are to provide accountability, transparency and stability. There are standard rules as to what may constitute a Fiscal Responsibility Law leaving a wide interpretation of what is included in the design and content of the law. The Fiscal Responsibility Law requires the Government to set objectives and policies for total revenues and expenditure, the overall fiscal balance and public debt. There is usually a short time period set for achieving the various objectives, with year by year targets, occasionally this may be for medium terms, to a maximum of between three and five years. Debt targets are expressed in terms of quantitative or qualitative targets usually as a percentage of GDP. In some instances there may be limits placed on government guarantees since lack of control of these contingent liabilities can compromise fiscal sustainability objectives. The main point of the fiscal responsibility approach is to enhance parliamentary scrutiny. This links transparency and accountability together in order to minimise irresponsibility of the executive. Invariably this may involve some external mechanism for the purposes of validation.

The necessity for a Financial Responsibility Law in the United Kingdom comes from the banking and financial crisis in 2008. The UK is currently forecast by the OECD to have the tenth highest debt of the 31 leading economies.[17] UK gross public debt increased from 46.0 per cent of GDP in 2006 to 82.2 per cent in 2010. The effect of the financial crisis on state debt is likely to be of long standing. In 2012 gross public debt is forecast to be 97.2 per cent of GDP and in 2013 to be 102.3 per cent. The UK is running a budget deficit set in 2011–12 to be £576 billion with government spending forecast to be £703 billion. Primarily the budget deficit is financed through the sale of government bonds. One factor that has contributed to government debt is the support provided by the Government to the banks. This took the form of share purchases, loans and guarantees with an inevitable effect on government finances. It is hard to estimate the extent of government support but it is calculated to be around 5 to 6 per cent of the deficit in 2008 and 2009. Attempts to address this problem took a number of forms. In July 2007, the Government, in its Green Paper, *The Governance of Britain*,[18] announced steps to simplify financial reporting to Parliament. The aim was to align the different bases on which financial information was reported to Parliament and ensure continuity between different formats. This builds on the principles laid before Parliament in the 1988 Treasury's Code for Fiscal Stability comprising transparency, stability, responsibility and fairness and efficiency in the formulation of fiscal policy. The Alignment (Clear Line of Sight) Project undertaken by the Treasury engages with the aims of greater transparency. The Fiscal Responsibility Act 2010 strengthened the Code and parliamentary scrutiny by requiring the Treasury to undertake a number of key measures:

---

[17] See HC Standard Note SN/EP/6054 Government borrowing and debt: international comparisons (27 January 2012). See also HC Standard Note SN/EP/6167 The budget deficit: a short guide (20 December 2011).

[18] Secretary of State for Justice, *Green Paper: The Governance of Britain* (Cm 7170) July 2007, available at www.official-documents.gov.uk/document/cm71/7170/7170.pdf; also see the earlier document by Cabinet Office, *White Paper: Modernising Government* (Cm 4310) March 1999.

- Between 2011–16 the Treasury must ensure that the public sector borrowing as a percentage of GDP is reduced from the previous year.
- Overall by the end of the financial year 2014, the Treasury has a duty to ensure that borrowing is reduced by at least a half from the financial year 2010.
- To secure sound finances, the Treasury has duties to apply the fiscal stability principles to the public finances.
- The Treasury must make regular progress reports to Parliament to ensure that the strategy to provide reductions in borrowing and sound finances are examined in the relevant Economic and Fiscal Strategy Reports and Pre-Budget reports.

The Fiscal Responsibility Act 2010 has been replaced by the Budget Responsibility and National Audit Act 2011 with a new Charter for Budget Responsibility setting out the Treasury's rules for the constraint of debt. There are debt management objectives and targets for fiscal policy, otherwise known as the fiscal mandate. This supersedes the previous arrangements. There is to be an annual Financial Statement and Budget Report containing the details of the Government's policy. The Coalition Government has adopted two fiscal rules to constrain government behaviour as follows:

- Fiscal Mandate: the structural current budget must be forecast to be in balance or in surplus at the end of the five-year Parliament;
- The supplementary target states that public sector net debt as a share of national income should be falling by a fixed date of 2015–16.

Meeting the above requirements will be hard. The Coalition Government set up the independent Office of Budget Responsibility (OBR) under the Budget Responsibility and National Audit Act 2011 to ensure compliance. There is considerable uncertainty in achieving these goals because of many variables such as oil prices, the stability of the Eurozone, the performance of the economy and income receipts. In constitutional terms the creation of the Office of Budget Responsibility is an innovation marking out the necessity for an independent body to oversee the Government's handling of the economy and to act as a check on the Treasury. This serves to underline one of the foundations of UK government accountability.

The Act provides Parliament with the potential to vote on the Government's medium-term fiscal plans including proposed borrowing and debt totals. The Coalition Government faces the need to meet the borrowing expectations in the Act. The nature of any parliamentary scrutiny, however, is uncertain as the Coalition Government operates under a fixed-term, five-year Parliament. Fixed-term parliaments provide a lock on opposition debate from taking a vote of no confidence in the Government of the day.

The financial crisis has also had profound effects on the way banks are regulated and the effectiveness of constitutional scrutiny. It is important to consider these questions in the context of banking regulation in the UK, the soon to be replaced tripartite arrangements under the Financial Services and Markets Act 2000 – the Bank of England, the Treasury and the Financial Services Authority

(FSA). The Coalition Government made major architectural changes to this tri-partite arrangement of financial regulation including making the Bank of England the key financial regulator with the abolition of the FSA and the splitting up of its functions.[19] This adds considerable uncertainty especially in the unproven nature of these changes. Political tinkering is much in evidence in choosing the most appropriate form of regulation: whether this will prove effective is very much open to debate. Could outcome based regulation offer a more effective form of regulation or is the Government's desire to return to a light touch form of principles based regulation moving the goal posts once more? The adoption of the Fiscal Responsibility Act highlights the importance of political accountability as one of the main tenets of fiscal transparency and accountability. Such a law puts a legal code in place rather than a set of legally enforceable judicially interpreted rules. This gives rise to political and economic flexibility rather than too much legal rigidity. It also facilitates responding to unforeseen and unpredictable events, which frequently arise with economic problems.

As explained above, the UK did not agree the EU's Inter-governmental Agreement, the Fiscal Compact or the TSCG. UK objections included the fact that it was outside the Eurozone and did not feel obliged to agree a treaty that might ultimately 'create an unfair disadvantage for Britain'. Above all, the UK feared an expansion in the role of EU institutions particularly in implementing the Fiscal Compact; that the Treaty had insufficient safeguards and that there was more merit in 'the flexibility of a network, not the rigidity of a bloc'.[20] The failure to meet their obligations may give rise to their being enforced through the European Commission and the ECJ.[21] This does not sit easily with the UK's approach to debt.

VI. Is there a Role for Debt Limits in Addressing the Current Financial Crisis?

Setting debt limits is seen as a major part of any budget strategy. One way is to adopt some form of Financial Responsibility Law that includes debt limits. This

---

[19] See Sixth Report Treasury and Civil Service Committee, *The Regulation of Financial Services in the UK* HC 1994–95 332-I. See NAO, IIC 676 Session 2010–11, *Report of the C&AG, Maintaining the financial stability of UK banks: update on the support schemes* (London, HM Treasury, 2010). The various banks include some Scottish banks, Dunfermline Building Society and various Icelandic banks. R Leigh-Pemberton, *Report of the Committee set up to Consider the System of Banking Supervision* (Cm 9550) June 1985.

[20] See 'Now it's a Three Speed Europe and Were left on the Hard Shoulder', *The Guardian* 11 December 2011; HC Debs 12 December 2011 c 520; 'Europe's hopeless last stand in defence of a single currency', *The Guardian* 13 December 2011; House of Commons Library: *The Treaty on Stability, Coordination and Governance in the Economic and Monetary Union: political issues* Research Paper 12/14 (27 March 2012).

[21] P O'Brien, 'The European Fiscal Treaty: Constitutionalising "The Road to Serfdom"?' Constitutional Law Group, 24 February 2012, available at www.ukconstitutionallaw.org/2012/02/24/.

offers a less legalistic way to control debt than the German example. It has the benefits of offering a law of limited scope that elaborates various budget principles on the basis of accountability, transparency and stability. The influential IMF has considered the role of Fiscal Responsibility Laws in addressing fiscal deficits. The main principles that support Fiscal Responsibility Laws are fiscal discipline and transparency. The main aim is to impose fiscal responsibility through law. This is contentious as not everyone is agreed that this is workable or desirable. There is no commonly agreed formula or definition but it is generally accepted that common elements are to be found. The IMF has identified some of the main requirements.[22] These include annual financial statements that relate to whole government accounts and a mid-year formal review of budget outcomes. Regular, timely and high quality fiscal reports are regarded as essential. There are many reasons why countries have been reluctant to adopt a Fiscal Responsibility Law, especially amongst advanced countries. The UK, along with New Zealand, adopted a narrowly defined form of the Financial Responsibility Law. The IMF regard the most effective are those where there is a strong political commitment and institutional support. This is an essential prerequisite for success.

VII. Conclusions

Germany has led the way in Europe, as its strongest economy and by adopting a constitutional rule that seeks to apply a debt brake in a legally binding way. The German debt brake offers the possibility of a legally enforceable and effective break on profligacy in government spending. This appears attractive since it offers assurances to financial institutions and banks. It is also attractive in prescribing in legal form the determination of the German Government to address historic debts through future promises of greater rigidity in financial controls that are legally binding. Any doubts about the rigidity of the debt brake and its effectiveness have to be considered in the context that the debt brake is seen by some as preferable to a debt crisis that might spiral out of control. In the German context the debt brake is largely dependent on the acceptance of a working assumption that borrowing needs to be limited to exceptional circumstances for specific and limited reasons. These assumptions have to be considered within the cultural context of government at Länder and federal levels. Failure to adopt the debt brake is likely to lead to constitutional disputes that fall to be adjudicated by the German Constitutional Court. The framework of the debt brake regulates public borrowing, but the Länder are free to adopt their own budget. This may lead to conflict and further constitutional quarrels. Interpretation of the scope

---

[22] I Lienert, 'Should Advanced Countries Adopt a Fiscal Responsibility Law?' IMF Working Paper 10/254 (November 2010), available at www.imf.org/external/pubs/ft/wp/2010/wp10254.pdf.

and application of the debt brake is also likely to be contentious and lead to constitutional challenges. Linked to the use of legal rules that apply economic instruments are issues related to the legitimacy of the legal system and the empowerment of political decision making.

The United Kingdom has taken a less formalistic and legalistic approach to addressing debt than Germany. The adoption of Fiscal Responsibility Act 2012 and its continuation by the Coalition Government places an emphasis on setting targets, increasing transparency and providing verification of budget planning and debt reduction. This falls short of the legally enforceable debt brake operational in Germany. The UK has no formal legally binding debt brake but there are some similarities in the aspiration of reducing debt and increasing budget responsibility. Instead of supervision by a Constitutional Court as in Germany, the United Kingdom has parliamentary supervision preserved within the general terms of financial targets. Government policy is easily adjusted to take account of unpredicted and unforeseen events. Outside the Eurozone, the UK has flexibility over exchange rates and borrowing and government policy-making requirements. Yet this flexibility has to be considered in the UK's anxiety over the Eurozone. Trade is depressed, at present, two-fifths of UK shipments go to Eurozone countries, and British banks have considerable exposure to banks in Ireland, Spain, Italy, Portugal and Greece to the extent of $300 billion, nearly 12.7 per cent of GDP, considerably greater than Germany.[23] The United Kingdom approach fits within a strong parliamentary tradition and visible and externally validated economic data under the OBR. There are lessons to be gained from the application of a Fiscal Responsibility Law.

Lessons from the German experience are too early to assess. The shift from historically lax public debt to tighter financial controls has yet to be made and at a period of financial instability in the Eurozone, financial stability has to be established following Germany's example. Germany is the bulwark of European financial stability and its future decisions will be heavily influenced by its approach to the debt brake. The European Fiscal Compact is likely to be heavily influenced by Germany, possibly with the willing agreement of Member States. Rigid debt brakes may not be feasible in many weaker EU economies. The longer term economic predictions of sovereign debt and fragility within the Eurozone might give rise to an unpredictable financial crisis that may not be best suited to legally enforceable debt brakes. This in turn might bring into question the effectiveness of operational debt brakes throughout Europe. Many commentators see the German example as an opportunity to address systemic weaknesses in budgets and in avoiding debt gains through credible controls.[24] Designing the framework for government spending within the debt brake is likely to require careful

---

[23] 'Chained to trouble', *The Economist* 23 June 2012.

[24] M Hüther, 'Debt Brakes Are the Best Way Out of The Crisis' *Der Spiegel* (8 November 2011), available at www.spiegel.de/international/business/opinion-debt-brakes-are-the-best-way-out-of-the-crisis-a-779655.html.

judgement and adjustment.[25] Transposing the debt brake into constitutional and legally enforceable rules marks an important shift in the role of law and the use of legal rules to enforce economic policy and instruments. This places considerable burdens on the role of judges in the constitutional arrangements that were hitherto the preserve of politicians. There may be doubts about the appointment and competence of judges in the context of economic and political issues. Debt brakes potentially provide for a system of governance that sits uneasily between the rule of law upheld by courts and political forms of governance accountability through elected politicians.[26]

[25] E Mayer and N Stähler, 'The Debt Brake: Business Cycle and Welfare Consequences of Germany's New Fiscal Policy Rule' Deutsche Bundesbank Discussion Paper 24/2009, available at www.bundesbank. de/Redaktion/EN/Downloads/Publications/Discussion_Paper_1/2009/2009_08_28_dkp_24.pdf?__ blob=publicationFile.

[26] See F Johns, 'Financing as Governance' (2011) 31 *OJLS* 391.

Part II

Europe

6

Why the ECB Cannot Save the Euro

PAUL YOWELL*

Introduction

At an investment conference in London in July 2012, Mario Draghi, the President of the European Central Bank (ECB), said the bank would 'do whatever it takes to preserve the euro'. The pledge reverberated around the world and changed the dynamic of the Eurozone crisis.

Draghi's words were more nuanced than suggested by the promise quoted out of context. He qualified his pledge by referring to the ECB's mandate, but at the same time hinted at a revised conception of that mandate that sees the ECB as responsible for financial stability and the continuity of the Euro:

> When people talk about the fragility of the Euro and the increasing fragility of the Euro, and perhaps the crisis of the Euro, very often non-euro area member states or leaders, underestimate the amount of political capital that is being invested in the Euro. And so we view this, and I do not think we are unbiased observers, *we think the Euro is irreversible*. And it's not an empty word now, because I preceded saying exactly what actions have been made, are being made to make it irreversible. But there is another message I want to tell you. *Within our mandate*, the ECB is ready to do whatever it takes to preserve the Euro. And believe me, it will be enough.[1]

The ECB has a strict legal mandate that makes price stability its overriding objective and prohibits it from using monetary policy to finance public spending. The US Federal Reserve, in contrast, has a broader mandate that includes the level of employment; and since it is not prohibited from monetary financing, it is considered a lender of last resort to the US Government. Many understood Draghi's pledge as an attempt to transform the ECB and make its role more like that of the Federal Reserve. Less than two weeks after the London statement, Draghi announced the

---

* I am grateful for the research assistance of John Menzies.

[1] M Draghi, Speech at the Global Investment Conference in London (26 July 2012) www.ecb.int/press/key/date/2012/html/sp120726.en.html, accessed 22 May 2013 (emphasis added). Draghi pencilled in the last two sentences of this quotation just before the speech. B Blackstone and M Walker, 'How the ECB Chief Outflanked German Foe in Fight for Euro' *The Wall Street Journal* (2 October 2012).

Outright Monetary Transaction programme (OMT), which confirmed that the ECB would shoulder responsibility for the survival of the Euro by committing to buying government bonds of distressed countries in potentially unlimited amounts, conditional on a country requesting relief committing to certain fiscal adjustments and structural reforms. One effect of Draghi's pledge and announcement of OMT was a dramatic fall in yields of bonds in Italy and Spain. By December 2012 yields on Italian two-year bonds had fallen to approximately 2 per cent and on Spanish bonds to 3 per cent, from peaks of around 5 per cent and 7 per cent, respectively.[2] By April 2013 Italian 10-year bond yields had fallen from a peak of over 6 per cent to below 4 per cent.[3] Many financial analysts have credited Draghi with saving the Euro from collapse.

The main argument in this chapter is that the ECB's legal mandate precludes it from acting as a lender of last resort to sovereign governments. This is a role that some economists have urged the ECB to undertake in order to prevent financial calamity and the break-up of the Eurozone. Draghi himself denied that this is a proper role for the ECB when he was appointed as its president, and he now contends that the OMT programme does not amount to monetary financing of public debt. I will argue that the objectives that Draghi outlined for the OMT programme go beyond the ECB's legal mandate.

The chapter proceeds as follows. I consider the basic legal structure of the European Monetary Union in section I, and show that it expressly excludes fiscal union and constrains the role of the ECB accordingly. In section II, I explain the ECB's legal mandate and criticise arguments that the ECB should act as a lender of last resort to governments put forth by Paul de Grauwe, the leading academic economist supporting this view. In section III, I argue that the OMT programme amounts to monetary financing of government debt and appears to include aims that exceed the ECB's legal mandate; and I consider and reject the claim that it would be justified to engage in such illegal monetary financing in an attempt to avert financial calamity.

I. Design of EMU

The European Economic and Monetary Union (EMU) was designed as a currency union without political or fiscal union. EMU thus consists of one monetary authority but many fiscal authorities. Control over the single currency and monetary policy was given to the European Central Bank, which was structured to operate independently of control by either Member States or the political institutions of the EU. The ECB operates in conjunction with the 17 national central

---

[2] See L Barber and M Steen, 'FT Person of the Year: Mario Draghi' *Financial Times* (London, 13 December 2012). In naming Draghi as Person of the Year, the *Financial Times* made his London pledge the centrepiece of this article and observed that the effects of the pledge were 'immediate – and durable'.

[3] C Forelle, 'European Bonds Defy Gravity' *The Wall Street Journal* (25 April 2013).

banks of the Eurozone who implement its monetary policy; together they form the 'Eurosystem'. The EU Treaties make no provision for collective debt issuance ('Eurobonds'), and prohibit one Member State (and the Union itself) from assuming or guaranteeing the debts or liabilities of any other Member State in Article 125 of the Treaty on the Functioning of the European Union (TFEU).

Member States retained power over their own fiscal policy. Each country sets its own taxing and spending levels, determines its public budget, and issues its own sovereign debt.[4] Member State fiscal powers, however, are limited to some degree by the EU Treaties, including Article 121 TFEU, which states the Member States shall 'regard their economic policies as a matter of common concern and shall coordinate them within the Council', and Article 126 TFEU, which provides that Member States 'shall avoid excessive deficits'. Both Articles were first adopted in the Maastricht Treaty of 1992 along with a Protocol on excessive deficit procedure, which was later complemented by the 1997 Stability and Growth Pact (SGP), a resolution of the Amsterdam European Council. The SGP provides that a Member State's annual deficits shall not exceed 3 per cent of GDP and that overall public indebtedness shall not exceed 60 per cent of GDP. The SGP has been persistently flouted by a number of Eurozone states, and most – including among larger countries not only Italy and Spain, but also France and Germany – are currently in breach with regard to public debt as a percentage of GDP.

The ECB's monetary policy is determined by the President of the ECB along with five other members of the Executive Board; all six are appointed for non-renewable eight-year terms. The Governing Council, composed of the Executive Board plus the governors of the 17 central banks of countries in the Euro area, is responsible for general decision making. The mandate of the ECB is established and constrained by the EU Treaties. The ECB's primary objective is 'to maintain price stability', according to Article 127 TFEU. In 1998 the Governing Council adopted a definition of price stability as a year-on-year increase of below 2 per cent over the medium term and stated that 'monetary policy strategy will focus strictly on this objective'.[5] In 2003 the Governing Council clarified the inflation target as being 'below, but close to, 2 per cent, over the medium term'; and it has remained committed to that level since then.[6] The ECB's objectives also include supporting the general economic policies of the EU 'with a view to contributing to the achievement of the objectives of the Union' as set forth in Article 3 of the Treaty on European Union (TEU), which include, inter alia, promotion of 'economic, social and territorial cohesion, and solidarity among Member States'.[7] Support of these wider objectives, however, must be 'without prejudice to the objective of price stability'.[8]

---

[4] Member States also retained general responsibility for regulating banks and providing depositor insurance at the national level.

[5] ECB press release, 'A stability-oriented monetary policy strategy for the ESCB' (13 October 1998) www.ecb.int/press/pr/date/1998/html/pr981013_1.en.html, accessed 29 May 2013.

[6] ECB strategy statement, 'The definition of price stability' www.ecb.int/mopo/strategy/pricestab/html/index.en.html, accessed 29 May 2013.

[7] Article 127 TFEU.

[8] ibid.

The Treaty law of the EU explicitly prohibits the ECB (1) from directly purchasing bonds or any kind of debt instrument from Member States and (2) from extending any form of credit to support public undertakings. Because this law has been overlooked or misconstrued by many economists and analysts, it is worth paying close attention to the black letter of the Treaties. Article 123 TFEU provides (emphasis added):

1. Overdraft facilities or *any other type of credit facility with the European Central Bank* or with the central banks of the Member States (hereinafter referred to as 'national central banks') in favour of Union institutions, bodies, offices or agencies, central governments, regional, local or other public authorities, other bodies governed by public law, or public undertakings of Member States *shall be prohibited, as shall the purchase directly from them by the European Central Bank or national central banks of debt instruments.*

2. Paragraph 1 shall not apply to publicly owned credit institutions which, in the context of the supply of reserves by central banks, shall be given the same treatment by national central banks and the European Central Bank as private credit institutions.

Two points should be noted. Although (1) the outright prohibition on purchasing debt from Member States applies to direct purchases rather than purchases in the open market, (2) the ECB is prohibited not only from direct purchases of government debt but also from entering into *any credit facility* in favour of Member State government (central, regional or local) or the public undertakings (spending commitments, etc) of Member States.

The ECB may, in fulfilling its mandate, purchase marketable instruments (including Member State bonds) in open market and credit operations, as set forth in Article 18 of the Statute of the European System of Central Banks (ESCB):

18.1. In order to achieve the objectives of the ESCB and to carry out its tasks, the ECB and the national central banks may:

– operate in the financial markets by buying and selling outright (spot and forward) or under repurchase agreement and by lending or borrowing claims and marketable instruments, whether in Community or in non-Community currencies, as well as precious metals;
– conduct credit operations with credit institutions and other market participants, with lending being based on adequate collateral.

18.2. The ECB shall establish general principles for open market and credit operations carried out by itself or the national central banks, including for the announcement of conditions under which they stand ready to enter into such transactions.

Traditionally, the ECB's standard tool in open market operations has been the reverse repurchase agreement or collateralised loan, in which a bank obtains cash from the ECB by making a short-term sale of debt paper (eg, government bonds)[9] to the ECB. The bank repurchases the debt paper from the ECB at an agreed time

---

[9] The ECB publishes a list of approved collateral, which typically includes only the sovereign debt of certain Eurozone countries.

(say, after two weeks) and discount interest rate.[10] Determining this interest rate is the ECB's main instrument for transmitting its monetary policy (controlling the money supply and inflation rate) – which should, according to the mandate set by the EU Treaty law, have price stability as its overriding object.

Recently the ECB has engaged in non-traditional kinds of transactions. Against the backdrop of the financial crisis and rising yields on bonds in some countries, in 2010 the ECB began purchasing significant quantities of Member State bonds and retaining them on its balance sheet through its Securities Market Programme (SMP).[11] Soon after Draghi was appointed president of the ECB he announced a new form of Long-Term Refinancing Operations (LTRO), which provided around €1 trillion to banks in late 2011 and early 2012, mostly in three-year loans with reduced collateral requirements.[12] In September 2012 Draghi announced the OMT programme, which was discussed in the Introduction and will be analysed in more detail in section III.[13]

Prior to the implementation of the LTROs by the ECB, EU Member States attempted to address the joint sovereign debt and banking crises through various institutional mechanisms. In May 2010, the Member States approved the creation of the temporary[14] European Financial Stability Facility (EFSF), which could provide assistance to Member States in financial difficulty. The EFSF was superseded by the European Stability Mechanism (ESM), which began operations in October 2012.[15] The ESM was established by means of two treaty agreements: one is between the 17 Eurozone Member States establishing the ESM as an international

---

[10] The ECB performs four main types of open market operations: main refinancing operations, longer-term refinancing operations (LTROs), fine tuning operations, and structural operations. In addition to open market operations, the ECB provides two standing facilities to eligible institutions in order to provide (and absorb) liquidity: the Marginal Lending Facility and the Deposit Facility. The former is used by counterparties to access liquidity on an overnight basis from national central banks (NCBs) against eligible collateral and acts to cap overnight lending rates. The latter provides a floor on the overnight lending rates.

[11] See Decision of the European Central Bank of 14 May 2010, establishing a securities markets programme (ECB/2010/5) (2010/281/EU).

[12] The announced LTROs were a marked break from previous policy. Since 1999 the ECB had performed LTROs that were typically three-month collateralised loans. The shift to full allotment 36-month LTROs was somewhat gradual. In October 2008, the ECB announced that the collateral list would be expanded and published an updated schedule for new LTROs. The LTROs that Draghi announced in December 2011 were two full allotment LTROs maturing in 36 months, with the option of repayment after one year; and the ECB again expanded the definition of acceptable collateral by reducing the rating threshold for asset-backed securities. NCBs were allowed, as a temporary solution, to accept certain credit claims as collateral.

[13] This brief exposition omits other milestones in the evolution on ECB policy, including the Covered Bond Purchase Programme (CBPP), whose stated goal was to reduce money market term rates, ease funding conditions, encourage credit institutions to expand lending, and improve liquidity.

[14] Had the facility not been accessed, it would have dissolved in June 2013. Since it was accessed by both Portugal and Ireland, it will remain in existence until the loans are repaid. See A-18 of European Financial Stability Facility FAQ at www.efsf.europa.eu/attachments/faq_en.pdf, accessed 7 June 2013.

[15] The ESM also superseded the European Financial Stabilisation Mechanism (EFSM), which had been developed by the European Commission with the backing of Member States, and had the capacity to raise up to €60 billion in order to contribute to interventions that preserve the financial stability of the Union.

organisation headquartered in Luxembourg,[16] and there is a separate treaty between all 27 EU Member States to amend Article 136 TFEU. The ESM is intended to act as a permanent crisis resolution mechanism[17] by providing 'stability support on the basis of a strict conditionality, appropriate to the financial assistance instrument chosen if indispensable to safeguard the financial stability of the Euro area as a whole and of its Member States'.[18] The ESM currently has a maximum lending capacity of €500 billion.[19] This amount is widely perceived to be sufficient to deal with crises in smaller states such as Portugal or Ireland but not for larger states such as Spain or Italy.

Some have argued that the ECB's ability to purchase government bonds in the open market creates a way for the ECB to circumvent Article 123's prohibition on direct purchase of government bonds and to supplement the limited amounts available under the EFSF/ESM. The ECB could use this power to affect the price of bonds with the aim of ensuring that Member States can continue to borrow in the credit markets the funds needed for government spending and avoid defaulting on existing bonds. An article in the *Investor's Chronicle*, for example, states:

> There is, in principle, a straightforward solution to the Euro area's debt crisis. The ECB could simply print sufficient money to buy as many bonds as necessary to drive down their yields. There is, in theory, no limit at all on how much money a central bank can create.[20]

The article urges the ECB thus to 'monetize the debt' of troubled Member States, acknowledging that Article 123 TFEU 'prohibits the ECB from directly buying national governments' debt', but adding, 'However, this article says nothing about buying in the secondary market'.[21]

Arguments of this sort, which are met frequently, overlook the broad prohibition on any 'credit facility' in favour of Member States in Article 123 and other basic features of EMU and the law governing the ECB. First, in authorising the purchase of bonds in secondary markets, Article 18(1) permits this only to 'achieve the objectives of the ESCB'; and, as we have seen, the EU Treaties establish price stability as the overriding objective. Second, EU law defines the terms of Article 123 in such a way as to bar the financing of the public sector through any third party, in Council Regulation 3603/93, which reads (emphasis added):

---

[16] The Treaty Establishing the European Stability Mechanism (TESM).

[17] More information on the institutional structure of the ESM can be found in European Stability Mechanism FAQ at www.esm.europa.eu/pdf/FAQ%20ESM%20041020121.pdf, accessed 7 June 2013.

[18] Preamble (6) TESM, www.esm.europa.eu/pdf/esm_treaty_en.pdf, accessed 7 June 2013.

[19] The combined lending capacity of the EFSF and ESM is nearly €700 billion. See ibid for more information.

[20] C Dillow, 'What's wrong with monetising the debt?' *Investor's Chronicle* (21 November 2011) www.investorschronicle.co.uk/2011/11/21/comment/chris-dillow/what-s-wrong-with-monetizing-debt/article.html, accessed 22 May 2013.

[21] ibid.

1. For the purposes of Article 104 of the Treaty [now Article 123 TFEU]:[22]

   (a) 'overdraft facilities' means any provision of funds to the public sector resulting or likely to result in a debit balance;
   (b) *'other type of credit facility'* means:

      (i) any claim against the public sector existing at 1 January 1994, except for fixed-maturity claims acquired before that date;
      (ii) *any financing of the public sector's obligations vis-à-vis third parties*

This Regulation, which has been largely overlooked by the financial press and by many economists writing on the ECB, is key to understanding the ECB's powers and the purposes for which it can exercise them. The Regulation clarifies that Article 123 is not a mere technical provision regarding direct lending to states and direct purchases of government debt, with a large loophole allowing indirect routes to the same end. The Regulation makes it clear that the *intent* or *purpose* for which the ECB acts is a relevant – indeed, a central – consideration, broadly forbidding any act that has the purpose of 'financing the public sector's obligations vis-à-vis third parties'. This language applies to buying Member State bonds in secondary markets as well as providing loans to banks. The ECB cannot legally carry out either of these kinds of transactions with the aim of financing government spending or public undertakings, capping yields, or otherwise underwriting sovereign bond markets.[23] The Regulation thus has the important effect of making the 'spirit of the law' part of the law itself, insofar as the spirit of Article 123 is to constrain the objectives for which the ECB can act and to preclude the monetary financing of public debt. The ECB has stated in several formal opinions that Article 123 precludes monetary financing, sometimes explicitly reading Article 123 in conjunction with Council Regulation 3603/93.[24] Several economists have overlooked this Regulation. Daniel Gros and Thomas Mayer say that bond purchases intended to fund government deficits violate the 'spirit' of Article 123 but not its 'letter' so long as they are made in secondary markets.[25] Willem Buiter argues that the ECB cannot pursue the role of lender of last resort through primary market purchases but can

---

[22] The original Article 104 of the Maastricht Treaty, which was adopted in the run up to adoption of the Euro, became Article 101 after the Treaty of Amsterdam and Article 123 after the Treaty of Lisbon.

[23] Whether or not a central bank transaction amounts to monetary financing of debt depends on the aim for which it is made, and not solely on factors such as the size of the purchase or whether it is made in primary or secondary bond markets. See D Thornton, 'Monetizing the debt' *Economic Synopses* (29 May 2010) www.research.stlouisfed.org/publications/es/10/ES1014.pdf, accessed 22 May 2013.

[24] See Opinion of the European Central Bank of 18 October 2010 (on an increase of the New Arrangements to Borrow with the International Monetary Fund); Opinion of the European Central Bank of 23 July 2012 (on a stabilisation fund for banks) (referring in section 3.3 to 'the monetary financing prohibition contained in Article 123 of the Treaty in connection with Council Regulation (EC) No 3603/93'); Opinion of the European Central Bank of 17 July 2012 (on the strengthening of financial supervision and establishment of a financial stability committee) (referring in section 3.2 to 'the prohibition of monetary financing under Article 123(1) of the Treaty, read in conjunction with Council Regulation 3603/93/EC').

[25] D Gros and T Mayer, 'Towards a Euro(pean) Monetary Fund' (2010) Centre for European Policy Studies www.papers.ssrn.com/sol3/papers.cfm?abstract_id=1615478, accessed 5 June 2013.

do so via secondary market purchases; the latter are 'less effective, but at least they are legal in the sense of not forbidden by the Treaty'.[26] Paul de Grauwe, whose positions will be considered in section II, makes similar claims.[27] All of these claims contravene the letter of the law as expressed in Regulation 3603/93.

Mario Draghi showed awareness of EU Treaty terms and the legally limited mandate of the ECB in an interview that he gave in December 2011 shortly after being appointed President of the ECB. The interviewer suggested that the ECB should engage in bond-purchasing programmes like those of the US Federal Reserve. In response Draghi states that monetary financing of public debt is illegal under the EU Treaties:

> Question: Why is it so impossible for the ECB to act like the other central banks, like the Federal Reserve System or the Bank of England? Why do you not act more directly to help European countries by buying up the debt on a massive scale?
>
> Draghi: As I said before, we have a Treaty and *the Treaty states what our primary mandate is, namely to maintain price stability. Also, the Treaty prohibits monetary financing.* I am old enough to remember that, when this Treaty was written in the early 1990s, some of the countries around that table were actually doing what you suggest doing now, namely some of the central banks of these countries were financing the government expenditure of their governments through money creation, and the consequences were there for all of us to see.[28]

One of these countries is Draghi's own Italy, whose economy faltered in the 1970s after a period of strong growth. As a doctoral student at the time, Draghi sought to understand the cause of decline and concluded 'that Rome's habit of force-feeding its central bank with public debt was debasing the lira. He became convinced Italy needed more German-style rigor'.[29]

The overall design of EMU, with its commitment to price stability and low inflation, the bar on monetary financing of public debt, and the agreement to keep budget deficits and total indebtedness low in the Stability and Growth Pact, reflects the 'hard money' approach of the German, post-Second World War tradition. The independence of the ECB resembles that of the Bundesbank, which the German Basic Law protects from manipulation by the political branches. A number of southern tier countries, in contrast, have traditionally taken a 'soft money' approach that – as Draghi recalled – leans toward monetisation of public debt and tolerates higher inflation in the long run; and before joining EMU they had central banks more subject to political control than the Bundesbank.

---

[26] W Buiter and E Rahbari, 'The European Central Bank As Lender of Last Resort for Sovereigns in the Eurozone' (2012) 50 *Journal of Common Market Studies* 6.

[27] See P de Grauwe, *The Economics of Monetary Union*, 9th edn (Oxford University Press, 2012) 199 (stating that Article 123 prohibits primary market bond purchases but not secondary market purchases).

[28] M Draghi, Introductory statement to the press conference (with Q&A) (8 December 2011) www.ecb.europa.eu/press/pressconf/2011/html/is111208.en.html, accessed 22 May 2013 (emphasis added).

[29] See B Blackstone and M Walker, 'How the ECB Chief Outflanked German Foe in Fight for Euro' *The Wall Street Journal* (2 October 2012) (discussing Draghi's background before becoming ECB President).

In the same December 2011 interview Draghi insisted that opposition to monetary financing of public debt is both a matter of sound of economic policy and of EU Treaty law, and said that attempts to circumvent the law or violate its spirit should be rejected. He argued, however, that the Securities Market Programme (SMP) was consistent with this understanding of the mandate (emphasis added):

Question: Mr Draghi, speaking in Parliament you also emphasized that the ECB would ensure price stability in both directions. Does that mean that there is a fear of deflation? My second question is, from a purely legal point of view, do you think there is any limitation on the ECB regarding the amount of government bonds that can be bought, as long as it can be justified on the basis of monetary policy considerations.

Draghi: At the present time we do not see a high probability of deflation. That is one point to keep in mind. The second point is, as I have said many times, that the purpose of the SMP is to reactivate the transmission channels of monetary policy. As I said in the statement to the European Parliament, the SMP is neither eternal nor infinite. *We must keep this in mind and we do not want to circumvent Article 123 of the Treaty, which prohibits the monetary financing of governments.*

Question: . . . And secondly, you have mentioned Article 123 in the Treaty. Would you consider *active buying at around the time certain instruments are issued to be something that would be state financing, and would you regard that as being against ECB law?*

Draghi: On the first issue, we are aware of the technical complexities that would arise with the SMP having an infinite size, but we will think about this. As for the other question, one can construct many different cases. But, as I said before, the key thing is that we should not try to circumvent the spirit of the Treaty. *No matter what the legal trick is, I think what matters for the people and what matters for the confidence and credibility of the institution is the spirit of this provision of the Treaty.* [30]

In an earlier press conference in November 2011, Draghi made a similar point (emphasis added):

Question: Are you prepared now to make a commitment that you will do whatever is necessary to keep the Euro area in one piece, including – if necessary – becoming the lender of last resort to governments?

Draghi: I have a question for you: what makes you think that the ECB becoming the lender of last resort for governments is what is needed to keep the Euro area together? *No, I do not think that this is really within the remit of the ECB.* The remit of the ECB is maintaining price stability over the medium term. [31]

There is a tension (i) between these remarks and Draghi's promise a year later to 'do whatever it takes to save the euro'; and (ii) between the understanding of the legal mandate of the ECB he exhibits in December 2011 and what is contemplated in the commitment to engage in potentially unlimited purchase of Member State bonds in the OMT programme. It is important to understand (and to track any

---

[30] Draghi, Introductory statement to the press conference (8 December 2011) (n 28).
[31] M Draghi, Introductory statement to the press conference (with Q&A) (3 November 2011) www. ecb.int/press/pressconf/2011/html/is111103.en.html, accessed 2 June 2013.

possible changes in) Draghi's views on monetary financing of governments because of the power he holds to lead the Executive Board and Governing Council in setting the ECB's monetary policy. He is the person with the chief responsibility to ensure that the ECB complies with Article 123 and Council Regulation 3603/93 and stays within its legal mandate. The ECB is deliberately structured to be immune from influence by the Commission, the Council, and Member State political authorities. While it might be possible to have judicial review of the ECB's decisions, generally there are not readily available mechanisms for holding central banks to legal account.

II. The ECB as Lender of Last Resort

Paul de Grauwe, professor of European political economy at the London School of Economics and author of *Economics of Monetary Union*, argues that the ECB should act as a lender of last resort in sovereign bond markets. Paul Krugman, Martin Wolf, and other economists and financial journalists have endorsed his argument, and Wolf has said that Draghi's announcement of the OMT programme 'marks belated acceptance of strong arguments' made by de Grauwe.[32] De Grauwe has actively set forth these argument in a series of recent newspaper editorials and articles in online publications, and the updated edition of his *Economics of Monetary Union* (2012) collects different threads of the argument.

In section 6.1 of the textbook, captioned 'The role of the central bank: lender of last resort', de Grauwe bases his argument for the ECB to act as a lender of last resort in sovereign bond markets on an analogy to a traditional central bank's role of lender of last resort for banks. In a fractional reserve banking system, there is a standing risk of bank runs because the cash a bank has on hand to pay depositors is vastly exceeded by the full amount of obligations it has to depositors.

> When deposit holders run to the bank together to convert their deposits into cash, the banks that hold relatively illiquid assets cannot produce the cash to pay out the deposit holders. As a result, the banking sector is very sensitive to movements of distrust that can create a self-fulfilling liquidity crisis. As banks try to find cash they sell assets, thereby lowering the price of their assets. This can lead to a solvency crisis.[33]

As de Grauwe points out, 'The nice feature of this lender of last resort function is that when depositors are confident that the central bank will exert this function they will rarely run to their banks, so that the central bank rarely has to step in to provide cash to banks'.[34] De Grauwe draws an analogy between bank liabilities and public debt:

---

[32] M Wolf, 'Draghi alone cannot save the euro' *Financial Times* (London, 11 September 2012).
[33] De Grauwe, *The Economics of Monetary Union* (n 27) 120.
[34] ibid.

Governments' assets and liabilities in a monetary union have the same structure as those of the banks. Governments' liabilities are liquid while most of their assets are illiquid (e.g. infrastructure, claims on taxpayers). Thus, when bondholders massively sell bonds, these governments may not be able to generate enough cash to pay out bondholders at maturity.[35]

De Grauwe claims that liquidity crises are avoided in 'stand-alone countries that issue debt in their own currencies mainly because the central bank can be forced to provide all the necessary liquidity to the sovereign'.[36] This 'creates an implicit guarantee for the bondholders that they will be paid out when the bond matures'.[37] In a monetary union, de Grauwe contends, a central bank should have the role of supplying 'the necessary liquidity in the different sovereigns' bond markets', and this would provide the same outcome of assurance against default:

> This creates an implicit guarantee for bondholders that they will always be paid out at maturity, as is the case in the bond market of stand-alone countries. By eliminating the threat of a liquidity crisis it can also prevent the market from pushing the member countries towards a bad equilibrium. Thus, in a monetary union there is a role of central bank as a lender of last resort in the domestic bond markets. By guaranteeing that the liquidity will always be available *it reduces the fragility of an incomplete monetary union.*[38]

Let us set aside for the moment the economic merits of de Grauwe's analogy and policy argument, and consider its context.

The reference to 'incomplete monetary union' in the previous paragraph is significant. I have been quoting from chapter six in de Grauwe's textbook, which is titled, 'How to Complete a Monetary Union?'. In chapter five, 'The Fragility of Incomplete Monetary Unions', de Grauwe describes the EMU as an *incomplete monetary union* and explains certain risks of bad equilibria which can lead to default on sovereign debt. He mentions two main devices for completing a monetary union: (1) entrusting the role of sovereign lender of last resort to a central bank, and (2) consolidating Member State national debt into a shared, common debt fund, which would amount to a budgetary union. He then states: 'As will be shown in the following chapters, [these two] possibilities are really part of one package that is *necessary to make an incomplete union like the Eurozone sustainable.* As will be argued, the lender of last resort function of the ECB is needed to deal with crisis situations, while the budgetary consolidation is necessary to make the Eurozone robust in the long run' (emphasis added).[39]

De Grauwe's argument in section 6.1 that the ECB should act as a lender of last resort is a proposal regarding an improved model for EMU. In the context of the textbook as a whole, this improved model is seen as a departure from the actual structure of EMU. In chapter eight, 'The European Central Bank', de Grauwe

---

[35] ibid.
[36] ibid.
[37] ibid.
[38] ibid (emphasis added).
[39] ibid 117.

describes the ECB as structured on the German model for a central bank, which has price stability as its primary objective, precludes monetary financing of public debt, and places a strong emphasis on political independence.[40] In the Anglo-French model, as described by de Grauwe, the central bank 'pursues several objectives, e.g. price stability, stabilization of the business cycle, the maintenance of high employment, and financial stability'.[41] This is 'very different' from the German model, de Grauwe says; in the Anglo-French model 'price stability is only one of the objectives and does not receive any privileged treatment'.[42] De Grauwe says that part of the explanation for the adoption of this model is that it was a condition for Germany's agreement to join EMU: 'The German authorities faced the risk of having to accept higher inflation when they entered monetary union [and] insisted on having an ECB that gives an even higher weight to price stability than the Bundesbank did. Our analysis of the statute of the ECB confirms that the German monetary authority succeeded in achieving this objective.'[43]

In de Grauwe's recent online articles and newspaper editorials, the same arguments presented in his textbook for changing the legal structure of EMU to bring it in line with his improved model, become strongly worded prescriptions for what the ECB must do – and must do *now* – in order to avert financial calamity. The following argument by de Grauwe, which counsels urgent action because of the connection of the debt crisis to the banking crisis, is representative; though lengthy the excerpt deserves careful attention because of the possibility that (as Martin Wolf suggests) it is de Grauwe's arguments that have persuaded Draghi to propose the OMT programme:[44]

> The sovereign debt crisis has degenerated into a banking crisis. . . . To stop the downward spiral *a floor has to be put on the price of government bonds in the eurozone. . . . To prevent further drops in government bond prices, the [ECB] should announce that it is ready to intervene in the market. The ECB is the only institution capable of doing this because it can create money without limit.* In announcing its unconditional commitment, the bank would stop the spiral of decline. And when investors were convinced of the resolve of the ECB, they would stop selling sovereign bonds because they would trust that *a floor had been put on their prices.* The beauty of this outcome would be that the ECB would not have to buy government bonds any more.

> Today the ECB does not reap this benefit because it has made it clear that *it thoroughly dislikes being a lender of last resort* and that it would like to stop as soon as possible. Why would bondholders, who are uncertain about the future value of their bonds, stop selling these when the ECB continues to signal that it does not trust these bonds either?

> Many objections are raised against the idea that the ECB should act as a lender of last resort in government bond markets. One is that it amounts to monetary financing of

---

[40] ibid 151.
[41] ibid.
[42] ibid.
[43] ibid 155–56.
[44] P de Grauwe, 'Europe needs the ECB to step up to the plate' *Financial Times* (London, 19 October 2011).

budget deficits, which in turn leads to inflation. This is unfounded. When the ECB buys government bonds in the secondary markets it provides liquidity, not to governments but to the financial institutions that sold the sovereign bonds. When these financial institutions sell government bonds they are in search of a safe asset, and this is primarily central bank money. That money is hoarded and is not used to expand credit and the money supply, and so does not lead to inflationary pressures.

The only reasonable objection to a lender of last resort role for the ECB is moral hazard. By announcing its readiness to provide liquidity in the government bond markets, the ECB creates the risk that governments may reduce their efforts at cutting deficits and debts. That is why binding rules that would force governments to bring their budgetary house in order must complement the ECB's role of lender of last resort. These rules are now being put into place. . . .

> *The ECB has no excuse not to act. In trying to keep its monetary virginity intact, the bank threatens to destroy the eurozone. If that happens, nobody will be able to profit from its virginity.* (Emphasis added.)

De Grauwe discusses opposition to the ECB acting as a lender of last resort primarily in terms of policy choice and without explicitly acknowledging the ECB's legal mandate as a reason for opposition to his plan.

This stands in stark contrast to his description of the ECB's role and mandate in chapter eight of his textbook. There he states that the ECB's primary objective is price stability and that other objectives cannot interfere with that.[45] He describes the ECB as being even more politically independent than the Bundesbank and explains that independence as 'a necessary condition for price stability'.[46] Without independence, de Grauwe states, *'the central bank can be forced to print money to finance government deficits. This is the surest way to inflation. In order to exclude this, the following sentence was included in the Treaty'* (emphasis added).[47] De Grauwe then quotes Article 123 as follows: 'Overdraft facilities or any other type of credit facility with the European Central Bank or with the national central banks of the Member States . . . with Community institutions or bodies, central governments, regional or local authorities, public authorities . . . shall be prohibited, as shall the purchase of directly from them by the ECB or national central banks of debt instruments'. This description of the law governing the ECB in chapter eight contrasts directly with de Grauwe's argument for an improved model for monetary union in chapter six, where he stated that countries with their own central bank do not stand in risk of default 'because the central bank *can be forced to provide all the necessary liquidity to the sovereign'* (emphasis added).[48]

This tension between chapter eight of *Economics of Monetary Union* and de Grauwe's more recent arguments can be explained as follows. De Grauwe's argument in section 6.1 about the need for the ECB to be a lender of last resort in the sovereign bond market is a new addition that appears for the first time in the

[45] De Grauwe, *The Economics of Monetary Union* (n 27) 155–56.
[46] ibid 152.
[47] ibid.
[48] ibid 120.

ninth edition of the book. The description of the ECB's structure, role, and legal mandate in chapter eight, however, are largely the same as in earlier editions of the book. Section 6.1 does not contradict chapter eight because the argument in 6.1 is for *changing* the existing structure of EMU. In his recent articles in online journals and newspapers, however, removed from the context of the textbook, those arguments become calls for the ECB to act as if the legal change that de Grauwe recommends has in fact already occurred.

De Grauwe might respond by claiming that monetary financing arises when central banks purchase bonds directly from Member States but not from bond purchases in secondary markets. In his textbook, in a section appearing for the first time in the new ninth edition and thus after the ECB initiated the SMP, de Grauwe states that when buying government bonds in secondary markets, 'the ECB does not provide credit to governments'.

> What it does is to provide liquidity to the holders of these government bonds. These holders are typically financial institutions. In no way can this be interpreted as monetary financing of government budget deficits.
>
> In contrast, the prohibition on buying debt instruments directly from national governments is based on the fact that such an operation provides liquidity to these governments and thus implies a monetary financing of the government budget deficit.[49]

De Grauwe cites two Articles of the ECB Statute: Article 18, which allows purchase of government bonds in secondary markets for the purpose of open market operations as discussed above in section I; and Article 21, which incorporates the prohibitions in Article 123 TFEU on providing 'overdrafts or any other type of credit facility' to public entities and on the direct purchase of debt instruments from Member States.[50]

De Grauwe's argument that buying bonds in secondary markets cannot be monetary financing of public spending is untenable and, as we have already seen in section I, rejected by Council Regulation 3603/93, which interprets 'other type of credit facility' in Article 123 to include 'any financing of the public sector's obligations vis-à-vis third parties'. *Credit facility* has a broader meaning than direct purchase of government debt, and Regulation 3603/93 confirms this and extends the definition explicitly to third-party transactions. One method by which the central bank can extend credit to governments by open market purchases is by pegging interest rates, for example by setting a floor price to Spanish 10-year bonds of 3 per cent above German 10-year bonds. De Grauwe has proposed this method, stating that 'the ECB should announce a cap on the spreads of the Spanish and Italian government bonds, say of 300 basis points'.[51] As long as the price floor is credible and set above the market rate, it is immaterial whether the central bank buys the bonds directly from the government or some financial intermediary shortly after

---

[49] ibid 199.
[50] See ibid.
[51] P de Grauwe, 'Why the EU summit decisions may destabilise government bond markets' *VoxEU* (2 July 2012) www.voxeu.org/article/why-eu-summit-decisions-may-destabilise-government-bond-markets, accessed 2 June 2013.

they have been issued.[52] A less direct kind of monetary financing could consist in secondary market bond purchases at some date after the issue and without any firm or announced cap or yield rate. If the central bank purchases bonds in a targeted manner and sufficient quantities – and especially if it signals its willingness to purchase unlimited quantities with the aim of making the Euro irreversible, as in the OMT programme – it increases the demand for the bonds and thereby lowers the Government's borrowing costs. If the central bank's aim in such purchases is to enable or underwrite public spending, this also is monetary financing forbidden by Article 123 and Regulation 3603/93. Crucially, the bonds issued to finance government operations do not end up being held by the public but by the ECB, regardless of the intermediary process.[53]

Despite de Grauwe's argument recounted above, elsewhere he accepts that bond-buying can amount to monetary financing of public debt. When Jens Weidmann, president of the Bundesbank, condemned Draghi's OMT proposal as 'being tantamount to financing governments by printing bank notes', de Grauwe criticised him in the *Financial Times*:

> This guerrilla warfare by the Bundesbank president is based on a failure to understand the role of a central bank in a modern economy. Central banks were created to deal with the endemic problem of financial capitalism: its instability and the impact this has on the banking system. This has led to the consensus that the central bank should be a lender of last resort in the banking system to ensure that the bubbles and crashes that are part and parcel of capitalism do not bring down the banking system.
>
> *Should this role of lender of last resort also be extended to the government? It must be, if financial stability is to be maintained, because the sovereign and the banks hold each other in a deadly embrace.* When the banking system collapses, this threatens the solvency of the sovereign. When the sovereign defaults on its debt, it pulls the banks into default. This means that the banking sector cannot be stabilised if the sovereign is unstable. *A central bank that wishes to stabilise the banking sector is condemned to also stabilise the government bond market.* Failure to do so leads to a banking crisis, forcing the central bank to provide huge amounts of liquidity to banks that it refuses to provide to the sovereign. (Emphasis added.)[54]

De Grauwe here acknowledges that buying bonds in the secondary market – as contemplated in Draghi's OMT proposal – can be a way of acting as a lender of last resort *for governments*. He proceeds to characterise the OMT programme as transforming the ECB into this kind of lender of last resort:

---

[52] See F Mishkin, *Money, Banking, and Financial Markets*, 9th edn (Addison Wesley, 2010) 628.

[53] It might be objected, with regard to the SMP and OMT programmes that they are *sterilised* bond purchases, which prevents the ECB from financing peripheral government debt using the unlimited creation of high-powered money. Instead of selling existing assets, such as German bonds, the ECB created new money (bank reserves) but encouraged banks to hold this as one-week fixed deposits, which are also counted as reserves. By choosing to sterilise bond purchases in this manner, there is no limit to the amount of peripheral government debt the ECB can accumulate on its balance sheet. For further discussion of this issue see G Fuzesi, 'ECB's failure to sterilize bond purchases is a red herring' *J.P. Morgan Economic Research Note* (2 December 2011).

[54] P de Grauwe, 'Stop this campaign against ECB policy' *Financial Times* (London, 22 October 2012).

Standalone countries such as the US and the UK understand [the need for a central bank to stabilise the government bond market] and have an implicit contract between the government and the central bank, whereby the latter *will always provide liquidity to the government in times of crisis.* Without such a contract, financial stability cannot be guaranteed.

The eurozone did not have such a contract between the sovereigns and the common central bank, explaining its fragility. It now has one with the OMT programme. Without such a contract, the eurozone cannot be stabilised. (Emphasis added.)[55]

Thus de Grauwe now acknowledges what he previously denied. In chapter six of his textbook he claimed that buying bonds in secondary markets 'provide[s] liquidity to the holders of these government bonds', who are typically financial institutions, and that '[i]n no way can this be interpreted as monetary financing of government budget deficits'.[56] There he equates providing liquidity to government with financing of government deficits.[57] Now he states in the article quoted above that the OMT bond-buying programme is a way of 'provid[ing] liquidity *to governments*' (emphasis added). Such a role conflicts with the ECB's legal mandate, as de Grauwe himself shows in chapter eight of his textbook, where he states that Article 123 was adopted in order to prevent a situation in which 'the central bank can be forced to print money to finance government deficits'.[58]

Because this chapter is primarily about the legality of the ECB acting as a lender of last resort in sovereign bond markets rather, I have not yet addressed the merits of de Grauwe's argument with regard to economic theory. In concluding this section, however, I will briefly canvass counter-arguments to his position regarding its economic merits.

1. The Aptness of the Analogy of Lender of Last Resort

In the wake of the financial crisis many economists and financial analysts have flocked to the idea that a central bank must act as a lender of last resort to sovereign governments, but any such proposal remains controversial, as de Grauwe acknowledges in his textbook.[59] The role of lender of last resort to the banking system and financial sector, as popularised by Bagehot,[60] has as its main function the prevention of a catastrophic collapse of the money supply due to illiquidity in the financial sector.[61] An important but ancillary effect is to reduce the risk of a run on any given bank. The lender of last resort provides liquidity to solvent but

---

[55] ibid.

[56] De Grauwe, *The Economics of Monetary Union* (n 27).

[57] ibid 199 ('In contrast, the prohibition on buying debt instruments directly from national governments is based on the fact that such an operation provides liquidity to these governments and thus implies a monetary financing of the government budget deficit'.)

[58] ibid 152.

[59] ibid 121.

[60] W Bagehot, *Lombard Street: A Description of the Money Market* (1873).

[61] TM Humphrey, 'Lender of Last Resort: The Concept in History' (1989) 75 *FRB Richmond Economic Review* 8.

illiquid institutions at a penalty rate, and it is premised on the ability of a financial regulator to distinguish (though not without possibility of error) between solvent and insolvent institutions, and to unwind insolvent ones. In the Eurozone, the ECB fulfils the role of lender of last resort to the financial system through the NCBs.[62] One problem with extending the role of lender of last resort to sovereigns is that it is more difficult to distinguish a solvency crisis from a liquidity crisis for a sovereign than it is for a financial institution. De Grauwe acknowledges the difficulty of distinguishing between liquidity and solvency crises in sovereigns but argues that the former can change quickly into the latter due to the link between banks and sovereigns, and that this helps to justify the role of sovereign lender of last resort.[63] Many economists, however, argue that a sovereign's illiquidity is a strong indicator of its insolvency.[64] Makinen and Woodward examined episodes of sovereign illiquidity during the interwar period and concluded:

> Although sovereign bond borrowing exhibits many aspects of bank runs (and hence an appeal to lender of last resort seems somewhat plausible) there is no historical evidence of spontaneous 'debt runs' on sovereigns. In all cases [examined in the paper] wrong debt management policies were the driver of crisis.[65]

When a private institution fails to manage its debt, the financial regulator can wind it down, but there is no such accountability for a sovereign government. Moreover, when the mechanism whereby a central bank functions as lender of last resort to a sovereign is purchasing its bonds in the open market – as proposed by de Grauwe – there is no possibility of receiving good collateral on the loan. Thus, basic conditions on which the function of lender of last resort to the financial system is premised do not apply to the proposed role for the ECB as lender of last resort to sovereigns.

An additional problem with de Grauwe's argument is his claim that creditors of nations with central banks that act as a sovereign lender of last resort need not fear default. In fact, there are numerous historical examples of such nations defaulting on sovereign debt in whole or in part.[66] Indeed, in most instances, the use of the

---

[62] National central banks can create short term, emergency lending facilities (ELAs) in order to provide liquidity to illiquid but solvent institutions that can no longer access the traditional standing facilities. These ad hoc collateralised loans have many safeguards to prevent their abuse (and hence partially mitigate the moral hazard problem). They require approval of the ECB's Governing Council but need not be disclosed to the public. Importantly, the ELA remains a responsibility of the issuing NCB and must receive a sovereign indemnity guarantee. Thus, the losses of a failing institution remain with the sovereign of the domestic country. Although the ECB provides liquidity through the NCBs, this does not transfer losses from bank failures across Member States or redistribute the risk of such losses. As we will see in section III, the OMT programme could result in such a redistribution of loss and risk thereof.

[63] See de Grauwe, 'Why the EU summit decisions may destabilise government bond markets' (n 51).

[64] See CM Reinhart and KS Rogoff, *This Time is Different: Eight Centuries of Financial Folly* (Princeton University Press, 2009) ch 4, for a discussion on the problem of distinguishing a sovereign that is unwilling to pay from a sovereign that would pay if it could access funding.

[65] G Makinen and T Woodward, 'Funding Crises in the aftermath of World War I' in R Dornbusch and M Draghi (eds), *Public Debt Management: Theory and History* (Cambridge University Press, 1990).

[66] See CM Reinhart and KS Rogoff, 'The Forgotten History of Domestic Debt' (2011) 121 *The Economic Journal* 319 (documenting 68 cases of overt domestic default in a historical sample ending in 2005).

printing press can be seen not so much as preventing default but as facilitating a partial default.[67]

2. Inflation Risk

Since the Eurozone crisis began in 2008, there has been a massive increase in the money base in the Eurozone due to the ECB purchasing assets to provide liquidity to financial institutions, and in part due to ECB government bond purchases. As de Grauwe observes, this has not led to inflation because the money supply has become disconnected from the money base:

> When the central bank buys government bonds (or other assets) it increases the money base (currency in circulation and banks' deposits at the central bank). This does not mean that the money stock increases. In fact, during periods of financial crisis both monetary aggregates tend to become disconnected.... [P]rior to 2008 both aggregates were very much connected in the Eurozone. From October 2008 on, however, the disconnect becomes quite spectacular. In order to save the banking system, the ECB massively piled up assets on its balance sheets, the counterpart of which was a very large increase in the money base. This had no effect on the money stock (M3).... The reason why this happened is that banks piled up the liquidity provided by the ECB without using it to extend credit to the non-banking sector. A similar phenomenon has been observed in the US and UK.[68]

De Grauwe, however, acknowledges that the increased money base creates a future risk of inflation, stating that when the economy begins expanding again, 'the extra liquidity held by banks could be used to expand credit'.[69] He argues that the central bank 'can then withdraw the liquidity by selling government bonds', counter-acting the inflation risk.[70] However, what should the ECB do once the money base is no longer divorced from the money supply? Should the ECB continue to be available as lender of last resort to sovereigns? If so, the ECB could give up effective control of monetary policy.

De Grauwe's argument that a central bank can forestall inflation by selling bonds assumes that the central bank maintains control of inflation through monetary policy. According to the fiscal theory of the price level (FTPL), however, a central bank can lose that ability. Economists Michael Woodford and Chris Sims, key proponents of FTPL, contend that the price level is not determined solely by the money stock; it is also affected by the Government's budget constraint, that is,

---

[67] ibid.

[68] De Grauwe, *The Economics of Monetary Union* (n 27) 121.

[69] ibid 122.

[70] ibid. Christian Noyer, governor of the Bank of France and member of the ECB Governing Council, is not as confident of the ability to control the inflation risk in the future: 'Although [asset purchases] may help to eliminate upward pressure on interest rates in the short term, they will also affect price and financial stability in the medium run.... Such risks will not necessarily materialise, but when they do the repercussions are immense'. See D Flynn, 'ECB to protect banks but won't step up bond buying' *Reuters* (21 December 2011) www.reuters.com/article/2011/12/19/eurozone-noyer-idU-SL6E7NJ11P20111219, accessed 22 May 2013.

the condition that the real value of the Government's stock of debt must be equal to the present value of future primary fiscal surpluses.[71] The real value of government debt changes as the price level changes. The strategic interaction between monetary and fiscal authorities can result in two outcomes:[72] (1) the central bank determines the price level and the fiscal authority responds by setting future primary surpluses so as to meet the budget constraint or (2) inflation is determined by fiscal policy and the monetary authority responds by monetizing the Government's debt. By choosing to act as the sovereign lender of last resort, the ECB opens the possibility of being pushed into the second outcome.

Although FTPL remains controversial, it calls attention to the dynamic between fiscal and monetary authorities and shows a potential danger of the OMT programme. The ordinary function of lender of last resort to the financial system does not conflict with, but rather complements, a central bank's objective of maintaining control of the money supply. However, the role of lender of last resort to sovereigns is not clearly congruent with that objective. If OMT were to involve pegging interest rates in crisis countries – as proposed by de Grauwe – the ECB could risk losing control of the price level. Currently, market evidence suggests that the ECB remains in control of monetary policy: inflation and inflationary expectations remain low in the Eurozone. Nonetheless, FTPL suggests that it is still legitimate to worry that inflationary expectations could become unanchored. A proponent of OMT might object that the requirement of submitting to bail-out conditions will counteract any tendency toward active fiscal policy. This strategy, however, draws the ECB into the role of directing and overseeing fiscal policy, which, for reasons I will explore in section III, is an imprudent role for a central bank and beyond the mandate of the ECB.

3. Moral Hazard

A danger of a central bank acting as lender of last resort to sovereigns is moral hazard, that is, the creation of incentive to accumulate more debt and avoid needed reforms. The previous subsection on inflation risk raises a question about moral hazard and the OMT that will be explored in more detail in section III. Here I will frame the problem in general terms.

Jens Weidmann explains how the central banks' response to the current crisis has created moral hazard for both the financial system and sovereigns:

> As a result of the measures taken, central banks now play a fundamentally different role. Before the crisis they provided scarce liquidity; now they serve as a regular source of funding that replaces or displaces private investors.

---

[71] M Woodford, 'Monetary Policy and Price Level Determinacy in a Cash-in-advance Economy' (1994) 4 *Economic Theory* 345; CA Sims, 'A Simple Model for Study of the Determination of the Price Level and the Interaction of Monetary and Fiscal Policy' (1994) 4 *Economic Theory* 381.

[72] EM Leeper, 'Equilibria under "active" and "passive" monetary and fiscal policies' (1991) 27 *Journal of Monetary Economics* 129.

This breeds the risk of some banks becoming overly dependent on central bank funding, thus reducing incentives to reform business models. . . . Regulators need to keep up pressure on banks to proceed with the restructuring of the financial sector, particularly by unwinding unviable banks and retaining earnings to build up capital.

By the same token, relieving stress in the sovereign bond markets eases imminent funding pain but blurs the signal to sovereigns about the precarious state of public finances and the urgent need to act. Macroeconomic imbalances and unsustainable public and private debt in some member states lie at the heart of the sovereign debt crisis. It may appeal to politicians to abstain from unpopular decisions and try to solve problems through monetary accommodation. However, it is up to monetary policymakers to fend off these pressures.[73]

De Grauwe acknowledges the danger of moral hazard. In one article he calls liquidity operations 'necessary' but not 'sufficient' because they do not address underlying structural problems. He draws an analogy to fire-fighting, contending that arguments against the ECB acting as a lender of last resort in sovereign bond markets are like arguments that the fire brigade should not put out fires if a city has underlying structural problems that lead to constant house fires (eg, a pyromaniac, or inadequate building codes):

These structural problems will have to be addressed. But does that mean that if a new fire erupts, the firemen should not extinguish it? The fact that pouring water on the flames does not resolve the structural problems and that other fires will rage cannot be a reason to conclude, as critics of the ECB do, that the fire brigade should not try to extinguish the fire. It should. This is necessary to prevent a worse outcome, and to avoid more innocent victims. Extinguishing the fire is necessary but not sufficient. Similarly, the interventions of the ECB are necessary but not sufficient.[74]

What this analogy fails to capture is that if the ECB acts as a lender of last resort to sovereigns, this may not only fail to solve the crisis, but may also discourage needed reforms and exacerbate the underlying problems, thus prolonging the crisis and magnifying its destructive potential.

In briefly canvassing these objections to a central bank acting as lender of last resort to sovereigns, my aim has not been to provide a definitive economic argument against that role but to show that the case is more debatable than some proponents of the ECB as lender of last resort to sovereigns have acknowledged. It is wrong to argue, as some financial analysts now do, that since a central bank is a 'lender of last resort' in a general sense, it must also be a lender of last resort to sovereigns. The latter is substantially different from the former, and any argument for it must contend with the downside risks and the political and institutional consequences of having a central bank that is operationally independent but can be 'forced', as de Grauwe says, to provide liquidity needed for government spending. My discussion of economic policy objections has mainly been in general terms applicable in a single-state setting. In a monetary union like the EMU, the political

---

[73] J Weidmann, 'Monetary policy is no panacea for Europe' *Financial Times* (London, 7 May 2012).
[74] P de Grauwe, 'The ECB, the OMT, and Austerity' *Social Europe Journal* (13 September 2012) www.social-europe.eu/2012/09/the-ecb-the-omt-and-austerity/, accessed 22 May 2013.

and institutional aspects loom larger, for reasons that will be explored in more detail in section III. The prohibition on monetary financing in Article 123 is concerned at least as much with preserving Member State sovereignty over fiscal powers as it is with economic policy. In any event, whether the economic merits of the argument for the ECB to act as a lender of last resort to sovereigns are strong or weak, this role was rejected when the law regarding the ECB was established. This is a fundamental feature of the EMU compact, and it was crucial to reaching agreement. In his initial press conferences after his appointment, Draghi showed that he understood and was committed to the ECB's legal mandate of price stability as the overriding aim, and that he agreed with the rejection in the EU Treaties of monetary financing of public debt and the role of the ECB as lender of last resort for governments (as discussed above in section I). That law still governs the ECB and is what Draghi should choose to follow.

III. The OMT Programme and the ECB's Mandate

Mario Draghi announced the OMT programme on 6 September 2012, soon after his promise in London to do '[w]ithin our mandate . . . whatever it takes to save the euro'. The programme has two key elements, according to the statement Draghi made to the press. First, the ECB stands ready to purchase Member State bonds in unlimited amounts in order to 'preserve the singleness of our monetary policy' and transmit it to the 'real economy', and to 'have a fully effective backstop to avoid destructive scenarios with potentially severe challenges for price stability in the Euro area'.[75] The purchases would be of bonds with a one- to three-year maturity, targeting the shorter range of the yield curve. Second, the ECB will purchase bonds only if a Member State first requests assistance from the ESM and submits to its conditions regarding fiscal discipline and macroeconomic adjustments, as well as to monitoring by the IMF.[76] Here is the summary justification in Draghi's words:[77]

> [W]e need to be in the position to safeguard the monetary policy transmission mechanism in all countries of the Euro area. We aim to preserve the singleness of our monetary

[75] M Draghi, Introductory statement to the press conference (with Q&A) (6 September 2012) www.ecb.int/press/pressconf/2012/html/is120906.en.html, accessed 22 May 2013.

[76] The ECB press release, 'Technical features of Outright Monetary Transactions' (6 September 2012) describes conditionality as follows: 'A necessary condition for Outright Monetary Transactions is strict and effective conditionality attached to an appropriate European Financial Stability Facility/European Stability Mechanism (EFSF/ESM) programme. Such programmes can take the form of a full EFSF/ESM macroeconomic adjustment programme or a precautionary programme (Enhanced Conditions Credit Line), provided that they include the possibility of EFSF/ESM primary market purchases. The involvement of the IMF shall also be sought for the design of the country-specific conditionality and the monitoring of such a programme.' www.ecb.int/press/pr/date/2012/html/pr120906_1.en.html, accessed 22 May 2013.

[77] Draghi, Introductory statement to the press conference (6 September 2012) (with emphasis added) (n 75).

policy and to ensure the proper transmission of our policy stance to the real economy throughout the area. OMTs will enable us to address severe distortions in government bond markets which originate from, in particular, unfounded fears on the part of investors of the reversibility of the Euro. Hence, under appropriate conditions, *we will have a fully effective backstop to avoid destructive scenarios with potentially severe challenges for price stability in the Euro area.* Let me repeat what I said last month: we act strictly within our mandate to maintain price stability over the medium term; we act independently in determining monetary policy; and the Euro is irreversible.

The most significant thing that Draghi has said is not that the ECB would 'do whatever it takes to save the euro' but (i) that 'the Euro is irreversible' and (ii) the ECB can intervene in bond markets to price out a premium based on investor fears of the break up the Euro. The reason this is so significant is that concerns about the solvency of a Eurozone state credibly raise fears among investors that the state will either be forced to leave the Euro or do so on its own accord – and that the exit of even one member could lead to a break up of the common currency. Draghi is therefore signifying that it is within the mandate of the ECB to ensure that Member States do not have to leave the Euro.

But Draghi and the governors of the ECB do not have the responsibility or authority to decide whether the Euro is irreversible or which states should remain within the Eurozone. That is a decision for elected politicians, who alone are accountable to the people – not only because this is in keeping with the principle of democracy, one of the pillars of the EU, but because the ECB is authorised to act only within its legal remit. That remit does not include ensuring that the Euro remains the currency used by Member States in the Eurozone, or acting to prevent a sovereign default that might cause a country to leave the Eurozone. The Member States of the EU are sovereign states,[78] and only the political authorities of those states can decide whether the Euro is irreversible.

Draghi claims that there are 'severe distortions' in government bond markets, which he attributes in particular to 'unfounded fears on the part of investors of the reversibility of the euro'. He has acknowledged, however, that it is not within the ECB's mandate to price out the 'default premium' that investors demand when purchasing sovereign bonds, that is, the premium demanded due to the risk that a sovereign will not honour the full real value of its debts.[79] For the ECB to buy sovereign bonds with the aim of reducing yields and thus pricing out the default premium would clearly amount to monetary financing of sovereign debt in violation of Article 123 TFEU. How then does Draghi justify buying government bonds in order to make the Euro irreversible? His argument is that the 'monetary policy transmission mechanism' is broken or fragmented and in need of repair, and that the ECB must strive for 'singleness of monetary policy'. What this means is that the ECB's decisions on setting interest rates – traditionally its main instrument of monetary policy – have different effects in different countries,

---

[78] The right of states to leave the EU is recognised in Article 50 TEU: 'Any Member State may decide to withdraw from the Union in accordance with its own constitutional requirements.'

[79] Draghi, Speech at the Global Investment Conference in London (26 July 2012) (n 1).

and in some cases the ECB is unable to achieve results. A decision to lower rates may stimulate bank lending to businesses in some countries but fail to have effects in others.[80] At the 26 July 2012 London investment conference Draghi also referred briefly to the 'risk of convertibility',[81] which can refer to fears that a state will adopt a new currency and redenominate its liabilities in that (presumably weaker) currency, or use capital controls to keep money from leaving its banks. Draghi claimed that while it is not within the remit of the ECB to price out the default premium, it is within the remit of the ECB to price out a premium due to convertibility risk.[82] Although some ratings agencies and economists have proposed formulae for distinguishing the risk of convertibility from that of default, such an endeavour is notoriously uncertain.[83] A deeper problem, however, is that even if the risk of convertibility could be specifically ascertained and distinguished from the default premium, there is nothing special about the risk of convertibility that makes pricing it out within the remit of the ECB. In the Eurozone context, any fears that investors have regarding risk of convertibility derive from concerns about a sovereign's capacity to fulfil its real debt obligations or fears about (full or partial) sovereign default. Such concerns and fears are the primary reason for high yields on bonds in peripheral countries and thus for the divergent interest rates that impair the transmission mechanism.[84] When asked a question at the 6 September 2012 press conference about whether there could be a 'convertibility premium' on German bonds due to the expectation that the value of a new Deutschmark would rise relative to other currencies, Draghi agreed that this could be the case.[85] This answer shows that investors are not concerned about redenomination per se but whether they will receive back less than the value of their investment; the risk of this is determined fundamentally by a sovereign's solvency and capacity and willingness to repay its obligations – matters that are not within the remit of the ECB. While the difficulty in transmitting monetary policy is real, it is primarily caused by underlying fiscal and economic problems which do not fall within the remit of the ECB. Draghi's claim that the ECB cannot

[80] Draghi, Introductory statement to the press conference (6 September 2012) (n 75). Draghi has observed that in Europe 80% of credit intermediation goes through banks, in comparison to the US where 80% is through capital markets. B Appelbaum, J Ewing and others, 'Central Banks Act With a New Boldness to Revitalize Economies' *The New York Times* (28 May 2013).

[81] Draghi, Speech at the Global Investment Conference in London (26 July 2012) (n 1).

[82] ibid.

[83] W Watts, 'Draghi's "convertibility" fears set ECB tough task' *The Wall Street Journal: MarketWatch* (31 August 2012) www.marketwatch.com/story/draghi-convertibility-worries-set-ecb-tough-task-2012-08-31, accessed 9 June 2013.

[84] It might be argued (i) that investor fears are driven not only by underlying indicators such as a country's debt figured as a percentage of GDP but also involve fears related to panics or self-fulfilling crisis; therefore, (ii) pricing out the premium owing specifically to such panic-based fears is in the remit of the ECB. But this argument is circular to the extent that the panic-based fears arise from the absence in the Eurozone of a sovereign lender of last resort like the US Federal Reserve, which can resort to monetary financing. The argument in (i) could be used to criticise the legal structure of EMU for the absence of such a backstop. But since the limited legal mandate of the ECB is, ex hypothesi, driving the panic, (i) is not a valid argument for concluding that pricing out the panic-based premium is in the remit of the ECB.

[85] Draghi, Speech at the Global Investment Conference in London (26 July 2012) (n 1).

price out default risk but can buy bonds of distressed countries to reduce their yields is like an insurance company stating in its policy that it does not cover diabetes (as a pre-existing condition), but later covering insulin pumps for all those who need them. The one is derivative of the other. Spreading the risk of paying for insulin pumps among policyholders is spreading the risk of the costs of diabetes. The broken transmission mechanism and risk of convertibility are due to high bond yields in the peripheral countries that are in turn due to underlying problems of economic performance and fiscal management.[86] If the ECB uses its bond-buying power to 'repair the transmission mechanism' and price out convertibility risk, it will do so by taking risky assets onto its balance sheet – the bonds of distressed Eurozone states – and spreading the risk among the Eurozone members. This is using monetary policy to underwrite sovereign debt.

Another argument that could be made in favour of the legality of OMT is that it is necessary to maintain price stability. A 'destructive scenario' of the kind contemplated by Draghi could cause prices to be unstable in any number of ways – and directions. This argument is flawed, however, because the prohibition on monetary financing laid down in Article 123 TFEU is a 'hard' rule – an independent side-constraint – not simply a 'soft' principle that can be overridden for the sake of a more generally formulated goal such as transmission of a single monetary policy, repairing a broken transmission mechanism, or even price stability. Someone might argue that the ECB can have recourse to monetary financing of public debt if this is necessary for price stability (or for financial stability), and thus that monetary financing is permissible if necessary to assuage investor fears about the break up of the Eurozone. This argument, taken to its logical conclusion, would remove all constraints on how the ECB could use its balance sheet, so long as the action could plausibly be justified as 'necessary to avoid a destructive scenario and thus maintain price stability'. For example, if the United States were in danger of defaulting on its sovereign debt, and this threatened to engulf the Eurozone in a global financial crisis of greater magnitude than that of 2008, then the ECB could purchase US treasuries in order to drive down yields and help the US Government service its debt – thereby helping to maintain price stability in the Eurozone.

It is not the case that EU Treaty law prohibits monetary financing except when it is necessary for price stability. The law prohibits monetary financing of public debt full stop. This is expressed in Article 123 TFEU in terms of a bar on extending any 'credit facility' to Member States. Draghi addressed Article 123 at the 6 September press conference in the following terms:

> [W]e are sure that we are acting within our mandate, that we are not violating Article 123. It is pretty explicit: it says for purchases on the primary market, this is a violation, not for purchases on the secondary market as I have stated this programme will work.[87]

---

[86] This is not all necessarily due to a country's unsustainable long-run fiscal imbalance. In the case of Ireland, for instance, the sovereign instability was largely caused by the domestic political decision to assume the private liabilities of the financial sector.

[87] Draghi, Introductory statement to the press conference (6 September 2012) (n 75).

This is the argument that de Grauwe made in his textbook,[88] but, as shown in section I, it ignores Council Regulation 3603/93, which prohibits 'any financing of the public sector's obligations vis-à-vis third parties'. Draghi's reading of Article 123 in September 2012 stands in stark contrast to his press conference in December 2011, when questions were raised about whether the ECB could, in keeping with the law, purchase bonds in unlimited amounts in open markets. Draghi firmly rejected monetary financing of public debt and the notion that the ECB should act as a lender of last resort to sovereigns, and he said that the ECB should not attempt to 'circumvent' Article 123: 'No matter what the legal trick is, I think what matters for the people and what matters for the confidence and credibility of the institution is *the spirit of this provision of the Treaty*.'[89] Perhaps in anticipation of the pressure ECB governors might feel to circumvent Article 123 TFEU, and to act contrary to its spirit through transactions in secondary markets, Regulation 3603/93 guarded against the kind of interpretation of Article 123 offered by Draghi in September 2012.

Someone might object to my argument's insistence on strict adherence to the detail of the law. What if monetary financing of public debt by the ECB is the only available means to prevent sovereign default and the financial calamity that could result from the Eurozone unravelling, with all the disastrous consequences of the collapse of a common currency? Would the motivation of averting such a catastrophe justify the ECB in violating its legal mandate? To answer this question, we first need to go back to the formation of EMU and, in light of its founding principles and basic structure, consider criticisms made at the time and some of the problems that unfolded, especially after the financial crisis of 2008.[90]

As shown in section I, the EU Treaties, while allocating certain economic powers to EU institutions and monetary authority to the ECB, preserved the sovereignty of Member States with regard to decisions about public spending and taxation. Thus EMU was designed as a currency union without fiscal or political union. At the launch of the Euro, many economists warned that this system was ill designed and questioned whether it could survive. Milton Friedman, in an address to the Canadian Central Bank in 2000, said: '[T]he Euro is one of the few really new things we've had in the world in recent years. Never in history, to my knowledge, has there been a similar case in which you have a single central bank controlling politically independent countries. . . . I think the Euro is in its honeymoon phase. I hope it succeeds, but I have very low expectations for it.'[91] Another Nobel

---

[88] De Grauwe, *The Economics of Monetary Union* (n 27) 121.

[89] Draghi, Introductory statement to the press conference (8 December 2011) (emphasis added) (n 28).

[90] For detailed analysis of these matters see A Hinarejos, 'The Euro Area Crisis and Constitutional Limits to Fiscal Integration' in C Barnard and M Gehring (eds) *Cambridge Yearbook of European Legal Studies*, vol 14 (Oxford, Hart Publishing, 2012); A Scott, 'Does Economic Union Require Fiscal Union' in NN Shuibhne and LW Gormley (eds) *From Single Market to Economic Union: Essays in Memory of John A. Usher* (Oxford University Press, 2012); P Krugman, 'Can Europe be Saved?' *The New York Times* (12 January 2011).

[91] M Friedman, 'Canada and Flexible Exchange Rates' Bank of Canada Keynote Address (November 2000) www.bankofcanada.ca/wp-content/uploads/2010/08/keynote.pdf, accessed 28 May 2013.

Prize-winning economist, Chris Sims, said that 'an attempt to create a central bank and a monetary unit that have no corresponding fiscal authority . . . appears to carry with it great dangers'.[92] As Friedman explains, a basic problem is the Eurozone countries have distinct labour markets and economic conditions with very different features:

> [T]he various countries in the Euro are not a natural currency trading group. They are not a currency area. There is very little mobility of people among the countries. They have extensive [internal] controls and regulations and rules, and so they need some kind of an adjustment mechanism to adjust to asynchronous shocks – and the floating exchange rate gave them one. They have no mechanism now. . . .
>
> I think that differences are going to accumulate among the various countries and that non-synchronous shocks are going to affect them. Right now, Ireland is a very different state; it needs a very different monetary policy from that of Spain or Italy. On purely theoretical grounds, it's hard to believe that it's going to be a stable system for a long time.[93]

Economists generally agree that the Eurozone does not meet the criteria for an optimal currency union.[94] Moreover, in a monetary union, a central bank is generally unable to counteract non-synchronous shocks.[95]

The honeymoon phase Friedman referred to lasted until 2007, but with the financial crisis of 2008 the fault lines in EMU began to emerge. By 2010 Greece, Portugal, and Ireland had all been forced to seek bail-out funds due to high interest rates that made raising funds in private markets untenable. The EFSF and ESM were initiated in order to make bail-out funds available to countries in crisis situations, as discussed in section I. By 2011 the yields on 10-year bonds in Spain and Italy had reached 6 per cent and were creeping toward levels economists consider unsustainable for the long term. In the spring of 2011 fears were heightening that Spain and Italy would eventually be unable to meet financing needs; that contagion was spreading, affecting sovereigns as well as banks and locking them in what de Grauwe called a 'deadly embrace'; and that the exit of even one member (whether voluntarily or – a particular concern for Greece – by expulsion) could set a precedent leading the Eurozone to unravel and the currency to collapse. It is important to note that the sovereign debt crisis was not solely caused by Member

---

[92] CA Sims, 'The Precarious Fiscal Foundations of EMU' (1999) 147 *De Economist* 415. See also H Uhlig, 'One Money, but Many Fiscal Policies in Europe: What Are the Consequences?' (2002) CEPR Discussion Paper No 3296 at www.papers.ssrn.com/sol3/papers.cfm?abstract_id=310474, accessed 9 June 2013.

[93] Friedman, 'Canada and Flexible Exchange Rates' (n 91).

[94] See P Krugman, 'Revenge of the Optimum Currency Area' *Paul Krugman Blog, The New York Times* (24 June 2012) www.krugman.blogs.nytimes.com/2012/06/24/revenge-of-the-optimum-currency-area/, accessed 30 May 2013.

[95] When a country controls its own currency, it can use monetary policy in responding to economic fluctuations. Its currency can fluctuate to stimulate exports and address competitive imbalances, which help the economy return to its long-run potential. A country that joins a monetary union gives up these tools. It retains, however, the power to use fiscal policy (borrowing and spending) to respond to financial shocks. In EMU this creates a risk of free-riding on countries with lower interest rates. See Uhlig, 'One Money, but Many Fiscal Policies in Europe: What Are the Consequences?' (n 92).

States' decisions about spending. The causes of the crisis are several and inter-related. Ireland and Spain, for example, had relatively low debt levels in the run-up to the crisis; it was enormous losses in the domestic financial sector that fundamentally led to the enormous increase in sovereign debt. Fiscal problems in these and other countries have been further exacerbated by competitive imbalances related to labour market and other factors.

The SMP temporarily kept yields in Spain and Italy from climbing higher, with the ECB spending over €200 million buying government bonds; and political transitions (an election in Spain, and the resignation of Silvio Berlusconi and appointment of Mario Monti to lead a technocratic government in Italy) bolstered market confidence to some degree. The ECB officially maintained that the aim of the SMP was to transmit monetary policy in the face of market fragmentation.[96] In December 2011 Draghi announced a modified form of the ECB's Long-term Refinancing Operations (LTRO), which allowed banks to obtain three-year loans at 1 per cent interest, with substantially reduced collateral requirements.[97] The ECB loaned out around €1 trillion through this programme. Nicolas Sarkozy told reporters at the December 2011 summit in Brussels 'This means that each state can turn to its banks, which will have liquidity at their disposal.'[98] The idea that banks could borrow from the ECB at 1 per cent and purchase, say, Spanish bonds yielding 5 per cent, was dubbed by financial journalists the 'Sarkozy carry trade'. The ECB, however, again maintained that the aim of the LTRO was to provide liquidity to banks because of the financial crisis rather than to support government spending.

Political leaders, meanwhile, pushed forward with the ESM and a renewed Stability and Growth Pact with a more vigorous enforcement mechanism, which was agreed to in December 2011. The ESM, however, probably lacks funds sufficient to bail out a country as large as Spain or Italy. And the renewed SGP targets have already been missed by several countries.[99] During the first half of 2012, there was a growing consensus among EU leaders that the only ultimate solution for the present crisis lies in taking steps toward increased fiscal and political union. The president of the Commission, José Manuel Barroso, said, 'The crisis has shown that without stronger governance in the Euro area it will be difficult, if not impossible, to sustain a common currency.'[100] A series of summit meetings proposed steps toward a common bank regulator and common fund for rescuing or winding down undercapitalised banks; centralised oversight of Member State budgets; and increased

---

[96] Lecture by Peter Praet, Member of the Executive Board of the ECB, at the International Center for Monetary and Banking Studies, Geneva (20 February 2012) www.ecb.int/press/key/date/2012/html/sp120220.en.html, accessed 12 June 2013.

[97] See n 12 for more detail.

[98] P Taylor, 'ECB limits bond buying, Eurozone looks to banks' *Reuters* (9 December 2011) www.uk.reuters.com/article/2011/12/09/uk-eurozone-ecb-idUKTRE7B80OA20111209, accessed 12 June 2013.

[99] B Fox, 'Brussels gives seven states more time to fix budgets' *EU Observer* (13 May 2013) www.euobserver.com/economic/120302, accessed 8 June 2013.

[100] J Ewing and S Castle, 'Weak Sale of Bonds Tests Germany's Stature in Crisis' *The New York Times* (23 November 2011).

political integration. Few observers, however, believe that EU citizens have the democratic will for such union. De Grauwe calls this the 'deep variable' in a monetary
union and notes that it was present at the unification of Germany in 1990: 'There
can be no doubt that such a comprehensive political union came about as a result of
common purposes and an intense feeling of belonging to the same nation.'[101] But he
acknowledges that this variable is weakly developed in the EU. 'Without a sense of
common purpose it is very doubtful that further progress towards political union
will be made. And as we have argued, without these steps towards political union
the monetary union will remain a fragile construction.'[102]

Thus we come to the claim that only the ECB can save the Euro, which many
economists and financial analysts have made in the last two years.[103] De Grauwe
argues that because the ECB is the only institution in the Eurozone that can set a
floor to bond prices, it must do so in order to prevent the downward spiral threatening banks and sovereigns together.[104] But does this emergency justify the ECB in
breaking the law and exceeding its mandate? No.

Even if some legal actors are justified in certain emergencies in violating
the law, we should be especially reluctant to consider independent central banks
justified in going beyond their legal mandate. Central banks are protected from
political accountability in order to allow them to pursue medium- and long-term
objectives without the interference of short-term pressures, and without the
incentive to withhold or grant benefits to entities (banks, financial institutions,
public spending programmes) for partisan or political purposes. Independent
central banks have a strong obligation to remain within their legal mandate
because the assumption that they will stick to that mandate is what justifies the
decision to make them independent in the first place. If it is true that the ECB is
the only institution that can save the Euro, this is because political leaders per-
ceive a lack of a spirit of co-operation or democratic will to take the political steps
toward fiscal integration that are necessary to preserve monetary union. An
important conclusion follows from this: if the ECB is the only institution that can
save the Euro, *then that is a strong reason for it not to attempt to save the Euro.* A
monetary union should not be held together by an independent central bank
operating outside its legal charter, relying on technical expertise rather than democratic and political support.

This general principle is even stronger in the EU than in the setting of a single
country because of the extreme difficulty of changing EU law. The ECB is significantly more independent than the Federal Reserve, the Bundesbank, or the Bank of
England because there is no straightforward way of holding the ECB to account,

---

[101] De Grauwe, *The Economics of Monetary Union* (n 27) 132.
[102] ibid.
[103] eg J Warner, 'Only the ECB can save the Euro now' *The Telegraph* (London, 30 May 2012); A Evans-
Pritchard, 'Only Mario Draghi's ECB can avert global calamity before the year is out' *The Telegraph*
(London, 29 July 2012); B Chu, 'Only the ECB can calm crisis, but is still dragging its feet' *The Independent*
(9 December 2011); L Knight, 'Will the European Central Bank save the Eurozone?' *BBC Business News*
(13 November 2011).
[104] De Grauwe, 'Europe needs the ECB to step up to the plate' (n 44).

or changing its structure or operations, through legislative means.[105] The first president of the ECB, Wim Duisenberg, observed that 'There is no bank in the world as independent from politics as the European Central Bank'.[106] The Federal Reserve, although operationally independent from the executive and legislative branches in the US, is legally accountable to the US Congress, which can change the statutes under which the Federal Reserve operates. Congress created the Federal Reserve in 1913 in response to financial panic and amended the Federal Reserve Act several times over the years in response to the Great Depression and other crises, most recently in 2010. The Bundesbank and Bank of England are legally accountable to their national parliaments in a similar way. But who can call the ECB to account? What if it continues to accrue liabilities on its balance sheet yet fails to prevent a sovereign default? The troubling – indeed frightening – prospect is that the EU has no body corresponding to a national legislature and executive that can address complex financial problems by means of ordinary lawmaking, changing the structure or mandate of a central bank, or creating new legal institutions. Neither the Commission, the Council, nor the European Parliament have the capacity – separately or in concert – to take the kind of decisive, swift action that a national legislature could take in such a situation. The ordinary lawmaking processes of the EU are far more cumbersome and complex than those of national parliaments and require a higher degree of consensus. And many processes for legal change in the EU require the unanimous agreement of 27 Member States, including the enhanced co-operation procedure of Article 352 TFEU, the revised Treaty amendment procedure of Article 48 TEU, and normal Treaty amendment procedures. The rules that prohibit the ECB from monetary financing of public debt and that prohibit assuming or guaranteeing the debts of Member States are Treaty Articles (123 and 125 TFEU) that can be changed only through unanimity. These rules thus have a similar status to national constitutional law but are far more difficult to amend than any national constitution. Unanimous agreement among the leaders of 27 States is an extraordinarily high barrier to legal change. Even if agreement on Treaty amendment could be reached, there are further barriers at the Member State level. Following the German Federal Constitutional Court's *Lisbon Treaty* judgment in 2009, which conditioned approval of the Treaty on the preservation of democratic control over certain subjects, Germany adopted a law that requires approval by the Bundestag and Bundesrat of measures that extend EU competences or deepen integration but are not subject to the regular Treaty ratification process.[107] The UK's EU Act 2011 requires that increases of power or competence of EU institutions must, if they affect the UK, be approved in a popular referendum before they can be ratified by the Government; if they do

---

[105] See S Berman and KR McNamara, 'Bank on Democracy: Why Central Banks Need Public Oversight' (1999) *Foreign Affairs* 2.

[106] M Persson, 'Euro crisis: After the Cyprus bank raid fiasco, Germany is being painted as the EU's chief villain' *The Telegraph* (30 March 2013).

[107] For discussion of this law see European Union Bill (HC Bill 106 of 2010–11) Research Paper 10/79 *House of Commons Library* (2 December 2010) www.parliament.uk/briefing-papers/rp10-79.pdf, accessed 11 June 2013.

not affect the UK, they must still be approved by Parliament, requiring the Government to deal with the strong eurosceptic bloc.[108]

Someone might turn this argument around with the following objection. Precisely because of the difficulty of obtaining unanimous consensus to amend the EU Treaties and the long time that would take, the ECB does not have the luxury of waiting. It must take measures to enable the Eurozone to survive while giving political leaders more time to agree to greater fiscal and political integration and enact the necessary legal changes. In the meantime, pressure can be brought to bear on the more heavily indebted states that will set them on the path to reform and restore market confidence.

This argument should also be rejected. The strategy of buying time is flawed because even if the people of the EU were willing to pursue fiscal union, the constitutional and institutional obstacles to this seem insurmountable for the foreseeable future. Alicia Hinarejos has explained some of the interrelated barriers to EU fiscal integration.[109] It would involve changing the fundamental tenet of EU governance from one of conferral, that is, that the EU can act only within the competences affirmatively granted to it under the Treaties.[110] Instead, the EU would need to assume general competence for lawmaking and policy like that of a national parliament. This increased competence, which would include power to make decisions about taxation and redistribution of wealth and public resources, would require a much greater degree of democratic legitimacy than EU institutions now possess. Fiscal measures, particularly the 'power to impose positive obligations on citizens to contribute taxes' and decide how such wealth is to be distributed, 'speak very directly to the link between citizen and the state'.[111] Hinarejos argues that the EU's present methods of democratic consultation and national accountability may be sufficient for the legitimacy of its core powers relating to the common market and regulation of trade, but that the magnitude of redistributive transfers in a fiscal union would 'necessitate a degree of political contestation and of connection between the citizen and the state that is currently lacking at the EU level, either through representative or deliberative democracy'.[112] Hinarejos adds that these barriers exist not only at the supranational level, but also at the level of Member State constitutions; several constitutional courts have held that 'there must be limits to European integration because certain areas are too integral to the sovereignty of the state' to be handed over to the EU.[113] These include fiscal powers, she argues, noting that the German Constitutional Court has been especially vocal about protecting the 'constitutional identity' of the German State, and that 'reserved domains' include 'fundamental fiscal decisions on public revenue and expenditure, [and] decisions on the shaping of the social

---

[108] See P Yowell, 'EU Act 2011: Law and Politics' *UK Constitutional Law Group* (19 January 2012) www.ukconstitutionallaw.org/2012/01/19/paul-yowell-eu-act-2011-law-and-politics/, accessed 25 May 2013.

[109] Hinarejos, 'The Euro Area Crisis and Constitutional Limits to Fiscal Integration' (n 90).

[110] ibid.

[111] ibid.

[112] ibid.

[113] ibid.

state'.[114] To Hinarejos's observations I would add the following. Solving the problem of democratic legitimacy in a federal union is inherently complicated by the need to represent Member States qua sovereign states while at the same time representing the people as a whole; there are correlative dangers of (i) diluting the individual vote of a citizen of a populous state by giving small countries more voting power, and (ii) of overriding the sovereignty of small countries by giving more power to the populace as a whole. The present system of qualified majority voting in the EU reflects this tension. The United States overcame this problem – which had been a major block in the 1787 constitutional convention – by adopting a bicameral legislature giving states equal representation in the Senate and the people equal representation in the House of Representatives. No such simple compromise appears available for the EU, in part because of its relative lack of a common language and culture.

If the ECB does not step in to save the Euro, the risks of default by a Member State and a currency break up are real. But the OMT programme does not fully remove that risk. So long as the Eurozone lacks political and fiscal union, the claim that the Euro is irreversible is little more than wishful thinking. If the ECB tries to save the Euro by monetary financing of debts of states in financial distress and fails, the consequences for the Eurozone could in the end prove more disastrous than if the ECB were to let matters take their course. This is not only because of financial considerations such as moral hazard, but also because of the institutional and political dimensions of the ECB assuming this role. Europe could find itself with an institution wielding vast powers and holding trillions of Euros in liabilities, which no legal or political authority has the means to call to account or to reform. Those liabilities have potential redistributive consequences because they are ultimately the responsibility of the Member State stakeholders in the ECB; however, they would rest on a shaky legal foundation, having been accumulated in violation of the ECB's legal mandate. The ECB could in effect become a kind of fiscal authority operating outside its mandate and without oversight.

The bar on monetary financing of public debt is not just an issue of policy, but something that goes to the heart of the federal structure of the EU. The absence of political and fiscal union in the EU Treaties, while dubious from the point of view of economic theory, is the logical counterpart of Member State sovereignty over matters of taxing, spending, welfare and other aspects of the public purse. It is therefore central to the compact to which the Member States and their citizens gave their assent.[115] As the ECB accumulates bonds of distressed countries on its balance sheet at above-market prices, it redistributes the cost of the risk of sovereign default. This amounts to a kind of fiscal union through the back door. This is not full mutualisation of public debt as in certain proposals for Eurobonds, but it carries many of the consequences of fiscal union. Among them is an effective

---

[114] ibid (quoting BVerfGE 123, 267 [252]).

[115] Under Draghi's predecessor, an ECB formal opinion referred to the exclusion of monetary financing in Article 123 as 'one of the basic pillars of the legal architecture of EMU'. Opinion of the ECB of 17 March 2011 (CON/2011/24) (2011/C 140/05).

assumption by one Member State of the debt obligations of another Member State – which is prohibited by Article 125 TFEU, another of the linchpins of the federal structure of EMU. Sir Mervyn King, governor of the Bank of England, explained this in the course of defending Draghi's rejection (at his first press conference discussed above in section I) of the proposal that the ECB should become a lender of last resort in the manner contemplated by de Grauwe:

> This phrase 'lender of last resort' has been bandied around by people who it seems to me have no idea what lender of last resort actually means, to be perfectly honest. It is very clear, from the origin, that lender of last resort by a central bank is intended to be lending to individual banking institutions, and to institutions which are clearly regarded as solvent. And it's done against good collateral and at a penalty rate. . . . That is a million miles away from the ECB buying sovereign debt of national countries which is used and seen as a mechanism for financing the current account deficit of those countries, which inevitably – if things go wrong – will create liabilities for the surplus countries. In other words, it would be a mechanism of transfers from the surplus to the deficit countries. And that's why the European Central Bank feels, I think – and with total justification – that it's not the job of a central bank to do something which a government could perfectly well do itself, but doesn't particularly want to admit to doing.[116]

It might be objected that King's proviso – 'if things go wrong' – is misplaced because central banks, by definition, cannot fail. Indeed de Grauwe has criticised the ECB for decisions to raise capital from member countries and finds it 'surprising that the ECB attaches so much importance to having sufficient equity'.[117]

> [T]his insistence is based on a fundamental misunderstanding of the nature of central banking. The central bank creates its own IOUs. As a result it does not need equity at all to support its activities. Central banks can live without equity because they cannot default. The only support a central bank needs is the political support of the sovereign that guarantees the legal tender nature of the money issued by the central bank. This political support does not need any equity stake of the sovereign.[118]

This argument assumes the basic point in contention, which is whether or not the political leaders – and the people – of the EU and the Member States have the political and democratic will necessary to sustain the common currency and to keep the Eurozone from unravelling. That is not a foregone conclusion, and it should not be treated as one by the ECB. The ECB must assume that it is possible for the common currency to disintegrate and must recognise that the liabilities on its balance sheet would then become an effective transfer of wealth between countries.

Questions of legality aside, the OMT programme poses three distinct risks of moral hazard. The first is that backstopping bonds with one- to three-year maturities provides enormous incentive to distressed countries to shorten the maturity

---

[116] See N Pratley, 'Hard truths about the Euro from Mervyn King', *The Guardian Blog* (16 November 2011) www.guardian.co.uk/business/nils-pratley-on-finance/2011/nov/16/mervyn-king-ecb-intervene, accessed 10 June 2013 (quoting remarks made by King at a press conference on 16 November 2011).

[117] De Grauwe, 'Why the EU summit decisions may destabilise government bond markets' (n 51).

[118] ibid.

structure of their debt, increasing the amount they must roll over on a regular basis. Draghi has recognised this risk and promised that the ECB would monitor it, but suggests that it is minimal because a country that made such a move would unbalance a maturity structure that took many years to achieve.[119] The second risk of moral hazard regards the reputation of the ECB itself. The reputation of a central bank is a crucial tool in its ability to keep inflationary expectations low and address the problem of time-consistent monetary policy.[120] The OMT programme raises a question as to whether the ECB can abide by the statutes and the Treaty law governing it. If it cannot bind itself to the mast of its own legal mandate, it raises doubt regarding its ability to abide by any commitments. Draghi has of course argued that the OMT programme is within the ECB's mandate, but it is difficult to reconcile (1) his December 2011 statements about the legality of bond purchases, when he insisted on avoiding monetary financing and sticking to the letter and spirit of Article 123 with (2) his September 2012 claim that Article 123 applies only to bond purchases directly from states and permits unlimited purchases of bonds of distressed states with the aim of reducing yields.

A third risk of moral hazard is that it provides a temptation to governments to continue to accumulate debt and to avoid reforms, knowing that the central bank stands ready to step in if the market loses confidence. The obvious rejoinder to this is the conditionality of the OMT programme: it can be accessed only if a country requests a bail-out from the ESM and submits to fiscal discipline and IMF monitoring. Without conditionality, the moral hazard of OMT would be an explosive danger. But the conditionality plan has manifold problems. In the first place, the moral hazard is now; it arises directly from Draghi's promise while the tempering effect of conditionality starts only once a state requests aid from the ESM. But no state has done so yet. It is now a commonplace in the financial press that Draghi has taken the risk of sovereign default off the table. As long as yields are kept down because the markets are confident of the ECB's backstop, then why should a government seek a bail-out from the ESM? Financial journalist Simon Nixon has recently argued that governments are backtracking from debt-reduction measures because 'market pressure to rapidly shrink budget deficits has eased, largely in response to the European Central Banks's promise to buy the bonds of countries that have agreed to a bailout package. Bond yields have fallen sharply in crisis countries, even as their economies deteriorate.'[121]

If a state does seek aid from the ESM, it is questionable whether this conditionality will have the desired effect, because the ECB's bond purchasing will begin on the basis of its agreement to abide by the strictures imposed. But what if the Member State fails to keep its promise? The dismal record of Member States in keeping to the covenants in the SGP, even among the fiscally stronger states and in better economic times, provides no great assurance that a state in distress will

---

[119] Draghi, Introductory statement to the press conference (6 September 2012) (n 75).

[120] See RJ Barro and DB Gordon, 'Rules, discretion and reputation in a model of monetary policy' (1983) 12 *Journal of Monetary Economics* 101.

[121] S Nixon, 'In place of austerity: what comes next?' *The Wall Street Journal* (29 April 2013).

keep its promises. Indeed, de Grauwe questioned conditionality on the ground that its demands could be too painful and even economically counter-productive:

> The [ECB] has made the purchase of government bonds conditional on further budgetary cuts in Southern countries. Most of these countries have made dramatically deep cuts. We now know that all too impetuous cuts are counterproductive, and can push countries into an economic and social abyss. Thus, one can hope that the ECB will use common sense and will not ask the Southern countries first to jump into the abyss before it helps them out with more cash.[122]

In another article, however, de Grauwe countered the moral hazard objections against the ECB acting as a lender of last resort by commending the conditionality in the OMT programme:

> By announcing its readiness to provide liquidity in the government bond markets, the ECB creates the risk that governments may reduce their efforts at cutting deficits and debts. That is why binding rules that would force governments to bring their budgetary house in order must complement the ECB's role of lender of last resort. These rules are now being put into place.[123]

The tension in de Grauwe's two comments reflects the very fine line the ECB is trying to navigate, promising 'unlimited' support to distressed states but on a strictly conditional basis.

If a Member State seeks aid under the OMT programme but then fails to keep to the conditions, then that may be because the state has fallen into further financial distress rather than because of profligacy or mere stubbornness. And what will the ECB do then? The ECB has said that bond purchases would terminate 'when there is non-compliance with the macroeconomic adjustment or precautionary programme'.[124] To take this step, however, would be to revert to the very risk that justified the creation of OMT in the first place – sovereign default that could lead to a break up of the Euro. It seems doubtful that the ECB would, at the end of the day, cut a state loose rather than keeping the flow open for further funding. Instead, it seems possible that the ECB would become actively involved in setting or adjusting the conditions under which a state may continue to participate in OMT, or at least influencing such decisions and providing oversight as to whether the conditions have been met. If so, then it will have taken on yet another role beyond its mandate: regulator of Member State fiscal policy. This would represent further accumulation of power in an institution that is not only operationally independent, but, as outlined above, cannot be effectively held to account or changed by ordinary lawmaking mechanisms. It is worth noting here that under recent EU agreements on the first part of the 'Banking Union', the ECB is set to assume responsibility for supervising banks in the Eurozone in mid-

---

[122] P de Grauwe, 'The ECB, the OMT, and Austerity' *Social Europe Journal* (13 September 2012) www.social-europe.eu/2012/09/the-ecb-the-omt-and-austerity/, accessed 12 June 2013.

[123] De Grauwe, 'Europe needs the ECB to step up to the plate' (n 44).

[124] See ECB press release, 'Technical features of Outright Monetary Transactions' (6 September 2012) (n 76).

2014,[125] though in this role (unlike that of monetary policy) the ECB will be answerable to policymakers, namely the European Parliament.

In the final analysis, the conditionality plan suggests that the ECB's promise to buy potentially unlimited amount of bonds has the aim of monetary financing of public debt, because it sets the promise in the context of distressed states seeking a bail-out. In the terms of EU law the OMT purchases will be a 'credit facility' in favour of Member States (barred by Article 123 TFEU), accomplished by means of 'financing of public sector obligations vis-à-vis third parties' (Regulation 3603/93). If the OMT programme were a legitimate form of monetary policy and necessary to achieve price stability, there would be no need for the ECB to subject its actions to decisions of the Member States. If pricing out the premium for convertibility risk is necessary and in the ECB's mandate, then why would the ECB allow the convertibility risk to persist until the country requests that it be priced out? If the OMT programme is needed to repair faulty transmission channels, then why would the ECB use it to extract fiscal concessions from states? Draghi has argued that in the absence of macroeconomic reform and fiscal discipline, the bond-buying under the OMT programme will not have its desired effect of repairing the transmission mechanism.[126] But this again suggests that the underlying reasons for the broken transmission mechanism are the interrelated problems of fiscal management in the peripheral countries and their weak economic performance relative to that of Germany and other countries with better growth and employment rates.

The conditionality of the OMT programme and linking of it to the ESM give a strong indication that OMT is not fundamentally motivated by reasons of monetary policy. There are grounds to think that, instead, OMT is a back-door bail-out vehicle. This impression is strengthened when one considers that before Draghi announced the OMT programme, some political leaders and financial analysts were calling for the ESM to be given a banking licence and to be deemed an eligible counter-party for borrowing from the ECB. This was seen as a solution to the problem of the limited funds of the ESM and the limited willingness of political leaders to contribute more. The ECB ruled this out in a formal opinion in March 2011 signed by its former president, Jean-Claude Trichet.[127] The opinion stated that a banking licence for the ESM would contravene Article 123 and the prohibition on monetary financing, which it called 'one of the basic pillars of the legal architecture of EMU'.[128] Nonetheless, Willem Buiter, chief economist at Citigroup, proposed in a May 2012 paper that one possible solution to the Eurozone crisis would be to make the ESM able to borrow from the ECB, 'using its claims on

---

[125] See European Council, Summit conclusions of 28/29 June 2012, EUCO76/12; 'An important step towards a real banking union in Europe: Statement by Commissioner Michel Barnier following the trilogue agreement on the creation of the Single Supervisory Mechanism for the Eurozone', Press Release of 19 March 2013, www.europa.eu/rapid/press-release_MEMO-13-251_en.pdf.

[126] Draghi, Introductory statement to the press conference (6 September 2012) (n 75).

[127] Opinion of the ECB of 17 March 2011 (CON/2011/24) (2011/C 140/05).

[128] ibid.

[Euro area] sovereigns as collateral'.[129] Under such a scheme, presuming the ECB's collateral rules would be expansive enough, the ESM could buy Spanish bonds, then pledge them as collateral in order to borrow cash from the ECB, and buy more Spanish bonds (this is what is meant by the ESM 'leveraging' its funds through the ECB).[130] Buiter acknowledged, however, that the proposal would face legal and political hurdles: (i) Article 123 might need to be amended, and (ii) the size or duration of the ESM's exposure as lender of last resort might violate 'constitutional requirements for budgetary sovereignty of national parliaments, including but not limited to the German parliament'. Draghi himself rejected the idea of a banking licence to the ESM on 5 July 2012, stating: 'I don't think there is anything to gain by asking the institution to act outside the limits of its mandate, thereby destroying its credibility.'[131] But that was before his promise in London on 26 July to do 'whatever it takes' to save the Euro. A few days after that promise, Mario Monti stated that a banking licence for the ESM 'will help, [and] I think this will in due course occur'.[132]

Paul de Grauwe has argued that: 'The only way to stabilise the government bond markets is to involve the ECB, either *indirectly* by giving a banking license to the ESM so that it can draw on the resources of the ECB (see Gros and Mayer 2010), or by *direct interventions* by the ECB' (emphasis added).[133] Calling the ECB a 'money-creating institution' with 'an infinite capacity to buy government bonds', de Grauwe contends that 'The fact that resources are infinite is key to be able to stabilise bond rates. It is the only way to gain credibility in the market.'[134] Was the OMT programme designed as an alternative means of allowing the ESM to draw on the resources of the ECB? *Financial Times* columnist Gavyn Davies has noted the close similarity between OMT and allowing the ECB to leverage liquidity provided by the ECB: 'Although the ECB claims that it is not bailing out governments through monetisation, which was the reason it originally declared proposals to leverage the ESM to be against the Treaties, it has ended up doing almost exactly the same thing. It will now increase its balance sheet to buy government bonds, alongside the ESM's activities. What is the difference between this and a leveraged ESM? Not much.'[135] Buiter characterises OMT as involving a

---

[129] W Buiter and E Rahbari, 'The European Central Bank As Lender of Last Resort for Sovereigns in the Eurozone' Centre for Economic Policy Research, Discussion Paper No 8974 (May 2012); also published in (2012) 50 *Journal of Common Market Studies* 6.

[130] See S Suoninen and P Carrel, 'ECB's Nowotny sees merits to leveraging ESM bailout fund' *Reuters* (Frankfurt, 25 July 2012) www.reuters.com/article/2012/07/25/us-ecb-nowotny-idUSBRE86O 0J820120725, accessed 9 June 2013.

[131] M Draghi, Introductory statement to the press conference (with Q&A) (5 July 2011) www.ecb. europa.eu/press/pressconf/2011/html/is111208.en.html, accessed 2 June 2013.

[132] D Wall, 'Monti Pushes for ESM Banking License' *The Wall Street Journal* (1 August 2012).

[133] De Grauwe, 'Why the EU summit decisions may destabilise government bond markets' (n 51).

[134] ibid.

[135] G Davies, 'Eurozone building blocks are falling into place' *Financial Times* (London, 12 September 2012) www.blogs.ft.com/gavyndavies/2012/09/12/eurozone-building-blocks-are-falling-into-place/#axzz269ufnIBk, accessed 2 June 2013.

degree of 'mutualisation' of debt,[136] and de Grauwe claims that, as a result of OMT, the Eurozone now has the sovereign lender of last resort that it lacked before.[137] Whatever the motivation for the OMT programme, its effect will be to transfer credit risk to the shareholders of the ECB and to impose on them open-ended potential liability in an amount that will depend on fiscal decisions of countries who access the OMT programme.

This dangerously compromises the integrity of the ESM (since OMT access is linked to ESM conditionality and supervision) and could even jeopardise its legality. The German Federal Constitutional Court has held that the principle of democracy in the German Basic Law – its constitution – prohibits Germany from entering into Treaties that would relinquish its national budget autonomy. The '*Bundestag* may not deliver itself up to any mechanisms with financial effect' which may result in burdens on the national budget that cannot be calculated.[138] There must be a means for 'prior mandatory consent', whether the burdens are expenses or losses of revenue.[139] These statements were made in a preliminary ruling considering whether the ESM was consistent with the Basic Law in an opinion in early September 2012, almost the same time as Draghi's announcement of the OMT programme in London.[140] The Court provisionally upheld the ESM, pending a final ruling, but under conditions. The Court held that Germany's contribution to the ESM would be strictly limited to the agreed upon €190 billion unless the Bundestag voted specifically to approve a greater amount.[141] The Court, moreover, relied on the fact that the ESM did not have a banking licence, citing the ECB's March 2011 opinion rejecting it; and it stressed the importance of this and the centrality of Article 123's prohibition on monetary financing.[142] The Court approved the amendment to Article 136 TFEU allowing for the ESM on the ground that 'There is no danger that the Federal Republic of Germany will, without the prior mandatory consent of the German Bundestag, be placed at the mercy of a mechanism with financial effect which is capable of resulting in complex burdens with budgetary significance or in unavoidably accepting liability for decisions of other states'.[143] When the OMT programme is activated, however, it could have similar effects. Could this lead the Court to conclude that the nature of the ESM itself has been transformed by OMT?

If the ECB cannot save the Euro, this does not mean it is doomed. The ESM is now operating as a valid vehicle for transferring any amount necessary to rescue Member States in financial distress. If the ESM's funding is insufficient, this does

---

[136] See D Keohane, 'Buiter on good news, bad news' *Financial Times Alphaville* (24 September 2012) www.ftalphaville.ft.com/2012/09/24/1174231/buiter-on-good-news-bad-news/, accessed 9 June 2013.
[137] P de Grauwe, 'Stop this campaign against ECB policy' *Financial Times* (London, 22 October 2012).
[138] BVerfG, 2 BvR 1390/12 (12 September 2012).
[139] ibid.
[140] See, on this ruling, the contributions by Huber and Eleftheriadis, chs 2 and 3 in this volume.
[141] ibid.
[142] ibid.
[143] ibid.

not justify drawing on the money creation powers of the ECB for this purpose. Rather, a lack of funding would be an indication that the Member States presently lack the political solidarity and democratic will needed for fiscal union. This could be connected to an absence of legal and institutional structures such as a common resolution authority for banks and common deposit insurance. As the German Constitutional Court observed, 'If the monetary union cannot be achieved in its original structure through the valid integration programme, new political decisions are needed as to how to proceed further. . . . It is for the legislature to decide how possible weaknesses of the monetary union are to be counteracted by amending European Union law.'[144] If the Member States lack the spirit of cooperation for pursuing such legal change, then it looks all the more dangerous to vest powers with implications for national budgets in an independent, unaccountable central bank. The justification for this is to preserve monetary union, but as de Grauwe has said, 'There can be little doubt that the survival of the Eurozone depends on its capacity to embed itself into a political union'.[145] Perhaps, however, we have overlooked another possibility. Could the sought after union be sustained by the steadying hand of the ECB itself, exercising its technical competence to control monetary policy, oversee national budgets, and regulate banks? If so, then the EU will have become based on a principle of governance by independent experts rather than democracy.

IV. Conclusion

Article 123 TFEU forbids the ECB not only from direct purchases of Member State bonds but from extending any 'credit facility' in favour of Member State governments and their public undertakings. Council Regulation 3603/93 clarifies that the prohibition on monetary financing of public debt may reach transactions conducted with third parties, such as ECB loans to banks or purchases of government bonds in open markets. Article 125 TFEU prohibits the EU and Member States from guaranteeing or assuming the debt of any Member States. The OMT programme, when considered in light of the specific objectives Draghi has laid down for it, appears to exceed the legal mandate of the ECB in contravention of Article 123 and Council Regulation 3603/93, and perhaps Article 125 as well.

Someone might respond to my arguments as follows: 'Whether the OMT programme is technically legal is not the point. We should look to its effects. The beauty of Draghi's promise is that, without spending a single Euro, it has reduced yields in Spain and Italy to sustainable levels, reversed the flight of capital from periphery banks, and restored confidence in the markets.' Many positive eco-

---

[144] ibid.
[145] P de Grauwe, 'How to embed the Eurozone in a political union' *VoxEU* (17 June 2010) www.voxeu.org/article/eurozone-needs-political-union-or-least-elements-one, accessed 9 June 2013.

nomic indicators in the past several months could be cited to sustain this claim, and some of them can be linked to Draghi's promise by tracing the turnaround to the date of his announcement. The stock market has risen, and investor confidence is up. Spain and Italy are not only meeting their funding needs for the shorter term covered by OMT, but successfully going forward with the sale of long-term bonds. In recognition of all this, the *Financial Times* named Draghi 'Person of the Year'. The article celebrating his achievement focuses on that crucial day in London when he promised to do 'whatever it takes'.

If these effects are indeed due to Draghi's promise – and I have no reason to doubt that – then this should be a cause of concern rather than comfort, for it means that bond and stock markets are being distorted by the expectation of monetary financing of public debt and a belief that the ECB has now become a lender of last resort in sovereign bond markets. The reason to call this market distortion is that, no matter how strong the desire of some for the ECB to have that role, and no matter how cogent the theoretical economic arguments are in favour of it, that role was rejected when the law governing the ECB was settled. It remains illegal for the ECB to engage in monetary financing of public debt. If Spain or another country requests relief under the OMT programme, its legality might then be tested. So long as it is not tested, the distortion in the markets will remain and intensify.

It is no part of my aim to predict the consequences of the ECB engaging in monetary financing of public debt or its failure to do so. I also do not aim to predict what decision will be reached in the event that the legality of OMT is tested. It may well be that the political pressures to maintain OMT will, by that time, be so great that legal authorities will be influenced more by that than by the law. My aim in this chapter has not been to anticipate what will happen but to put forth an argument about what should happen. I have argued that, according to law, the ECB should not engage in monetary financing of public debt or act as a lender of last resort in sovereign bond markets. I have also addressed the argument that the financial crisis is an emergency that justifies the ECB in exceeding its legal mandate, and have shown that it fails. It follows, from those conclusions, that Draghi's promise to save the Euro, 'whatever it takes', cannot be justified in retrospect by its supposed positive effects in the bond markets.

The attitude toward EU Treaty law expressed in the objections above should be resisted. One reason is that it undercuts ongoing attempts to address the Eurozone crisis through negotiation. A basic purpose of law is to relate the past to the future in a way that promotes co-ordinated action around agreed, specified norms. Legal compacts facilitate a valuable kind of co-operation not available through other means, and this is one of the things that makes the rule of law a key component of any healthy economy. In the EU context, the highest form of legal pre-commitment is Treaty law. If Treaty law is to be cast aside according to what the exigencies of the moment seem to dictate in the eyes of economists, this eviscerates the trust needed to solve problems by deliberation and agreement; and the rule of law would be replaced by the rule of experts.

7

A Governance Crisis?
Treaty Change, Fiscal Union and the ECB

CHRISTOPH OHLER

I. The Constitutional Crisis of the EU

The ongoing sovereign debt crisis in Europe is simultaneously both a constitutional and an economic crisis. Its constitutional side is intricately linked to the leading principles of EU law: the principle of conferral (or enumerative competences) under Article 5(1) of the Treaty on European Union (TEU) and the principle of unanimous consent of all Member States for any amendment of the Treaties as stipulated under Article 48 TEU.[1] Late in 2009, when the debt crisis evolved in Greece, Ireland and Portugal out of the preceding financial crisis, it became clear that the Treaties did not provide much flexibility in their emergency measures to fight the crisis effectively. This meant that the EU was limited in the instruments at its disposal in order to appropriately react to an economic crisis of such magnitude. At the same time, from a practical perspective, it was impossible to amend the Treaties at the speed which the Member States and the EU organs felt were necessary; the 'ordinary revision procedure' under Article 48(2) to (5) TEU would have required convening a convention prior to an intergovernmental conference. The ratification procedure would have triggered referenda in some Member States with an uncertain political outcome. Finally, it was unclear whether the members of the Eurozone and the Member States outside the Eurozone would have been able to reach a consensus on how to revise the monetary constitution of the EU. While in hindsight it is not difficult to identify structural weaknesses in the legal architecture, the ex ante analysis of the Maastricht Treaty was different. From its birth, the European Economic and Monetary Union (EMU) was a political and economic experiment, but the legal architecture seemed to be robust and its rules were considered to be strict and coherent. In particular, nobody would have

---

[1] Similar analysis by C Herrmann, 'Staatsbankrott in der EU: Versagen, Bewährung oder Chance der Europäischen Währungsverfassung' in K von Lewinski (ed), *Staatsbankrott als Rechtsfrage* (Baden-Baden, Nomos, 2011) 29, 41. See also C Ohler, in E Grabitz, M Hilf and M Nettesheim (eds), *Das Recht der Europäischen Union* (Munich, CH Beck 2011) Article 48 TEU para 4.

believed that a small Member State, at least in economic terms, could trigger a deep economic crisis of the Euro area as a whole.[2] Today, 20 years after the signing of the Maastricht Treaty, the impression is that the contracting parties overestimated the capacity for the law to ensure regulatory discipline and underestimated the risks involved in serious legal breaches by individual Member States.

The first result of this constitutional dilemma was that the organs of the EU, including the European Central Bank (ECB), stretched the ambit of primary law to an unprecedented extent which in turn raised massive doubts on the legality of the measures taken. These doubts referred particularly to the establishment of the European Financial Stabilisation Mechanism (EFSM) under Regulation 407/2010[3] and to the Securities Markets Programme (SMP) of the ECB.[4] The second result was that the Member States established variable 'coalitions of the willing' and agreed by means of public international law on material reforms of EMU which fell outside the ambit of EU law. The Member States of the Euro area devised the Treaty establishing the European Stability Mechanism of 2 February 2012 (ESM Treaty)[5] whereas the Treaty on Stability, Coordination and Governance in the Economic and Monetary Union of 2 March 2012[6] was signed by 25 Member States with the UK and the Czech Republic excluded.[7]

II. Monetary Emergency Measures

The ECB introduced the Securities Markets Programme in May 2010 as a response to 'the current exceptional circumstances in financial markets, characterised by severe tensions in certain market segments which are hampering the monetary policy transmission mechanism and thereby the effective conduct of monetary policy'.[8] Under this programme, the ECB purchased government bonds from the Eurozone Member States on the secondary market and securities issued by private debtors of the Eurozone on the primary and secondary markets.[9] By May 2012, the programme had reached a total volume of €214 billion. As far as purchases of government bonds are concerned, critics of the ECB argued – with a view to the amount and intention of the programme – that it would violate Article

---

[2] cf R Smits, 'The European debt crisis and European Union law: comments and a call for action' (2012) 49 *CML Rev* 827, 828.

[3] Council Regulation (EU) No 407/2010 of 11 May 2010 establishing a European financial stabilisation mechanism [2010] OJ L118/1.

[4] Decision of the ECB of 14 May 2010 establishing a securities markets programme (ECB/2010/5) [2010] OJ L124/8.

[5] Text available at www.european-council.europa.eu/media/582311/05-tesm2.en12.pdf (accessed 30 April 2013).

[6] Text available at www.european-council.europa.eu/media/639235/st00tscg26_en12.pdf (accessed 30 April 2013).

[7] For an initial analysis see Editorial Comments, 'Some thoughts concerning the Draft Treaty on a Reinforced Economic Union' (2012) 49 *CML Rev* 1.

[8] Decision ECB/2010/5 (n 4), recital 2.

[9] ibid Article 2.

123 of the Treaty on the Functioning of the European Union (TFEU).[10] This provision prohibits 'the purchase directly from [Member States] by the European Central Bank or national central banks of their debt instruments'. The aim is to prevent a monetary financing of state debts by the central bank.[11] One line of reasoning refers to the question of when purchases of bonds become 'direct' as Article 18(1) of the Statute of the ESCB and ECB permits buying and selling outright marketable instruments in the financial markets.[12] For this reason, the restriction imposed by Article 123 TFEU is read as referring to the primary market only.[13] Secondary market operations would accordingly be considered as being legal as long as they are not used to circumvent the objective of the prohibition.[14] A second line of reasoning refers to the need of any central bank to maintain the conditions necessary to carry out its monetary policy operations. In this regard, the objective of financial stability plays a major role. It is mentioned in Article 127(5) TFEU which reads that 'the ECB shall contribute to the smooth conduct of policies pursued by the competent authorities relating to the prudential supervision of credit institutions and the stability of the financial system'. If Article 127(5) TFEU is interpreted narrowly then the role of the ECB in maintaining financial stability would be rather limited. However, this interpretation reduces the complexities surrounding the issue of financial stability to an extent that is incommensurate with the real problems. The financial crisis revealed that financial stability is a public good, which had been underestimated for too long by monetary policy and prudential supervision. Therefore, there is little doubt that protection of financial stability is one of the central tasks of the ECB[15] even if this is not expressly spelled out by Article 127(1) TFEU. It is also the real reason behind its purpose as a lender of last resort for solvent (albeit illiquid) banks.[16] Accordingly, the monetary analysis by the ECB includes the question of whether financial markets are sufficiently stable for the proper operation of monetary policy. Based on the results of this analysis, its monetary measures under Article 127 TFEU may also aim at stabilising financial markets without infringing Article 123 TFEU.[17]

---

[10] F Schorkopf, 'Europas politische Verfasstheit im Lichte des Fiskalvertrags' (2012) *Zeitschrift für Staats- und Europawissenschaften* 1, 18; critical assessment also by M Ruffert, 'The European Debt Crisis and European Union Law' (2011) 48 *CML Rev* 1777, 1787.

[11] M Selmayr, *Das Recht der Wirtschafts- und Währungsunion* (Baden-Baden, Nomos, 2002) 228.

[12] The Statute of the European System of Central Banks and of the European Central Bank is contained in protocol 4 to TEU and TFEU, see [2010] OJ C83/230.

[13] R Smits, *The European Central Bank* (The Hague, Kluwer, 1997) 75.

[14] Recital 6 of Regulation (EC) No 3603/93 of 13 December 1993 specifying definitions for the application of the prohibitions referred to in Articles 104 and 104b (1) of the Treaty [1993] OJ L332/1.

[15] cf R Lastra, *Legal Foundations of International Monetary Stability* (Oxford, Oxford University Press, 2006) 302; T Padoa-Schioppa, *Regulating Finance* (Oxford, Oxford University Press, 2004) 109; R Smits, 'The European debt crisis and European Union law: comments and a call for action' (2012) 49 *CML Rev* 827, 829.

[16] cf R Lastra, 'The Role of the European Central Bank with Regard to Financial Stability and Lender of Last Resort Operations' in C Goodhart (ed), *Which Lender of Last Resort for Europe?* (London, Central Banking Publications, 2000) 199ff.

[17] C Herrmann, 'EZB-Programm für die Kapitalmärkte verstößt nicht gegen die Verträge' [2010] *Europäische Zeitschrift für Wirtschaftsrecht* 645, 646.

There are two fundamental problems; the first consists of the monetary analysis which could be based on either incomplete facts or a badly estimated risk assessment of the actual risks for the proper functioning of the markets. From a legal point of view however, the ECB enjoys a wide margin of discretion under Article 127 TFEU,[18] meaning only in cases of grave and evident misjudgement would its decisions be considered as a violation of primary law. It is also important to note that the relevant perspective of the ECB is ex ante and not ex post. This implies that the legality of the measures taken is dependent upon the facts and circumstances at the time they were actually made.

The second fundamental problem of the discussed monetary stance concerns its effects. The central bank must face the fact that with financial markets the private creditors and the sovereign debtors are intensely intertwined.[19] It is practically unavoidable that stabilisation measures implemented for the benefit of the creditors will also result in favourable economic side-effects for the debtors. This creates a moral hazard both for market participants and the ailing states. Governments of these states could be induced to rely on this monetary policy and slow down their reform efforts. Investors could start believing that they would bear no risk when purchasing government bonds of countries in trouble. Both effects would be counterproductive both for budgetary and market discipline and, in the end, bring monetary policy into a vicious circle of growing monetisation of public debts. Therefore, the principle of proportionality demands that such emergency programmes avoid creating any automatism, thus requiring such programmes to be limited in time, reflecting as realistically as possible the market situation and do not give an impression that financial institutions are immune to bearing the credit risks of their debtors.

In the period between May 2010 and late 2011, there were sufficient economic signals, as reflected in credit default swap (CDS) spreads and interbank market activity, that markets were under massive strain. As a consequence, there was sufficient evidence for the reasoning of the ECB that the SMP was necessary to calm down the markets, ensure their proper operation and thereby safeguard the monetary transmission mechanism.[20] This does not mean however, that individual monetary decisions taken during that time were necessarily correct from an economic point of view – in particular, if one applies an ex post perspective. Legally however, they were still covered by the margin of appreciation which Article 127 TFEU provides in favour of the ECB.

---

[18] Smits, 'The European debt crisis and European Union law' (n 15) 829.
[19] C Ohler, 'Finanzkrisen als Herausforderung der internationalen, europäischen und nationalen Rechtsetzung' [2011] *Deutsches Verwaltungsblatt* 1061, 1063.
[20] Smits, 'The European debt crisis and European Union law' (n 15) 829.

III. Fiscal Emergency Measures

The constitutional dilemma of EMU becomes also visible with regard to the European Stability Mechanism (ESM). When the Member States, following conclusions of the Ecofin Council of 10 May 2010,[21] established the predecessor of the ESM known as the European Financial Stability Facility (EFSF), they did so in order to restore confidence in the financial markets and to signal that the EU would not accept a breakdown of EMU. It also closes the gap between monetary and fiscal policy that had opened in the course of the debt crisis. The gap exists because Article 123 TFEU prohibits the ECB from recapitalising insolvent banks[22] and from funding ailing Member States. The insolvent banks and Member States that are unable to get access to financial markets may trigger another financial crisis if their breakdown creates a systemic risk. The purpose of the EFSF and the ESM was therefore to prevent a further deterioration of market stability. Again, the distinction between objectives and effects of this emergency mechanism allows different views on its legality. Many critics of the measures argued that the operation of the EFSF violated Article 125 TFEU, which prohibits Member States from being liable for or assuming the commitments of other Member States.[23] In a literal sense, granting guarantees to a special purpose vehicle and extending loans via this vehicle to an ailing Member State is not included in the list of financial techniques mentioned under Article 125 TFEU.[24] But, if the purpose of this provision is taken into account – that market discipline must be upheld and may not be distorted by financial assistance of other Member States – then the ring-fencing under the EFSF/ESM must be considered as falling under the ambit of Article 125 TFEU.

Inevitably, the extensive interpretation of the 'no bail-out' clause leads to the question whether financial assistance would be available at all in the event of a severe financial crisis. In other words, does Article 125 TFEU oblige the Member States to step aside once a Member State threatens bankruptcy? Before we can reach a definite answer, the economic effects of the decision on the functioning of EMU must be considered. Without accounting for the effects implied in the interpretation of Article 125 TFEU, the provision would become the pivotal norm of EMU under which any other legal objectives of EMU would be disregarded. The record of economic history and the international state practice demonstrates to a sufficient extent that a state insolvency affects not only the state in question and

---

[21] See www.consilium.europa.eu/uedocs/cms_data/docs/pressdata/en/ecofin/114324.pdf (accessed 30 April 2013).

[22] European Central Bank, Convergence Report 2008, 24, available at www.ecb.int/pub/pdf/conrep/cr200805en.pdf (accessed 30 April 2013).

[23] M Ruffert, 'The European Debt Crisis and European Union Law' (2011) 48 *CML Rev* 1777, 1785; F Schorkopf, 'Gestaltung mit Recht' (2011) 136 *Archiv des öffentlichen Rechts* 323, 336ff.

[24] R Bandilla, in E Grabitz, M Hilf and M Nettesheim (eds), *Das Recht der Europäischen Union* (Munich, CH Beck, 2011) Article 125 TFEU para 11; C Herrmann, 'Griechische Tragödie' [2010] *Europäische Zeitschrift für Wirtschaftsrecht* 413, 415.

its population – but, causes a negative impact on the international creditors like banks, insurance companies and pension schemes. In the internal market of the EU, where capital controls are abolished due to Article 63 TFEU, a state insolvency *may* produce widespread contagion effects to the disadvantage of other market participants, even if they are not creditors of the insolvent Member State. These effects are particularly relevant as long as neither international law nor European law provide a proper basis for an orderly insolvency proceeding of states and internationally operating banks. Against this background, the interpretation of Article 125 TFEU requires a restriction, at least in the case of severe financial crises which threaten to destabilise the Euro area as a whole.[25] The proper functioning of EMU is an objective justified by Article 3(4) TEU and Article 127 TFEU. The EMU forms an essential part of the EU policies and supplements the internal market. Therefore, if the objective of financial assistance is to prevent a disorderly state insolvency from unfolding and producing grave negative effects for markets and other Member States, this policy should not be considered as a violation of Article 125 TFEU.

Once Article 136 TFEU is amended by a new paragraph (3),[26] it will suspend the current tension between Article 125 TFEU on the one hand and the state practice of the Member States on the other hand.[27] The new provision will expressly permit the activation of the ESM 'if [it is] indispensable to safeguard the stability of the euro area as a whole'. It also makes clear that the granting of any financial assistance will be made subject to strict conditionality. Under Article 48 TEU, this Treaty revision will not be considered as a conferral of competences but remains a simple amendment of primary law pursuant to Article 48(6) TEU. An important consequence will be that the ESM forms an institution referred to, yet not established, by the Treaties. It will be bound by EU law, in particular by Article 136(3) TFEU, but due to the restriction imposed by Article 48(6) TEU, it will not become an institution of the Union.[28] Its establishment as an international organisation under public international law also demonstrates that Member States may still enter into legal relations amongst themselves alongside the framework of primary law. The legality of the international treaties between Member States depends however on the competence of the Member States under Article 4(1) TEU – unless primary law provides an express permission.[29] Since the competence to establish an emergency mechanism for ailing Member States of the Euro area has not yet been conferred on the EU, the Member States still enjoy the right to enter

---

[25] U Häde, in C Calliess and M Ruffert (eds), *EUV/AEUV Kommentar*, 4th edn (Munich, CH Beck, 2011) Article 125 TFEU para 8.

[26] European Council Decision 2011/199/EU of 25 March 2011 amending Article 136 of the Treaty on the Functioning of the European Union with regard to a stability mechanism for Member States whose currency is the euro [2011] OJ L91/1.

[27] B Kempen, in R Streinz (ed), *EUV/AEUV*, 2nd edn (Munich, CH Beck, 2012) Article 136 TFEU para 1; H Kube, 'Rechtsfragen der völkerrechtlichen Euro-Rettung' [2012] *Wertpapiermitteilungen* 245.

[28] C Ohler, 'The European Stability Mechanism: The Long Road to Financial Stability in the Euro Area' (2011) 54 *German Yearbook of International Law* 47.

[29] cf J Schwarze, 'Das allgemeine Völkerrecht in den innergemeinschaftlichen Rechtsbeziehungen' (1983) 4 *Europarecht* 1, 5.

into the ESM Treaty.[30] Nevertheless, the ESM will introduce considerable tensions into the constitutional arrangement of the EMU because the Member States must rely heavily on the troika formed by the International Monetary Fund (IMF), ECB and Commission.[31] This will entail difficult questions concerning the Commission's democratic accountability because the European Parliament does not enjoy the right to control the Commission under the ESM Treaty.[32] Only decisions taken by the Board of Governors of the ESM will be legitimated and controlled by the respective national parliaments.

IV. Austerity and Growth

So far, the existing treaty framework is based on the strict division of powers in the field of monetary and fiscal policy. This fundamental distribution of competences is not blurred by the reforms currently envisaged.[33] Fiscal policy remains the exclusive realm of the Member States where they act autonomously as far as their right to decide on budgetary revenues and expenditures is concerned. Budgetary autonomy is also part of the reason why Member States must bear the fiscal costs of their economic policy decisions, as well as earning the yields of their policies. This autonomy is limited by two mechanisms only: the participation in the economic policy coordination mechanism under Article 121 TFEU and the prohibition of excessive deficits under Article 126 TFEU. The first limitation was not felt on a practical basis as the Member States did not pay much attention to form and content of the co-ordination mechanism. Legally, they had no reason to do more since the recommendations of the Council under Article 121(3) TFEU were neither binding nor politically enforceable. In practice therefore, the economies of most Member States tended not to converge but rather to diverge increasingly. This can be seen paradigmatically in the development of the services sector where the differences between the Member States deepened considerably since the end of the 1990s. Those Member States that fostered the services industries at the same time lost their economic strength in the goods producing sector. Today, the macroeconomic heterogeneity within the EU seems to be even bigger than at the beginning of EMU.

The second limitation, which is the prohibition of excessive deficits, was initially reinforced under the Stability and Growth Pact of 1997 but later weakened by the Member States themselves when they reformed the Pact in 2005.[34] The long-term negative effects of this policy were not felt until autumn 2008 when the financial crisis gravely hit Europe and Northern America. Sharply rising debts and deficits

---

[30] M Ruffert, 'The European Debt Crisis and European Union Law' (2011) 48 *CML Rev* 1777, 1789.
[31] cf Article 13 ESM Treaty.
[32] Ruffert, 'The European Debt Crisis and European Union Law' (n 30) 1790.
[33] ECB, *Monthly Bulletin* (July 2011) 71.
[34] F Schorkopf, 'Gestaltung mit Recht' (2011) 136 *Archiv des öffentlichen Rechts* 323, 332.

were a symptom of the crisis in all Member States of the EU, but the problems seemed to be more serious in those Member States that had long-lasting difficulties with their international competitiveness. Aggravating fiscal problems also appeared in Member States with an oversized banking sector where the governments were forced to bail out insolvent banks to avoid a breakdown of the financial system. The necessary means had to be raised by higher public indebtedness which overstrained, as the case of Ireland demonstrates, the financial capacity of the state.

The EU tried to overcome the structural problems underlying these developments by introducing two major reforms. The first step was to revise and amend the Stability and Growth Pact.[35] The main elements of this reform consisted of: a new technique of 'reverse voting' in the Council, the introduction of sanctions in the preventive arm of the Pact, a better focus on debt reduction next to deficit reduction, and the establishment of a mechanism against macroeconomic imbalances. Nearly all elements of this reform seem to be politically reasonable and correspond to problems that were identified in the wake of the crisis. From a legal point of view, it is very doubtful however, whether the legal basis of Article 136 TFEU permits the introduction of reverse voting in general and the imposition of financial sanctions outside the scope of Article 126 TFEU.[36] Another major political step was the signing of the Treaty on Stability, Coordination and Governance in the Economic and Monetary Union of 2 March 2012 with the so called 'Fiscal Compact' as its centrepiece.[37] The Fiscal Compact creates the obligation for the contracting parties to introduce a 'debt brake' in their national laws with numerical restrictions of the annual deficit and a more or less automatic correction mechanism. In addition, the contracting parties agree to reduce their debt in annual steps in circumstances where the ratio of debt to GDP exceeds 60 per cent.[38] Both obligations are useful and strengthen the ideas of the revised Stability and Growth Pact further. However, the essential question will be whether the Member States have actually learnt their lesson on the debt crisis; it is urgent that they reduce their immense debt burden if they want to survive as autonomous political entities. There is a high risk that the new provisions constitute a compact without impact and that they will experience the same fate as the original Stability and Growth Pact. The latter was ignored once the economic conditions did not seem to correspond with legal obligations. This was fostered by the political structure of the decision-making process in the Council, where the Commission plays a minor role only. In contrast to this model, the new Fiscal Compact will be directly enforced by the European Court of Justice (ECJ) which relies solely on

---

[35] Regulations (EU) No 1173–1177/2011 [2011] OJ L 306/1 (see below); Council Directive 2011/85/EU of 8 November 2011 on requirements for budgetary frameworks of the Member States [2011] OJ L 306/41.

[36] Ruffert, 'The European Debt Crisis and European Union Law' (n 30) 1800. For an extensive interpretation of Article 136 see JC Piris, *The Future of Europe: Towards a Two-Speed EU?* (Cambridge, Cambridge University Press, 2012) 107; R Smits, 'The European debt crisis and European Union law: comments and a call for action' (2012) 49 *CML Rev* 827, 829.

[37] Article 3(1) of the Treaty.

[38] Article 4 of the Treaty.

legal aspects and not on economic considerations. However, what seems to be a step towards depoliticising the review procedure and to lessen the grip of the Member States on issues of budgetary autonomy could become a merely formalistic exercise. The wording of Article 8 of the Treaty does not allow for the conclusion that the ECJ is empowered to review the annual budget of a contracting party in any detail. The enforcement mechanism is restricted to an ex post control on whether a contracting party introduced and applied the debt brake at all. This does not suggest that the rule of law will play a stronger role in budgetary policy in the future.[39]

While in economic terms, the reform of the Stability and Growth Pact and the Fiscal Compact seem to herald a new age of austerity in Europe,[40] another debate started over the need for cultivating stronger economic growth. Elements of this classical tension can already be found in the new Regulation on the prevention and correction of macroeconomic imbalances.[41] Its objective is to detect economic imbalances between the Member States and find ways to increase competitiveness. Again, it remains entirely unclear how the EU wants to spur economic activity in the Member States or prevent bubbles from occurring. Even if booms and busts of an economy arise domestically, their origins stem from the economic decisions of market participants and not of the state. Legislative measures taken by the state may play a role, but in a market economy, the effects of legislation on economic behaviour are mostly of an indirect nature. Against this background, the technical system of sanctions employed on Member States in an effort to correct macroeconomic imbalances[42] does not seem to promise much practical impact.

V. Towards a Fiscal Union?

The constitutional dilemma discussed in this chapter leads to the conclusion that legal solutions ultimately can only be found in the revision of the Treaties. The economic dilemma that Europe faces requires solutions for a multitude of problems which boil down jointly, to a lack of competitiveness and the over-indebtedness of many Member States. In addition, many Member States experience negative demographic developments because their populations shrink and get older on average, which will weaken their ability to grow in economic terms. While it is legally possible to revise the Treaties, so long as the requirements of Article 48 TEU and of

---

[39] See in detail Rudolf Streinz, 'The Limits of Legal Regulation', ch 14 in this volume.

[40] cf Smits, 'The European debt crisis and European Union law' (n 36) 830.

[41] Regulation (EU) No 1176/2011 of the European Parliament and of the Council of 16 November 2011 on the prevention and correction of macroeconomic imbalances [2011] OJ L306/25.

[42] Regulation (EU) No 1174/2011 of the European Parliament and of the Council of 16 November 2011 on enforcement measures to correct excessive macroeconomic imbalances in the euro area [2011] OJ L306/8.

national constitutional law are observed, it is a much more complicated political question whether a strengthened EU will be able to cope with the aforementioned challenges. Over-indebtedness of the Euro area does not disappear because the EU enjoys additional fiscal competences or has a larger budget. The economy will not grow simply because further legislative competences in the field of tax law, social law and labour law are conferred to the EU. No legislator can easily solve the intricate problems of demography, since first and foremost they require societal and cultural changes. Does more supra-nationalisation help in this context? While it would be useful to consolidate the Fiscal Compact within the framework of primary law and to improve the coherence of EMU in general, considerable doubts remain as to whether a further conferral of competences in the fields of economic, tax and budget policies would solve the current problems.

8

State Aid and the Financial Crisis

CONOR QUIGLEY

I. The Financial Crisis and the Need for State Aid Control

Financial institutions in almost all Member States were affected by the crisis that erupted on the global financial markets in the years following the summer of 2007. Up to mid-2008, the crisis manifested itself as an acute liquidity shortage among financial institutions. The initial public response was aimed at ensuring that banks remained liquid and, in particular, were able to cope with their debts. Following the demise of Lehman Brothers in September 2008, the crisis developed into a systemic collapse of confidence that created intense risks as stock markets fell and liquidity seized up. In particular, the total amount of long-term debt securities with a maturity of over one year issued by financial institutions in the Eurozone decreased by 40 per cent in the third quarter of 2008 compared to the previous quarter, resulting in increased fears that other major institutions could collapse causing severe difficulties for the entire financial system. Subsequently, the crisis developed into sovereign debt at national level, thereby creating a new order of threat to national economies. Greece, Ireland, Portugal, Spain, Italy and some of the Baltic states caused particular concerns, but significant problems also arose in, for example, the United Kingdom, Belgium and Germany.

Action was taken at both national and European level in order to deal with the effects of the crisis. Initially, national financial rescue policies focused on restoring liquidity and capital of banks and the provision of guarantees. The European Central Bank (ECB) and national central banks outside the Eurozone adjusted the provision of liquidity to the banking system and cut interest rates to unprecedented low levels. Policy action on the demand side was based on the European Economic Recovery Plan,[1] a discretionary fiscal stimulus of some €200 billion, entailing a budgetary expansion by Member States of €170 billion and EU funding of €30 billion, aimed at boosting demand and stimulating confidence over

---

[1] European Commission, *Communication from the Commission to the European Council: A European Economic Recovery Plan* COM (2008) 800, 26 November 2008.

2009–10. A European Financial Stabilisation Mechanism was established allowing for up to €500 billion to be provided to Member States in exceptional difficulty. In addition the European Commission adopted a strategy, particularly with regard to approving State aid, that recognised the special importance to the economy of the banking sector. Apart from the fact that the largest banks are so much bigger than the largest non-bank businesses, no other sector has a comparable share of debt in their funding compared to equity, given that banks are largely financed through a limited amount of equity supplemented by funds provided by creditors. It follows that markets in which banks operate may be subject to systemic risk due to the massive negative externalities that a bank failure, or its anticipation, may generate on competitors and the economy at large. This assumption that a bank failure would cause systemic reactions throughout the financial and economic world lies at the heart of all the subsequent actions by the European institutions, notably the European Commission and the ECB, as well as the Member States.[2]

II. State Aid Control by the European Commission

To a significant degree the national financial support measures put in place as a response to the crisis constituted State aid within the meaning of Article 107(1) of the Treaty on the Functioning of the European Union (TFEU). State aid is generally incompatible with the internal market and prohibited unless it has been notified to and approved by the Commission pursuant to Article 107(3) TFEU. Initially, in 2007, the Commission considered State assistance to a handful of financial institutions, such as Northern Rock in the United Kingdom and Sachsen LB in Germany, as rescue aid within the scope of Article 107(3)(c), which had hitherto been the normal basis for allowing rescue and restructuring aid that was deemed necessary to facilitate the development of the banking sector. However, as the crisis entered its systemic phase, it became apparent that the scale of the necessary liquidity and restructuring measures called for special treatment. In particular, much of the aid could not be approved under Article 107(3)(c) in accordance with the general rescue and restructuring guidelines, since these required the recipient to be in financial difficulty, whereas the problem was often based not on the financial strength of the financial institutions in question but on wider systemic liquidity and related matters. In order to avail itself of a much greater degree of freedom of action, the Commission called into play the hitherto rarely used provision in

---

[2] For a summary of the Commission's analysis of the State aid measures adopted to deal with the financial crisis, see the Commission Staff Working Paper: The effects of temporary State aid rules adopted in the context of the financial and economic crisis, 5 October 2011 SEC (2011) 1126 final. This Working Paper was the subject of a review in C Quigley, 'Review of the Temporary State Aid Rules Adopted in the Context of the Financial and Economic Crisis' (2010) 3 *Journal of European Competition Law & Practice* 237, much of the details of which are set out in the present chapter.

Article 107(3)(b) allowing for aid to remedy a serious disturbance in the economy of a Member State. By invoking this provision the Commission not only afforded itself a greater flexibility but also pre-empted any possibility that the Member States themselves might seek to take control of State aid supervision through the Council, as permitted in exceptional circumstances pursuant to Article 108(2) TFEU.

The Commission's State aid policy during the financial crisis pursued the twin objectives of restoring financial stability and returning to functioning financial markets. As regards financial stability, State aid was approved with a view to restore confidence in the banking sector, ensure inter-bank lending, limit the systemic risk of insolvency and avoid contagion between Member States. A return to functioning financial markets was envisaged through measures to stimulate lending to the real economy and to ensure long-term viability of the banking sector. In order to seek to impose a degree of consistency on the various measures that Member States intended to apply, and to ensure that external effects on competition in other Member States were taken into account and reduced, the Commission adopted a series of Communications setting out the principles that it intended to apply to State guarantees, recapitalisations, impaired asset relief and restructuring aid. The main guiding principles throughout were that approval of State aid would require the beneficiaries to pay an adequate remuneration to the State and that adequate burden sharing from beneficiaries would be required to curb moral hazard. The Commission concluded that these rules, taken as a whole, would result in an approach centred on the overall balance of the compatibility conditions, based on a comprehensive assessment of the three pillars of viability, burden sharing and competition remedies. Subsequent recourse to State aid support for the banking sector was widespread throughout most of the Member States, with some 95 per cent of the EU banking sector being eligible to access aid schemes. The amount of aid pledged by individual governments varied from more than €500 billion (United Kingdom, Germany) to less than €3 billion (Cyprus, Latvia). As a percentage of the financial sector in the national economy, aid pledged varied between more than 30 per cent in Ireland to less than 1 per cent in Italy. However, it should also be noted that five Member States (Bulgaria, Czech Republic, Estonia, Malta and Romania) did not adopt any specific measures, three (Poland, Slovakia and Lithuania) did not actually use any of the measures that they adopted, and use by Finland of its adopted measures was marginal.

The aid that was actually used was concentrated in the Member States where the banking sectors are the largest. The top three banking markets, the United Kingdom, France and Germany, accounting for 60 per cent of the EU banking sector as a whole, received 60 per cent of the total amount of aid granted. However, those Member States were not where the aid was highest in relative terms, that is, as a share of the total banking sector size. Whereas Member States granted on average the equivalent of 2.9 per cent of the total assets of their national financial institutions, France, Germany and the United Kingdom were close to that average at 2.0 per cent, 3.8 per cent and 3.1 per cent respectively. By contrast, Greece (11.8 per cent), Ireland (8.9 per cent), Latvia (8.0 per cent), Slovenia (5.6 per cent) and the Netherlands (4.3 per cent) were substantially higher than the EU average. A total of 215 financial institutions received some form of aid. Of the 114 that received asset support relief, with the singular exception of Denmark which supported a very large number of beneficiaries (47), in general aid was concentrated on a small number of critical banks. In 12 Member States, the three major beneficiaries of aid received more than 80 per cent of the total aid granted. The United Kingdom gave asset support aid only to four banks, France to eight and Germany to nine. The 10 largest beneficiaries of asset support aid received two-thirds of the total asset support in the EU, whilst the 10 largest beneficiaries of liability support received about half of all liability support. Nevertheless, it is clear that many of the largest banks in the EU did not require support. Out of the top 25 banks in the EU, 10 did not receive any direct State aid.

As regards the actual quantities of aid granted over the period September 2008 to December 2010, the headline figure suggested by the Commission is that Member States committed a total of nearly €4,300 billion representing 36 per cent of EU GDP or 10 per cent of the total assets of the European banking sector. Significantly, the Commission concedes that most of the State aid did not have direct effects on public finance since support was essentially contingent, although it nonetheless brought additional uncertainty on the public budget and increased the risks attached to Member States' financing. It follows that placing a realistic figure on the amount of aid actually made available is impossible from an economic perspective, even if the legal criteria are fulfilled in respect of the figures cited by the Commission. Some 75 per cent of all pledged aid was in respect of guaranteeing financial institutions' senior liabilities. Of the remainder, 13 per cent was committed for potential direct capital support, 9 per cent for impaired asset relief measures and only 3 per cent for liquidity support. As to the calculation of the amount of aid actually granted during this period, the Commission proposes that the figures are €1,240 billion, representing 10.5 per cent of GDP and 2.9 per cent of total assets of the EU financial sector. On this basis, €757 billion (61 per cent) was in the form of guarantees, €303 billion (24 per cent) constituted capital injections, €104 billion (8 per cent) was spent on impaired asset relief and €77 billion (6 per cent) on liquidity measures.

The Commission adopted more than 200 State aid decisions relating to the financial sector, either in the form of schemes or ad hoc support. In the light of the Commission's Communications, the vast majority of the decisions (other than final restructuring aid decisions) were approved, without the Commission raising objections, on the basis of Article 107(3)(b) TFEU. In the early stages of the financial crisis, a significant number of cases were approved on a temporary basis to enable the delivery of the emergency rescue measures, while making them conditional on the submission of a restructuring plan which involved an in-depth investigation procedure. In accordance with its declared principles, the Commission reviewed each proposed State aid measure for its appropriateness, necessity and proportionality. State aid was to be appropriate to achieve the objective of remedying the serious disturbance in the economy, in accordance with Article 107(3)(b) TFEU, by being targeted to restoring financial stability. The criterion of necessity required that aid be limited both in time and in scope, thus ensuring that all measures were temporary and had a pre-defined and reasonable budget. Proportionality required that the positive effects of aid should be properly balanced against the resulting distortions of competition in order for the latter to be limited to a minimum. The Commission practice focused on three points: (i) ensuring that aid provided by Member States was adequately remunerated and where possible incentivised exit from State support; (ii) ensuring that sufficient safeguard conditions were attached to the aid to limit distortions of competition; and (iii) ensuring that remuneration and safeguard conditions were stricter for distressed banks than for safe banks, with in-depth restructuring where appropriate.

III. Guarantees

The first of the Commission's communications, the Banking Communication,[3] issued on 13 October 2008, made the authorisation of State aid in the form of guarantee, capital, asset relief or liquidity support dependent on respect for various essentials. Access to aid was to be non-discriminatory, limited in time, clearly defined and limited in scope. An appropriate contribution was to be provided by the beneficiary. In certain cases behavioural rules, such as a ban on aggressive expansion, and/or follow-up restructuring measures were to be imposed. Liquidity support in the form of emergency liquidity assistance from central banks was not regarded as State aid, as this was considered to be a general measure available to all banks in cases that needed it. In its decision on Northern Rock,[4] the Commission set out four criteria that had to be met for no State aid to arise: (i) the financial institution must be solvent and the liquidity assistance must not be part of a wider financial package; (ii) the facility must be fully secured by collateral to which haircuts must be applied; (iii) the central bank must charge a penal rate for the facility; and (iv) the measure must be taken at the central bank's initiative and without a counter-guarantee by the State.

Subsequently, the Commission approved guarantee schemes in 20 different Member States, each with the objective of supporting the short- and medium-term financing needs of solvent financial institutions which faced increasing difficulty in accessing liquidity. Guarantees were required to be open to all systemically relevant solvent financial institutions in the State concerned, including subsidiaries of

---

[3] European Commission, 'Commission Communication: The application of State aid rules to measures taken in relation to financial institutions in the context of the current global financial crisis' [2008] OJ C270/8.
[4] Commission Decision NN 70/2007, *Northern Rock* [2008] OJ C43/1.

foreign institutions (although some Member States excluded branches of foreign banks). The solvency criterion aimed at mitigating the potential effects of the guarantees on the budget of the Member States by reducing the risks that the guarantees would be called on. By offering State guarantees to newly issued debt instruments of the banks, the Member States aimed to make them more attractive to investors, to restore confidence in solvent financial institutions and to improve lending to the real economy. Most guarantee schemes showed a clear preference for guaranteeing instruments representing senior (as opposed to subordinated) liabilities, in the hope that, in case of default, the State would be entitled to a degree of compensation. Schemes were initially limited to an entry period of six months (which was subsequently prolonged) and guaranteed debt issuance with a maturity of a maximum five years. Since the guarantee was available for all systemically important banks, whose difficulties arose from the collapse of the wholesale funding market, the provision of the guarantee was not considered a structural measure. Nevertheless, if the guarantee had to be called on by a financial institution, a restructuring plan was required.

In order to minimise distortions of competition, pricing of the guarantees was at estimated market rates. The Commission's general approach was that a guarantee was presumed when the beneficiary bank could not find any independent private operator on the market willing to provide a similar guarantee. Moreover, following long-standing practice in relation to non-market guarantees, the Commission took the view that the actual amount of aid granted in the form of guarantees is the volume of the liability covered by the State. On this basis, the amount of aid estimated by the Commission was some €757 billion, even though this greatly exceeded the actual costs borne by the Member States. Given that the guarantees given to banks had to be paid for at a price that is an estimated market price linked to functioning market rates, it is odd that the Commission did not attempt an alternative formulation in the light of the special characteristics of guarantees in the crisis period. In particular, the reason for putting guarantees in place in the financial sector was not with a view that the guarantees would be called on, thereby placing full financial liability on the State for the amounts covered, but precisely the opposite – to engender a market expectation that the financial institutions in question would be able to continue operating. The guarantees constituted, therefore, a form of confidence building measure with no immediate call on State resources.

Moreover, from an economic perspective, the guarantees clearly did not involve a financial burden on the Member States equal to the amounts guaranteed. On the contrary, the Commission insisted on a pricing formula based on a recommendation of October 2008 from the ECB which provided that the price of State guarantees on bank debt with maturities exceeding one year should be based on the risk profile of the beneficiary plus an add-on fee. The risk profile is measured through the median five-year senior debt credit default swap (CDS) spread in the reference period 1 January 2007 through 31 August 2008. The CDS spread is a widely available and liquid measure of the perceived market assessment of the credit risk associated with individual banks. The add-on fee was valued at 50 basis points and was imposed to cover the operational costs incurred by the Member State for guaranteeing the beneficiary's debt as well as to represent a premium on State support. The add-on could be lower where the guarantee was collateralised since the risk taken by the Member State in that event was lower. The price of State guarantees on bank debt with maturities of less than or equal to one year was to be equal to an overall flat fee of 50 basis points. A flat fee for short-term debt was considered appropriate since CDS spreads might not provide an adequate measure of credit risk for such debt. In 2010, the price of State guarantees was increased in order to induce banks to seek private sector solutions by bringing the pricing of State support closer to current market conditions and to better reflect individual banks' creditworthiness.[5] Member States largely implemented the ECB recommendations. Small modifications to the pricing mechanism for short-term debt were introduced in the Cypriot and Irish schemes, which reduced the fee to 25 basis points, and the French and Slovenian schemes reduced the fee when liabilities were collateralised. For long-term debt only Sweden introduced a reduced add-on of 25 basis points on top of the five-year historic CDS median.

Various additional safeguards were introduced, relating to behavioural constraints and exit incentives, in order further to counteract distortions of competition. An advertisement ban of the fact that the bank could issue State guaranteed debt was included in all schemes. Most schemes featured a limitation of balance sheet expansion or a ban on aggressive commercial policies. Several countries, such as France, Ireland and the Netherlands, introduced limitations in the remuneration payable to the management of financial institutions. Others included commitments as regards the use of the new funding for the real economy (eg Austria, Cyprus) or a dividend ban (eg Denmark, Poland). Some Member States provided for exit incentives in the remunerations mechanism as an incentive aimed at limiting guarantees for only short- and medium-term debt. For example, Italy provided for a step-up clause in the remuneration for maturities longer than two years and Portugal reserved the right to revise the fee if the market situation were to improve. In order to phase out the guarantee regime after 30 June 2010, schemes had to include thresholds of 5 per cent of total outstanding guaranteed liabilities to total liabilities and of €500 million for the absolute amount of guaranteed liability. If those thresholds were exceeded, the Member State concerned had to submit a review demonstrating the bank's long-term viability to the Commission within three months, unless the bank was the subject of restructuring proceedings.

---

[5] The increase was required to be at least 20 basis points for banks with a rating of A+ or A, 30 basis points for banks rated A- and 40 basis points for banks rated below A-.

IV. Recapitalisation

The Recapitalisation Communication of 5 December 2008[6] provided guidance on the pricing of capital injections made by the State into banks. The pricing of capital was to be reasonable and linked to properly functioning markets so that recapitalisation was to differentiate between banks that were fundamentally sound and those that were distressed. The price of capital injections was to be linked to the risk profile of the beneficiary bank, the type of capital injected by the State (in particular its subordination) and the nature of any safeguards against abuse. Recapitalisation of banks in distress posed a greater risk of distortions of competition, so they were in principle to be required to pay more for State support and be subject to stricter safeguards. Restructuring to restore long-term viability was an essential requirement for distressed banks, a requirement that was extended to all bank beneficiaries of recapitalisation from 1 January 2011. Moreover, in order to keep the duration of State involvement to a minimum, exit mechanisms had to be included to ensure a timely redemption of injected State capital, in particular by providing that remuneration for State capital should increase over time.

The Commission approved recapitalisation schemes in 15 Member States between October 2008 and December 2010, the majority being adopted by June 2009. The primary aim of the schemes was to restore financial stability and to ensure lending to the economy by providing Tier 1 capital injections so as to allow beneficiaries to continue their lending activity. These schemes were in compliance with the principles of adequate and increasing remuneration coupled with behavioural safeguards to restrain beneficiaries from using State aid at the expense of competitors. Nevertheless, the schemes displayed significant differences in detail. In schemes targeted to ensure additional credit to the real economy, access to State capital was generally explicitly restricted to sound and solvent banks, whereas schemes that were in principle open to distressed banks required such beneficiaries to submit a restructuring plan within six months of recapitalisation.

Pricing of recapitalisation was the subject of an ECB recommendation of November 2008 which required that remuneration should be based on the risk level of the beneficiary and on the nature of the capital injected. The ECB recommendation provided a price corridor for Tier 1 capital, with lower and upper bounds depending on criteria such as seniority in profit and loss, voting conditions, etc. The lower bound was defined by the required rate of return on preferred shares and other hybrid instruments having economic features similar to subordinated debt (ie not redeemable by the issuer before a fixed period and

---

[6] European Commission, 'Communication from the Commission – Recapitalisation of financial institutions in the current financial crisis: limitation of the aid to the minimum necessary and safeguards against undue distortions of competition' [2009] OJ C10/2.

redeemable at par value). This was calculated as the sum of the relevant government bond yield, the issuing bank's five-year historic CDS spread on subordinated debt and an add-on fee of 300 basis points per annum to cover operational costs. The upper bound was defined by the required rate of return on preferred shares and other hybrid instruments having features similar to those of ordinary shares (ie non-cumulative, without the responsibility of pay back, or perpetual instruments with convertibility to ordinary shares). This was the sum of the relevant government bond yield, an equity risk premium of 500 basis points per annum and an add-on fee of 100 basis points per annum. As a result, the average price corridor in mid-November 2008 for the average Eurozone bank for Tier 1 capital instruments was between 7 and 9.3 per cent. As with valuation of State guarantees, the Commission opted for a maximalist valuation of State aid for recapitalisation, based on aid being equal to the nominal value of the recapitalisation, being a total of €303 billion as aid used for capital injections. Once again, the capital injections are considered aid on the sole ground that this level of financing was not available at the time on the commercial markets due to the contraction of the wholesale market. In fact, in all schemes, the indicative entry rates of remuneration were in compliance with the minimum rate provided for by the ECB recommendation and in some cases even exceeded the upper rate. Most Member States also included in their schemes step-up clauses aimed at increasing the remuneration over time in order to provide an incentive for banks to redeem the State support in favour of capital from the commercial market. For example, the German and Spanish schemes provided for an annual increase in the remuneration rate of between 15 and 20 basis points.

Behavioural safeguards were introduced in order to limit distortions of competition with banks that did not receive State capital, including a ban on advertising the fact of State support. In the first schemes approved by the Commission (in the United Kingdom, Germany and Greece) a cap was imposed on the growth rate of the beneficiaries' balance sheets in order to limit potential aggressive expansion. However, these limits were dropped for fundamentally sound banks following the adoption of the Recapitalisation Communication since they could impede the lending activities of beneficiaries. Subsequent schemes contained mechanisms to ensure that State capital would be used to increase lending to the real economy. Some schemes imposed structural limitations on beneficiaries in the form of maintaining an increased capital adequacy ratio or included a ban or a limitation on the payment of dividends. All schemes included potential changes in the governance of the beneficiary and its executive compensation policy, including constraints of remuneration of top management. Some Member States imposed the appointment of new board members or their direct participation in the board, in some cases with veto powers on key decisions.

V. Impaired Assets Relief

On 25 February 2009, the Commission adopted the Impaired Assets Communication,[7] providing guidance on how relief measures could be applied to remove impaired or toxic assets. Asset relief could take either the form of asset purchase, in which case the State would buy the impaired asset portfolio at a determined price higher than the market price, which constituted the aid, or asset guarantee, whereby the State would take a share of the risk of default or loss relating to the asset. Asset relief schemes were to be conditional on the following: there must be full disclosure of impaired assets and the costs must be shared between the Member States, shareholders and creditors of the financial institutions; identification of eligible assets and valuation of assets must be made on a co-ordinated basis; and distressed beneficiary banks must be the subject of restructuring measures so as to ensure a return to normal market conditions. Only a small number of Member States availed themselves of impaired asset relief measures, mostly on an ad hoc basis, the only effective scheme being applied in Ireland through the controversial National Assets Management Agency (NAMA). The Commission's assessment of these measures focused on ensuring, in line with the Impaired Assets Communication, an appropriate remuneration for the aid and an appropriate burden sharing by the beneficiaries. The value of the State aid granted by this type of measure was intended to be the difference between the transfer value paid to the beneficiary and the market value of the asset. On the basis of estimated values at the time of the asset transfers, the Commission valued all impaired asset relief aid at €104 billion. Austria adopted a support mechanism in the form of an asset guarantee, only to be drawn in the case of insolvency of the beneficiary. This amounted to a capital injection of the value of the guaranteed asset and was treated similarly to recapitalisation. The German scheme allowed financial institutions to transfer structured securities to a special purpose vehicle (SPV) for a period of 20 years, while ultimately bearing the full risks of losses related to the assets. The Lithuanian scheme consisted of an asset purchase with a minimum haircut of 20 per cent off the real economic value.

A major difficulty in assessing the worth of impaired asset relief measures was the introduction of the notion of the real economic value of assets, being an estimated market value in the longer term contrasting with the present depressed market value in the financial crisis. Where, as with the Irish NAMA scheme, the toxicity of the impaired assets taken over by the State is such as to eliminate any realistic long-term valuation, the notion of real economic value becomes theoretical rather than practical. Irish bank lending to the construction sector rose from €5.5 billion in 1999 to €96.2 billion in 2007. It was initially estimated in the first draft NAMA Business Plan that the total value of loans coming within

---

[7] European Commission, 'Communication from the Commission on the treatment of impaired assets in the Community banking sector' [2009] OJ C72/1.

NAMA's purview would amount to some €77 billion, including €9 billion of rolled-up interest, the book value of these assets being €88 billion. It was estimated that Irish property prices had fallen by around 47 per cent from the 2007 height, thereby reducing the present market value to €47 billion. This present market value was then increased by 15 per cent to reflect what was anticipated as long-term economic value. Thus, the total price to be paid by NAMA to the banks, in the form of government bonds that were to be secured with the ECB in return for cash, was €54 billion. It is intended that NAMA will sell off these properties over a 10-year period. In its Working Paper, the Commission happily records that for the first tranche of transferred assets in August 2010, the real economic value of the transferred assets was estimated to be more than 10 per cent higher than the transfer price paid by NAMA, thus ensuring its adequate remuneration, along with an almost 50 per cent haircut which imposed an appropriate burden sharing on the beneficiaries. In fact, when NAMA issued its first audited annual report in July 2011, it transpired that it had paid a total of €30.5 billion for assets with an original face value of €72.3 billion. NAMA conceded that it had overpaid for its loans by €1.485 billion and that the long-term value of the assets had been too optimistic. In the meantime, the Irish property market had crashed even further.

VI. Restructuring

On 22 July 2009, the Commission adopted the Restructuring Communication[8] setting out detailed restructuring conditions for those banks that received large amounts of aid and that had unsustainable business models. Those banks had to demonstrate strategies to achieve long-term viability without State support under adverse economic conditions. The restructuring plan had to include a thorough diagnosis of the bank's problems, including a stress test to demonstrate that a restructured bank would be able to withstand adverse macroeconomic conditions. It was anticipated that in many cases divestments would be essential, either to ensure viability of core businesses or to compensate for the negative competitive impact of aid on key markets. Banks would be required to contribute to the costs of restructuring as much as possible from their own resources in order to reduce moral hazard and to create appropriate incentives for future behaviour. As with recapitalisation measures, restructuring was required to be accompanied by appropriate measures to ensure that distortion of competition was limited. The Restructuring Communication allows for a number of variations to the requirements applicable

---

[8] European Commission, 'Commission communication on the return to viability and the assessment of restructuring measures in the financial sector in the current crisis under the State aid rules [2009] OJ C195/9. For difficulties arising under this Communication, see FC Laprevote, 'Selected issues raised by Bank Restructuring Plans under EU State aid rules' (2012) 11 *European State Aid Law Quarterly* 93.

under the general rescue and restructuring guidelines.[9] In particular, the restructuring period could last for up to five years, as opposed to the normal period of two years, and the general requirement that the beneficiary meet 50 per cent of the restructuring costs was set aside so that difficulties in accessing private capital could be taken into account. The one-time last-time rule was also temporarily lifted. Because the new rules are sectoral, the Commission was able to specify in greater detail the type of information required to determine whether the proposed restructuring measures were apt to restore a bank's long-term viability. In certain cases, a monitoring trustee was to be appointed, a practice common to merger control but hitherto rarely used in State aid supervision.

Over 50 financial institutions have been the subject of restructuring measures since the start of the credit crisis. Approximately 85 per cent of banks that received recapitalisation aid and all banks that received impaired asset relief support were restructured or have submitted a restructuring plan. The 15 largest beneficiaries are from a small number of Member States: the United Kingdom (RBS and Lloyds Banking Group); Ireland (Anglo Irish Bank and Allied Irish Bank); Belgium (Fortis, supported also by the Netherlands and Luxembourg, and Dexia, supported also by France and Luxembourg); Germany (Bayern LB, Commerzbank, HSH Nordbank, IKB, LBBW and West LB); and the Netherlands (ING and ABN Amro). By the end of 2010, of the 26 banks from 12 Member States in respect of which a decision had been taken by the Commission, all but four were restructured, with the remainder being liquidated (Fiona in Denmark, Kaupthing Luxembourg in Luxembourg and Dunfermline and Bradford & Bingley in the United Kingdom). Subsequently, Portugal's BPP was liquidated and Ireland's Anglo Irish Bank (which had been instrumental in leading the property development boom) was renamed the Irish Bank Resolution Corporation and stripped of its trading capacity.

Detailed restructuring conditions, as required by the Commission on a case by case basis, were aimed at restoring the long-term viability of the restructured institution. Commerzbank, for instance, agreed to reduce staff numbers by some 20 per cent, whilst other banks reduced administrative or IT costs. Divestment of ailing subsidiaries or loss-making activities was a central element in the restructuring process in many cases. Dexia, for instance, had to sell its US subsidiary FSA as well as some non-core businesses. Business constraints for the duration of the restructuring period (which was generally for between two and five years) were imposed in certain cases, restricting the bank's investment policy, pricing policy or even the nature of its activities. Where capital buffers were found to be insufficient, a bank would have an acquisition ban imposed on it in order to aim to recapitalise. Similarly, constraints in respect of the bank's investment portfolio were imposed where it was found that the bank's viability had been endangered by previous risky investment strategies. In order to ensure a more prudent invest-

---

[9] European Commission, 'Communication from the Commission – Community guidelines on State aid for rescuing and restructuring firms in difficulty' [2004] OJ C244/2.

ment strategy in the future, the Commission required commitments that the bank would follow investment guidelines describing the acceptable level of risk. In some cases, such as ING, where the Commission received evidence that aggressive pricing and commercial practices had contributed to structural difficulties, a price leadership ban was imposed.

Restructured financial institutions were required to contribute towards the costs of restructuring so as to ensure that the bank and its capital holders bore an adequate responsibility for the consequences of their past behaviour and in order to counteract moral hazard. Contribution by existing shareholders could be made indirectly through an increase in State shareholding, since State aid in the form of capital injections diluted the ownership and control of existing shareholders, most notably in the case of full nationalization. The degree of dilution depended on the type of capital injected, with injections through ordinary shares being more effective in that regard than the issue of preferred shares. Some 45 per cent of capital injected by the Member States in restructured banks was in the form of ordinary shares, while 47 per cent was Tier 1 capital mostly in the form of preferred shares. In most cases the Commission imposed restrictions on the payment of dividends or coupons to shareholders or other investors, or on repurchases or calls of the instruments, in order to ensure that banks could not use State aid to remunerate own funds (equity and subordinated debt) when those activities did not generate sufficient profits. This restriction was in some cases loosened whenever required by contractual or legal provisions.

Apart from the few cases where liquidation was required by the Commission, structural measures intended to limit distortions of competition included the divestment of subsidiaries. The initial decision authorising aid to West LB required the German authorities to sell their stake in the restructured bank. In some cases, the bank was required to be split between a good bank and a bad bank, the former being sold whilst the latter would be run down. In addition, beneficiaries were sometimes required to divest certain portfolios of customers or specific assets or were prohibited from acquiring new business during the restructuring period. An analysis of the restructuring decisions shows, however, that there was no set ratio of divestments required across the board for all restructured banks, but that this was applied on an individual case by case basis. Dexia, for example, was prohibited from acquiring 5 per cent or more of the capital of any financial institution, whereas Fortis Bank was merely precluded from acquiring control. In certain cases, restructuring was accompanied by measures addressed to the Member State to open up markets. For instance, Ireland was ordered to facilitate the entry into the market of competitors through enhanced electronic banking, so as to counter the high cost of maintaining a network branch. Lloyds Banking Group and RBS were each required to divest a 5 per cent market share in the UK to a new entrant or small existing competitor on the market. As with guarantees and recapitalisation, additional constraints, such as price or margin limitations were sometimes imposed in order to ensure the aid was being used to lower prices and increase market share. For instance, a price leadership ban was imposed on ING and on Commerzbank. A minimal marginal percentage was imposed on Dexia and ABN Amro.

VII. Temporary Framework for the Real Economy

In order to complement the four Communications on aid to the financial sector, the Commission also adopted a temporary framework for State aid measures to stimulate the real economy, principally so as to deal with difficulties of businesses' access to finance.[10] The main measures set out in the temporary framework were the possibility of Member States granting a limited amount of aid up to €500,000 per undertaking, subsidised loans and guarantees, more flexible risk capital funding and trade financing. Member States committed in total some €81 billion, as approved by the Commission, but in fact only about a quarter of that was actually taken up by businesses in the EU, most SMEs. Nevertheless the Commission believes that the adoption of these temporary measures by the Member States sent a signal to the markets that they were willing to meet potential demand. However, the Commission acknowledges that it is difficult to assess how effective the temporary framework has been. In particular, the fact that the most popular measure, the grant of up to €500,000, was implemented through schemes that did not require investment or a link to any specific objective meant that it was not possible to assess its impact on long-term recovery. The temporary framework expired at the end of December 2011.

VIII. Strategies for Withdrawing from State Aid

As of the end of 2010, the worst case scenario of the collapse of systemic financial institutions had been avoided. The amount of aid used by financial institutions fell significantly during 2010 and only four Member States (Germany, Greece, Spain and Ireland) were granting large amounts of aid in the last quarter of 2010. This decrease in the use of aid was paralleled by the gradual exit from support schemes by Member States as market conditions reasserted control. For instance, the emissions of State guaranteed long-term debt securities, which had picked up in the beginning of 2009, fell in 2010 as banks were increasingly able to finance themselves on wholesale markets without State support. This decrease in the use of State guaranteed bonds was also driven by the fact that they were more expensive that commercial bonds. State support also helped to decrease the risk of default of European financial institutions, as measured by CDS spreads. That

---

[10] European Commission, 'Communication from the Commission – Temporary Community framework for State aid measures to support access to finance in the current financial and economic crisis' [2009] OJ C16/1.

decrease in the perceived risk of default of major banks was deemed essential for a swift return to stability in the financial sector since it contributed to increasing the confidence that banks placed on their counterparts and thus to a refuelling of short-term and longer-term funding markets. However, longer-term effects were not so clear, in particular due to the increase in sovereign debt risks and CDS spreads resumed a sharp upward trend in 2010 to reach levels similar to those at the peak of uncertainty in 2009.

The solvency of financial institutions did not significantly decrease in the course of the financial crisis. On the contrary, the average Tier 1 capital ratio of both aided and non-aided banks increased, due significantly to public recapitalisations. From mid-2009 onwards, there was no visible difference in the evolution of the solvency of aided and non-aided banks, with both categories improving their Tier 1 capital and reaching an average solvency ratio of 11.5 per cent at the end of 2010. State aided recapitalisation measures were particularly aimed at ensuring that banks could finance loan activity, which was successful in the case of household loans but less so in the case of loans to non-financial corporations until well into 2010. The Commission accepted that no link could be established between State aid in the form of capital and the evolution of loans to non-financial corporations. Nevertheless, recapitalisation was considered a success. As of the end of 2010, about €35 billion of recapitalisation investments by the Member States had been repaid by the beneficiaries, representing more than 10 per cent of Member States' investments in banks' capital, and was redeemed mostly in France, Belgium, the Netherlands and the United Kingdom. The Commission took the declining dependence of State-backed debt as another indicator of the return to normal functioning of the financial markets.

In order to encourage exit from State aid schemes, the Commission instigated a process of tightening up on the approval conditions in its Communications. From 1 July 2010, the conditions of access to guarantees were made more stringent.[11] The guarantee fee was increased by 20/30/40 basis points depending on the beneficiary's rating as compared with the pricing set out in the ECB's October 2008 recommendation. In addition, banks issuing new or renewed guaranteed debt which took or maintained their overall reliance on State guarantees beyond 5 per cent of their total outstanding liabilities or a total amount of €500 million would have to undergo a viability review by the Commission. In December 2010, the crisis regime was extended by the Prolongation Communication, which recognised the continuing need to approve aid pursuant to Article 107(3)(b) TFEU and which extended the Restructuring Communication – the only one of the original Communications without a specific expiry date – on amended terms until 31 December 2011.[12]

---

[11] European Commission, *DG Competition Staff Working Document: the application of State aid rules to government guarantee schemes covering bank debt to be issued after 30 June 2010* (30 April 2010), available at www.ec.europa.eu/competition/state_aid/studies_reports/phase_out_bank_guarantees.pdf.

[12] European Commission, 'Communication from the Commission on the application, from 1 January 2011, of State aid rules to support measures in favour of banks in the context of the financial crisis' [2010] OJ C329/7.

Henceforth, every beneficiary of a recapitalisation or impaired asset measure would be obliged to submit a restructuring plan for approval by the Commission. This effectively did away with the distinction between sound and distressed banks that had been recognised since the beginning of the crisis. Instead, since the banking sector now faced fewer difficulties in raising capital on the markets or through retained earnings, most banks could meet their capital needs without recourse to State aid, with the result that those banks that continued to need State support should be required to undertake the necessary restructuring efforts and return to viability without undue delay. The Prolongation Communication was intended to signal that banks had to prepare for a return to normal market mechanisms without State support when market conditions permitted and the financial sector gradually emerged from crisis conditions.

The Commission concludes in its Working Paper that the State aid granted to restore financial stability and a normal functioning of financial markets has achieved its objectives during the period mid-2008 to the end of 2010 and that the EU's co-ordinated response, including State aid control by the Commission, has contributed to preserving the Single Market throughout the crisis. Unfortunately, 2011 did not turn out as expected, with pressures on the financial markets emanating from the sovereign debt crisis leading to fresh difficulties of access to funding markets. Accordingly, in December 2011, the Commission once again prolonged the application of its Communications, with amendments applicable from 1 January 2012.[13] In particular, this Second Prolongation Communication supplements the Recapitalisation Communication, by providing more detailed guidance on remuneration for capital instruments that do not bear a fixed return and for fees payable in return for guarantees on bank liabilities, as well as explaining how the Commission will undertake the proportionate assessment of the long-term viability of banks.

IX. Conclusions

It remains difficult to say whether the Commission's flexible approach to State aid during the financial crisis has been successful. Indeed, has State aid control been of any use whatsoever? Comparison with the position in the United States, where there is no equivalent control, is not necessarily favourable. Whereas the EU banks had only repaid 10 per cent of recapitalisation debt by the end of 2010, more than 90 per cent of government capital in the United States had been reimbursed by beneficiaries of the Troubled Assets Relief Program (TARP) by then. The onset of the sovereign debt crisis in 2011, which has engulfed several Member

---

[13] European Commission, 'Communication from the Commission on the application, from 1 January 2012, of State aid rules to support measures in favour of banks in the context of the financial crisis' [2011] OJ C356/7.

States as well as appearing to endanger the survival of the Euro itself as a viable currency, also increased pressures on bank capitalisation. The Commission's Working Paper has little to say as to whether smaller banks in certain Member States should have been allowed to go bust, with their position on the market being taken over by banks from other Member States. By contrast, in the United States, there was much less reliance on the notion that banks were systemically important. In the US banking sector, hundreds of small and medium sized orderly bank failures had been allowed, whereas only a handful of European banks of a similar size have been allowed to fail. It might be wondered whether, if banks had been allowed to fail across the EU, other banks would not have quickly filled their place on the market without the need for huge amounts of State aid.

Burden sharing is another aspect of the credit crisis where some difficult questions go begging. This is particularly the case in respect of banks in Germany and France that had lent to banks in the troubled periphery, notably Greece, Ireland, Spain and Portugal which, as estimated by the Bank for International Settlements, owed them a little under €800 billion. The negotiations with Greece eventually led to bondholders being required to take a very significant haircut on their debts. In its negotiations with Ireland, by contrast, the ECB and the European Commission insisted that Ireland repay, on behalf of the Irish banks that had fuelled the local property boom, all of the money that they had borrowed from other banks in order to lend on to Irish property developers, which included €99 billion owed to German banks and €30 billion owed to French banks.

Despite the huge impact of the Commission's programme of State aid control, it is noticeable that there has been very little challenge to its decisions in front of the General Court. The Commission was defeated in one minor respect in relation to its decision approving aid to ING in Case T-33/10, but otherwise the structure put in place by the Commission has largely survived intact. This may of course be largely explained by the fact that Member States and their banks were largely grateful to receive Commission approval, with the Commission asserting in public that it was protecting the position of competitors by requiring the Member States to show good reason for the quantities of aid being proposed. Also, by relying on the hitherto largely unused Article 107(3)(b) TFEU, the Commission was able to determine a wide ranging discretionary power for itself that was difficult to challenge. It is trite law that the European courts will not interfere with the exercise of such a discretion except in the case of manifest error, and it might be expected that the General Court would certainly not relish having to second-guess the Commission's analysis.

Nevertheless, the fact is that banks in Europe are presently largely organised on national rather than European lines. Future developments of an internal banking market and pan-European regulation might mean that a similar situation as arose in 2007 will be unlikely to be repeated and that cross-border banks would be better able to deal with global liquidity difficulties in the same way as the major US banks acted. From the Commission's perspective it was merely responding to requests from Member States to adopt financial support measures and seeking to impose a framework that would prevent national action from resulting in protectionist subsidies. It is certainly too early yet to tell whether this was the right policy. But it was the only policy tool immediately available to the Commission at the time.

9

State Aid for Banks in the Financial Crisis: The Commission's New and Stronger Role

THOMAS ACKERMANN

I. The Legal Fall-out from the Crisis

The financial crisis and the sovereign debt crisis that followed it have put the EU constitutional framework to the test. The EU competition rules are a minor, but not totally insignificant part of this framework. While the crisis did not have a large impact on the application of Articles 101 and 102 TFEU and of the rules of EU merger control, the Commission's implementation of State aid control under Article 107 TFEU was deeply affected by the crisis. The sheer scale of aid granted by Member States to their banks in order not only to save ailing financial institutions, but also to prevent a meltdown of financial markets, as well as the urgency of the measures, stretched the legal framework to breaking point. Conor Quigley has shown in his contribution to this volume how the Commission confronted this immense task. He also sheds some light on the somewhat doubtful economic effects which Member States' measures accepted by the Commission had on the recovery of the financial sector. In particular, I fully agree that the ominous term 'systemic relevance' was rather widely applied, and that this may have led to an unnecessarily generous use of taxpayers' money in support of financial institutions. However, my focus will not be on the financial and economic impact of the decisions that have been made, but on the legal fallout from the crisis as far as State aid rules are concerned. In my opinion, the most important outcome is a strengthening of the position of the Commission. The Commission increasingly acts like a regulator with a broad margin of judicially uncontrolled discretion. This became evident in the progression from the rescue stage to the restructuring stage of the process. As Neelie Kroes, then EU Commissioner for Competition, nicely put it: 'In plain English, the price of State support is that you must submit a restructured business to us.'[1] The

[1] Speech by Commissioner Kroes at the 36th Annual Conference on International Antitrust Law and Policy, Fordham University New York, 24 September 2009, available at www.eu-un.europa.eu/articles/en/article_9019_en.htm (last visited 6 June 2013).

weakening of State aid control that could be observed in the early stages of the crisis may have no enduring consequences, but there will perhaps be a permanent shift in the Commission's role.

II. Weakening of State Aid Control as a Temporary Phenomenon

In order to prevent losing control of the State aid regime in the rescue stage of the crisis, the Commission was prepared to adjust the legal framework in several respects. Most obviously, procedures were accelerated to a great degree. Normally, there is a preliminary examination period for notified aid of two months,[2] followed by a formal investigation period of 18 months.[3] During the crisis, decisions not to raise objections were made within weeks, sometimes within a few days. However, there were more important adaptations relating to the substance of State aid control. Only in the early stages of the crisis, the Commission stuck to its regular approach under Article 107(3)(c) TFEU and the Guidelines on State aid for rescue and restructuring of 2004 (R&R Guidelines).[4] The Commission then changed its strategy by turning towards Article 107(3)(b) TFEU, according to which State aid may be considered permissible to remedy a serious disturbance in the economy of a Member State. This provision was not only applied to general schemes, but also to individual cases. Subsequently, the Commission clarified its approach in four communications (the Banking Communication, the Recapitalisation Communication, the Impaired Assets Communication, and the Restructuring Communication) that were aptly summarised in Conor Quigley's contribution.

While the Commission's new approach to State aid in the financial sector left the main principle of the R&R Guidelines intact that no rescue aid would be allowed without restructuring, it also led to a softening of the legal framework in several respects, which may however not have a lasting impact beyond the crisis:[5]

- According to the R&R Guidelines, aid may only be granted to undertakings in difficulty, that is, to companies which will go out of business in the short or medium term if they do not get support. In contrast to that, the Banking Communication

---

[2] Article 4(5) of Regulation 659/1999.

[3] Article 2(6) of Regulation 659/1999.

[4] Communication from the Commission – Community guidelines on State aid for rescuing and restructuring firms in difficulty, [2004] OJ C444/2.

[5] A deeper analysis than this comment is provided by H Gilliams, 'Stress Testing the Regulator: Review of State Aid to Financial Institutions after the Collapse of Lehman' (2011) 36 *European Law Review* 3; U Soltész, 'Von der Beihilfekontrolle zur Neugestaltung des Marktes – Schafft die Kommission eine 'bessere Bankenwelt'?' [2010] *Wirtschaft und Wettbewerb* 743; D Zimmer and M Blaschczok, 'Die Banken-Beihilfenkontrolle der Europäischen Kommission: Wettbewerbsschutz oder Marktdesign?' [2010] *Wirtschaft und Wettbewerb* 142.

allowed State aid also to be granted to fundamentally sound financial institutions with liquidity problems. This was certainly justified, but owed to the special situation of the crisis, which did not only hit particular undertakings, but financial markets as such.

- The R&R Guidelines follow the concept that aid is a temporary and reversible assistance. As a consequence, after six months, the aid must either be reimbursed or a restructuring plan must be notified. On the other hand, under Article 107(3) (b) TFEU, many rescue measures (eg capital increases) are not reversible, and restructuring is not a necessary prerequisite. Again, this is a deviation from regular cases that takes account of the urgency and the depth of the crisis and is thus unlikely to lead to a permanent change of the general approach to State aids.

- As a general rule laid down in the R&R Guidelines, rescue aid may only be granted once every 10 years. Once again deviating from general standards, the Banking Communication allowed the provision of aid during the restructuring period (following the initial aid) if justified by reasons of financial stability. However, it follows from this condition that this is not meant to be precedent for State aid control under regular circumstances.

III. Shift in the Commission's Role

During the crisis, it turned out that the State aid rules granted more leeway to the Commission than was previously assumed. The Commission used its discretion to develop the legal framework in a way that put the Commission into the role of a quasi-regulatory authority with discretionary powers. While the particular rules for the financial sector will lose their importance after a while, this newly developed self-conception of the Commission may be here to stay.

One aspect supporting this suspicion is a potential broadening of the scope of the State aid rules so that a wider array of State measures is subject to the Commission's scrutiny. According to Article 107(1) TFEU, '[s]ave as otherwise provided in the Treaties, any aid granted by a Member State or through State resources in any form whatsoever which distorts or threatens to distort competition by favouring certain undertakings or the production of certain goods shall, in so far as it affects trade between Member States, be incompatible with the internal market.' Four requirements must be fulfilled for the classification of a measure as State aid: first, there must be an intervention by the State or through State resources; second, this measure must be liable to affect trade between Member States; third, it must confer an advantage on the recipient, and fourth, it must distort or threaten to distort competition. The third criterion requires an answer to the question how an advantage for the recipient can be identified. The conventional solution is the private investor test. According to this test, the Commission has to assess whether a private investor acting in a market economy would have acted in the same way as the State. However, a crisis that hits a whole market makes it excessively difficult to apply this test properly because there cannot be an evaluation under market conditions if the market has collapsed. This was the case with the financial crisis as there were no longer investors who gave banks fresh capital, or buyers who were interested in toxic assets. Therefore, the Commission decided not to use the private investor test. This led to sweeping conclusions as can be seen in the example of the *ING* case that has recently been decided by the General Court (joined cases T-29/10 and T-33/10). The Dutch bank ING had received a capital injection of €10 billion. Subsequently, the repayment terms were changed, which potentially led to an additional advantage of €2 billion. Without applying the private investor test, the Commission found that this constituted additional aid. The General Court did not accept this and held that 'the Commission misinterpreted the concept of aid by not assessing whether, by accepting the amendment of the repayment terms, the Netherlands State acted as a private investor would have done in a similar situation'.[6] However, this criticism by the General Court is unlikely to have a large impact as a restriction on the Commission's discretion in assessing the classification of a measure as State aid in situations where markets have collapsed.

Another aspect that is even more important as a foundation for the Commission's stronger role concerns the legal consequences of State aid decisions, in particular as far as commitments and conditions attached to these decisions are concerned. Generally speaking, the approval of aid for banks could be linked with behavioural and structural measures. For example, in the above-mentioned case, ING was ordered to reduce its balance sheet by 45 per cent within five years so that ING had to divest itself of its insurance branch and other entities. Furthermore, a three-year ban on acquisitions was imposed on ING, and ING was prohibited from acting as price leader for certain products and certain markets. Finally, ING had to face restrictions on dividends and on advertising as well as salary caps. While each of these measures may be justified as a means to keep the risk of pernicious side-effects of the aid granted to the bank in check, it can hardly be denied that these measures will rarely be contested by those concerned. The urgency of the situation usually forces States and banks to accept whatever the Commission demands from them, irrespective of whether these measures serve a legitimate aim and whether they are necessary and proportionate with regard to this aim. Once aid has been granted, incentives are often low to contest the Commission decision even if the conditions attached to it seem unduly burdensome. So only few cases (such as *ING*) reach the General Court. This leaves a legal vacuum in which the Commission is free to impose structural and behavioural measures without having to fear limits set by the judiciary. If these measures cover a sufficiently large number of important players in a given market, as happened during the banking crisis, they tend to merge into a quasi-regulatory regime. In other words, the State aid rules can then provide the Commission with a lever to re-organise an economic sector such as the banking

---

[6] Joined Cases T-29/10 and T-33/10 *Kingdom of the Netherlands (T-29/10) and ING Groep NV (T-33/10) v European Commission*, para 125 (nyr).

sector as we would normally only expect from a regulatory authority with far-reaching discretionary powers. Admittedly, this can only be an ad hoc regulation which comes to end at the moment when State measures cease. But considering the large impact the State aid decisions have had in sum on the structure and conduct of the banking industry, one may have doubts whether it was legitimate for the Commission to interpret its mandate under the State aid rules in such a broad way. Market regulation should be entrusted to authorities on the basis of proper legislation. The difficulties of establishing a European banking union show that this is not an easy task. However, the State aid rules should not be used to bypass these processes by introducing elements of regulation by stealth.

Part III

Regulation

10

Comparing Apples and Oranges?
Public, Private, Tax, and Criminal Law
Instruments in Financial Markets Regulation

ALEXANDER HELLGARDT[1]

I. Introduction

Financial markets are currently undergoing the most severe reforms since the 1930s. Those parts of the financial industry that were not significantly affected by the financial crisis itself will most likely be reshuffled by the new wave of regulation that followed it. In April 2009, the Group of Twenty (G20) agreed at their London summit to 'extend regulation and oversight to all systemically important financial institutions, instruments and markets'.[2] Thereafter, many previously unregulated parts of the financial system came under supervision for the first time. Most of the new legislation however, is concerned with the reform of regulation pre-existing the financial crisis. These reforms exemplify that it was not only deregulation that caused the crisis; the problems of financial crisis stem from two distinct sources: (1) grave deficiencies of existing regulation as such and (2) major failures by public agencies in the administration of the existing rules.[3]

---

[1] I would like to thank the participants of the Oxford conference and especially my commentator John Vella for helpful comments and suggestions.

[2] Group of Twenty, 'The Global Plan for Recovery and Reform' (London Summit, 2 April 2009) para 15, fourth bullet point.

[3] It is beyond the aim of this chapter to analyse the causes of the recent crisis (or, in fact, the crises, as one might want to distinguish between the disruptions of 2007–09, starting with the breakdown of the US subprime market, and the 2010– sovereign debt crisis). However, the existing reports on the 2007–09 crisis broadly seem to support the claim that regulatory failure played an important role in the run-up to the crisis. From a US perspective see eg The Financial Crisis Inquiry Commission, 'The Final Crisis Inquiry Report. Final Report of the National Commission on the Causes of the Financial and Economic Crisis in the United States' (Official Government Edition, 2011) xviii. From a German perspective see eg M Hellwig, *Finanzmarktregulierung – Welche Reformen empfehlen sich für den deutschen und europäischen Finanzsektor?*, Gutachten E zum 68. Deutschen Juristentag (Munich, CH Beck, 2010) 35–49. From a UK perspective see eg Financial Services Authority, *The Turner Review. A Regulatory Response to the Global Banking Crisis* (FSA 2009) www.fsa.gov.uk/pubs/other/turner_review.pdf at 11–49.

Yet, the discussion concerning the reform of financial regulation centres on the substantive standards of the new rules and neglects the problem of choosing the right regulatory instruments. If the subject of legal forms is discussed at all, the debate is biased toward very few and traditional instruments. For example, consider the European Commission's Communication in December 2010 on '[r]einforcing sanctioning regimes in the financial services sector';[4] the paper only focuses on administrative fines, criminal sanctions, and the power of public authorities. Accordingly, the Communication was followed by extensive reform proposals for a Market Abuse Regulation,[5] a Sanctions Directive[6] and a reform of the Transparency Directive[7] – all of which are confined to administrative and criminal sanctions. Think of somebody who owns a garden with a variety of grown fruits. Yet, this same person chooses to consider only recipes for making apple pie. As it is, the Commission's diet actually encompasses a whole variety of 'fruits'; an example includes the new Credit Rating Agencies (CRA) Regulation, which has introduced civil liability claims for investors who have relied on misleading ratings.[8] The Commission proposal states that this new liability provision aims at 'ensuring compliance with the rules of the CRA Regulation'.[9] Another example features fiscal measures like the financial transaction tax[10] or the bank levy.[11] In its respective proposals, the European Commission explicitly refers to the regulatory function of these instruments.[12]

[4] European Commission, 'Communication: Reinforcing Sanctioning Regimes in the Financial Services Sector' COM(2010) 716 final, 8 December 2010.

[5] European Commission, 'Amended Proposal for a Regulation of the European Parliament and of the Council on Insider Dealing and Market Manipulation (market abuse)' COM(2012) 421 final, 25 July 2012.

[6] European Commission, 'Amended Proposal for a Directive of the European Parliament and of the Council on Criminal Sanctions for Insider Dealing and Market Manipulation' COM(2012) 420 final, 25 July 2012.

[7] European Commission, 'Proposal for a Directive of the European Parliament and of the Council Amending Directive 2004/109/EC on the Harmonisation of Transparency Relation to Information about Issuers whose Securities are Admitted to Trading on a Regulated Market and Commission Directive 2007/14/EC' COM(2011) 683 final, 25 October 2011.

[8] See Article 35a of the Regulation (EC) No 1060/2009 of the European Parliament and of the Council of 16 September 2009 on Credit Rating Agencies' [2009] OJ L302, 1 (as amended by Regulation (EU) No 462/2013 of the European Parliament and of the Council of 21 May 2013).

[9] European Commission, 'Proposal for a Regulation of the European Parliament and of the Council Amending Regulation (EC) 1060/2009 on Credit Rating Agencies' COM(2011) 747 final, 15 November 2011, 11.

[10] European Commission, 'Proposal for a Council Directive implementing enhanced cooperation in the area of financial transaction tax' COM(2013) 71 final, 14 February 2013.

[11] See proposed Article 94 in European Commission, Proposal for a Directive of the European Parliament and of the Council establishing a framework for the recovery and resolution of credit institutions and investment firms and amending Council Directives 77/91/EEC and 82/891/EC, Directives 2001/24/EC, 2002/47/EC, 2004/25/EC, 2005/56/EC, 2007/36/EC and 2011/35/EC and Regulation (EU) No 1093/2010 COM(2012) 280 final, 6 June 2012.

[12] ibid 35 (bank levy shall 'provide incentives to operate under a less risky model'). See also European Commission, COM(2013) 71 final, 14 February 2013, 32 (proposal is meant 'to create appropriate disincentives for transactions that do not enhance the efficiency of financial markets'); European Commission, 'Communication: Taxation of the Financial Sector' COM(2010) 549 final, 7 October 2010, 3 ('Additional taxes could indirectly and in addition to regulation contribute to the goal of improving the stability of the financial sector by dissuading it from carrying out certain risky activities').

The short survey illustrates how the European Commission employs a variety of regulatory instruments in financial markets regulation; but there does not seem to be a system directing the use of different legal tools. The choice appears to be arbitrary and idiosyncratic to the respective Directorate-General which is in charge of a proposal. As far as I am aware, there is no systematic discussion of regulatory instruments and no comparison of their relative strengths and weaknesses in the context of financial regulation. This is especially problematic if one agrees with the European Commission's own diagnosis that regulatory failures during the past crisis were not only due to a lack of rules but also to ineffective enforcement.[13] This chapter is intended to be a first step towards a comparative analysis of public, private, tax, and criminal law instruments in financial markets regulation.

In what follows, I will focus on four basic instruments of law enforcement and take three examples of regulatory options in financial markets regulation. Using a number of different yardsticks for comparison, I will analyse the relative strengths and weaknesses of the four instruments and finally employ a cost-benefit analysis. Before I embark on this analysis, it is however necessary to briefly recall the characteristics of European financial markets regulation.

II. European Financial Markets Regulation

As in several fields of business law, financial markets regulation pursues very broad and diffuse goals like 'financial stability'[14] or 'market integrity'.[15] Even concepts such as 'investor protection', which at first blush seem slightly more clear-cut become vague when applied to diverse groups of investors such as hedge funds on the one hand and workers saving for their retirement on the other hand. Private investors are heavily reliant on protection by means of regulation, while professional investment managers are mostly able to safeguard their own interests.[16]

While it is easy to prohibit any violation of a person's physical integrity, it is not feasible to stipulate a rule that bans any infringement of a market's integrity; the

---

[13] See European Commission, COM(2010) 716 final, 8 December 2010, 2 ('The financial crisis has put into doubt whether financial market rules are always respected and applied as they should be across the Union.').

[14] See European Commission, COM(2013) 71 final, 14 February 2013, 32 ('The Commission's multiannual strategic objective targeted by the proposal: Financial stability').

[15] See Recital 2 Directive (EC) 2003/6/EC of the European Parliament and of the Council of 28 January 2003 on insider dealing and market manipulation (market abuse) [2003] OJ L96, 16 (Market Abuse Directive).

[16] There are, however, attempts to cope with different abilities of investors to safeguard their own interests by introducing different classes of clients ('professional clients' v 'retail clients'), see Annex II of the Directive (EC) 2004/39/EC of the European Parliament and of the Council of 21 April 2004 on markets in financial instruments amending Council Directives 85/611/EEC and 93/6/EEC and Directive 2000/12/EC of the European Parliament and of the Council and repealing Council Directive 93/22/EEC [2004] OJ L145, 1 (MiFID).

exact meaning of concepts such as 'market integrity' is debated. The ambiguity of the concept is rooted in the broadness of the idea.[17] In other cases, the meaning of concepts like 'systemic risk' is subjected to ongoing academic debate.[18] In order to obtain operational definitions, the broad objectives of financial markets law have to be made concrete and transformed into a regulatory strategy. In the course of this process, regulatory goals change: instead of safeguarding a public good like 'financial stability', concrete rules aim to prevent specific patterns of behaviour that infringe the ultimately protected public or private interest. It is obvious that the extent to which basic objectives like 'market integrity' are achieved depends on the regulatory strategy pursued. Once a regulatory strategy has been chosen, the question arises how a specific prohibition or duty within this strategy should be enforced; through fines or criminal sanctions or civil liability in case of infringement? The remaining sections of this chapter will be confined to the analysis and comparison of these instruments of law enforcement.

The general objectives of financial markets regulation are predominantly subject to international or European law. The regulatory strategy, that is, the prohibited or mandated behaviour – such as the usage of inside information, the dissemination of misleading capital market information, or the mandated disclosure of certain financial information – is often defined at the European level. Yet up until the crisis, Member States were responsible for selecting enforcement mechanisms. Some Directives contained fairly broad standards such as 'Member States shall ensure . . . that at least the appropriate administrative measures may be taken or civil and/or administrative penalties imposed in respect of the persons responsible'[19] or even stipulated the Member State's duty to impose some sort of civil liability on infringers.[20] But, in general Member States enjoyed free choice of legal forms in Directive transposition and enforcement.[21] In response to the crisis, this system is about to change.

The European Commission has identified 'divergences and weaknesses in national sanction regimes' as a major shortcoming of the existing European financial markets law.[22] As a consequence, the Commission proposes harmonisation of the sanctioning regime.[23] When the sanctioning rules in financial markets

---

[17] See Recital 2 of the Market Abuse Directive which defines 'market integrity' as '[t]he smooth functioning of securities markets and public confidence in markets'.

[18] See the comprehensive overview by DO Edwards, '(Systemic) Risk and Taxation' (2011) 31 *Virginia Tax Review* 331, 344–49.

[19] Article 28(1) of the Directive (EC) 2004/109/EC of the European Parliament and of the Council of 15 December 2004 on the harmonisation of transparency requirements in relation to information about issuers whose securities are admitted to trading on a regulated market and amending Directive 2001/34/EC [2004] OJ L390, 38 (Transparency Directive).

[20] See Article 7 of the Transparency Directive; Article 6 of the Directive (EC) 2003/71/EC of the European Parliament and of the Council of 4 November 2003 on the prospectus to be published when securities are offered to the public or admitted to trading and amending Directive 2001/34/EC [2003] OJ L345, 64 (Prospectus Directive).

[21] See eg Case C-352/92 *Milchwerke Köln/Wuppertal eG v Hauptzollamt Köln-Rheinau* [1994] ECR I-3400, para 23.

[22] See European Commission, COM(2010) 716 final, 8 December 2010, 6–9.

[23] ibid 10–16.

law will be Europeanised and thereby unified, it reinforces the need for consideration of different enforcement options.

III. Comparison of Legal Instruments: Regulatory Options

This chapter focuses on a particular category of enforcement mechanisms – instruments that aim to prevent a particular harm from occurring.[24] In the field, there are four basic choices of regulatory instruments.[25] These instruments are: (1) administrative sanctions; (2) civil liability; (3) corrective taxation; and (4) criminal sanctions. The four enforcement mechanisms are usually discussed separately. Continental lawyers in particular are reluctant to treat civil liability and taxation on an equal footing with administrative or criminal law as law enforcement mechanisms[26] – following the conventional wisdom that apples and oranges cannot be compared. Such a judgement might be the result of the comparative analysis; it should, however, not forestall the exercise of comparing regulatory tools altogether. In the pages that follow, I will analyse three examples of regulatory options in the pursuit of financial markets regulation. Each example belongs to a class of regulatory options.

The first example is the prevention of unsuitable investment advice.[27] This example concerns the relationship between investment firms and retail investors. As many individuals lack the knowledge and experience to develop their own

---

[24] See S Shavell, 'The Optimal Structure of Law Enforcement' (1993) 36 *Journal of Law & Economics* 255, 256–61. Shavell distinguishes between acts and harms and, based on this distinction, classifies legal instruments in categories that aim to prevent an act, that impose sanctions based on the commission of an act (regardless of its consequences), and that impose harm-based sanctions. The approach taken here encompasses all of these categories insofar as they ultimately strive to prevent a particular harm from occurring.

[25] Note there is no suggestion that there are no other instruments – I am in fact sure that there is a whole battery of additional instruments in the field of private law alone (Shavell, 'The Optimal Structure of Law Enforcement' (n 24) 259–61 for instance, includes injunctions in his analysis). The four instruments noted here are the ones most commonly used when containing harms. If one broadens the view of regulatory goals beyond the control of possible harms, the number of instruments increases. For a classification of legal instruments see eg T Daintith, 'Law as a Policy Instrument: Comparative Perspective' in T Daintith (ed), *Law as an Instrument of Economic Policy* (Berlin and New York, Walter de Gruyter, 1988) 3, 31–32, 51; R Mayntz, 'The Conditions of Effective Public Policy' (1983) 11 *Policy and Politics* 123, 128. See also A Shleifer, 'Understanding Regulation' (2005) 11 *European Financial Management* 439, 442 who takes an even broader view by listing four instruments to control businesses: market discipline, private litigation, public enforcement through regulation, and state ownership.

[26] For a doctrinal critique of corrective taxation see P Kirchhof, 'Lenkungssteuern' in K Tipke and H Söhn (eds), *Gedächtnisschrift für Christoph Trzaskalik* (Cologne, Otto Schmidt Verlag, 2005) 395; for a critique of civil liability as a regulatory tool (using the example of anti-discrimination laws) see E Picker, 'Antidiskriminierung als Zivilrechtsprogramm?' [2003] *Juristenzeitung* 540, 543–44.

[27] For an overview of the European regulation of investment advice, see N Moloney, *EC Securities Regulation*, 2nd edn (Oxford, Oxford University Press, 2008) 599–609, 614–21.

investment strategy, they rely upon banks and investment advisers. In the case that the advice provided is unsuitable for investors' needs, it not only hurts the client, but may eventually lead to a loss of confidence in financial markets as a whole. I have chosen this example because it is considered typical in two respects: first, it involves public as well as private interests and second, the particular harm is relatively small in each individual case (though it might be large in the aggregate) but can only be assessed on a single-case basis.

My second example is the prevention of insider trading.[28] Insiders exploit their superior knowledge of circumstances relevant to the pricing of a security to make extra profits. Insider trading violates the principle of equal opportunity for all investors. It may cause a loss of confidence and increases the volatility of the market. In the end, companies listed on such a market will attract less capital and will have to pay higher risk premiums.[29] I have chosen insider trading because it is considered 'victimless crime';[30] while it adversely affects both investors and companies that issue financial instruments, the harm is indirect and the infringement is often hard to detect.

The last example features financial institutions as such. It is about deterring banks from growing 'too big to fail'. The financial crisis of 2007–08 highlighted the dangers of private companies growing so big that states were forced to bail them out to prevent their default. Such bail-outs not only burden public budgets, but also increase the moral hazard problem of bank managers incurring excessive risks.[31] I have chosen this example because of the complexity in the structure of the harm to be deterred.

In the following, I will use the aforementioned examples to compare regulatory instruments in their different respects. Some people prefer orange juice to apple juice, however their appetite for entire fruits may favour apples to oranges. Hence, before embarking on the overall cost-benefit analysis, it is important to investigate single aspects.

1. Functioning

The functioning of the enforcement mechanisms is the first and most significant criterion for comparative analysis.

---

[28] As to the European prohibition of insider dealing, see ibid 951–67.

[29] For an analysis of the reasons to ban insider trading see eg GA Ferrarini, 'The European Market Abuse Directive' (2004) 41 *CMLR* 711, 713–15.

[30] For the argument that insider trading does not hurt investors see eg SM Bainbridge, 'Insider Trading: An Overview ' in B Bouckaert and GD Geest (ed), *Encyclopedia of Law and Economics*, Vol III (Cheltenham, Edward Elgar, 2000)772, 785–86.

[31] See A Admati, P DeMarzo, M Hellwig, P Pfleiderer, 'Fallacies, Irrelevant Facts, and Myths in the Discussion of Capital Regulation: Why Bank Equity is Not Socially Expensive' (2013) Rock Center for Corporate Governance at Stanford University Working Paper No 86, available at www.ssrn.com/abstract=1669704 at 22.

a) The Example of Unsuitable Investment Advice

In case of investment advice, the suitability of a financial instrument for a certain investor has to be assessed on a single-case basis.[32] This renders enforcement by means of corrective taxation problematic. If a tax is designed to influence human behaviour, it needs a tax base that is easily comprehensible. Ideally, there should not be much ambiguity as to legal elements constituting the tax base as such.[33] Yet, assessing the suitability of financial instruments for a particular investor is essentially a qualitative judgement that depends on a multitude of factors. Tax authorities need to review every single investment recommendation and decide whether to levy the tax or not based on normative criteria. The tax would consequently transform into an administrative fine. Corrective taxation is therefore an inappropriate enforcement instrument to deter misleading investment advice.

The complex structure of the harm to be deterred also poses a problem for administrative law. While it is theoretically possible to employ financial supervisors to monitor investment advice, considerable practical problems arise. To effectively prevent misleading investment advice requires the close scrutiny of single investment recommendations and of the underlying consultations between bank and investor. This is hardly feasible in a mass business like retail banking. In practice, public supervision is therefore restricted to controlling procedural standards and general principles of plausibility.[34] Thus, supervision may fail to help every single investor suffering losses due to unsuitable investment advice. Nevertheless, it secures general compliance with the applicable standards, which might be valuable for the public interest goal of investor confidence.

The options to use criminal law to regulate investment advice are even more confined. Due to their severity, criminal sanctions have to be restricted to few and grave law infringements. Unsuitable investment advice features only a low degree of unlawfulness. Instead of deterring misleading recommendations, the threat of criminal sanctions would most likely impede the market for investment advice as bank employees might be reluctant to engage in such a risky business. Still, criminal punishment may be used to sanction outright fraud and personal enrichment. In these cases, the private benefit derived from the misleading advice must be set off by a credible threat of punishment. By contrast, civil liability, which generally only obliges the defendant to repay the sum invested in reliance on the misleading advice, cannot effectively deter personal enrichment.[35]

---

[32] The concept of suitability is laid down in Article 19(4) of the MiFID; see Moloney, *EC Securities Regulation* (n 27) 615–16.

[33] See S Shavell, 'Corrective Taxation versus Liability as a Solution to the Problem of Harmful Externalities' (2011) 54 *Journal of Law & Economics* S249, S255–56. Shavell argues that corrective taxes can only handle few variables.

[34] On the differences between the (supervisory) requirements by MiFID and (German) contract law with regard to investment advice, see P Mülbert, 'The Eclipse of Contract Law in the Investment Firm-Client-Relationship: The Impact of the MiFID on the Law of Contract from a German Perspective' in G Ferrarini and E Wymeersch (eds), *Investor Protection in Europe* (Oxford, Oxford University Press, 2006) 299, 316–19.

[35] cf R Cooter and T Ulen, *Law & Economics*, 5th edn (Boston, Pearson/Addison-Wesley, 2008) 493.

When employing civil liability, the enforcement mechanism depends on the degree of fault that is required to trigger liability. On the one hand, there is strict liability, on the other hand, liability based on negligent behaviour.

Strict liability shifts all economic consequences onto the infringer, irrespective of personal responsibility. Such a standard is only suitable when the relevant risks emanate from the infringer's sphere of responsibility. In that case strict liability should induce the potential law infringer to exercise socially optimal care, as he will have to bear all economic consequences anyway.[36] Yet, in case of investment advice, investors' losses will often have causes other than the misleading recommendation, notably a decline in the financial instrument's price. Hence, a regime of strict liability would provide investors with insurance against investment losses in general, which extends beyond the regulatory goal. Strict liability is therefore not an appropriate standard to deter unsuitable investment advice.

By contrast, liability for negligence is only triggered when a court finds the advice that caused the investor's loss to be sub-standard. Negligence liability allows courts to deduce special due diligence rules out of the general duty of care. As these special rules are developed using real cases, the resulting standards tend to be more so aligned with actual industry practice. Civil liability thus allows not only for an enforcement that is tailored to the individual case, but it also enables every single investor who suffered a loss to bring his case. Financial supervision and civil liability thus perform complementary functions.[37]

b) The Example of Insider Trading

Insider trading is a clearly defined offence.[38] Therefore, enforcement through administrative law works very well. Financial supervisors do not need to wait until they suspect insider trading to react as they have manifold possibilities to install upfront detection tools.[39] In this vein, the authorities may for instance oblige issuers and financial intermediaries to name persons with access to inside information.[40] In an investigation, trading data may be compared to these insider lists.

---

[36] S Shavell, *Foundations of Economic Analysis of Law* (USA, President and Fellows of Harvard College, 2004) 179–80.

[37] This speaks against the (economic) soundness of Mülbert's view that the MiFID bars EU Member States from applying higher standards of contract law as compared to the standards set by Article 19(4) MiFID in cross-border cases. See Mülbert, 'The Eclipse of Contract Law in the Investment Firm-Client-Relationship' (n 34) 319.

[38] For a detailed analysis of the European regulation of insider dealing see Ferrarini, 'The European Market Abuse Directive' (n 29) 718–24, 728–29. See also Moloney, *EC Securities Regulation* (n 27) 951–67.

[39] Here, I do not count the issuers' duty to 'inform the public as soon as possible of inside information' according to Article 6(1) of the Market Abuse Directive as such a preventive measure. Even though these 'ad hoc disclosures' are an important instrument of preventing insider dealings, they are also part of the companies' disclosure obligations and in this respect they themselves form primary duties which have to be enforced by one of the mechanisms discussed in this chapter. For an analysis of the regulatory goals of Article 6(1) of the Market Abuse Directive, see A Hellgardt, 'The notion of inside information in the Market Abuse Directive: Geltl' (2013) 50 *CMLR* 861, 868–70.

[40] cf Article 6(3)(3) Market Abuse Directive (stipulating a duty to 'draw up a list of those persons . . ., who have access to inside information').

By contrast, civil liability cannot remedy insider trading. Trading on inside information does not *directly* harm other investors but erodes market integrity as such – a public interest. Even if we allow for gain-based damages, without showing loss to the claimant, civil damages for insider trading are not feasible as claims cannot be attributed to specific investors. As long as private claimants are not treated as private Attorney-Generals as is the case in the US '*qui tam* action',[41] civil liability requires some kind of connection to a single person. It has been proposed, however, to grant a claim to those investors who traded in the relevant securities at the same time as the insider.[42] Yet considering that insider trading does not directly harm particular investors, but leads to a loss of investor confidence in general and to an increase in the issuers' cost of capital, there does not seem to be a compelling justification for entitling just those investors who coincidentally happen to trade simultaneously with the insider.

Theoretically, insider trading could be deterred by a penalty tax. In this setting, insider trading would be considered legal, but insiders would have to pay a high tax on the gains from expropriating their informational advantage. If the tax is calculated correctly, the incentive to trade on inside information should disappear. However, there are many practical problems with such a penalty tax. First, in order to effectively deter insider trading, the tax rate would have to be either very high (100 per cent in cases where an insider sells shares that are actually worthless) or must be calibrated on an individual basis, siphoning off the excess return of each insider transaction. But even more important, voluntary compliance with such a penalty tax is very unlikely. If actions are not readily identifiable – as is the case with insider trades – enforcement would have to rely primarily on the voluntary declaration of the gains in a tax return. As information asymmetries between insiders and other investors are the essential characteristic of inside information, it is comparatively easy to conceal insider dealing. Thus a penalty tax would need complementary criminal enforcement mechanisms for tax evasion, which would most likely become more important than the actual tax.

Criminalising insider trading directly is a more straightforward solution than the previously mentioned proposal of levying a tax and punishing tax evasion. One may nevertheless ask whether there is in fact a big difference between an administrative fine, a tax, and a criminal fine. The economic analysis of law for instance, treats criminal penalties as prices by employing a formula that multiplies the monetary amount with the probability of conviction.[43] However this approach to criminal punishment may be viewed as incomplete. Criminal fines

---

[41] On the '*qui tam* action' (short for *qui tam pro domino rege quam pro se ipso in hac parte sequitur*), see J Fisch, 'Class Action Reform, Qui Tam, and the Role of the Plaintiff' (1997) 60 *Law & Contemporary Problems* 167.

[42] C Kirchner, 'Zur zentralen Rolle der zivilrechtlichen Sanktionen im Recht des Insiderhandels' in HG Leser and T Isomura (eds), *Wege zum Japanischen Recht – Festschrift für Zentaro Kitagawa* (Berlin, Duncker & Humblot, 1992) 665, 680.

[43] This idea was originally developed by G Becker, 'Crime and Punishment: An Economic Approach' (1968) 76 *Journal of Political Economy* 169. For an analysis of the differences between prices and sanctions see R Cooter, 'Prices and Sanctions' (1984) 84 *Columbia Law Review* 1523.

involve a strong social stigma, and a criminal record often entails serious consequences such as expulsion from the job market.[44] In fact, it makes a huge difference whether somebody is held liable by a court to either pay the amount X in
civil damages, in tax liability, or as a criminal fine. In the former cases, people do
not hesitate to complain to their social environment about 'overregulation' or
'judicial errors'. In the latter, most people prefer to observe secrecy. From a law
enforcement perspective, the lack of a direct effect on private interests in the case
of insider trading militates in favour of using criminal sanctions. The increased
deterrent effect of criminal punishment substitutes the lack of private surveillance
(since investors have no incentives to detect insider trading when they cannot sue
for damages) and the low probability of detection.

c) The Example of Banks Too Big to Fail

My last example, the problem of banks growing too big to fail, poses a serious
challenge to regulation. It is difficult or even impossible to objectively define the
point a financial institution reaches the realm of systemic relevance.[45] The assessment of whether a bank is systemically relevant or not has to be updated from
time to time for each bank.

This indeterminacy of systemic risk is a problem to criminal law. Human rights
guarantees like Article 7 of the European Convention on Human Rights (ECHR)
demand that criminal offences be clearly defined by the law; the definition must
not be changed retrospectively.[46] Considering the stigma associated with a criminal conviction, these rules seem justified from an economic point of view. Bank
managers might behave overcautiously in fear of losing their social status. The
criminal law has therefore to rely on clear and predefined prohibitions. Yet, there
are difficulties in drafting a criminal offence that prohibits banks from growing
systemically important. The reason is that the way business is conducted at banks
which are deemed too big to fail does not differ from the business conduct of
smaller banks. It is simply the accumulation of transactions at a single financial
institution which makes the difference, but the relevant threshold cannot be
clearly defined ex ante. All of this indicates that the field of criminal law is unsuitable for preventing systemic risk.

---

[44] K Svatikova, 'Economic Criteria for Criminalization: Why Do We Need the Criminal Law?' (2009)
RILE Working Paper No 2008/12 www.ssrn.com/abstract=1150689 at 18. Svatikova uses the stigma
effect as a criterion to distinguish the use of criminal law from administrative law.
[45] For an overview of criteria that lead financial institutions to become systemically relevant, see
International Monetary Fund and the Bank for International Settlements, and the Financial Stability
Board, 'Guidance to Assess the Systemic Importance of Financial Institutions, Markets and
Instruments: Initial Consideration' (Report to the G-20 Finance Ministers and Central Bank
Governors, 2009), www.imf.org/external/np/g20/pdf/100109.pdf. See also N Tarashev, C Borio and
K Tsatsaronis, 'The Systemic Importance of Financial Institutions' (September 2009) *BIS Quarterly
Review* 75; M Brunnermeier, A Crockett, C Goodhart, A Persaud and H Shin, *The Fundamental
Principles of Financial Regulation* (London, Centre for Economic Policy Research, 2009) 13–23.
[46] See eg *Streletz, Kessler and Krenz v Germany* App no 34044/96, 35532/97 and 44801/98 (ECtHR,
22 March 2001) s 50 with further references.

Even though systemic risk is hard to define, this does not imply it cannot be regulated. Economists have identified the size of balance sheets, equity, and liquidity as variables that influence the systemic relevance of financial institutions.[47] Unlike insider trading or unsuitable investment advice, the variables are only sufficiently detrimental when they rise above or fall below certain thresholds. The regulator's task is to ensure that the relevant variables stay within an acceptable range that is subject to readjustment from time to time. There are different instruments for controlling variables that range from taxation to relative and absolute quantity regulation.

The softest approach is to levy a tax on variables. The so called bank levy for instance, charges a tax on either certain liabilities, on the balance sheet total or on risk-weighted assets.[48] A peculiar feature of these corrective taxes is that they shift the power to decide from the state onto the businesses. Corrective taxes increase the price of economic activities only, and do not place prohibitions on the activities. A regulatory agency does not decide whether a certain transaction is concluded or if a financial structure is permissible; the economic calculus alone provides bank managers with the incentives to go ahead or to stop.[49] If the externality in question is nonlinear – as is arguably the case where the systemic banks enjoy a funding advantage due to the implicit bail-out guarantee (which increases with the size of the bank)[50] – the steering effect can be intensified through the use of progressive tax rates.[51]

The next step is the use of relative quantity regulation.[52] Under relative quantity regulation, the legislator does not place absolute limits on an activity but obliges financial institutions to maintain certain ratios. Basel II and III are essentially about relative limits. But there are differences even within relative quantity regulation. To guarantee enforcement, it is crucial for the variables constituting the ratio be readily observable. Basel II sets the target standard ratio to 8 per cent of capital to assets, but the value of the assets is calculated not at face value but on a risk-weighted basis. Such an approach renders precisely tailored ratios for each asset. However, a

---

[47] See above n 45.

[48] For an overview of different models of bank levy see *n.a.*, 'Financial Resolution Arrangements to Strengthen Financial Stability: Bank Levies, Resolution Funds and Deposit Guarantee Schemes' (June 2011) ECB Financial Stability Review 149, 150 (table D.I). The bank levy was first brought forward by the IMF in a report for the G-20; see International Monetary Fund, 'A Fair and Substantial Contribution by the Financial Sector' (Final Report for the G-20, IMF 2010) www.imf.org/external/np/g20/pdf/ 062710b. pdf at 13–16.

[49] This concept of corrective taxation goes back to the seminal work, AC Pigou, *The Economics of Welfare*, 4th edn (London, Macmillan, 1932).

[50] See eg the model in M Keen, 'The Taxation and Regulation of Banks' (2011) IMF Working Paper 11/206 www.imf.org/external/pubs/ft/wp/2011/wp11206.pdf at 18.

[51] For a discussion of corrective taxes with nonlinear tax rates see L Kaplow and S Shavell, 'On the Superiority of Corrective Taxes to Quantity Regulation' (2002) 4 *American Law and Economics Review* 1 (the authors argue that where a single firm undertakes harmful activities, corrective taxation with nonlinear tax rates is superior to quantity regulation).

[52] The discussion of the relative merits of quantity regulation as compared to the usage of prices (a corrective tax can be seen as a price on an economic activity) goes back to ML Weitzman, 'Prices Vs. Quantities' (1974) 41 *The Review of Economic Studies* 477. In the context taxation and regulation of banks see Keen, 'The Taxation and Regulation of Banks' (n 50) 22–29.

huge scope of regulatory discretion is thereby introduced into the system, which might lead to loopholes. The zero risk-weight for EU Member States' sovereign bonds[53] is a telling example of a misguided political intervention causing a major regulatory loophole. Therefore, one of the aims of the new Basel III framework is to introduce complementary ratios based on objective measures like an overall leverage ratio or a liquidity coverage ratio.[54] Another differentiation can be introduced by employing graded ratios. In this vein, the Basel III framework contains plans to levy capital surcharges on systemically important financial institutions.[55]

The last step in controlling variables is absolute quantity regulation. While the infringement of capital ratios can be remedied by raising equity, the transgression of absolute quantity targets mandates enforcement action. In case of financial institutions growing too big to fail, this could mean a break-up once the size of a bank exceeds a pre-defined threshold, for example, a certain balance sheet total. Pursuant to section 121(a)(5) of the Dodd-Frank Act,[56] the Board of Governors of the Federal Reserve are granted the power to decide with a two-thirds majority whether to 'require the company to sell or otherwise transfer assets or off-balance-sheet items to unaffiliated entities' if it is necessary in the effort to mitigate a threat to the financial stability of the United States. A similar proposal has been endorsed by the Deutscher Juristentag,[57] but is not currently on any European reform agenda.

Finally, civil liability may play an important role in containing the excessive risk-taking behaviour of individual managers. Personal liability is an accepted and well-proven tool for inducing managers to internalise the external effects of their decisions. However, it is difficult to introduce a norm stipulating personal liability in situations where the size of a bank's balance sheet, equity, or liquidity exceeds certain thresholds. There is no direct and measurable harm which arises from the crossing of certain thresholds, but only an enormous increase in systemic risk. If this risk materialises in the form of bankruptcy or bail-out, the personal funds of nearly every manager will be only sufficient enough to cover a fraction of the resulting damage. Hence, civil liability might complement corrective taxation or capital regulation, but as a stand-alone measure, it is not suitable to deter banks from growing too big to fail.

---

[53] cf Directive (EC) 2006/48/EC of the European Parliament and of the Council of 14 June 2006 relating to the taking up and pursuit of the business of credit institutions (recast) [2006] OJ L177, 1 annex VI part 1 para 4. Even the new Article 114(4) of the Regulation (EU) No 575/2013 of the European Parliament and of the Council of 26 June 2013 on prudential requirements for credit institutions and investment firms and amending Regulation (EU) No 648/2012 [2013] OJ L176, 1 retains this problematic rule.

[54] Basel Committee on Banking Supervision, 'Basel III: A Global Regulatory Framework for More Resilient Banks and Banking systems' (Bank for International Settlements, June 2011) 4, 9.

[55] ibid 7.

[56] Dodd-Frank Wall Street Reform and Consumer Protection Act § 121(a)(5), 12 U.S.C. § 5331(a) (5) (2012).

[57] Resolution 4a of the Abteilung Öffentliches und Privates Wirtschaftsrecht, 68. Deutscher Juristentag Berlin 2010. See also D Zimmer, *Finanzmarktregulierung – Welche Regelungen empfehlen sich für den deutschen und europäischen Finanzsektor?, Gutachten G zum 68. Deutschen Juristentag* (Munich, CH Beck, 2010) 25–40. The Deutscher Juristentag is the Association of German Jurists, which meets biannually to discuss legal policy problems and to issue recommendations to the legislator.

2. Law Enforcement Agent

The second criterion for comparison is the agent of law enforcement, that is, the person or authority in charge of an enforcement mechanism. In this comparison, I shall focus on two key aspects: the difference between private and public agents of law enforcement, and the role assumed by courts.

a) Public v Private Enforcement

In all the examples previously discussed, that is, unsuitable investment advice, insider trading, and banks growing too big to fail, administrative law mechanisms are enforced by a financial supervisory body like the Financial Conduct Authority (FCA) and the Prudential Regulation Authority (PRA) in the UK or the Bundesanstalt für Finanzdienstleistungsaufsicht (BaFin) in Germany. These authorities supervise investment firms and securities markets and enforce prudential banking regulation like Basel II. As public bodies, financial supervisors are generally required to prosecute all cases of law infringements. Yet there are exemptions intended particularly to capture cases where the law is over-inclusive, that is, its wording covers cases which – according to the spirit of the law – should be left unregulated. In these cases, public supervisors may abstain from enforcing the law, while private persons who are under the incentive of monetary compensation tend to make a claim nevertheless.[58] In other cases, private persons may abstain from enforcing their claim although the pursuit of enforcement would be beneficial from a societal point of view. The danger of over- or under-enforcement arising from this 'discretion' private parties enjoy, must however be contrasted with the higher rate of detection. Private persons will normally notice when they suffer losses due to misleading investment advice,[59] while public authorities will only detect a fraction of all law infringements.

Taxes are regularly administered by fiscal authorities that lack special knowledge of financial markets; however, this is counterbalanced by the lack of discretionary power in tax law. Also, the use of tax returns heavily reduces the need for investigative efforts by the tax authorities. Yet, to ensure taxation yields a corrective effect, the possibility of tax evasion must be minimised either through the taxable event being highly visible or by way of employing additional criminal investigators.

Public prosecutors also lack specialised knowledge of financial markets but by virtue of the procedural guarantees of criminal law,[60] they are required to conduct extensive investigations.[61] Therefore, criminal enforcement will be least stringent.

---

[58] L Klöhn, 'Private versus Public Enforcement of Laws: a Law & Economics Perspective' in R Schulze (ed), *Compensation of Private Losses* (Munich, Sellier European Law Publishers, 2011) 179, 194.

[59] See Shavell, 'The Optimal Structure of Law Enforcement' (n 24) 267.

[60] These are especially warranted because of the stigma effect that is associated with a criminal conviction. See above section III(1)(b).

[61] However see Klöhn, 'Private versus Public Enforcement of Laws' (n 58) 188. Klöhn argues that a centralised public enforcement system like the public prosecutors can achieve economies of scale. It is, though, unclear whether these advantages outweigh the extra costs associated with criminal investigations as compared to standards of proof in civil litigation or administrative proceedings.

b) The Role of the Courts

Courts are central to the enforcement of legal regimes. Sometimes courts and regulatory agencies are contrasted with one another. This is based on the assumption that agencies themselves have the power to regulate, while private parties have to utilise courts in order to secure their rights.[62] This setting is, however, incomplete in two regards: First, private parties can also settle their claims outside court and very often do so. Since the result of such negotiations will be determined by the belief of both parties how a court might decide their case, this is still an effect of the regulatory function of civil liability.[63] Second, regulators' actions generally can also be challenged in court. While it is true that many administrative cases never reach courts, there is at least the theoretic possibility of applying for the judicial review of agencies' decisions.

Depending on the enforcement mechanism, cases of regulatory infringement may be decided by criminal courts, civil courts or – in continental Europe – specialised tax or administrative courts. From a law enforcement perspective, these differences matter because they have important implications for the procedural and evidence standards. The burden of proof and the standard of review employed by courts might prove decisive for the effectiveness of an enforcement instrument.[64] Instruments of criminal law for instance, might turn out to be very ineffective in financial markets regulation if high procedural standards aggravate the proof of insider trading or market manipulation. Also, the prospect of settlement – either in or outside court – factors into the effectiveness of an enforcement regime.

3. Complexity and Information

Complexity and information are also criteria for comparing enforcement instruments. 'Complexity' has been defined as a function of information costs and bounded rationality.[65] In the following, I will discuss several elements of complexity. Thereby I will try to account for the different dimensions that have to be taken into account within single regulatory instruments and when using a combination of multiple instruments. Then I will compare the information needs that are triggered by using particular regulatory instruments.

---

[62] For an extensive comparison see R Posner, 'Regulation (Agencies) versus Litigation (Courts)' in D Kessler (ed), *Regulation versus Litigation: Perspectives from Economics and Law* (Chicago, Chicago University Press, 2011) 11. Others argue that the comparison should be between regulation by ex post litigation and regulation by ex ante rule making, see F Schauer and R Zeckhauser, 'The Trouble with Cases' in D Kessler (ed), *Regulation versus Litigation: Perspectives from Economics and Law* (Chicago, Chicago University Press, 2011) 47, 49 with fn. 7.

[63] See R Cooter, R Marks and R Mnookin, 'Bargaining in the Shadow of the Law: A Testable Model of Strategic Behavior' (1982) 11 *Journal of Legal Studies* 225.

[64] See L Kaplow, 'Burden of Proof' (2012) 121 *Yale Law Journal* 738 (Kaplow gives an extensive analysis of the burden of proof's implications on social welfare).

[65] D Awrey, 'Complexity, Innovation, and the Regulation of Modern Financial Markets' (2012) *Harvard Business Law Review* 235, 242–45.

a) Single v Multi-variable Instruments

The first aspect of a regulatory instrument which affects its complexity pertains to the number of variables it is able to process. The more variables an instrument can control the more complex the regulatory functions it can perform.

Corrective taxation is an enforcement mechanism of very low complexity. It can only handle one or a few variables which constitute the tax base.[66] Examples are corporate income or single balance sheet items that can be easily assessed on a quantitative basis. The bank levy is based on the assumption that the systemic relevance and interconnectedness of banks can be measured with regards to certain liabilities, notably short-term funding. If the legislator fails to correctly define systemic risk however, a levy based on incorrect variables could lead to serious market distortions and even exacerbate the problem of systemic risk.[67] The utility of corrective taxation decreases as the number of variables increase. Therefore taxation is unsuitable for complex tasks like deterring unsuitable investment advice. The suitability of investment recommendations depends on a multitude of factors that are connected to the individual investor and the financial instrument in question. It is therefore impossible on a practical level, to draft a tax base that considers all these factors ex ante, that is, at an abstract and generalised level.

The problem of choosing the correct tax rate is also related. Even in cases where there are few variables – the tax base is defined correctly – the desired steering effect hinges on the selection of the correct tax rate. If the tax rate is set too low, it will not deter effectively the socially undesirable accumulation of risk and if it is set too high, there will be hampering of desirable economic activity.[68] Moreover, there are cases where every market participant has an idiosyncratic utility function. This is true for insider trading, where the excess return due to the informational advantage depends on the individual circumstances of the particular case. While it might be theoretically possible to set nonlinear tax rates that capture many of these situations,[69] in practice it will be impossible to identify the correct progressive tax rate.

The field of criminal law is also restricted to controlling only a small number of variables. This is mainly due to the requirement that criminal offences must be clearly defined in the law, a point discussed earlier.[70] Due to this necessity, norms stipulating criminal offences must exhibit a high degree of foreseeability. This sets natural limits on the number of factors guiding the desired behaviour.

By contrast, legal instruments in the fields of administrative law and civil liability can handle multiple variables. Because courts and public supervisors are able to develop customised rules for a multitude of situations, the extent to which private

---

[66] Shavell, 'Corrective Taxation versus Liability' (n 33) S255–56.

[67] See Edwards, '(Systemic) Risk and Taxation' (n 18) 377–78.

[68] For a detailed analysis of the Government's problems in implementing a corrective tax see RH Coase, 'The Problem of Social Cost' (1960) 3 *Journal of Law & Economics* 1, 39–42.

[69] cf Kaplow and Shavell, 'On the Superiority of Corrective Taxes to Quantity Regulation' (n 51) 7–10.

[70] See above section III(1)(c).

and administrative law can accommodate circumstances idiosyncratic to particular cases significantly exceeds the abilities of tax and criminal law.

b) Regulatory Mix and Unintended Consequences

The complexity greatly increases when different regulatory instruments are combined to prevent the same harm from occurring. First, there is concern over how the instruments may become redundant or that the joint impact of both instruments may lead to over-deterrence.[71] Secondly, a problem arises when the regulatory mix yields unintended consequences.

Systemic risk regulation is a good example. The German and the UK bank levy provide banks with incentives to change from short-term debt to long-term finance, especially equity. But it begs the question: what are the consequences of a bank shifting its funding from debt to equity? In all likelihood, this will lead to an asset substitution effect:[72] Basel II works like a scale, the more equity a bank possesses, the more risky assets it may hold according to the capital adequacy rules. Increasing equity lowers a bank's leverage and thereby negatively influences its rate of return. In order to stay profitable, the bank has to increase the risk on the asset side of the balance sheet.

Theoretically, this kind of phenomenon is explained by the different legal instruments which lack a full overlap in regulatory goals despite being partially aimed at deterring the same harm. These different legal goals can be played off against one another such that the realisation of one hampers the adherence to the other.[73]

Unintended consequences do not arise only from cases where multiple instruments are used. Here again systemic risk regulation provides an instructive example. The German bank levy is not based on the consolidated balance sheet but assesses each corporate entity separately. This makes it possible to halve the levy base simply by splitting the company into two. Since the levy's rate is progressive, such a split would have a major impact on the total charge due but – depending on the group structure – does not imply a necessary risk reduction.

c) Information Needs

These examples of complexity point to the underlying problem of information. Legislators and the law enforcement agents require quite different kind of information, depending on which law enforcement mechanism they are employing.

Corrective taxation features the highest ex ante informational requirements as it sets up an enforcement concept of its own. The tax base and rate must be devised in such a manner that incentivises the targeted industry to make business decisions which are optimal for a firm as well as for society. Therefore, in the

---

[71] These problems are discussed by John Vella, 'Regulatory Choice: Observations on the Recent Experience with Corrective Taxes in the Financial Sector', ch 11 of this volume.

[72] M Devereux, 'Will the Bank Levy Meet Its Objectives?' (2011) 1 *British Tax Review* 33.

[73] L Katz, 'A Theory of Loopholes' (2010) 39 *Journal of Legal Studies* 1, 11–25.

drafting process a legislator requires extensive information on the nature of an externality (in order to develop a suitable tax base) and the extent or the damage caused respectively (in order to set the optimal tax rate).

A legislator drafting administrative law provisions also needs detailed information about the part of the financial industry which is going to be regulated. This is mainly due to the (constitutional) requirement that administrative laws need to be clearly stipulated and predictable.[74] Regulation by means of administrative law thus has the effect of homogenising and thereby standardising behaviour.[75] Therefore, legislators are required to reflect carefully when drafting administrative rules because of their anticipated impact on business behaviour. Regulatory frameworks like Basel III are drafted by banking experts, leading to unsurpassed degrees of complexity.

Civil liability and criminal law rules by contrast erect comparatively simple regulatory standards and shift the complexity onto the judge handling a given case. The questions as to whether somebody indeed traded on inside information or whether a particular piece of investment advice was unsuitable may raise complicated issues. When employing criminal or civil liability regimes, these problems are however reduced to questions of fact. Since the judge need only deal with the problems at hand, this strongly reduces complexity and information needs. Albeit such a strategy runs the risk of losing consistency with the regulatory approach. The legal rules devised by case law tend to satisfy the specific demands of the decided case rather than the necessities of the regulated area as a whole.[76]

IV. Cost-Benefit Analysis

Having compared colour, sweetness and juiciness of apples and oranges, the decisive question is of course: which is better in absolute terms? I am unable to fully answer this question. However, the relationship between an instrument's effects and the input required to set up the instrument seems central to the overall assessment. A classification of enforcement instruments according to their cost-benefit ratios might help legislators when drafting new provisions, but might also serve courts as a basis for judging the proportionality of employing a particular legal instrument to a given regulatory problem. In the following, I will thus try to develop some preliminary ideas about an overall cost-benefit analysis of the different enforcement instruments.

---

[74] In German law, this is called 'Bestimmtheitsgebot'. According to this requirement, the persons concerned must be enabled to understand the law and to align their behaviour with the legal requirements; see *Bundesverfassungsgericht*, BVerfGE 108, 186, 235.

[75] A Shleifer, 'Efficient Regulation' in D Kessler (ed), *Regulation versus Litigation: Perspectives from Economics and Law* (Chicago, Chicago University Press, 2011) 27, 38.

[76] See Schauer and Zeckhauser, 'The Trouble with Cases' (n 62) 61–64.

1. Benefits-Side

The benefits-side of the scale consists of the effectiveness of an instrument. The effectiveness of an instrument can be described as measuring the extent to which it achieves its intended objectives.[77] The ultimate goal of any law enforcement instrument is to induce a high level of compliance. But since an individual's motives for complying with the law are not observable, the relationship between enforcement threats and compliance cannot be tested directly. Therefore, the analysis shall be confined to those aspects that are solely rooted in the legal process, that is, to the effectiveness of the enforcement as such.

In this respect, administrative law and civil liability lead the field, as they both generate outcomes which are specifically tailored to individual cases. Financial supervisors as well as civil courts can consider all circumstances of a given case. This reduces the problem of over- and under-inclusiveness of norms and permits optimal implementation of the regulatory goals. When comparing both, civil liability enjoys the advantage of a higher detection rate, while administrative law yields speedy results.

Instruments of tax law by contrast are very inflexible. They lack the ability to react to special circumstances and hence, are in danger of setting severe disincentives in times of crisis. It might be true that rapid adjustment is not only difficult in case of corrective taxation, but also for quantity regulation.[78] But the enforcement concept of corrective taxation completely relies on the incentives emanating from statutory law, while administrative law is concretised by financial supervisors, who detect market turmoil quickly and are able to react more swiftly than any legislator could.

As an enforcement mechanism, criminal law is the least effective. The threat of a criminal conviction may be indispensable in many cases to induce compliance. Yet when looking at the actual enforcement, only a small fraction of all violations will lead to a conviction. This is due to the high procedural burdens and the limited resources of public prosecutors.

2. Costs-Side

On the costs-side of the calculation, one may distinguish between: the cost of law making, the financial industry's compliance cost and the cost of law enforcement.[79]

The cost of law making is especially high in administrative law and taxation. Instruments like Basel III or the bank levy already embody a complete enforce-

---

[77] L Salamon, 'The New Governance and the Tools of Public Action: An Introduction' in L Salamon (ed), *The Tools of Government* (Oxford, Oxford University Press 2002) 1, 23.

[78] cf Kaplow and Shavell, 'On the Superiority of Corrective Taxes to Quantity Regulation' (n 51) 6.

[79] Salamon, 'The New Governance' (n 77) 23.

ment concept. Therefore, the main input takes place at the stage of law making. By contrast, norms stipulating civil or criminal liability are much easier to draft. The standards they set are often only general. Criminal law in particular seldom aims to comprehensively regulate a whole part of the financial industry. Rather, it is employed to fill regulatory gaps in cases where people would otherwise have strong incentives to break the law.

The industry's compliance costs depend on the concrete instrument. Yet in generalised analysis, it appears that administrative regulation and civil liability will entail high compliance costs. This is the downside of the instruments' specificity. Implementation expenditures will increase as regulators are increasingly able to target single players in the financial markets. By contrast, corrective taxes – due to their simple structure – should often necessitate few adjustments. While the financial impact of these adjustments might turn out to be severe (like a change in a bank's finance structure), this impact does not count towards implementation cost; it should result from the implementation of the primary legal rule and independently of the way this rule is enforced. Finally, criminal law simply demands the implementation of a basic business organisation. Its main impact should lie at the level of individual behaviour and should not in principle, affect firms as such.

The law enforcement component of criminal law and administrative law is very costly for the state. The state must establish agencies and employ public servants. The administration of corrective taxes however does not require higher amounts of investment. Taxpayers will be forced to file tax returns that often include information relevant to tax calculation. Finally, civil liability involves only moderate costs for public budgets, as litigants bear most of the costs themselves.[80] Also, it allows for out-of-court settlements, so that public costs may not be accrued at all.

3. Result

After weighing all these aspects, we can now answer the question: which option is more functional, apples or oranges?

All in all, while civil liability is limited in its scope of application,[81] it exhibits the best cost-benefit ratio. It can be used to achieve highly precise outcomes but places only moderate costs on public budgets. Instruments of criminal law seem very inefficient. Such instruments are extremely costly and can be mainly justified by the voluntary compliance they induce. However, the deterrent effect of criminal sanctions may be overestimated given the actual detection rate of financial crimes. Arguably only a fraction of white-collar crimes are detected and

---

[80] Yet, it is sometimes argued that if private litigation is subsidised at all, this might lead to an excessive level of litigation, see Klöhn, 'Private versus Public Enforcement of Laws' (n 58) 196. While this danger is certainly real, other enforcement alternatives feature similar problems; eg public choice problems (like the ambition to maximise one's own budget) might lead supervisory agencies to engage in excessive enforcement actions.

[81] See above section III(1)(b).

prosecuted. The fields of administrative law and corrective taxation are considered the second best regulatory options. They exhibit high costs, but also often render valuable enforcement results. Hence, the return from using such instruments must be assessed on a case-by-case basis.

V. Conclusion

In conclusion, a comprehensive overview of law enforcement mechanisms is still outstanding. However, the current findings of comparison might be of use next time one enters the 'fruit shop' of financial market regulation.

The good performance of civil liability may give reason to consider private enforcement alternatives. Most cases involving investors, like many parts of capital market regulation, allow for private law remedies. This includes subjects like market manipulation or misleading capital market information, where the European Commission has detected law enforcement deficiencies.[82]

I also suggest against heavy reliance on corrective taxation. Corrective taxes are inflexible enforcement instruments which can be easily avoided when poorly drafted. A financial transaction tax, for example as currently discussed in France and Germany, is a weak regulatory instrument.[83] Yet if properly designed, it may raise significant tax revenue. Also, it may relieve public outrage over the financial sector. And these are – even though not regulatory in nature – also honourable goals of legislation.

---

[82] See European Commission (n 4) 7 and (n 7) 9.

[83] For a critical assessment of the recent European plans to introduce a financial transaction tax, see J Vella, 'The Financial Transaction Tax Debate: Some Questionable Claims' (2012) 47 *Intereconomics* 90.

11

Regulatory Choice: Observations on the Recent Experience with Corrective Taxes in the Financial Sector

I. Introduction

Despite being well-known instruments in the regulatory toolbox, corrective taxes have been traditionally restricted to a few fields. Before the onset of the recent financial crisis, little attention, for example, had been given to these taxes in the field of financial regulation. The financial crisis marked a significant change in this respect as it sparked widespread interest, both academic and practical, in the application of this regulatory tool in the field of financial regulation. Indeed, in the past few years various corrective taxes on the financial sector have been proposed to achieve a wide range of regulatory goals, including: tackling remuneration practices in the banking sector which are thought to lead to excessive risk taking, addressing concerns with banks' leverage and liquidity, and creating disincentives for transactions which are thought not to add to the efficiency of markets. A number of these taxes have been adopted; some on a temporary basis, such as the UK tax on bank bonuses, and some on a permanent basis, such as the bank levies introduced by 13 EU Member States.

The use of corrective taxes in the field of financial regulation is an interesting development that requires careful examination. Alexander Hellgardt's chapter in this volume contributes to this examination by setting out a broad theoretical framework to evaluate regulatory choice in the financial sector. It provides illuminating insights into the strengths and weaknesses of tax as a regulatory tool. This chapter contributes three observations on the recent experience with corrective taxes in the financial sector. These observations are an attempt at drawing some immediate and practical lessons from this new development. Undoubtedly, many

---

[1] I would like to thank Michael Devereux and Alexander Hellgardt for helpful discussions and comments. The usual disclaimers apply.

further lessons will be drawn in the years ahead. They can be added to the theoretical considerations involved in choosing between different regulatory options to provide a more complete picture of regulatory choice.

The first observation is that care must be taken when corrective taxes are adopted concomitantly with regulation seeking to achieve the same regulatory goals. As shall be seen, this is because one instrument can affect the other. Secondly, whilst some taxes may purport to have both regulatory and non-regulatory goals, a careful look at the design or calibration of the tax can suggest that in reality the regulatory goals are only of secondary importance. Indeed, the specific design of a tax or the setting of its rates might blunt its corrective function. Thirdly, regulatory goals can be employed as powerful arguments when making the case for a tax. Worryingly, in the recent crisis, a regulatory goal was used to 'sell' a controversial tax despite the uncertainty surrounding the goal itself.

II. Using Tax and Regulatory Instruments Concomitantly

Thinking about regulatory choice requires weighing up one instrument against another. In practice, however, the question might not be which of two instruments ought to be chosen, but whether an instrument ought to be introduced given the existence of another. In such cases, care must be taken as to whether and how the two instruments interact. The bank levies introduced in the aftermath of the crisis provide an interesting example.

Banks tend to have high leverage ratios, thereby making them inherently fragile institutions. This fragility increases the likelihood of failure, and bank failure, as has become painfully clear in recent years, produces considerable negative externalities. For this reason, bank capital has been subject to regulation for a number of years primarily through the Basel Accords which are agreed at an international level by the Basel Committee on Banking Supervision (BCBS) and implemented through national legislation.[2] This regulation requires banks to hold a certain amount of capital against their risk-weighted assets. Capital is defined rather broadly, and includes instruments that fall into categories of decreasing loss-absorbency,[3] thus ranging from equity to subordinated debt.

Banks' excessive leverage can also be addressed through a corrective tax. Whilst regulation lays down the amount of capital which banks are required to hold relative to their risk-weighted assets, a tax could be imposed on banks' liabilities thus giving them an incentive to hold more equity (which is the most loss-absorbing form of capital). As both regulation and tax could be employed to achieve the same

---

[2] The Committee is made up of 27 Member States. The first Basel Accord (Basel I) was produced in 1988 (and amended in 1996). Basel II was produced in 2004. For further information see www.bis.org.
[3] Core Tier 1, non-core Tier 1 and Tier 2.

goal, the first question to ask is which of the two should be chosen.[4] Despite being of considerable theoretical interest, this is not a choice that arises in practice. Indeed, in the aftermath of the crisis, as it transpired that existing regulation was inadequate, it was clear that capital regulation would be improved but not abandoned in favour of a tax.[5] The decision to be made was not whether a corrective tax should replace capital regulation but whether a tax should be added to the regulation.

In many countries the decision was taken to introduce the corrective tax in addition to the regulation. In the EU, 13 Member States introduced the corrective tax in question, known as a bank levy, and others are expected to follow. These bank levies differ in terms of tax base, rates and even objectives, however they generally follow the model proposed by the International Monetary Fund (IMF) in its report of June 2010 to the G20.[6]

Bank levies are not exclusively corrective. Indeed, as shall be argued below, there are reasons to believe that, at least in some instances, the corrective function was only of secondary importance. Setting that to one side for the time being, if both instruments are in place simultaneously the question then arises as to how they interact.

It has been noted that the introduction of a bank levy, given the existence of capital requirements, could produce an asset substitution effect; meaning that the ratio of capital to total assets increases but the ratio of capital to risk weighted assets remains the same.[7] This requires some further explanation. The Basel rules require banks to hold a certain percentage of capital against their assets, however assets are weighted according to risk, so that the capital banks are required to hold increases with the riskiness of the asset. Viewed in another way, for a given amount of capital, a bank can hold a certain amount of risk-weighted assets. If a bank levy is successful in incentivising banks to hold more capital, that would produce 'spare capacity' to hold riskier assets. They can thus respond by substituting assets, which are low risk with others which are high risk.

The UK bank levy can be used to provide a more concrete example.[8] The levy encourages banks away from riskier funding by having the full levy imposed on

---

[4] See eg IMF, 'Financial Sector Taxation: The IMF's Report to the G-20 and Background Material' (June 2010), Appendix 3, available at www.imf.org/external/np/g20/pdf/062710b.pdf and M Keen, 'The Taxation and Regulation of Banks', IMF Working Paper, WP/11/206 (August 2011) available at www.imf.org/external/pubs/cat/longres.aspx?sk=25196.0. The websites referred to in this chapter were accessed on 12 June 2012.

[5] Basel Committee on Banking Supervision, 'Basel III: A global regulatory framework for more resilient banks and banking systems', December 2010 (rev June 2011) available at www.bis.org/publ/bcbs189.pdf.

[6] IMF, 'Financial Sector Taxation' (n 4).

[7] European Economy Advisory Group, 'Taxation and Regulation of the financial sector' in EEAG, *The EEAG Report on the European Economy 2011* (CESifo, Munich 2011) 147, available at www.cesifo-group.de/ifoHome/policy/EEAG-Report/Archive/EEAG_Report_2011.html. The initial results of on-going empirical work suggest that asset substitution can be observed following the introduction of bank levies in EU Member States. M Devereux, N Johannesen and J Vella, 'Can Taxes Tame the Banks? Evidence from the European Bank Levies' (2013), mimeo, Oxford University Centre for Business Taxation.

[8] The bank levy was introduced through Schedule 19 of Finance Act 2011 and SI 2011/1785. For more information see HMRC, *Bank Levy Manual*, available at www.hmrc.gov.uk/budget-updates/autumn-tax/bank-levy-manual.htm.

'riskier' sources of funding, with 'less risky' sources not subject to the levy or only subject to a lower rate. Technically, this is achieved by imposing the levy on total chargeable equity and liabilities then subjecting certain liabilities to a lower rate or excluding them altogether. Tier 1 capital (which includes equity and is the most loss-absorbing category of capital) is excluded from the levy thus giving banks an incentive to hold such capital. If this incentive is effective and banks hold more Tier 1 capital, they could also respond by increasing the risk profile of their assets by substituting zero or low risk-weighted assets with higher risk-weighted assets up till the point allowed under the Basel requirements. If this is done, their Tier 1 to total assets ratio increases but their Tier 1 to risk-weighted assets ratio remains the same. At first glance this suggests that if banks respond in this manner, they would not be safer despite having increased their Tier 1 capital. On the other hand, there are known deficiencies in the risk-weighting procedures.[9] For example, certain government debt has a zero risk-weighting, a regulatory decision recently exposed as fundamentally flawed. To this extent, increasing the ratio of Tier 1 capital to total assets whilst the ratio of Tier 1 capital to risk-weighted assets remains unchanged, might not be a bad outcome. Indeed, this is one of the reasons motivating the introduction of a leverage ratio in Basel III, even if it is equally susceptible to the asset substitution effect described here.[10]

III. How Seriously is the Corrective Objective Pursued?

Taxes can have multiple objectives, only one of which is corrective. The main taxes on the financial sector proposed in the aftermath of the crisis have multiple objectives. For example, the Financial Transaction Tax (FTT) proposed by the EU Commission has the corrective objective of creating disincentives for transactions which are thought not to add to the efficiency of markets. However, it is also meant to raise revenue from the financial sector, to avoid the fragmentation of the internal market and to pave the way towards a global introduction of the tax.[11]

Taxes which have a plurality of objectives, only some of which are corrective, merit careful examination as this might reveal that the corrective objectives are only of secondary importance. The experience with the UK bank levy is instructive in this respect.

As seen above, the UK bank levy has the objective of encouraging banks 'to move away from riskier funding' but it is also meant to 'ensure that banks make a

---

[9] M Hellwig, 'Capital Regulation after the Crisis: Business as Usual?' Working Paper Series of the Max Planck Institute for Research on Collective Goods 2010_31, Max Planck Institute for Research on Collective Goods, 2010, available at www.coll.mpg.de/pdf_dat/2010_31online.pdf.

[10] Basel Committee on Banking Supervision, 'Basel III: A global regulatory framework for more resilient banks and banking systems' (n 5) 4.

[11] European Commission, 'Proposal for a Council Directive on a common system of financial transaction tax and amending Directive 2008/7/EC' COM(2011) 594 final, 28 September 2011, available at www.ec.europa.eu/taxation_customs/taxation/other_taxes/financial_sector/index_en.htm.

contribution that reflects the potential risk to the UK financial system and wider economy from bank failures and consequent loss of consumer and investor confidence.'[12] This objective can be interpreted in at least two ways. One interpretation holds that the levy is a payment for the implicit bail-out guarantee enjoyed by some banks. The consultation document on the bank levy rejects this first interpretation,[13] due to moral hazard concerns. An alternative, albeit less sophisticated interpretation, views the tax as simply ensuring that the banking sector makes a larger contribution to the public purse. The evidence given by the Chancellor of the Exchequer to the Treasury Select Committee favours the second interpretation:

> [T]he other reason, [for the introduction of the levy] to be absolutely frank, was for reasons of equity. Asking the general population to accept a VAT rise, asking them to accept that there were going to be changes to welfare eligibility and the like, doing these things is a difficult thing for any government to do but I thought it would be totally inappropriate not to ask the banking sector to make a contribution as well. I think it is appropriate to have a tax on banks and I have tried to do it in a way that follows international best practice. When it is fully operational the bank levy is going to raise £2.5 billion and we made it clear that we are targeting a revenue sum rather than a particular rate because we think that is an appropriate contribution that balances fairness with the competitiveness of the UK banking sector. That sum of money, when it is put alongside some of the impacts of capital requirement changes, is relatively small.[14]

Apart from shedding light on the meaning of the second objective, this quote is interesting for our purposes because of its explanation of the manner in which the rates of the levy were set. For a tax to produce the desired corrective effect, not only must it be designed with care, but its rates must also be set at the right level. This does not appear to have been done in the UK. A political decision was taken to raise £2.5 billion, and then, given the tax base, the rates were set by working backwards from that revenue target.

The target sum of £2.5 billion is also interesting. It is here described as a sum which is thought to balance fairness with the competitiveness of the UK banking sector. A cynic might note that this sum is just higher than the net amount raised by the one-off bank payroll tax introduced by the previous (Labour) Government. By raising this sum through the bank levy, the Conservative–Liberal Democrat Government, put itself in good stead to counter criticism that it was being 'softer' on banks.[15]

---

[12] HM Treasury, *Bank Levy: a consultation* (July 2010) para 1.8, available at www.hm-treasury.gov.uk/d/consult_bank_levy_condoc.pdf.

[13] ibid para 1.9.

[14] HC 350 2010/11 Qs270, 272 (Ev 39-40).

[15] The initial proposal, laid out in the June Budget of 2010, to stagger the introduction of the levy was abandoned on 8 February 2011, when the Chancellor announced that the lower rates envisaged for 2011 would not be continued thus raising a further £800 million. The decision was officially justified on the grounds that the banks' economic performance had picked up, however, it was widely seen as a political move by the Chancellor as the announcement was made on the day he was to face the new, and more pugnacious Shadow Chancellor, Ed Balls. See G Parker, 'Politics helps illuminate Osborne's dawn raid' *Financial Times* (London, 9 February 2011).

The lesson from this observation thus is that even if the promoters of a tax claim that it has a corrective objective, one has to look carefully at its design and the way its rates are set, to determine how seriously the corrective objective is being pursued.

IV. The Use of Regulatory Goals to Make the Case for a Tax

It might be thought that little help is required to advance the case for a tax on the financial sector at a time of sustained and deep public anger towards the sector. However, in the face of industry opposition and justifiable concerns about the possible negative effects on the economy, being able to appeal to the corrective effects of a proposed tax can be of significant political utility. Of itself, this is not a matter of concern. If revenue is required, designing a tax which produces a desirable corrective effect, and hence a double dividend, can only be welcome. However, concern can arise in at least two scenarios. The first is if a regulatory goal is relied upon heavily in advancing the case for the tax but then is not pursued seriously. The second is if a corrective function that is given considerable importance in making the case for the tax turns out to be of questionable foundation. The current debate over the FTT provides an example of the second scenario.[16]

In the aftermath of the financial crisis, the EU Commission decided that the financial sector should pay a substantial contribution to public finance. The question remained as to which approach was best suited for these purposes.[17] The Commission examined a number of options, and despite an early preference for a Financial Activities Tax (FAT) over an FTT,[18] it eventually proposed an EU-wide FTT.[19] This proposal proved extremely divisive. A number of Member States, headed by Germany and France were strongly in favour of it, whilst others, headed by the UK, were strongly opposed to it. The required unanimity in favour of the proposal could not be achieved and, therefore, at the time of writing, the sub-group of Member States in favour of the tax are seeking to adopt the tax through

---

[16] The author considered this issue in J Vella, 'The Financial Transaction Tax Debate: Some Questionable Claims' (2012) 47 *Intereconomics* 90.

[17] House of Lords, EU Economic and Financial Affairs and International Trade Sub-Committee, 'Financial Transaction Tax, Oral and Written Evidence' 248, available at www.parliament.uk/documents/lords-committees/eu-sub-com-a/FinancialTransactionTax/FTTFINALWeb.pdf.

[18] European Commission, 'Communication from the Commission to the European Parliament, the Council, the European Economic and Social Committee and the Committee of the Regions – Taxation of the Financial Sector' COM(2010) 549 final, 7 October 2010, 8, available at www.eurlex.europa.eu/LexUriServ/LexUriServ.do?uri=COM:2010:0549:FIN:EN:PDF.

[19] European Commission, 'Proposal for a Council Directive on a common system of financial transaction tax and amending Directive 2008/7/EC' (n 11).

the Enhanced Co-Operation procedure.[20] The debate thus rages on. Throughout the debate there have also been passionately held positions amongst several interest groups. A number of NGOs have been campaigning vigorously for an FTT for many years, but industry participants and representatives are resolute in their opposition to the tax. In the midst of such a heated debate, with deeply entrenched positions on either side, a powerful argument in favour of one's position can help to tilt the balance. The FTT's corrective function has undoubtedly been employed instrumentally to this end by the Commission and other supporters of the tax.

The Commission's original proposal explains that one of the goals of the proposed FTT is 'to create appropriate disincentives for transactions that do not enhance the efficiency of financial markets thereby complementing regulatory measures aimed at avoiding future crises.'[21] High-frequency trading (HFT) is the primary target here. Therefore, the basic thrust of the argument is that by adopting the FTT, HFT will be reduced and, consequently, so will the probability of a future crisis. This is a compelling argument at a time when the painful consequences of a crisis are being felt and, in fact, proponents of the FTT have employed the argument repeatedly. Commissioner Šemeta, for example, argued that:

> a second objective [of the FTT] is to discourage unwarranted and leveraged transactions such as high frequency trading which inflate market volumes in all segments. This should complement regulatory measures and expose financial market actors to price signals.[22]

In one of the series of newspaper articles published in different Member States, presumably to sway public opinion, he argued:

> [T]he economic case [for an FTT] is even clearer when one factors in the FTT's potential to discourage some forms of socially useless and high-risk trading, and *therefore to help prevent future crises.* (Emphasis added.)[23]

In explaining to the EU Sub-Committee of the House of Lords, the Commission's decision to favour an FTT over an FAT, Commissioner Šemeta identified two favourable factors, one of which was the ability of the FTT to deal with HFT.[24]

Some pushed this corrective function even further. A report commissioned by the Socialists and Democrats in the European Parliament argued that 'reducing High Frequency Trading could actually have *a positive long term effect on growth,*

---

[20] European Commission, 'Commission Proposal for a Council Directive implementing enhanced cooperation in the area of financial transaction tax', COM(2013) 71 final of February 14, 2013. See J Englisch, J Vella and A Yevgenyeva, 'The Financial Transaction Tax Proposal Under the Enhanced Cooperation Procedure: Legal and Practical Considerations' (2013) 2 *British Tax Review* 223.

[21] ibid 2.

[22] A Šemeta, 'Financial Transactions Tax: The Way Ahead' Meeting of Members of the Finance and Fiscal Committees in the Danish Parliament (Copenhagen, 19 March 2012), speech 12/196, available at www.europa.eu/rapid/pressReleasesAction.do?reference=SPEECH/12/196.

[23] A Šemeta, 'Rebalancing the Financial Transactions tax debate' *The Telegraph* (London, 9 February 2012). The article is available at www.telegraph.co.uk/finance/newsbysector/banksandfinance/9072297/Rebalancing-the-financial-transactions-tax-debate.html.

[24] House of Lords, EU Economic and Financial Affairs and International Trade Sub-Committee, 'Financial Transaction Tax, Oral and Written Evidence' (n 17) 248.

given that it could reduce systemic risk and thus the likelihood of crises' (emphasis added).[25] Again, this is a compelling argument at a time when the economies of many EU Member States are flat-lining and some are even in recession.

The Commission and other supporters of the FTT have relied heavily on this regulatory objective in making the case for this controversial tax. It is thus disconcerting to note that the Commission itself appears to acknowledge the questionable foundations of this objective. In the Impact Assessment it prepared to accompany its original FTT proposal, the Commission noted that 'the empirical economic literature is still *rather inconclusive* on effects from this trading form in terms of increased volatility or price deviations' (emphasis added).[26] In a consultation document on the review of the Markets in Financial Instruments Directive (MiFID), the Commission noted '[e]xisting evidence is *inconclusive* about the impact of HFT on market efficiency' (emphasis added).[27] Indeed, some studies have found that HFT improved market efficiency through tighter spreads and increased liquidity.[28]

The point here is not that HFT does not raise legitimate concerns. The flash crash of 6 May 2010 was a warning call that must be heeded and it is imperative that systems and processes are in place to address these concerns. In fact, this is being done at an EU level by the European Securities and Markets Authority through its guidelines and by the Commission through its revision of the MiFID. The point here is that the evidence on the effects of HFT is inconclusive.

After a review of the existing literature on the impact of computer trading (of which HFT is a subset) on liquidity, price efficiency/discovery and transaction costs, the Final Project Report on *The Future of Computer Trading in Financial Markets* concludes:

> CBT (computer based trading) is now the reality in asset markets. Technology has allowed new participants to enter, new trading methods to arise and even new market structures to evolve. Much of what has transpired in markets is for the good: liquidity

---

[25] S Griffith-Jones and A Persaud, 'Financial Transaction Taxes' (February 2012). This is available at www.socialistsanddemocrats.eu/gpes/media3/documents/3835_EN_Financial%20Transaction%20 Taxes_Griffith%20Jones%20and%20Persaud_February%202012.pdf.

[26] European Commission, 'Impact Assessment, accompanying the document European Commission Proposal of 28 September 2011 for a Council Directive on a common system of financial transaction tax and amending Directive 2008/7/EC, Vol.1' SEC(2011) 1103 final, 16, available at www.ec.europa. eu/taxation_customs/taxation/other_taxes/financial_sector/index_en.htm.

[27] European Commission, 'Public Consultation: review of the markets in financial instruments directive (MiFID)', December 2010, 14, available at www.ec.europa.eu/internal_market/consultations/ docs/2010/mifid/consultation_paper_en.pdf.

[28] See the literature reviewed in Foresight, *The Future of Computer Trading in Financial Markets – Final Project Report* (London, The Government Office for Science, 2012), available at http://www.bis. gov.uk/assets/foresight/docs/computer-trading/12-1086-future-of-computer-trading-in-financial-markets-report.pdf . The Commission's consultation paper on MiFID, cited above (n 26), continues '[S]ome studies suggest that HFT using market making and arbitrage strategies has added liquidity to the market, reduced spreads and helped align prices across markets. However, the average transaction size has decreased considerably and some participants question the value of the additional liquidity provided. They argue there may be improved liquidity for investors who trade retail-size orders but it is now more difficult for institutional investors to execute large orders. Also, there are different views about whether HFT increases or reduces market volatility.'

has been enhanced, transactions costs have been lowered and market efficiency appears to be better, or certainly no worse. The scale of improvements may be fairly small and, in the short term, they may have been obscured by the background of a very poor performance by Organisation for Economic Co-operation and Development (OECD) economies and stock market indexes in particular. However, there are issues with respect to periodic illiquidity, new forms of manipulation and potential threats to market stability due to errant algorithms or excessive message traffic that must be addressed. Regulatory changes in practices and policies will be needed to catch up to the new realities of trading in asset markets. *Caution must be exercised to avoid undoing the many advantages that the high frequency world has brought.* Technology will continue to affect asset markets in the future, particularly as it relates to the ultra-fast processing of news into asset prices. (Emphasis added.)[29]

The reduction of HFT simply cannot be portrayed as an unambiguously desirable goal. At present, the existing evidence on the effect of HFT on market efficiency is inconclusive and it is thus deeply worrying that the reduction of this form of trading (and the supposed reduction in the probability of a financial crisis it should bring) is being employed repeatedly in making the case for this tax.

The reasoning behind the conclusion that the FTT would lead to economic growth merits a closer look:

[P]ossibly the most important additional positive effect on future growth is that the FTT would somewhat reduce systemic risk, and therefore the likelihood of future crises. We are clearly not arguing that on its own, the FTT would reduce the risk of crises, as prudent macroeconomic policies and effective financial regulation as well as supervision also have a major role to play in crisis prevention. *However, by significantly reducing the level of noise trading in general and reducing (or eliminating) high frequency trading in particular, the FTT would make some contribution to the reduction of severe misalignments and hence the probability of violent adjustments.* Moreover, in financial crises 'gross' exposures matter more than the net ones, and financial transaction taxes will reduce the gap between the two . . . Should the FTT, for example, decrease the probability of crises by a mere 5%, (which is a very low assumption), and the cost of GDP lower growth in the long term due to crises were around 7 % which consistent with the above estimates, then the positive impact of the FTT on the level of GDP, due to crisis avoidance, could be a 0.35% of GDP. In that case, the net effect of the FTT on the level of GDP would be +0.25 % (if we combine the negative impact estimated by the Commission model of -0.1%, with the positive one just estimated of +0.35%). (Emphasis added.)[30]

This argument would carry significant weight if it were supported by evidence. No evidence is produced in support of the claim that the FTT can reduce the probability of financial crises. Nor is any evidence provided to support the assumption that it would reduce the probability by 5 per cent, despite its being described as a 'very low' assumption.

---

[29] Foresight, *The Future of Computer Trading in Financial Markets – Final Project Report* (London, The Government Office for Science, 2012), (n 28).

[30] S Griffith-Jones and A Persaud, 'Financial Transaction Taxes', (n 25).

The central lesson here is that a corrective function can be a powerful selling point for a tax. Unfortunately, this can be abused. In the case discussed here, the danger is that the FTT, which is primarily required as a revenue-raiser,[31] is 'sold' on the basis of a corrective function of questionable foundation. This should not be the argument which tilts the balance in favour of this controversial tax, particularly when other taxes, such as the FAT, might be preferable on other grounds, such as being less distortive, less susceptible to avoidance and more likely to hit its intended target.[32]

V. Conclusion

The use of corrective taxation in the field of financial regulation merits careful investigation. This chapter contributes by providing some practical observations on the recent debates and implementation of corrective taxes in this field. These observations hopefully add to the theoretical debate and assist in providing a more complete set of issues to consider when thinking about regulatory choice.

---

[31] The Commission proposed that two-thirds of the revenue raised would be used to finance EU expenditure. European Commission, 'The financial transaction tax will reduce Member States' GNI contributions to the EU budget by 50%', press release of 23 March 2012, ref IP/12/300, available at www.europa.eu/rapid/press-release_IP-12-300_en.htm?locale=en.

[32] See J Vella, C Fuest and T Schmidt-Eisenlohr, 'The EU Commission's Proposal for a Financial Transaction Tax' (2011) *British Tax Review* 607.

12

Banking Special Resolution Regimes as a Governance Tool

GUSTAF SJÖBERG[1]

I. Introduction

One of the main problems connected with handling failures of systemically important banks is the risk of creating moral hazard. Bailing out the owners and creditors of banks creates perverted incentives that increase the risk level in the financial system. To preserve financial stability and at the same time uphold (or create) market discipline (that is, to avoid moral hazard) is therefore of paramount importance.

It is essential for every jurisdiction to have legal mechanisms aimed at reducing moral hazard in systemically important institutions. One way of achieving that is to create a Special Resolution Regime (SRR) with the explicit objective of serving as a governance tool. An SRR designed with that objective in mind must make it credible that shareholders and debt holders will suffer losses if an institution fails, thereby inducing market discipline.

Nowadays everyone seems to agree that an SRR should be an important part of the legislative package used to control the behaviour of banks, or, more accurately, the decisions by people involved in banks, such as their owners, their management and other employees and their creditors. However, from a policy perspective it is important to have a clear picture of the precise role that an SSR is to play. A policymaker has to identify what the objectives are and how the SRR would fit in with the rest of the legislative package. When forming the overall picture it is paramount to have a realistic view on what actually can be achieved with an SRR.

The perspective in this chapter is one of legislative effectiveness and efficiency; the objective is to identify the most efficient solutions from the point of view of society as a whole. Banks are private institutions that fulfil important tasks in the

[1] Many thanks to Lars Hörngren, Chief Economist at the Swedish National Debt Office, for invaluable inspiration and help.

economy and the basic assumption is that they should conduct their business according to the conditions of the free market. However, negative external effects from failures call for legislation regarding the operation of their businesses and that legislation has to be designed with a societal perspective.

In my view, an SRR serves two equally important purposes. One of them is to provide the legal instruments necessary to deal with an ongoing crisis. The other is to help prevent crises; to serve as a tool affecting the governance of banks. The focus here will be on this latter goal and on what realistically can be expected from a resolution regime. Since corporate governance in general is a complicated matter and governance of banks perhaps even more so, it can be nothing more than a sketchy attempt to identify mechanisms that have the potential to affect the governance of banks. A more in-depth investigation should, among other things, go into the relationship between management and owners in the governance of banks, since that is a crucial question regarding the effectiveness of measures directed at shareholders, for example, write down of equity capital in a resolution process. This is a complex issue, not at least since the relationship between management and owners would be affected by the introduction of such mechanisms and a static analysis of present conditions would therefore not be sufficient. However, it feels safe to assume that increased risk for shareholders to lose money after a bank failure will affect shareholder incentives and perhaps also that it can be instrumental in tipping the balance of power between shareholders and management. The role of creditors in the governance of banks will not be analysed or discussed, except for the underlying assumption that an increased risk for creditors to lose money after a failure will affect governance.

It should be mentioned from the outset that an important restriction on an SRR is that it must not, from a societal perspective, be detrimental to the functioning of banks in normal times and to stability in times of stress.

Several countries have SRRs in place and others are well on their way to doing so. Perhaps the best examples of countries with existing systems are the USA and the United Kingdom. One notable example of far advanced preparations is the proposal for a European Directive on SRRs.[2] However, other countries and regions have hardly applied any efforts to developing SRRs. The Financial Stability Board's Key Attributes seek to give guidance to countries in the process of developing an SRR.[3]

The approach here is to discuss different features of an SRR that can make such a legal construction an efficient governance tool. The analysis is independent of any existing or proposed system. Hence, this is not primarily a comment on specific

---

[2] European Commission, 'Proposal for a Directive of the European Parliament and of the Council establishing a framework for the recovery and resolution of credit institutions and investment firms and amending Council Directives 77/91/EEE and 82/891/EC, Directives 2001/24/EC, 2002/47/EC, 2005/56/EC, 2007/36/EC and 2011/35/EC and Regulation (EU) No 1093/2010', COM(2012) 280/3, 6 June 2012.

[3] Financial Stability Board, 'Key Attributes of Effective Resolution Regimes for Financial Institutions' (Key Attributes) (October 2011) available at www.financialstabilityboard.org/publications/r_111104cc.pdf.

solutions but an effort to identify necessary elements in the legislative product and also in the legislative process. The discussion is to a large extent based on experiences in Sweden during the domestically created crisis of the 1990s and in the global crisis in 2008–09 and on subsequent inquiries and research. Cross-border considerations are not addressed. To make an otherwise abstract discussion more concrete examples are given, mainly from the proposed EU directive since it is close both in time and geographically.[4] However, it is fair to say that the examples most often are used to contrast the ideas brought forward here.

Of course the legislative product is of primary interest but I do believe it is also important to touch on the legislative process and subsequent policy perspective, since it is necessary to establish a level of ambition and clear goals for the legal system under construction. When it comes to the level of ambition it is simply not possible, in my view, to design a single system suited to handle crises of all magnitudes. The legislator will have to aim for a future system designed to suit specific situations. I will outline three different levels of crises, which call for different actions and hence different legal solutions. Of course, they are only rough sketches and in real life there are no clear distinctions between different levels or magnitudes of crises, but the models can serve as a starting point for a discussion. Since it is hardly possible to achieve all goals for crisis management with one single legal solution, it is important to have an idea ex ante what you want to achieve; what kinds of crises you would like to be able to handle.

The focus in this chapter will be on an SRR designed to handle individual systemically important banks and there will consequently be an effort made to identify some elements and instruments necessary for such a regime. However, when discussing the limits of such a regime questions regarding system wide events will also be touched upon.

Even though the primary perspective of this chapter is that of a legislator or a policymaker, the ideas brought forward can be used by others when evaluating existing SRRs or proposing new ones. In that way it is also academically oriented. As I see it, academics, both in law and economics, have to develop instruments suited to critically evaluate legal products independent of narrow legal methods or reasoning.

To sum up; this chapter aims primarily at identifying realistic goals for an SRR and discusses some key features of such a system to make it an effective governance tool. In the next section three different levels of crises are elaborated on in order to create a backdrop to the continued discussion. In the section after that the desired objectives of an SRR are discussed. The penultimate section deals with three key features of an SRR, namely: (i) the ex ante perspective; (ii) the need for immediate control of a bank in crisis; and (iii) the requirement that the

---

[4] This text was written a couple of weeks after the proposal was released in June 2012. Many of the opinions related to the proposal brought forward here are inspired by the Swedish National Debt Office's response to the proposal, available at www.riksgalden.se/Dokument_sve/om_riksgalden/remissvar/2012/Konsultation%20avseende%20EU-kommissionens%20f%c3%b6rslag%20till%20krishanteringsdirektiv%202012-1163.pdf.

system must function also in a full blown systemic crisis. Finally, conclusions are drawn.

II. Three Levels of Crisis Management

As mentioned above it is useful to identify beforehand what kinds of crises the proposed system should be able to handle. The measures and instruments necessary and suitable are quite different depending on the goals of the system. Below, three levels are set out and briefly discussed. The point is not to define or analyse different types of crises, but simply to sketch different possible scenarios, thereby creating a starting point for the analysis. Without a clear view of what kind of situations the system, at least primarily, sets out to handle there is an obvious risk of suboptimal solutions. A system designed to handle problems similar to those of the recent crisis, with a near melt down of the whole financial system, carries the risk of being inappropriate under more 'normal' crisis circumstances.

There are two related basic rationales behind state interventions to prevent banks from failing – in the sense that they become unable or very close to being unable to fulfil their obligations. Both aim at reducing the considerable social costs related with a failure. The first and by far most important rationale is to preserve the functionality of the financial system, most often called systemic stability. But the failure, or more accurately the closing down, of a viable banking business could also have other social costs, mainly in the form of loss of private information regarding the borrowers. Both these dimensions are touched upon below, but the focus of this chapter is on systemic stability.

There seem to be, at least, three possible levels of ambition for a system handling distressed banks, namely to handle:

- individual non-systemic banks
- individual systemic banks
- full blown systemic crises involving more or less all banks.

Level one (individual non-systemic banks) encompasses failures of banks that are so small that they cannot individually, under almost any circumstances, be of systemic relevance. An SRR designed for this level should be able to efficiently handle failures in non-systemic banks and probably focuses on depositor protection and issues related to what is known as regulatory forbearance.

It should be noted in this context that this chapter focuses on the governance of banks (and perhaps other financial institutions) but not on the entirely different issue of the governance of supervisory agencies.[5] Depending on the size and the market structure of the country in question an SRR created to deal with failures

---

[5] I see what is often called prompt corrective action foremost as a tool for supervisory agency governance.

on this level can meet quite different tasks. One example is the Federal Deposit Insurance Corporation (FDIC) in the USA that, via its resolution mechanisms, handle hundreds of insolvent banks every year. The FDIC system is virtually a factory for closing down relatively small banks as smoothly as possible.[6] Another example is the Danish system that more or less explicitly limits itself to non-systemic banks. The mechanisms used to take control over failing banks and the method of transferring liabilities and assets to another legal entity is not suited for banks of systemic importance. The Danish system has handled around 20 insolvent banks in recent years.[7]

Systems designed to handle level one situations seem in practice often not fit to handle situations at the second level, namely difficulties in one or several systemically important banks.[8] The reason for this is not clear, but it could be that it is much more complicated to handle systemically important institutions, so if the system is developed with non-systemic institutions in mind such mechanisms are avoided.

At level two (individual systemic banks), one or a few systemically important banks face difficulties, but there is no immediate danger of a total melt down of the financial system (level three) if the situation is handled promptly and correctly.

A few words must be said on the meaning of systemically important. Difficulties in a bank have systemic implications in two cases, namely when the bank itself is so large that its failure will create considerable disturbances to the functioning of the economy as a whole or when there is risk of contagion (when difficulties in one bank lead to problems in other banks).[9] A failure in a single large bank can cause disturbances in the overall economy, for example, if its depositors (temporarily) lose access to their accounts and are thereby unable to use the payment system or because of an ensuing credit crunch. Even though it may be important to establish that the failure of one single bank can cause systemic problems, it is hard to imagine a case where a large bank fails without any risk of contagion.[10] Contagion can be caused both by direct links (through contractual relations including credit exposures or the payment system) between banks and by indirect links such as via markets and/or rumours that the problems in one bank also are present in other banks. Direct links between banks mean that if one bank suddenly stops to fulfil its obligations there may be a chain reaction that brings down other banks depending on the size of the exposure. Therefore it is not possible to

---

[6] The list of banks that failed during 2009 names close to 150 banks and the list for 2011 names close to 100 banks, see www.fdic.gov/bank/individual/failed/banklist.html. FDIC employs almost 10,000 people, see its 2011 Annual Report at www.fdic.gov/about/strategic/report/2011annualreport/AR11final.pdf.

[7] See Finansiel Stabilitet, *Annual Report 2012*, available at www.finansielstabilitet.dk/Admin/Public/DWSDownload.aspx?File=%2fFiles%2fFiles%2fRapporter%2f2012_4K%2fFS_UK_AR12.pdf.

[8] It was, as far as I know, not even contemplated at the outset that the FDIC system would be able to handle the difficulties of the present crisis.

[9] For an extensive analysis of systemic risk, see SL Schwarcz, 'Systemic Risk' (2008) 97 *Georgetown Law Journal* 193.

[10] One such case could be that of a country with only one dominant bank which has few links abroad.

let a bank with such links (immediately) go bankrupt, in the sense that the bank's contractual relations are broken and the legal entity dissolved.

When a systemically important bank runs into acute problems, almost by definition, prompt action from the authorities is necessary. There are two possible alternative scenarios leading up to the acute phase of a crisis. One is a genuine balance sheet solvency problem which is our focus here, the other being pure liquidity problems (without connection to a solvency problem). If the bank is balance sheet solvent emergency liquidity assistance (ELA) from the central bank could be sufficient, but if the bank is not solvent (on its own or via a mechanism for support from a resolution scheme) ELA should not be provided, since that constitutes support to the owners of the bank.

An acute situation can appear suddenly without warning or, alternatively, the underlying problems may be known, to a smaller or larger extent, during a period before the acute phase. The focus here is on the acute phase, when a bank faces immediate difficulties in fulfilling its obligations and therefore poses a threat to the functioning of the financial system (and ELA is not sufficient or appropriate). The way this phase is handled is crucial to the functioning of a crisis management system. If the part of a system designed to handle this phase fails (or does not exist), the risk of moral hazard in the financial system increases and the credibility of supervision of troubled institutions and the efficacy of early intervention may be questioned. It goes without saying that if the initial phase of the crisis management process fails, there is not much use in an elaborate system for post-acute measures.

Level three (full blown systemic crises) means that substantial parts of the financial system in a country or, even worse, in the region or even in the world are in deep distress. The recent crisis is an example. The causes of the crisis are less relevant for the analysis here, but of course crucial when addressing the underlying problems. It should be pointed out that in globalised markets the causes of the crisis in one country (but not in all countries) can be entirely external. It must also be stressed that I do not suggest that any SRR (in the ordinary sense of the term) would be sufficient in a crisis of this magnitude. Other measures outside the scope of an SRR have to be employed when the whole financial system is at risk.

As was said above, difficulties due only to temporary liquidity problems can ideally be solved by pure liquidity support. In fact the possibility of avoiding large social costs with relatively simple means is the main explanation of the existence of a lender of last resort function. Even though this chapter focuses on situations where a systemically important bank encounters acute problems that have deeper roots than just temporary lack of liquidity, it should be noted that it is not always self-evident where to draw the line between ELA and other measures aimed at enhancing liquidity. In the recent crisis both traditional bank runs (depositors queuing in the streets and deposit withdrawals using more contemporary techniques) and withdrawals of wholesale funding occurred. This was accompanied by an almost total breakdown in the markets used for funding. In fact the lack of available funding (lending to the bank or the bank's sale of assets), regardless of the banks' economic health, was perhaps the most characteristic feature of the crisis. In this context, it is important to reiterate that even banks whose finances are in good order and which are perfectly viable businesses can be hit by a liquidity shortage that can rapidly develop into solvency problems if nothing is done. In the current crisis, we have learnt that liquidity problems, that under normal circumstances should have been very short-lived, lasted for long periods and affected the entire financial sector. For this reason also, it is clear that traditional ELA to individual institutions is not sufficient. Measures aimed at enhancing the liquidity situation generally may be needed as well as complementary mechanisms for dealing with (potential) solvency problems. During the recent crisis the measures aimed at generally enhancing the liquidity situation, at least in the Swedish financial system, was much more extensive than pure traditional ELA.

As noted above, an SRR designed with the objective of handling crises of every conceivable magnitude is, to my mind, not a reasonable option. Worst case situations frequently call for political ad hoc solutions on both domestic and international levels. A further difference between a second and a third level crisis is that a second level crisis could be dealt with using money paid by the banks to an insurance system of some sort, perhaps connected to depositor insurance systems or a resolution fund. A crisis on the third level frequently calls for state money to be used. Another way of expressing this, and perhaps to define the difference between the two types of situations, is that the latter situation is not insurable; the insurance premiums to cover a full blown crisis with a near melt down of the whole financial system would be so high that the banks could neither pay them ex ante, nor compensate the state for the costs it has incurred ex post.

The difference between level two and level three crises have an immediate bearing also on the governance of financial institutions. An SRR could and should be used as an instrument to curtail careless bank practices. This is one of the main points of this chapter. But, it is equally essential that legislation does not give the opposite incentive, namely to take on too little risk. If the framework gives the impression that drastic measures will also be taken against banks that end up in difficulties due to circumstances beyond their control, that will have effect on risk taking. Concern among owners and creditors that banks can be subject to drastic resolution measures without a clear connection to the behaviour of an individual bank will almost certainly have negative effects on the functioning of the banking sector.

Experience indicates that full blown systemic crises are also almost invariably caused by a significant amount of bad policy making, that is, circumstances outside the control of banks and their owners and creditors. The conclusion is that an SRR is much more likely to be an efficient and effective governance tool when directed at level two crises, since the chances are higher that the crisis is caused (at least to a large extent) by bad banking.

Even though a system designed to handle situations of the second level is not fit to take care of all problems connected with a full blown systemic crisis, the legal tools provided by such a system could be useful in parallel with other required state measures.[11] It can be said that a well-designed SRR is necessary but not sufficient to handle level three crises. In addition preparedness for ad hoc solutions and general measures are needed. One example is preparedness for situations where banks try to survive via shrinking balance sheets in a manner that causes a credit contraction that threatens to destabilise the economy. A minimum requirement is that an SRR developed to handle level two situations does not impede the handling of level three situations. Among other things this means that an SRR to be efficient in a level three context cannot rely too much on 'private solutions' since there may be no viable private actors around.

III. Objectives of a Special Resolution Regime

Regardless of the perspective on the task of designing an SRR, it is necessary to identify clear objectives for the system. Inevitably, there will be a number of difficult choices during the process; it may concern different possible legal solutions or other issues that can be decided in different ways. Without setting clear objectives for the intended system it is difficult or perhaps even impossible for a policymaker or legislator to handle the decisions that by necessity arise later in the process in a rational and consistent manner. In the same way it is meaningless for an academic to evaluate a system without the analytical base of clear objectives; it is not possible to say whether a system is good or bad if there is no clear yardstick.

There is no point in having an SRR if it is not successful in preserving systemic stability. As indicated above, I see a functioning financial system as included in the objective of systemic stability; it is not meaningful to say that there is financial stability if (critical) banking functions are not performed. However, it is not difficult to create financial stability (at least if the state's finances are in good order). The problem is how to do it without creating moral hazard. From this observation, the two overriding goals of an SRR can be formulated, namely, to preserve systemic stability and at the same time uphold (or create) market discipline (that is, to avoid moral hazard).

It should be noted that these goals are set for an SRR and consequently for crisis conditions. The balance struck between stability and efficiency in legislation applicable under normal circumstances is another difficult question that is not addressed here. However, as already mentioned, one important restriction on an SRR is that it should not negatively, from a societal perspective, affect banks risk taking during normal times. Or, to put it simply, it should not make banking services unnecessarily expensive.

Minimising the costs of resolving the situation, both to society and to taxpayers, is often mentioned as a separate objective of a system, but I believe that if

---

[11] eg legal instruments to gain control over banks and for valuation could also be used when state funds are needed for guarantees and to buy assets.

the two goals noted above are met, that will result in minimal overall costs to society. Taken literally, minimising costs to taxpayers (in that capacity) is a more or less pointless goal since taxpayers' money should be used if that could reduce the cost to society. Expressed in another way: the goal of minimising costs to taxpayers is connected with a risk that costs are shifted to the same persons in different roles, namely as banks' customers or counterparts, and also that the costs to society will be higher.

Another objective (or perhaps a restriction) is that the system (as well as the rest of the regulatory environment) has to allow a continuing development of the financial sector. That means that banks without a viable business could be forced to close down. In this context one qualification should be made regarding the first objective. Simply put, it can be said that the functioning of the financial system has to be preserved but not necessarily the institutions in existing form and absolutely not with the same owners.

Without doubt it is difficult to design a system for handling acute problems in banks. This, in combination with the temptation for legislators and regulators to refer to the need for 'flexibility' and room for 'practical solutions', is often used as an excuse for incomplete or unclear regimes. Such an approach can be dangerous for several reasons. Obviously there is a risk that banks can obtain support on overly favourable terms when there are no legal measures that can be used to put pressure on them in a negotiation. A lack of clear rules also exposes banks and their owners to the risk of unfair treatment. The position of a bank in a temporary liquidity crisis (perhaps caused by forces outside the bank's control) is dire. Moreover, public opinion in times of financial crisis often puts pressure on the authorities to 'act resolutely' towards the banking sector. From the perspective of legal certainty, it is better to have the procedures to be applied in these situations clearly set out ex ante in legislation. Sales over the weekend on ad hoc terms may seem to offer smooth solutions and give the government credit for being forceful but they are generally not desirable.[12] To put it in economic terms, quickly executed sales on ad hoc terms may be associated with substantial transaction costs and subsequent wealth transfers in the absence of legal certainty concerning the rights of different stakeholders.[13] When we discuss the goals of a crisis handling system, a given should therefore be that such a system meets high legalistic demands. However, I do not see legal certainty as a separate objective, but as a (very important) restriction.

[12] When the authorities force the incumbent owners of a bank to sell their shares and another institute under supervision to buy them (perhaps purporting that it is the institution's duty, in order to prevent mistrust in the financial system) both sellers and buyer are given reasons to question ex post the transaction on different grounds. Furthermore the forced selling of one institution to another unavoidably gives rise to a form of implicit guarantee from the authorities that the institution being sold meets some sort of qualitative minimum requirements and also that it fits together with the buying institution. Hence, a supervisor will have difficulty questioning the economic soundness of the new entity resulting from the amalgamation.

[13] Uncertainty about government policy can trigger a crisis. It has been pointed out that the sudden and unpredictable reversal in resolution policy that marked the failure of Lehman Brothers changed market expectations and led to a general flight to quality, which in turn decreased stability.

Article 26 of the proposed directive contains a list of items that are all defined as 'Resolution objectives'. It is stated that all items on the list are of equal signific-ance.[14] The six items on the list include inter alia continuity of critical functions and financial stability, which seem to be more or less the same thing. Included in the paragraph on financial stability is the objective of maintaining market dis-cipline.[15] The protection of public funds is set out as a separate objective as is protection of depositors covered by guarantee schemes and client funds and assets.[16]

As stated above, protection of public funds is a questionable objective and it is at least not equal to financial stability. From a societal perspective the protection of public funds can at most be seen as a constraint when pursuing the overriding objective of financial stability. Perhaps there is a difference between what are called resolution objectives and objectives for the process of designing an SRR, but I do not think so.[17] Listing so many different items and suggesting that they are equally important objectives is at best confusing and could, in the worst case scenario, paralyse the resolution authority. In my view, the existence of two over-riding objectives is sufficient, these being to preserve systemic stability and at the same time uphold market discipline.

It is stated in the Key Attributes that their implementation 'should allow authorities to resolve financial institutions in an orderly manner *without taxpayer exposure to loss from solvency support,* while maintaining continuity of their vital economic functions' (emphasis added).[18] Even though the Key Attributes seem to draw a sophisticated difference between the causes of the losses, there is a clear objective not to expose taxpayers to loss.[19]

IV. Three Necessary Features of a Special Resolution Regime

Below I focus on what I believe are the three most essential features for the func-tioning of an SRR as a governance tool although there are of course several other important (and necessary) ingredients when putting together a workable mixture of legal measures. The features dealt with are: (i) the ex ante perspective, (ii) the need for immediate control of a bank in crisis and (iii) the requirement that the system must also function in a full blown systemic crisis.

---

[14] Article 26(3).
[15] Article 26(2)(b).
[16] Article 26(2)(c) and 26(2)(e) and (f).
[17] Article 26(1) says that the resolution authorities shall have regard to the objectives when applying the resolution tools and exercising the resolution powers.
[18] Financial Stability Board, 'Key Attributes' (n 3) Foreword, 1.
[19] However, this standpoint seems mitigated by the wording in section 2.3, regarding objectives and section 6, regarding funding of firms in resolution.

1. Ex Ante Perspective

Apart from providing legal tools for dealing with a crisis at hand it is also necessary that an SRR is permeated with an ex ante perspective. This point is not strictly about the legal technical features of an SRR, but more about the mindset behind the design and the credibility of the end product. On the face of it, an ex ante perspective seems more or less self-evident, since one of the objectives is to avoid moral hazard and thus function as a governance instrument. However, the consistent application of a credible ex ante perspective on every aspect of a conceived system is easier said than done.

One of the major problems with systemically important banks is that shareholders and debt holders are not perceived to, and in reality do not, suffer losses when banks fail. This gives rise to an increased risk level in systemic banks. When deciding on risk levels and pricing shareholders and creditors take into account a more or less implicit state guarantee. As a consequence, there is not enough market discipline. This means that debt financing is too cheap from a societal perspective, which in turn results in too much debt financing and increased risk through the institutions' balance sheet composition. Consequently, one of the key attributes of an SRR has to be increased risk in debt financing or, to put it differently, the removal of the conceived state guarantee for debt holders. That calls for mechanisms that deprive debt holders of value in the resolution process, or in other words a mechanism for writing down debt even though the bank is not going through a bankruptcy. It goes without saying that this is technically very complicated in a systemically important bank, since losses incurred by debt holders is one of the major sources of contagion.

If a system contains mechanisms to deprive debt holders of value it is necessary also with mechanisms to deprive the shareholders of value. Writing down debt without eliminating shareholder value should not be considered, since this would set aside priority rights and give rise to awkward incentives. The possibility of wiping out shareholder value is important also, or perhaps foremost, from a governance perspective. Insofar as shareholders exercise control of risk levels, this can help to bring down risk in the financial system. A second order effect could be a larger portion of controlling shareholders in banks.

Both the Key Attributes and the proposed directive put much emphasis on the resolution tool called bail-in, as does the general debate regarding crisis management. The terminology is not entirely clear on this point, but it is clear that bail-in is something more than a write down of claims on banks. Bail-in has been used to describe both the increase of a financial institution's equity capital through the conversion of contingent convertible capital with a high trigger point, before it ceases to be a going concern, and recapitalisation of a financial institution that has reached the point of non-viability. Both the proposed directive and the Key Attributes use the term bail-in in the latter sense. Here the term bail-in is used mainly to contrast recapitalisation of a bank through the conversion of debt into equity capital to a pure write down of debt.

The bail-in mechanism is, as I see it, an amalgamation of two objectives, namely to decrease moral hazard and to facilitate recapitalisation. Again, it is not entirely clear how these objectives are supposed to be met in different situations.

One reason that a debt write down is combined with a recapitalisation seems to be to overcome the problem of attracting new equity capital in a situation where the economic status of the institution is uncertain, often described as the debt overhang problem.[20] A compulsory conversion of debt to equity makes a search for new (private) equity capital unnecessary. The process is easiest to envisage in the case where the losses have wiped out the entire equity capital and more, that is, when there is negative equity. The first step is to cancel existing shares; to wipe out the stake of incumbent shareholders. The second step is to write down debt until the 'hole' in the balance sheet has been filled. At this stage the institution has no equity capital (neither positive nor negative). This mechanism creates incentives for debt holders (incumbent and potential) to evaluate and monitor banks and is therefore a governance tool. The third step, bail-in, would be to convert enough of remaining debt claims into new equity to ensure that the bank meets relevant capital requirements. The third step makes the claim holders whose claims have been converted to equity the new owners of the bank.[21] The consequences of the third step, from a governance perspective, are hard to evaluate. Without going into detail, it can be said that it is a long leap from making the debt holders assume the losses of the institution (mimicking bankruptcy) to making them responsible for the recapitalisation and ownership of a bank. It cannot be assumed that the debt overhang problem can be solved without cost. Undoubtedly, a bail-in mechanism adds a layer of uncertainty, which can affect the dynamics of a crisis.

Another reason for combining a debt write down with a forced recapitalisation seems to be to minimise state intervention in the restructuring process. As was outlined in an article in the *Economist* the ideal seems to be that the capital restructuring process take place over a weekend and that the institution comes out newly capitalised and fully viable on Monday morning.[22] Obviously the enormous time pressure gives rise to different problems, including valuation of the institution. To be on the safe side the authority in charge will have to convert considerably more debt to equity than would be necessary with a slower and more careful valuation process. If too little debt is, or is perceived to be, converted the capital strength of the bank will probably be questioned when the bank re-opens again (Monday morning) and the bank will not be able to operate on its own.

The advantages of including a bail-in mechanism in an SRR should be compared with a system that, after a debt write down, allows for a slower recapitalisation process under the control (and temporary financing) of a resolution authority. This seems to be an example of where the objectives of the system dictate the choice of

[20] The concept of debt overhang was first formalised in SC Myers, 'The Determinants of Corporate Borrowing' (1977) 5 *Journal of Financial Economics* 147.

[21] The Key Attributes seem to recognise the different mechanisms involved in step two and three, see Key Attributes 3.5(i) and (ii).

[22] P Calello and W Ervin, 'From Bail-out to Bail-in' *The Economist* (28 January 2010) available at www.economist.com/node/15392186?story.

mechanisms used.[23] The objective governing here seems to be to limit state involvement, or at least what is called taxpayer costs, and the result is reliance on a mechanism for recapitalisation that is questionable in system-wide crises and insofar as it can affect the dynamics of a level two crisis.

Even without the bail-in step the possibility of a debt write down would affect the dynamics of a crisis. It seems unavoidable that a bank (that is under a write down regime) that is perceived to be in difficulties will face financing problems earlier than if write down or bail-in was not possible. Access to funding markets involving debt instruments that can be written down or bailed-in will be cut off. Here again, we come back to the difference between a level two and a level three crisis. If the market's response is isolated to one, or possibly a few banks, this might be manageable and perhaps even considered desirable. It would speed up the process and expose the institution to an immediate liquidity shortage. If the bank is about to become balance sheet insolvent, it can be brought into resolution and handled in an orderly manner.

However, if problems are not isolated to one bank but expose the entire system as a result of a common shock – a level three situation – speeding up funding problems is anything but desirable. It would also be very unfortunate if the market's response affected the dynamics of the crisis such that it tipped a level two situation into a level three situation. The impact of disturbances in funding markets is affected by many factors, including the liquidity buffers maintained by individual banks and by the actions that might be taken by central banks and others to support the funding of balance sheet solvent banks. This aspect is a good example of the need to consider at its inception how the SRR will work in different circumstances and how it will interact with other parts of the legal environment.

The Key Attributes do not address the issue of contagion through a bail-in. The proposed directive is surprisingly unclear in respect to bail-in. The Articles covering the implementation of the bail-in tool[24] make no clear distinction between debt write down and equity conversion. Write down and conversion are in several instances used as if they had equivalent effects and could be used interchangeably. This, of course, adds to the uncertainty. Furthermore, there is no description of the role of the holders of the new equity. They would seem to be the legal owners of the bank, but they appear to have no role in its management. Instead all the powers are to be given to an administrator, whose task it is to put the bank back on sound footing. From a governance perspective it may appear strange to block the new owners from exercising influence, even though they have been creditors of a failed institution. Separation of powers and economic interest for a prolonged period of time is seldom a good idea.[25]

---

[23] This is of course appropriate; the objectives should influence the choice of tools. The point being made here is that the wrong objectives give the wrong tools.

[24] Articles 41–47.

[25] It may also seem strange that the state, through administration, takes responsibility for reorganising a capitalised bank and then hands it back to private sector owners once the job is done, as the proposed directive seems to suggest. It is another thing if the value of the reorganisation work can be accounted for in the terms of a subsequent recapitalisation (see further below).

There is also an ex ante dimension regarding the scope of an SRR. From a policy perspective it is desirable to identify the truly important functions of the economy and the types of institutions that perform them and limit their exposure to other types of institutions. Such types of institutions should be included in the scope of an SRR. For example it can be argued that the identification (ex post) of AIG as a systemically important institution should not necessarily lead to the inclusion (ex ante) of that type of insurer in the scope of an SRR (or in tighter regulation). It can be argued that it would be better to limit the exposure of truly important institutions, such as banks, to other institutions thus preventing the latter from becoming so big that they can threaten ex ante systemic institutions.

In this context it is appropriate to say something very briefly about valuation. When reducing the claims of shareholders and debt holders the matter of valuation is always important. It is not only a question of legal certainty as to how the valuation process is designed. To clearly set out valuation principles and methods prevents a situation where present and potential shareholders (and creditors) do not take action to solve a difficult situation because it is impossible to calculate the risk of losing money in a subsequent rescue operation by the state. What is sometimes called constructive ambiguity seems not to be a palatable option in this area. It is not hard to imagine that it would be difficult to get incumbent shareholders and new investors to put up new capital if the terms of the investment are unclear.[26] It is important in this respect also to have an ex ante perspective.

One conclusion that may be drawn from what has been said above is that there is a clear link between the credibility of an ex ante perspective and the objectives of an SRR. If there is doubt that the technical solutions offered by the system will work in a level three crisis or that they risk tipping a level two crisis into a level three crisis that will cast doubt on the system's credibility. The ambition to take care of systemic wide disturbances as well could make the system less credible and thus less efficient as a governance tool.

2. Immediate Control of a Bank in Crisis

For several reasons, it is important that the state, through the relevant authorities, is able to assume immediate and absolute control of a bank in acute distress. A bank that poses a systemic threat is in a strong position in negotiations regarding the (necessary) measures to avoid a systemic crisis. This, in turn, means that the bank may be able to obtain support on overly favourable terms if a negotiating situation cannot be avoided. Avoiding the risk of not being able to agree on reasonable terms for support is one strong reason for assuming control. The need to assume control is not the same in all situations; the weaker the economic situation of the bank, the greater the need. The owners' incentive to take an unreasonable standpoint in negotiations is inversely proportionate to the value they have at

---

[26] Valuation will also be touched upon in the next section.

risk. If the bank's capital is zero or even negative there is not much to lose for the owners in driving a hard bargain; if it succeeds the bank is saved and if it fails there was nothing to lose anyway.

Another reason for assuming control in an acute crisis is the risk that the managers or owners of the bank raise the risk level dramatically, thus increasing the risk to the financial system and the potential costs to creditors and/or the state, in an attempt to gamble for resurrection. Such a change of risk level can be achieved in a very short time. In a state of unrest and confusion in the middle of a crisis, decisions that change the risk level can probably also be taken quite low down in the organisation.

Frequently, crisis management involves issuing guarantees of some sort for the bank's liabilities.[27] There is a clear advantage for the issuing authority if it or some other authority can exercise control over the guaranteed bank. Since central banks are supposed to extend ELA only to balance sheet solvent banks there should, in principle, be no need for a mechanism that provides control when banks rely solely on ELA for support. But as soon as it is in doubt whether the bank is solvent (with a consequent transfer to a separate crisis management regime) there is a need for control, for the above mentioned reasons. In practice, this may well be the most likely case as there is typically great uncertainty in such situations.

Even though the objective is immediate and absolute control of a bank, the legal tools used are important. The exact legal thresholds for when the authority can take control will not be discussed here, but it has to be made clear that it is necessary that control can be achieved without delay when a bank is in immediate need of support. Since it is typically large and complex entities that have to be governed with a view to possible continued business, it is a clear advantage to be able to (at least to some extent) use the existing legal structure created by corporate law (and internal regulations and instructions) instead of creating a new legal structure working in parallel with the existing one. To step into the shoes of the existing structure means that the authority in charge can use the parts of the structure that are useful and reliable, and, of crucial importance, more easily maintain continuity of service in systemically important parts. At the same time the authority in charge is given legal tools to change the other parts of the structure. In contrast, creating a new legal animal bears the risk of being less efficient in terms of governance and creating unnecessary ambiguity in relation to counterparties and potential counterparties.

It is necessary to be able to assume control of all aspects of the bank's business, including operations through subsidiaries. That has to include control over the bank's capital and business structure.[28] Control must also entail a possibility to

---

[27] If the bank in question faces more than temporary liquidity problems, which should be the minimum threshold for entering into an alternative regime, there are frequently doubts about the quality of the bank's assets which in turn warrants guarantees in many situations where an immediate closing of the operations is not possible.

[28] The Second Company Directive (77/91/EEG, Article 58(2)) requires decisions regarding a reduction of the share capital and new issues of shares to be taken by the shareholders. In a common European corporate law for banks (see below) this obstacle could be removed.

change the management (the people controlling the bank's business) as well as staff at a lower level if they are central to the running of the bank (eg people involved in risk control) if that is called for.[29] The legal tool used to take control must not raise any doubts as to whether the bank remains the same legal entity and whether contractual obligations will be honoured.[30]

When the option of creating an entirely new structure for decision making is ruled out two alternative basic principles for assuming control remain, namely to take over the ownership of the shares in the bank or to assume their voting rights. To assume the voting rights has several advantages. As a matter of principle, it seems right to choose the method that intervenes least in the incumbent owners' rights without jeopardising the means of the process, for example, creating moral hazard.[31] Under the presumption that the shareholders are treated fairly later in the process, that speaks for an assumption of the voting rights. If the incumbent owners can remain as owners during the process (temporarily without control) they can be offered the opportunity to voluntarily participate in a subsequent capital injection or other restructuring measures in that capacity.[32] That may mitigate the valuation problems always connected with involuntary measures. If it is possible to achieve an entirely voluntary solution regarding the terms of participation there will of course be no problems connected with valuation. Owners (and potential owners) with different views on the risks and possibilities connected with the holding of shares in the bank can trade in the shares and thereby further facilitate a private solution. A further advantage with the possibility of trading is that incumbent owners in need of cash can sell their shares (temporarily, at least, without voting rights).

Also, for more technical reasons, it seems better and easier to assume the voting rights. It has to be remembered that it must be possible to take control very quickly, often within hours. It can be presumed that most legal systems require more rigorous legal proceedings for a final and involuntary transfer of ownership of the shares in a bank than for a (temporary) transfer of voting rights. Lengthy legal battles in court must be avoided, at least as long as they hinder the immediate assumption of control over the bank. A decision by a relevant authority (a court or the authority in charge of crisis management) to take over the voting rights of the shares can be executed immediately and thus the authority can assume control of the bank.[33] This

---

[29] The proposed directive seems to make it compulsory to replace senior management in an institution under resolution (Article 29(1)(c)) which seems unnecessary. The assistance of (parts of) senior management could be very useful at least at the initial stages of the process.

[30] This does not mean that it should be impossible to include in a legal regime the option to write off certain types of debt under conditions clearly set out in the law, see above section IV.1.

[31] In the context of control after a bail-in, it was stated earlier that separation of powers and economic interest is seldom a good idea and this may seem to be a similar case. However, in this case control is assumed before the bank is recapitalised and the economic interest of the incumbent owners can more or less be neglected. After reorganisation and recapitalisation under state management, control of the bank should be given to the owners as promptly as possible.

[32] eg they can be offered the first right to subscribe to new shares.

[33] Depending on the legal system, different steps must be taken to utilise the voting power, but it is assumed that most systems make it fairly easy for a single controlling shareholder to gain control.

does not mean that there should be no possibility to legally challenge the authority's decision afterwards. However, mechanisms that require the authority to take certain steps, including valuation and ex post compensation to the shareholders, within a specified time frame may be a sufficient substitute.

If for some reason it is no longer necessary to have control over a bank or if a decision to assume the voting rights is reversed, it is simple to give the voting rights back. On the other hand, if the ownership has been transferred by the authorities, it is a complicated task to transfer it back to the final owners in different registers.

The assumption of the voting rights will in practical terms give the authority in charge of the crisis management all votes at the shareholders' meeting, thereby giving it the power a sole owner of a company would have. That will enable it to use a wide range of measures. However, it is necessary to give the state or the authority in charge additional tools outside the company law system that can directly affect the power over the bank under administration. The assumption of voting rights only gives the authorities the instruments that general company law provides, which do not include, for example, compulsory write down of debts or share capital.

The important objectives regarding the control aspect are that the authorities should be able to assume immediate control without unnecessarily jeopardising the rights of the incumbent shareholders.[34] A balance has to be struck between the need for the authorities to move quickly in the public interest and the interest of the incumbent shareholders to remain in control. Here it is important to note that the valuation problems can be sorted out later in a separate process (if it is not possible to find an amicable solution). Another important aspect is that the authorities' assumption of power must not jeopardise the bank's ability to continue its business activities if that is desired.

The Explanatory Memorandum to the proposed directive sets out that 'resolution authorities will have the power to take control over an institution that has failed or is likely to fail, take over the role of shareholders and managers, transfer assets and liabilities and enforce contracts'.[35] The memorandum thus recognises the need to take control, but the directive proposal itself directs much of the attention to what is called the resolution tools without much explanation of how the assumption of control will be achieved. Maybe this is partly a matter of exposition, but clarity in this respect is essential and by trying to describe the legal process of assuming control better in the directive one may also discover ways to improve it.

Regarding valuation, the directive proposal states, as a starting point, that an independent valuation should be completed *before* resolution action is taken.[36] It is questionable whether this is a realistic assumption. Experiences from Sweden during the 2008–09 crisis indicate that it can take several weeks to assess the value

---

[34] Some degree of infringement is necessary since ownership rights include control rights.

[35] Explanatory Memorandum, 12.

[36] Article 30(1).

of even a small bank. Where urgency necessitates it, the proposal leaves open the alternative to give the resolution authorities power to do the valuation. However, it does not seem possible to take resolution action without first making a valuation of the institution. This would not be an acceptable delay of the decision to assume control. Even though it may seem to be a technical point, this requirement could jeopardise the functioning of the SRR.

3. The System Must Also Function in a Full Blown Systemic Crisis

As noted at the beginning of this chapter it is not possible or at least not desirable to design an SRR that can take care of all conceivable crisis scenarios. However, it is important that a system designed mainly to manage what I have termed level two crises does not impair the handling of more serious disturbances to the financial system. It is, of course, also important that the system is not designed in a way that risks tipping a genuine level two crisis into a level three crisis. This is, as was the point regarding the ex ante perspective, more of a mind-set issue than a question of concrete technical solutions.

It is important that different ad hoc and general measures can be used as an extension of the SRR when it fails to meet the requirements of the situation. Or put differently, it is essential that the SRR can function and also be used in a level three crisis even though the solutions offered are not sufficient. Otherwise, a situation could arise where it is necessary to, more or less abruptly, abandon the SRR and rely entirely on ad hoc solutions, which could mean for example that the coercive measures necessarily entailed in the SRR cannot be used. In turn, this means among other things that the state's strength in negotiations is weakened and that support might be given on overly favourable conditions. This could, in the worst case scenario, be used by different actors to play the system in order to worsen the crisis and ultimately decrease the credibility of the system's ability to handle a crisis situation and once again create moral hazard.

A system that does not allow for state support in one form or another is not realistic. If the entire financial system is in deep difficulties it is not possible for an SRR to rely (entirely) on solutions that depend on private means or initiatives. The system must be designed to function and interact with different kinds of state measures, such as capital injections into individual banks or general measures to increase liquidity or lending capacity in the system.

When it comes to the proposed EU directive it is stated that both recovery and resolution plans covering individual banks should include preparations for systemic wide events.[37] It is further stated that plans shall not assume any extraordinary public financial support.[38] This runs against all experience, since by their very

---

[37] Articles 6(2)(b) and 9(2).
[38] With the exception of central bank facilities (Article5(3)), but central bank facilities for liquidity support are rarely so clearly defined and predictable that they can form the basis for an obviously credible recovery plan.

nature system wide events will trigger policy actions, for example, in the form of general public support measures. To make plans on an assumption to the contrary carries the risk that the entire planning will be in doubt when reality shows that measures not planned for are necessary. At worst this will mean that the entire system is abandoned and replaced with ad hoc solutions.

Another example from the proposed EU directive regards liquidity planning. Banks are required to hold liquidity buffers and it seems logical that the recovery planning could be based on the assumption that a bank can meet a liquidity squeeze by selling assets from the buffer. Otherwise it does not make sense to have the buffer and this is perfectly rational when it comes to individual banks in trouble, that is, level two crises. However, when it comes to a systemic crisis it is impossible for many banks to be sellers of the same liquid instruments at the same time without risking a breakdown of the markets for these instruments. Again, the measures (liquidity buffers and recovery planning) are primarily aimed at level two crises but are not fit to handle level three crises. It is difficult to say whether the authorities, on realising that the planning regarding liquidity is flawed, will be able to comply with other aspects of the recovery plan. The worst case scenario is again that both the planning and the system are abandoned altogether.

What is said above also means that a system that relies entirely on private restructuring measures of different kinds, for example, strong banks buying weaker banks or parts of them, is not credible in a more serious scenario. As has been touched on above, the use of different convertible instruments can also be questioned, mainly on the grounds that such instruments may enhance the risk of contagion in systemic crises. This could mean that the state has to step in and use public funds in order to disarm the risk of contagion.

A third example (very similar to the second) from the proposed directive can be used here. Again, the intended content of the detailed resolution plans is the starting point. It seems to be assumed that resolution plans should entail plans for the sale of assets and businesses to other institutions in an orderly and organised manner. This could be useful in the event of the failure of an individual institution. However, in a systemic crisis it is highly unlikely to find willing buyers of (parts of) failing institutions. In a situation like that, no private operator has the capacity to buy significant parts of other institutions. This should be recognised in the planning process and, consequently, planning with respect to individual institutions should be limited to idiosyncratic failures.

A difficult question is how the system should interact with liquidity support. Pure short-term liquidity support to single solvent institutions should pose no problem, but as soon as there is support for extended periods the need for interaction with the SRR comes into question. This question is not addressed here and nor is it addressed in the proposed directive.

V. Conclusions

As has been stressed above it is essential for every jurisdiction to have legal mechanisms with the explicit objective of serving as a governance tool and aiming at reducing moral hazard in systemically important institutions. To meet that objective using a Special Resolution Regime, it must be credible that shareholders and debt holders will suffer losses in the resolution process.

When designing an SRR it has to be recognised that there are fundamental differences between the handling of failing individual systemic institutions and the handling of full blown systemic crises that affect whole countries or regions (so called level three crises). It is potentially dangerous to pretend that SRRs designed also to take care of individual institutions would be sufficient in a system wide crisis. A crisis of this magnitude always calls for state intervention and this has to be recognised in the planning for such a situation and in the design of an SRR. It simply does not make sense to pretend that a system can be made credible without out the explicit backing of the state.

This puts the objectives of the system in focus. It is important to set clear objectives when designing the system. Inappropriate objectives carry the risk of taking the system in the wrong direction. If an important objective is to minimise the use of public funds the temptation to pretend that the state does not carry the ultimate responsibility for financial stability perhaps becomes too strong and hence the legal mechanisms try to minimise state intervention. The number of objectives should be kept to a minimum and strictly adhered to both when designing the system and when applying the SRR tools and powers.

The main point to be taken from this chapter is that SRRs could and should be used as a governance tool, in order to curtail careless bank practices. In order to achieve that, by reducing moral hazard, it is essential that the system is credible and realistic in the way it is set out to impose losses on shareholders and creditors. To work as a governance tool (and not as some sort of punishment) a credible system must be in place well before the breakout of a crisis. Also, in the interest of legal certainty, it is important to have the rules clearly set out in advance.

It is important to note that from a governance perspective there is a difference between a crisis in an individual bank and a systemic crisis, what are here referred to as level two and level three crises. Experience indicates that level three crises almost always are caused, to a large extent, by bad public policy, that is, circumstances outside the control of banks and their owners and creditors. The conclusion is that an SRR is much more likely to be an efficient governance tool when directed at level two crises, since the chances are higher that the crisis is caused (at least to a large extent) by bad banking. If the system gives the impression that drastic measures will also be taken against banks that end up in difficulties due to circumstances beyond their control, this will have a negative effect on desirable risk taking. This is a difficult balance to strike, not least in the immediate aftermath (or even in the midst) of a crisis, but it must be borne in mind that the aim is not to eliminate risk taking in financial institutions.

As noted earlier, it is necessary with mechanisms for eliminating shareholder value and for debt write down (not necessarily connected with bail-in). In a level two crisis there should be no problems connected with either of these mechanisms. In a level three crisis the risk of contagion could jeopardise the possibility of a debt write down and perhaps even of eliminating shareholder value. To refrain from a write down or just to make a partial reduction is a decision that has to be taken in the situation at hand. If, ex post, it turns out not to be possible to use the system in a level three crisis that is a pity but the ex ante governance effect should be obtained anyway.

When it comes to bail-in the consequences are much harder to predict. The primary reason to use bail-in, and not just debt write down, seems to be to reduce state involvement in the resolution process. However, there is a danger that a system heavily dependent on the bail-in tool cannot be used in a level three crisis and it might even be the case that the threat of a bail-in tips a level two crisis into a level three crisis. Bail-in should perhaps be left open as a legal option for a suitable situation, but the uncertainty added is considerable. It is questionable whether the lack of state commitment bail-in is supposed to create really makes up for the disadvantages connected with the bail-in tool.

A minimum requirement is that an SRR must not jeopardise the handling of a systemic crisis. Level three crises frequently call for general ad hoc measures and it is important that they can be implemented as an extension of the SRR when it fails to meet the requirements of the situation. Even though the solutions offered are not sufficient it is also essential that the SRR can function in a level three crisis. The SRR must leave room for flexible solutions and not be locked to rigid legal mechanisms that may fail to meet the situation at hand which could render the legal framework provided by the SRR entirely useless. That, in turn, would mean the authorities having to rely entirely on ad hoc solutions to solve difficulties in individual institutions, with grave consequences both for legal certainty and for the effective handling of failing institutions.

In conclusion, SRRs should be aimed at handling level two crises through simple and clearly defined legal mechanisms. In level three situations the system should be able to interact with general state ad hoc measures. The ultimate responsibility for the handling of financial crises always rests with the state. All legal solutions that pretend otherwise are doomed to fail at some stage. This is something that market players know and are prepared to use. The end result can thus turn out to be far more costly to taxpayers than a solution based on a realistic description of the role of the state.

13

Special Resolution Regimes for Banking Institutions: Objectives and Limitations

CHRISTOS HADJIEMMANUIL

If the global financial crisis has proven anything, it is that the financial system's image of efficiency, sophistication and strength can turn out to be highly deceptive. A great many banks, including some of the largest and most reputable global institutions, were shown to be in parlous state. In several countries, the troubles engulfed the whole banking system.

The manifest fragility of banks and banking systems impels the search for appropriate policy responses. For obvious reasons, the more conspicuous governmental decisions made at the height of the crisis were aimed at restoring normal conditions of operation in the financial markets through the provision of state guarantees or immediate financing support. However, the official reactions have also included a host of legislative and regulatory measures, seeking to establish the longer-term rules of the game for the banking industry in the post-crisis period. Amongst the flood of new institutions, rules and regulations, a range of novel arrangements for the resolution of failed banks stand out. How should the state respond, if one or several banking institutions show signs of severe financial and/ or operational weakness and are on the verge of collapse? What legal and administrative tools should it have in place, so as to be ready to address adequately the situation? These issues are central to the ongoing regulatory realignment.

Before 2008, most countries lacked specialised legal frameworks and clearly defined lines of governmental-administrative responsibility for the resolution of failed banks and, in particular, of systemic banking crises (section I). Due to the recent global troubles, this has now changed. In the new environment, the introduction of so called Special Resolution Regimes (SRRs) for banking institutions, with particular objectives and attributes, has developed into a global and European policy priority (section II). In the long run, this may well prove to be the most significant and noteworthy regulatory response to the crisis.

In his contribution to this volume,[1] Gustav Sjöberg seeks to establish at the conceptual level an SRR's proper purpose and general conditions of success (section

---

[1] Gustav Sjöberg, 'Banking Special Resolution Regimes as a Governance Tool', ch 12 in this volume.

III). In particular, Sjöberg considers that SRRs are not meant merely to provide appropriate tools for handling crises, if and when these erupt, but also to prevent them, thus playing a continuous role as 'governance tools' (section V). To meet their dual objectives, SRRs should possess, in his view, three key features, which are discussed in turn below (sections VI to VIII).

I. Bank Failures and their Resolution Prior to the Global Financial Crisis

The experiences of the period preceding the global financial crisis should have alerted policymakers to the increasing fragility of banking institutions. The apparently benign macroeconomic environment which prevailed, roughly, from the mid-1980s to the eruption of the US 'subprime mortgage' crisis in 2007 – the so called 'great moderation'[2] – coincided with a rapid increase in the incidence of bank failures, small and large, sometimes isolated but often of systemic proportions. These affected, at different points in time and with variable severity, most economies in the world.[3] This trend was closely connected to the liberalisation and internationalisation of financial markets, which created new opportunities for risk taking and profit making, added to the competitive pressures that banks face and resulted in a more fluid and unpredictable economic environment.

Remarkably, up till the recent crisis, the prevalence of bank failures had failed to incentivise the search for general and internationally consistent solutions. The global and national policy debates were primarily focused on the development, implementation and cross-country convergence of prudential norms, especially of standards of capital adequacy, with a view to ensuring the viability of banking institutions and preventing crisis situations. In contrast, they either ignored or, at best, paid limited attention to the practical and legal aspects of the ex post handling of bank failures, should these occur. The same was true of most academic commentary. This 'preventative'-prudential bias of the policy debate is not surprising. After all, in a heavily regulated industry like banking, the financial or

---

[2] B Bernanke, 'The Great Moderation', remarks at the meetings of the Eastern Economic Association (Washington, DC, 20 February 2004) available at www.federalreserve.gov/boarddocs/speeches/2004/20040220/default.htm.

[3] Examining the period 1970–2011, Laeven and Valencia identify 147 'systemic' banking crises; their definition of a 'systemic' crisis combines significant signs of distress in the banking system with significant public intervention measures in response to the losses suffered by banks; L Laeven and F Valencia, 'Systemic Banking Crises Database: An Update', IMF Working Paper No WP/12/163 (June 2012) available at www.imf.org/external/pubs/ft/wp/2012/wp12163.pdf. Interestingly, of all the systemic banking crises identified by Laeven and Valencia, only four occurred before 1980 (specifically, in 1976 and 1977), while from that point onwards crises become common, with clusters observed in the early 1980s, at three points in the 1990s (affecting, consecutively, the transition economies, Latin America and East Asia) and finally in 2008 (with the eruption of the largest ever number of incidents, namely, 22).

operational failure of the participating enterprises is considered to be, not a normal occurrence, but an aberration, which also counts as a failure of the legislative and regulatory authorities. Thus, in normal times it comes more naturally to the regulatory community to discuss and develop safety standards, which are supposed to prevent the materialisation of risks, than to contemplate failure as a likely scenario, requiring contingency planning. This attitude was abandoned only because of the global crisis. Its unprecedented intensity forced lawmakers and regulators to recognise that banking failures cannot be wished away, nor assumed to be fully preventable, no matter how robust the applicable prudential regime.

This does not mean that in the past there was complete lack of concern for the treatment of bank failures, but simply that this took place in the form of ad hoc, improvised crisis management, once a failure had already occurred. Common global or European standards for bank resolution were lacking, and even at the domestic level most countries had not developed sufficient permanent arrangements for dealing with this eventuality.

More precisely, at the domestic level, the public authorities with responsibility for the banking sector did not stand idly by when bank failures occurred. However, their responses were frequently based, not on preordained policies and stable rules, but on a combination of administrative actions taking place without the benefit of clear and precise legislative guidance and of discretionary financial interventions. In addressing banks' distress, a variety of official actors – governments, central banks, banking regulators, deposit insurers, courts or other insolvency officials – could apply in makeshift ways, and possibly with little co-ordination, a diverse range of tools and powers: financial support measures, extended by the government or the central bank either on the basis of special legislation or by utilising the general provisions of fiscal, central banking, contract or company law; supervisory and enforcement decisions made under the standing administrative mandate of the regulatory authorities; or restructuring or liquidation decisions made by the courts or the relevant insolvency officials after the opening of formal insolvency proceedings.[4] The overall approach to bank crisis management thus lacked a clear legal and administrative structure, and the outcome of the official interventions was almost always up for grabs.

Of course, the level of actors and the type of response would typically depend on the nature and systemic impact of each case. Thus, in financial crises of systemic proportions the key official decisions have almost always been made or, at least, approved by the political leadership. The handling of such crises was – and continues to be – treated essentially as a matter of discretionary macroeconomic policy, rather than as a microeconomic question of market ordering, which could be regulated in advance by way of standing legal norms. The official interventions usually take the form of financial support operations in favour of part or the

---

[4] See C Hadjiemmanuil, 'Bank Resolution Policy and the Organization of Bank Insolvency Proceedings: Critical Dilemmas', in DG Mayes and A Liuksila (eds), *Who Pays for Bank Insolvency?* (Basingstoke and New York: Palgrave Macmillan, 2004) 276–80.

whole of the banking industry (for instance, extension by the central bank of emergency liquidity assistance or, to use the traditional term, lending of last resort, or provision by the state of blanket guarantees over banks' assets or liabilities), possibly in conjunction with the nationalisation of institutions which are no longer able to operate independently.

In the past, an essentially similar approach was followed whenever the imminent failure of a large banking institution raised the fear of contagion. When institutions of this type (formerly called 'too big to fail', but lately going by the more neutral appellation of 'systemically important financial institutions', or 'SIFIs') fell in distress, their fate was invariably decided, not by strict application of the applicable regulatory or insolvency rules, which might mandate the revocation of their licence or their placing in liquidation, but through hastily arranged mergers, refinancing packages or restructuring schemes, initiated by the ministry of finance or the central bank. Interventions of this type frequently involved the participation of the failed institutions' private competitors; thus, from a legal viewpoint, they could often be carried out by using the tools of negotiation, implicit pressure and private contracting, without need for formal acts of public law.

In contrast, the isolated failures of less significant financial institutions were occasionally allowed to run their course. In other words, from time to time a bank might go into insolvent liquidation. In this case, the standing legislation on bank insolvency (together with the administrative norms on the withdrawal of a bank's licence) would come into operation. Some jurisdictions had in place special insolvency rules for banking institutions. Other countries applied to the failed banks the norms of general corporate insolvency law. Even in the latter case, however, the insolvency law was frequently supplemented by a deposit guarantee system, covering the claims of retail depositors. All in all, the standing legislation applicable to failed banks suffered from two fundamental shortcomings: first, it only regulated bank insolvency proceedings as such, but did not cover the financial participation of the state in the rescue and/or restructuring of failed banks; and secondly, it was usually fragmentary or underdeveloped and did not fully articulate bank regulation as an administrative activity, on the one hand, with bank insolvency proceedings (winding up and, possibly, rehabilitation through restructuring), on the other. This was a recipe for inconsistency and confusion.

A major exception has been the United States. There, in the aftermath of the 'savings-and-loan' (or 'S&L') financial crisis of the late 1980s, the Congress adopted the Federal Deposit Insurance Corporation Improvement Act of 1991 (FDICIA),[5] which introduced a novel, robust and quite rational resolution system for American depository institutions. Operated by the Federal Deposit Insurance Corporation (FDIC), the FDICIA system integrated into a single regulatory (as distinct from judicial) process the provision of protection to the eligible depositors of failed banks (a policy applicable in the US since the 1930s) with the orderly resolution of the latter through expedited quasi-insolvency proceedings, guided

---

[5] PL 102-242, 105 Stat 2236.

by explicit legal policies and criteria. Nonetheless, despite the precedent set by FDICIA, until the eruption of the global financial crisis, the domestic and international policy pronouncements on bank crisis management and, in particular, bank insolvency law were few and far between.

Naturally, the international financial institutions and regulatory fora had not failed to notice the global surge in bank failures. Thus, from around 2000 onwards, they introduced in their agendas the issue of bank insolvency law and engaged in some exploratory work on the subject. The main initiatives of this period included: a technical paper issued in September 2001 by the Financial Stability Forum (the precursor of the Financial Stability Board, or FSB), which provided guidance to countries seeking to set up a deposit insurance system;[6] the 'Weak Banks' report issued in March 2002 by the Basel Committee on Banking Supervision (BCBS), setting out a structured approach to the management of bank distress and failure;[7] and a report prepared jointly by the International Monetary Fund (IMF) and the World Bank in 2002–03, comprising a detailed checklist of the institutional options and technical solutions that a national framework for the treatment of bank insolvency should address.[8] Significantly, the BCBS's 'Weak Banks' report covered both the pre- and post-insolvency phases of bank distress. However, it failed to address the complex institutional issues involved in the post-insolvency phase or in situations of systemic crisis, when the banking supervisory authority may either lack jurisdiction or be restricted to specific actions, while other authorities – the judiciary, the government, the central bank, or the deposit insurer – assume distinct and critical roles. This shortcoming was inherent in the fact that this was a BCBS report: written by and for regulators, the 'Weak Banks' report could not speak to or guide the actions of non-regulatory decision makers. As for the IMF/World Bank paper, its drafting was effectively completed by early 2004, but it was not formally endorsed and published until after the global financial crisis, in April 2009.[9] Thus, it was unavailable to influence the development of the legal and institutional situation while there was still time. All in all, by 2008 the various international efforts had not yet yielded concrete results, and the regulatory community still had a long way to go in order to arrive to globally consistent solutions.

---

[6] Financial Stability Forum, 'Guidance for Developing Effective Deposit Insurance Systems' (September 2001) available at www.financialstabilityboard.org/publications/r_0109b.htm.

[7] BCBS, 'Supervisory Guidance on Dealing with Weak Banks: Report of the Task Force on Dealing with Weak Banks' (March 2002) (the 'Weak Banks' report) available at www.bis.org/publ/bcbs88.pdf.

[8] See RB Leckow, 'The IMF/World Bank Global Insolvency Initiative – Its Purpose and Principal Features' in DS Hoelscher (ed), *Bank Restructuring and Resolution* (Basingstoke and New York: Palgrave Macmillan, 2006) 184–98.

[9] IMF and World Bank, 'An Overview of the Legal, Institutional, and Regulatory Framework for Bank Insolvency' (17 April 2009) available at www.imf.org/external/np/pp/eng/2009/041709.pdf.

II. Special Resolution Regimes for Banks as a New Policy Priority

Evidently, the crisis has changed all that. Especially after the collapse of Lehman Brothers, states on both sides of the Atlantic sought to prevent the collapse of large banks and to reverse the freezing of interbank lending markets by putting together emergency bank-support (or bail-out) programmes of various descriptions and huge proportions, whose fiscal implications were profound and quite disturbing. Most bail-out packages were introduced in the final months of 2008. They relied on a variety of tools, such as blanket deposit guarantees, guarantees in favour of wholesale bank creditors, capital injections, special lending assistance by states, emergency liquidity assistance by central banks, asset guarantees and direct asset-purchase programmes, which operated in parallel with general macro-economic measures of monetary and fiscal easing.

As the market environment becomes more stable, the financial burden becomes a key incentive for governments and central banks to seek a rapid exit from the bail-out packages.[10] By the same token, the fiscal nexus exercises a strong influence on the longer-term official policy stance, since it induces states to make bail-outs less likely in the future, by endorsing novel legal and regulatory tools for the treatment of bank failures, with the specific aim of discouraging and constraining the application of public monies in bank rescue operations. This has turned out to be a top priority at all policy-making levels – the global, the European and the national.[11]

The UK was one of the first countries to adopt a special resolution regime (SRR) for banks in the wake of the crisis.[12] The basic elements of its new statute, which was enacted in February 2009, have been a source of inspiration (or rather, a usable legislative model) for other jurisdictions. Germany has adopted its own version of SSR in December 2010.[13]

Globally, the BCBS has acted by promulgating, in co-operation with the International Association of Deposit Insurers (IADI), revamped standards for deposit insurance systems[14] and issuing a report on the coordinated treatment of bank insolvencies with cross-border implications.[15]

---

[10] FSB, 'Exit from Extraordinary Financial Sector Support Measures: Note for G20 Ministers and Governors Meeting 6-7 November 2009' (7 November 2009).

[11] For a state of play as at mid-2011, see BCBS, 'Resolution Policies and Frameworks – Progress So Far' (July 2011).

[12] Banking Act 2009.

[13] Gesetz zur Restrukturierung und geordneten Abwicklung von Kreditinstituten, zur Errichtung eines Restrukturierungsfonds für Kreditinstitute und zur Verlängerung der Verjährungsfrist der aktienrechtlichen Organhaftung (Restrukturierungsgesetz) vom 9. Dezember 2010, BGBl. 2010, I, 1900. For a brief description in English, see BJ Attinger, 'Crisis Management and Bank Resolution: Quo Vadis, Europe?', ECB Legal Working Paper No 13 (December 2011) 28–34.

[14] BCBS and IADI, 'Core Principles for Effective Deposit Insurance Systems' (June 2009).

[15] BCBS, 'Report and Recommendations of the Cross-Border Bank Resolution Group' (March 2010).

The key global initiative, however, has taken the form of a new standard for countries' bank resolution frameworks. This was prepared by the FSB[16] and endorsed by the G20 at the Cannes Summit of November 2011.[17] The new standard requires the establishment of national SRRs, whose scope should cover '[a]ny financial institution that could be systemically significant or critical if it fails';[18] thus, in principle, it is not confined to banks, but can also apply to insurance companies and non-depository financial intermediaries, such as securities houses. The document sets out under 12 main headings, accompanied by four annexes on specific implementation issues, the 'key attributes', or 'essential features', of an effective resolution regime. Its provisions address questions relating to:

- the scope of the SRR,
- the designation of the national resolution authority,
- the resolution-related powers of the latter,
- the treatment of contractual arrangements and clients' assets in the course of the resolution process,
- the necessary safeguards for the protection of the legal rights and financial interests of failed banks' creditors and shareholders,
- the funding of banks in resolution, that is, the identification of the sources of financing which may be used to maintain a failed bank's essential functions during its resolution, as well as
- the legal arrangements for cross-border co-operation in the case of a resolution with extraterritorial effects, including access to information and information sharing.

In addition, the standard establishes a set of resolution-related prior planning requirements, applicable primarily to the world's very largest banks, now dubbed 'global SIFIs' or 'G-SIFIs'; an accompanying list identifies by name 29 G-SIFIs, for which these requirements will need to be met by end-2012.[19] These requirements are intended to prepare the ground for an orderly resolution, in the event of a G-SIFI's failure. They encompass the introduction of multi-jurisdictional crisis management groups, with the participation of the relevant national public authorities of the various countries in which a G-SIFI's group operates, the conclusion of institution-specific cross-border co-operation agreements between the home and relevant host authorities involved in the planning and actual resolution stages, the regular conduct of resolvability assessments by the resolution authorities responsible for G-SIFIs, and the preparation and regular review of recovery and resolution plans by G-SIFIs and the supervisory and resolution authorities

[16] FSB, 'Key Attributes of Effective Resolution Regimes for Financial Institutions' (October 2011) available at www.financialstabilityboard.org/publications/r_111104cc.pdf.
[17] G20, 'Cannes Summit Final Declaration: Building Our Common Future: Renewed Collective Action for the Benefit of All' (4 November 2011) para 28.
[18] FSB, 'Key Attributes' (n 16) para 1.1.
[19] FSB, 'Policy Measures to Address Systemically Important Financial Institutions' (4 November 2011). The list will be updated regularly and will eventually include, in addition to banks, insurers and non-bank financial entities of global systemic importance.

responsible for them, respectively. While the FSB and the G-20 demand the application of the resolvability assessment and recovery and resolution planning requirements only in relation to G-SIFIs, national authorities are free to extend this approach to local SIFIs or even to non-systemically-important institutions.

At the European level, the European Commission presented its comprehensive proposal for handling financially weak or insolvent banks, the Draft Recovery and Resolution Directive, in June 2012.[20] The proposed framework requires EU Member States to adopt provisions on preparatory and preventative measures (including the preparation of recovery plans by individual banks and resolution plans by their supervisors),[21] on early supervisory intervention in the event of breach of a bank's prudential requirements (including by way of appointing special managers),[22] and on special resolution powers and tools in situations where a bank is failing or likely to fail.[23] The establishment of 'resolution financing arrangements' (that is, dedicated resolution funds), which should be pre-funded by means of levies on the financial institutions subject to the resolution framework, is also envisaged to secure bridge financing for potential restructuring operations under the national SRRs.[24]

Essentially, the prototype for the various SRRs recently adopted or currently under discussion is FDICIA. This applies, most evidently, to the UK's SRR,[25] but is also true of the other systems and proposals mentioned above. Nonetheless, the SRRs of the new, post-crisis generation include additional elements, which go beyond the FDICIA model in significant ways. A good example would be the requirement of pre-crisis contingency planning for a potential situation of distress at the level of individual banks, in the form of so called 'recovery and resolution plans', colloquially known as 'living wills'. Another example would be the requirement that banks raise part of their funding in the form of convertible debt instruments (most famously, 'contingent convertible bonds' or 'CoCos'), whose unilateral conversion in the event of distress can permit a rapid debt-to-equity recapitalisation of the issuing institution, avoiding the need for public funding. Finally, one should not forget the creation of industry-wide resolution funds, which can provide large amounts of financing for restructuring operations, where necessary.

Given the economic importance of the matter and the novelty of the preferred solutions, it is no wonder that the adoption, under the rubric of SRRs, of new tools and powers for the restructuring (or, at least, going-concern liquidation) of

---

[20] European Commission, 'Proposal for a Directive of the European Parliament and of the Council establishing a framework for the recovery and resolution of credit institutions and investment firms and amending Council Directives 77/91/EEE and 82/891/EC, Directives 2001/24/EC, 2002/47/EC, 2005/56/EC, 2007/36/EC and 2011/35/EC and Regulation (EU) No 1093/2010', COM(2012) 280/3, 6 June 2012.

[21] Draft Recovery and Resolution Directive, Title II (Articles 4–22).

[22] ibid Title III (Articles 23–25).

[23] ibid Title IV (Articles 26–79).

[24] ibid Title VII (Articles 90–99).

[25] P Brierley, 'The UK Special Resolution Regime for Failing Banks in an International Context', Bank of England Financial Stability Paper No 5 (July 2009) 4.

failed banks generates considerable interest, theoretical as well as practical. It is in this context that one should examine Gustaf Sjöberg's contribution to this volume.

III. The Sjöberg Thesis

Sjöberg undertakes an advocacy of SRRs at the conceptual level. Specifically, he maintains that SRRs should be designed to address the situation of a systemically important bank facing acute problems (as distinct from the distress or failure of a small bank without systemic implications). They should serve two objectives: (a) at the time of crisis, to provide sufficient legal tools for dealing with the failed bank(s) while preserving systemic stability, in the sense of securing the continuous provision of the key functions of the financial system; and (b) ex ante, to create an appropriate set of incentives, so as to preserve market discipline and avoid moral hazard. An SRR with the aforementioned focus and objectives would have to display, in Sjöberg's view, three essential design features.

First, to ensure the SRR's operation as a 'governance tool' (which I take to mean that the SRR should establish appropriate incentive structures for bank stakeholders) and, in particular, in order to combat moral hazard, the rules should promise ex ante and in a credible way to inflict losses on shareholders and debt holders in the event that their bank fails. This would force such private stakeholders to behave more responsibly in normal times. It would equally reduce their room for negotiation with the authorities in times of crisis.

Secondly, the applicable rules should enable the authorities to take immediate and legally unchallengeable control over a bank facing acute distress. Beyond the purely managerial responsibilities, the authorities' control should enable them to decide irreversible on all appropriate corporate actions, including the transfer of the bank's ownership.

Finally, while the tools of the SRR may be insufficient to handle a fully-fledged systemic crisis (that is, one characterised by the disruption of large parts of the financial system), which may necessitate the adoption of ad hoc state support measures, they should still be applicable and functional in a situation of this type. The suspension of the SRR's applicability during systemic crises would be counterproductive, because it would strengthen the banks' stakeholders' hand in the negotiating table, probably resulting in more generous support packages than what is warranted. Moreover, the prospect of suspension of the SRR's operation in favour of ad hoc solutions would provide a reason for the various stakeholders of banking institutions (managers, shareholders and creditors) to behave strategically. Conceivably, the stakeholders might even allow a simmering crisis to reach systemic proportions, precisely in order to benefit from the SRR's suspension, the discontinuation of its strict resolution approach and the introduction of an exceptional support package more advantageous to their interests.

Despite Sjöberg's strong reservations about certain technical elements of the recently enacted or proposed SRRs mentioned above, his thinking and proposals to a large extent dovetail with the current policy trend. Nonetheless, they are not bereft of conceptual difficulties and internal tensions. I will try to address the issue from a limited number of angles. Following a short terminological comment (section IV), I will turn to Sjöberg's views on the proper objectives of SRRs (section V). I will then proceed to a discussion of the three levels of bank crisis management, and on Sjöberg's view that SSRs should prioritise the second (SIFI resolution) but also be available in the third (systemic crisis management) (section VI). I will continue with the resolution authorities' ability to immediately assume control over failed banks, which Sjöberg considers crucial, and on which apparently depends the achievement of his first key objective (section VII). Finally, I will comment on the ex ante perspective, which is thought to be a necessary element of a properly designed SSR, and which evidently relates to the achievement of the second key objective, that is, the containment of moral hazard (section VIII).

IV. The Ambit of Bank Resolution

Clarifying what one means by 'bank resolution' might help. The use of the term in the banking literature is not entirely consistent.

Two pioneering experts in bank insolvency law, Tobias Asser[26] and Eva Hüpkes,[27] use the term to describe the techniques that can be applied for the reorganisation, disposal or liquidation of banks in the context of formal bank insolvency proceedings, regardless of their precise legal basis (general insolvency law or special insolvency or administrative law) and of who is in charge (the insolvency courts or the banking regulatory authorities). In similar fashion, Sjöberg uses the term 'SRR' to denote the set of standing legal arrangements establishing insolvency and quasi-insolvency procedures for the liquidation and/or restructuring of banks facing financial difficulties. But in the case of systemic crises, he explicitly allows for ad hoc state interventions, outside the SRR framework, in support of the banking sector.

Of course, 'resolution' could be understood to include such interventions too. That is, the term could be used in a sense encompassing every conceivable response of the authorities when faced with a bank's actual or imminent failure

[26] TMC Asser, *Legal Aspects of Regulatory Treatment of Banks in Distress* (Washington, DC, International Monetary Fund, 2001) ch XI, especially 141: 'Bank resolution procedures are used to dispose of a bank. Generally, therefore, they come into play only while the bank is in receivership or when insolvency proceedings have been opened against the bank.'

[27] E Hüpkes, *The Legal Aspects of Bank Insolvency: A Comparative Analysis of Western Europe, the United States and Canada* (The Hague, Kluwer Law International, 2000) ch IV, especially 83: 'The resolution of a bank insolvency is accomplished, in a broad sense, in either of two fundamental ways – ie through the option of reorganization or through the option of a winding-up and liquidation of its assets.'

(in the sense of the insolvency and/or collapse of its business operation).[28] Many types of action would fall under this heading: administrative measures to deal with floundering banking organisations; formal insolvency proceedings aimed at restructuring or liquidating banks which have crossed the relevant legal threshold; private transactions that the authorities instigate and help organise informally, such as merger, acquisition or asset-sale transactions, leading to a transfer of the failed bank's operations, in whole or in part, to a viable institution and their continuation on a going-concern basis; and all sorts of bail-outs, leading to the survival of the failed banks with the support of public monies. This brings into the picture a variety of pre-insolvency actions (or, to use Sjöberg's terminology, actions that do not presuppose legal assumption of immediate and absolute control over a bank by the state authorities).[29]

Sjöberg's usage is consistent with the actual or proposed SRRs of recent vintage, which do not cover the whole field of bank resolution in the latter, wider sense. In essence, these are confined to matters of bank insolvency law, replacing the general corporate insolvency proceedings with a bank-specific system of formal resolution proceedings and tools. Within this narrower field, they prioritise particular schemes of action and seek to exclude others. This is justified, to the extent that, while descriptively the range of possibilities and policy alternatives relating to bank insolvency is very wide, from a prescriptive viewpoint a *properly constituted* system of bank resolution may justifiably rule out certain options or promote particular types of outcome.

For instance, in the European Commission's Draft Recovery and Resolution Directive, 'resolution' is defined as 'the restructuring of [a banking] institution in order to ensure the continuity of its essential functions, preserve financial stability and restore the viability of all or part of that institution'.[30] This legislative definition does not seek to provide a 'neutral' lexical meaning of the term; instead, it is a stipulative definition, limited to the purposes of the specific text or, at most, of European policy making. Significantly, by confining the term's use only to restructuring efforts directed to the stated objectives, the definition effectively constitutes an authoritative declaration of a policy preference. In this sense, it reflects the emerging consensus amongst international policymakers on the proper purposes of bank insolvency law.

---

[28] Thus, eg, M Dewatripont and X Freixas, 'Bank Resolution: Lessons from the Crisis' in M Dewatripont and X Freixas (eds), *The Crisis Aftermath: New Regulatory Paradigms* (London, Centre for Economic Policy Research, 2012) 106, define a 'bank resolution procedure' as 'any public intervention that is intended to restore the bank's normal business conditions or to liquidate it, thus restoring normal business conditions for all other banks'.

[29] This broad understanding of the term is consistent with its use by the BCBS 'Weak Banks' report (n 7) section 6.

[30] COM(2012) 280/3 (n 20), proposed provisions, Article 2(1).

V. Objectives of Bank Resolution

One can think of various reasons for which the enactment of a special set of insolvency rules for banking institutions may be desirable. Some of these could be valid, even if bank insolvency law had the same primary objectives as general corporate insolvency law. The latter is typically thought to pursue the protection of the assets of the insolvent estate from further dissipation, the maximisation of their collection value (whether through their piecemeal disposal or by means of the going-concern liquidation or a restructuring of the insolvent enterprise), the satisfaction of liability holders to the maximum possible extent and always in accordance with a specific order of priority (reflecting the prior contractual engagements and expectations of the liability holders, based on which these are pigeonholed in different classes) and, conversely, the apportionment of final losses in a principled and predictable manner.[31] The key problem here is the avoidance of a race for the assets of the insolvent enterprise by individual creditors, whose uncoordinated attempts to enforce their respective claims by grabbing and liquidating particular assets of the debtor enterprise is likely to result in an economically wasteful and unjustified diminution of the total value of its estate, including through the destruction of its going-concern surplus value. From this standpoint, the primary objective of insolvency law is to maximise the value of the common pool of assets (that is, the insolvent estate) for the benefit of all creditors – an objective pursued through the main institutions of insolvency law (moratorium on individual enforcement actions, collective proceedings, satisfaction of the creditors in order of priority between classes and on a pari passu basis within each class, etc).[32]

However, the effective implementation of the objective of realised-value maximisation may depend on the specific context, which may not be the same for banks as for industrials or commercial companies. If so, the purpose of the special banking regime would be to provide appropriate solutions to certain technical problems of bank insolvency which are not present in other cases. In particular, the nature of the financial assets and the liabilities in banks' balance sheets may justify appropriate derogations from the general rules of corporate insolvency, in

---

[31] cf IMF Legal Department, *Orderly & Effective Insolvency Proceedings: Key Issues* (Washington, DC, International Monetary Fund, 1999) 5–7.

[32] On the best-known theoretical model, these institutions should be understood as a putative 'creditors' bargain': if only they had the opportunity to bargain with each other before lending to the enterprise in question, creditors in general would be likely to converge voluntarily on something similar to the existing arrangements of mandatory insolvency law. See TH Jackson, 'Bankruptcy, Non-Bankruptcy Entitlements, and the Creditors' Bargain' (1982) 91 *Yale Law Journal* 857–907; and DG Baird and TH Jackson, 'Bargaining after the Fall and the Contours of the Absolute Priority Rule' (1988) 55 *University of Chicago Law Review* 738–89. For alternative views of US and English bankruptcy law, see, eg, BE Adler, 'Financial and Political Theories of American Corporate Bankruptcy' (1993) 45 *Stanford Law Review* 311–46; and RJ Mokal, *Corporate Insolvency Law* (Oxford and New York, Oxford University Press, 2005) ch 2.

order to increase the effectiveness of the stock-taking and collection effort and to avoid untoward secondary effects of the insolvency process. The need for special rules may be especially pressing in relation to the fate of transactions carried out through organised markets and/or payment and settlement systems: their abrupt discontinuation or unwinding as a result of the commencement of insolvency proceedings may involve significant negative externalities and undermine the smooth operation of such markets and systems. Thus, special rules have been introduced in the EU and elsewhere, which modify the time when the official pronouncement of insolvency comes into effect, or which exempt certain financial transactions from the operation of the moratorium, from the right of insolvency officials to step out of transactions, etc.[33]

More obviously, many countries have in place regimes of deposit insurance, whose effect is to provide a predetermined measure of protection to retail depositors, even when the value of an insolvent bank's estate does not suffice for this purpose.[34] Deposit insurance has a specific protective objective, unrelated to those of general corporate insolvency law; this objective can be pursued outside the otherwise applicable bank insolvency framework, through distinct structures and tools. Thus, payments out of the deposit insurance fund typically take place independently of the main insolvency proceedings. Of course, the effect of such payments may be to bring a particular class of liabilities outside the insolvency process or, alternatively, to cause the deposit insurer's subrogation to the claims of the original depositors. The objectives of the insolvency process per se are not necessarily altered as a result.

Even the wholesale exclusion of the general insolvency system and the subjection of banks to SRRs could be compatible with a continuing insistence on the normal objectives of insolvency law. Thus, SRRs could be justified by reference, not to any special objectives of bank resolution, but to the need to ensure administrative coherence and continuity across the banking supervisory, deposit insurance and resolution processes. Administrative streamlining and simplicity in the lines of communication and remedial action are particularly important in the case of transnational banks and banking groups. In this context, the complexities of cross-border bank resolution could also militate in favour of SRRs.

For Sjöberg, however, as for a great many other policymakers and academic students of banking, the reasons justifying SRRs are not technical or administrative. They go to the heart of resolution policy – that is, to its very objectives. The critical assumption here is that the famed 'specialness' of banks, which provides the justification for their prudential regulation, also dominates their post-failure treatment and determines its objectives.

---

[33] At the European level, see Directive 98/26/EC of the European Parliament and of the Council of 19 May 1998 on settlement finality in payment and securities settlement systems, OJ 1998 L 166/45, as amended; and Directive 2002/47/EC of the European Parliament and of the Council of 6 June 2002 on financial collateral arrangements, OJ 2002 L 168/43, as amended.

[34] At the European level, see Directive 94/19/EC of the European Parliament and of the Council of 30 May 1994 on deposit-guarantee schemes, OJ 1994 L 135/5, as amended.

It is commonplace to describe banking intermediation as a peculiar type of business activity, whose unique features render the banks especially vulnerable to crises. On the standard theory, individual banks can fall victim to crises of confidence (depositors' 'panics') precipitating runs on their deposits which destroy their funding base, even in situations where their underlying situation is otherwise sound. Moreover, banking crises, far from affecting one bank at a time, are notoriously contagious. This property of banking intermediation is untypical of other sectors. In most commercial and industrial fields, the failure of one firm is a boon for its competitors, not a cause of harm. In contrast, a bank's failure can be a source of troubles, with potentially fatal consequences, for some or all of its peers. Further, the failure of banking institutions, especially in the context of a generalised ('systemic') financial crisis, is thought to entail significant external costs, which go beyond the banking market. Over and above the losses suffered by the failed banks' immediate creditors (including depositors) and market counterparties, a systemic financial crisis can lead to large-scale unavailability of depositors' transaction accounts, a collapse of the monetary aggregates and the payments system, a severe disruption of the provision of liquidity to the real economy and a large-scale destruction of economically useful information relating to the failed banks' borrowers. In short, on this account, if bank failures were left unchecked to run their course, their effects could reach catastrophic proportions, inflicting huge loss of value and bringing the whole economy to a state of deep depression. Thus, it would seem imperative for the state to engage in prudential supervision of the banking institutions with a view to establishing their financial and operational soundness, to intervene by financial and other means in order to prevent banks from failing or, when this cannot be avoided, to ensure that their failure is orderly, of limited dimensions and unlikely to thwart the continuous performance of the financial system's critical functions. In other words, the 'systemic' rationale for intervention, to which Sjöberg subscribes explicitly, apparently dictates the special treatment of banks both preventatively (through prudential regulation) as well as reactively (through active crisis management and a special insolvency regime, that is, an SRR).

On this account, the objectives of bank resolution (including resolution in the narrow sense of the formal SRR) are inherently different from those pertinent to other business entities. In Sjöberg's formulation, an SRR should serve two overriding goals: (a) the preservation of systemic stability, including a continuing performance of all critical banking functions;[35] and (b) the simultaneous maintenance of market discipline.[36] According to Sjöberg, the former goal is not difficult to

---

[35] This raises the following question, which I do not intend to discuss here: What does it mean to preserve a 'functioning' financial system? Does this merely require the continuing supply of payment and account-related services to the depositing public? Or does it further involve a steady level of lending activity, so as to ensure the regular provision of liquidity to the real economy?

[36] Sjöberg recognises a subsidiary objective or, possibly, restriction of his proposed scheme, namely, that the SRR should allow 'banks without a viable business [to] be forced to close down', thus allowing 'a continuing development of the financial sector'. In fact, this is not a separate consideration, but a specific implication of the market-discipline principle.

achieve, at least as long as the state's financial position is strong – presumably because even deeply insolvent banks can be refinanced and/or recapitalised with taxpayers' money. This, however, may be a source of significant moral hazard, to the extent that the expectation of a state-financed bail-out reduces the incentives of bank managers and other stakeholders to behave prudently.

Sjöberg rejects the minimisation of costs to society and to the taxpayers as separate objectives, apparently on the ground that a successful resolution process achieving his two overriding goals necessarily entails least-cost solutions. Why exactly this is so, is not spelt out in detail. However, Sjöberg argues that placing undue emphasis on the absolute fiscal cost (costs to taxpayers) of resolution is wrong, since fiscal expenditure of any magnitude can be justified if it results in greater benefits (or greater reduction of costs, which amounts to the same thing) to society as a whole. One can agree that the objective of market discipline leaves no room for unnecessary transfers from taxpayers to bank stakeholders or for bank support packages that are not justified on an economy-wide cost-benefit analysis. The reverse, however, is not self-evident: even a parsimonious and well-calibrated expenditure of public resources in bank restructuring efforts can, nonetheless, include elements of subsidisation of the bank stakeholders and their risk-taking activities, thus negating Sjöberg's second goal.

This possibility raises a more fundamental question about the compatibility of the two objectives in the context of SRRs of the type under consideration. Is it truly possible to reconcile the strictures of market discipline with an SRR which prioritises, in the name of systemic stability and the uninterrupted provision of key financial services, the continuing survival, through mergers or restructuring, of banking institutions which have already proven unable to avoid failure (distress and/or insolvency)?

VI. Three Levels of Bank Crisis Management?

Sjöberg distinguishes between three types of situations that an SRR might be intended to handle, namely: (a) individual failures of banks of no systemic importance; (b) individual failures of systemically important banks, which have not (yet) triggered a fully-fledged systemic crisis; or (c) fully-fledged systemic crises, engulfing substantial parts of the national, or even the international, banking industry. Apparently, for each type (or 'level') of failure, different considerations apply and the official response should be based on different principles.

For first-level failures, the key issues are the establishment of rules on depositor protection and the avoidance of regulatory forbearance. Sjöberg claims that SRRs calculated to handle first-level failures may prove insufficient for second-level events: due to the scale and complexity of the institutions involved, the latter demand much more complicated technical responses. For this reason, the SRR should be designed with the second level in mind. As for fully-fledged systemic crises, Sjöberg suggests that they cannot be handled through an SRR 'in the ordinary meaning' (which apparently covers only standing, rule-bound resolution methods supported by predetermined financial resources); additional tools will be needed. Indeed, in contrast to a first- or second-level situation, a third-level crisis is said to be 'non-insurable', in the sense that its resolution cannot rely on financial resources set aside in advance by way of industry-based levies and commitments (say, in the form of deposit insurance premiums or prefunded resolutions funds). Moreover, level three crisis management cannot count on private-sector participation, since in the midst of serious systemic disturbances it may be impossible to find suitable private investors (meaning, in effect, other banks with sufficient resources and willingness to take up additional risk) who will pick up the pieces of the distressed banks by contributing in their recapitalisation, acquiring them or taking over their operations. Thus, a crisis of systemic proportions will often necessitate extraordinary solutions, based on ad hoc political judgement, not legal norms. These will typically include the extension of large-scale discretionary financial aid by the state. In Sjöberg's own words, '[a] system that does not allow for state support in one or another form is not realistic'.

Based on this analysis, Sjöberg concludes that (a) the SRR's standing norms should be sufficient for resolving effectively and at an early stage second-level failures (isolated failures of large, systemically important institutions) and (b) they should not contain elements inconsistent with the parallel adoption of any ad hoc measures which might be considered necessary ex post in view of the factual circumstances of a third-level crisis. The second criterion is intended to avoid the need for a formal suspension of the SRR before special measures – including the provision of State aid to individual institutions or to the banking industry at large – can be implemented. The mandatory tools of the SRR should be able to operate in conjunction with a wide variety of state measures for the recapitalisation of the banking sector and/or the enhancement of its liquidity.

In my view, the three-level framework, while useful for the exposition of the diverse challenges posed by different types of banking crisis, is not sufficiently robust, so as to be able to inform the design or the operation of the SRR. As Sjöberg himself admits, it is often impossible to distinguish between the various levels; nonetheless, not only the mix of tools, but even the objectives of resolution change (if they are not entirely reversed) as we move from the second to the third level. Thus, a potentially drastic shift in the preferred resolution approach comes to depend on an obscure and imprecise criterion.

More specifically, the distinction between systemically important and other banks is not at all clear. Admittedly, the failure of a small bank is less likely to trigger systemic problems than that of a large one. In particular, in the former case the direct transmission of losses to other banks through various counterparty exposures will be of little consequence. On the other hand, even a small bank's failure can cause informational contagion, if it is perceived (either accurately or with informational 'noise') as indicative of industry-wide problems. Assuming (as many authors appear to believe, but I very much doubt) that pure (irrational) panics are possible in banking, it may even trigger a baseless loss of confidence in other banks. Interestingly, Sjöberg does not deny that any number of factors can render a bank 'systemically important': 'Difficulties in a bank have systemic implications in two cases, namely when the bank in itself is so large that its failure will create considerable disturbances to the functioning of the economy as a whole or when there is risk of contagion (when difficulties in one bank lead to problems in other banks).' If so, depending on the circumstances almost any institution may generate systemic concerns and it is not possible to determine beforehand which individual institutions are systemically important. Systemic importance thus becomes a question of context and judgement. But then, no true distinction can be drawn between the first and second levels. What is left, is a reasonable call for rules of sufficient sophistication, which so as to enable rapid, decisive and orderly handling of failures even of large and operationally complex (rather than 'systemically important') banking institutions.

For similar reasons, the distinction between second- and third-level crisis failures does not depend on the intrinsic characteristics of the failed institutions, but on the intervening fact of contagion – or, more precisely, on the presence, nature and degree of common problems, afflicting the total banking industry or large segments thereof. A third-level crisis cannot always be prevented by handling 'promptly and correctly' the initial distress of particular bank, because in this situation the troubles are not transmitted sequentially. Instead, common underlying causes affect many banks in parallel and almost simultaneously. Typically, fully-fledged systemic banking crises (including, by the way, the latest, global one) represent the final phase of macroeconomic imbalances and asset bubbles. In terms of policy response, they require measures of general applicability, aimed at the restoration of macroeconomic and financial stability and the normalisation of market conditions, including through the recognition and absorption of the bad-debt overhang. For this purpose, the state authorities (meaning, in this context, not merely the various administrative authorities performing the tasks of banking supervision, deposit insurance and bank resolution, but primarily the senior economic decision makers in the government and the central bank) will need to be involved in a major way.

Bank restructuring certainly has a role to play in the context of a systemic crisis, but it is not the first priority. In the midst of a financial crisis characterised by liquidity squeezes and non-performing asset markets, it is difficult to distinguish between the non-viable ('insolvent') banks and those whose fortunes have taken a turn for the worse because of the negative macroeconomic environment, but which are otherwise viable and fundamentally sound. The ambiguous condition of many banks, in particular due to extraordinary funding difficulties beyond each individual bank's control, as well as the prevalence of fire-sale prices for assets, which impedes an accurate valuation of bank portfolios, becomes a matter of contestation, impeding the restructuring efforts. Moreover, a policy of harsh enforcement and immediate restructuring may aggravate in and of itself the situation. In normal periods, the official policies may insist on strict conditions for lending of last resort, limits on the cover offered by deposit insurance systems, early intervention in distressed banks and rapid resolution, including through unforgiving treatment of bank shareholders and managers, or even junior creditors. Once a systemic crisis has erupted, however, the emphasis shifts to measures intended to forestall further contagion, prevent a collapse of monetary circulation and the payment system, stop runs, pacify the market participants and sustain the flow of liquidity from the financial intermediaries to the real economy. In the latter context, it often appears imperative for the state to validate all and sundry financial claims. A host of extraordinary policies, all marked by the ex post relaxation of the supposed rigours of market discipline, thus come into play: emergency liquidity assistance by the central bank, with few strings attached;[37] blanket guarantees in favour of depositors and other creditors; and even guarantees in relation to new assets and special-purpose vehicles for the management of impaired existing assets, which seek to reduce the asset-side-risks faced by the banks themselves and to protect them from excessive losses.[38] In extreme cases of massive withdrawals of bank deposit liabilities, a mandatory change of the contractual terms of deposits may be attempted, in the form of 'bank holidays' or administrative restrictions in the withdrawal of deposits ('deposit freezes'). Such interventions take place in the name of minimisation of the wider costs of the systemic crisis, which threatens to disrupt profoundly the operation of the real economy and the society that the financial intermediaries are supposed to serve.

Sjöberg rightly points out that the financial resources on which an SRR is supposed to rely (that is, the resources of the deposit insurance fund and/or the pre-funded resolution fund, if such a fund exists, as well the resources that the private sector might be expected to commit) are bound to prove insufficient in the event of a systemic crisis. However, the SRR's tools of coercion may still prove useful and facilitate the implementation of the authorities' preferred response to the crisis. On this basis, Sjöberg recommends that the SRR should not rely exclusively on private solutions or pretend to disallow wider measures of state support.

Admittedly, in circumstances of systemic crisis an unduly restrictive SRR would have to be side-lined through special legislation. This could give rise to delays and uncertainties, which might worsen the developing crisis. It is less evident, however, that the suspension of the SRR per se would somehow weaken the state's hand in its negotiations with the banks' stakeholders, as Sjöberg fears, since the extraordinary legislation introduced to legitimise the crisis-related measures could always include equivalent coercive tools. In this case too, the main risk is not that the state lacks sufficient powers of coercion, but that it is unwilling to use them. In fact, in a systemic crisis the officials' bias towards forbearance becomes

---

[37] ie lending of last resort at low interest rates, with long periods for repayment and on relaxed collateral – exactly the opposite from Bagehot's celebrated formula of one and a half centuries ago. See W Bagehot, *Lombard Street: A Description of the Money Market*, 3rd edn (London, Henry S King & Co, 1873) 196–99.

[38] DS Hoelscher and S Ingves, 'The Resolution of Systemic Banking System Crises' in DS Hoelscher (ed), *Bank Restructuring and Resolution* (Basingstoke and New York, Palgrave Macmillan, 2006) 3–23.

especially acute, for two reasons already mentioned above: first, because it may not be clear that the banks in distress are individually blameworthy and/or unviable; and second, because strict enforcement can be self-defeating, since it can increase the risk of contagion. The main problem, then, with systemic crisis management is not simply that it requires very large amounts of financing, which exceed the SRR's ordinary resources, but that it results in a wholesale relaxation of the insolvency constraint. In essence, this amounts to an almost complete reversal of the policy priorities of the SRR, since in an isolated bank failure (even that of a 'systemically important' institution) the strict enforcement of the balance-sheet constraints may dominate the choices of the resolution authorities (at least in the form of the least-cost-resolution principle), while in a systemic crisis the preferred resolution approach will typically be marked by disregard precisely for such constraints. In Sjöberg's terminology, the two objectives of the SRR do not operate concurrently: while in the first two levels (that is, when the stability of the whole system is not yet under direct threat) the primary goal of the resolution process will be the preservation of market discipline, as soon as we move into the third level the objective of restoring systemic stability takes over, not in conjunction, but largely as a negation of the former objective.

Since the point of transition from the one level to the other is imperceptible and inherently contestable,[39] mingling the 'norm' of individual bank resolution with the 'exception' of systemic crisis management is tantamount to building into the SRR conflicting objectives and open-ended tools. This will have negative consequences for the incentives of the resolution authorities. In particular, explicitly allowing the SRR's tools to be utilised in conjunction with discretionary financing operations involving public funds (in other words, with bail-out packages) will operate as an open invitation to the resolution authorities to consider a relaxation of their policy stance, by casually claiming that the threshold of systemic crisis has been crossed or is about to be crossed. Sjöberg argues that the availability of the SRR's coercive tools in the context of a third-level crisis will be beneficial, because it will reduce bank shareholders' room for negotiation. However, if the SRR's procedural framework is used in all cases, but the objectives (or, at least, the priorities) and thus the preferred outcomes remain open for consideration, depending on the level of crisis, the main effect will probably be, not to reduce the room for negotiation in third-level cases, but to increase it in first- and second-level ones. The reason is that a discretionary choice as to the general direction of the official intervention will always be possible, but will simply be disguised as a discussion about the potential systemic repercussions of strict enforcement under the circumstances. This will reduce the automaticity of the SRR's operation and open the road to negotiation and, ultimately, to forbearance.

From this viewpoint, to the extent that it is intended to discourage forbearance (a necessity for an SRR aspiring to an ex ante role as a 'governance tool'!), the SRR

---

[39] ibid 12, where the authors point out that the diagnosis of banking sector conditions in a systemic crisis is typically hampered by data limitations.

will need to focus exclusively on individual bank failures and its available options will have to be confined to the orderly but strict enforcement of the insolvency constraint.[40]

VII. Immediate Assumption of Control Over Failed Banks: Trigger and Stakeholders' Rights

Sjöberg is on strong ground when he insists that the SRR should enable the resolution authorities to assume immediate and absolute control of failed banks. This is necessary both in order to preclude further deterioration of the situation and to ensure a more effective restructuring.

As a weak bank's net worth approaches zero, the shareholders and managers become increasingly risk-prone. Their incentives lead them to gamble for resurrection, because they have very little to lose and everything to gain by speculating with the resources still left under their control. This tendency becomes even stronger once the net worth has become negative. The probability that the stakeholders' gamble will be successful is very low; but the ensuing losses can be monumental and can accrue in a very short period of time. To avoid this development, the legal rules should enable banking regulators to take early and full control of banks in distress.

An additional consideration is that, since the resolution (in the wide sense) of banks in distress does not necessarily entail their placement in formal insolvency proceedings, not even the expropriation of the old shareholders, the latter are interested in solutions that will preserve the value of their shareholdings to the maximum extent possible. In particular, they will insist on solutions that ensure the continuing operation of their institution without change of legal form or cancellation of the existing shares, preferably with the benefit of state financial support. Similarly, senior bank managers will strive to remain in their place. To achieve this result, such stakeholders will act strategically, utilising any available legal means. The implication is that, insofar as certain solutions can be lawfully implemented only with their support or, at least, consent, old shareholders will tend to withhold such support, in expectation of a better deal. Knowing that the failure of their institution may cause embarrassment to the regulatory authorities and political cost to the government will play in their favour. Significantly, at this stage the old stakeholders will have a perverse incentive to amplify the scale of

---

[40] In Sjöberg's view, recent proposals place excessive emphasis on the handling of individual systemically important banks, eg through recovery and resolution plans, liquidity planning or CoCos, without taking into consideration that the proposed measures would not work well in a level three situation. This, however, is perfectly natural, since on Sjöberg's own account the SRR should be specifically directed to second-level situations! Even from the standpoint of the three-level distinction, it does not hold water to claim that an SSR should eschew principles and tools appropriate for handling level two situations, simply because these do not fit well with the discretionary bail-out or forbearance measures potentially required for crisis management in a level three situation.

systemic risk posed by their institution, in an attempt to hide its specific short-comings within a picture of market-wide problems and to force the hand of the regulators in the direction of a bail-out package on terms generous to them (retention of value in a recapitalised bank, retention of their position in its gover-nance). For this reason, the old stakeholders should not be left in control, nor be allowed to act as veto players in relation to the restructuring decisions of the reso-lution authorities. Instead, to be effective, the SRR must enable the resolution authorities to pursue without obstruction the restructuring and continuation of a failed bank's operations, where this is appropriate, including through the manda-tory sale of its business as a going concern (purchase-and-assumption trans-actions) or of the legal entity itself, or through the write down of share capital.

Sjöberg considers that, for this purpose, the assumption by the resolution authorities of voting rights will be equally effective with the direct assumption of ownership over the shares; it will also be preferable, as less intrusive to the incumbent shareholders' rights pending verification of the situation and precise valuation of the stakes.[41] Retention of the underlying title to the shares by the old shareholders makes possible a reversal of the situation and their restoration to their full rights in the event of a successful resolution of a non-balance-sheet-insolvent but nonetheless distressed bank. In addition, it enables the old owner-ship's participation in capital injections or the trading of their shares. In theory, this can facilitate the implementation of private solutions. However, it creates the risk that certain but not all old shareholders (or their successors) will exercise their pre-emption rights and participate in a potential recapitalisation, thus fail-ing to raise adequate funds for recapitalisation but still precluding a clean break with the past through an effective and complete change of ownership. The result-ing delays and uncertainties can dissuade new investors from taking over failed banks. In any event, the difference becomes theoretical, when the restructuring involves the mandatory sale of the business or of the legal entity. Sjöberg himself contemplates the utilisation of tools outside the system of corporate actions of company law, such as compulsory write down of share capital or debt. A com-plete expropriation of the shareholders is necessary in this case, both because we are already in the field of insolvency law and because it would be a gross violation of the order of priorities to write down debt without first exhausting the resources of the shareholders.

Sjöberg suggests that the immediate assumption of control by the resolution authorities is especially important in the case of banks suffering from underlying insolvency, while those subject to temporary liquidity problems, but otherwise viable could receive emergency liquidity assistance (ELA) from the central bank and survive while remaining under the control of the old stakeholders. The classification of bank problems as ones of liquidity, however, is the typical way in

---

[41] Sjöberg adds that most legal systems require more rigorous legal proceedings for a final and invol-untary transfer of ownership over the shares than for a temporary suspension of voting rights; but this distinction would only be acceptable insofar as such suspension does not include a power of the author-ities to sell or cancel the shares. Otherwise, the legal protections should be no less demanding.

which forbearance is exercised: the authorities turn a blind eye to the underlying problems of the distressed banks (in particular, to the presence of actual and potential non-performing loans) and extend new financial resources to them in the form of loans (liquidity assistance), without seeking to take over their control. Thus, the underlying problems are not resolved (or even acknowledged) and the longer-term position remains problematical.

This raises the issue of the trigger for official intervention under the SRR. This can take a variety of forms, including that of balance-sheet insolvency or negative net worth, breach of specific capitalisation thresholds even though the bank's net worth is still positive, or inability to repay debts as they fall due, that is, cash-flow insolvency. A bank's 'temporary' liquidity problems may amount to insolvency in the latter sense, which has a long and dominant pedigree in general insolvency law. From an economic viewpoint, too, a 'solvent' bank's prolonged inability to ensure refinancing from the market on reasonable terms places in question its viability. Thus, the problem of definition of the SRR trigger is by no means a secondary one or subsidiary to that of avoidance of delay. An imprecise or non-objective trigger may well result in the worst of all possible worlds: under its authority, the authorities' propensity towards forbearance may be combined with arbitrary or discriminatory enforcement against particular viable banks. Consequently, the legal specification of the trigger is prior to the discussion of the immediate effect or the particular tools of the official intervention.

Assuming that, to avoid perverse incentives and increase the effectiveness of the intervention, the trigger kicks in before the threshold of negative net worth has been reached, the economic claims of existing shareholders will need to be given full recognition.[42] More generally, to avoid delay and uncertainty, the assumption of control by the authorities and any ensuing restructuring actions under the SRR should not be subject to contemporaneous legal challenges. Nonetheless, this emphasis on immediate and decisive action raises the prospect of irreversible effects being produced, occasionally on grounds which are later found to be mistaken. The need for guarantees or protections for property rights thus becomes a key consideration for the SRR's design.[43]

Sjöberg relies on requirements of ex post valuation and compensation as a sufficient substitute for the lack of contemporaneous legal remedies. Even though this does not guarantee the full restoration of the pre-existing situation in the event that a bank is proven to have positive net worth and/or to be viable, it is a reasonable compromise position.

---

[42] See E Hüpkes, 'Special Bank Resolution and Shareholders' Rights: Balancing Competing Interests' (2009) 17 *Journal of Financial Regulation and Compliance* 277–301.
[43] ibid; and V Babis, 'Bank Recovery and Resolution: What About Shareholder Rights?', University of Cambridge Faculty of Law Legal Studies Research Paper No 23/2012 (September 2012).

VIII. The Ex Ante Perspective – and Why it Fails

For Sjöberg, a well-designed SRR can serve as a 'governance tool', curtailing moral hazard and thus contributing to the prevention of future crises. An SRR's propensity to serve in this manner is evidently linked to its form, that is, to its incorporation in a set of standing, preannounced rules. If the rules prescribe in advance and in a credible way particular outcomes, these will be taken into account by private actors, change their incentive structure and influence their actual behaviour. In contrast, an improvised, ad hoc response to a banking crisis which has already occurred would lack the necessary generality, permanence and constancy of a rule-based system. For this reason, in principle it would be less likely to influence future behaviour.

For an SRR to operate effectively in this manner, it must satisfy two conditions, namely, that (a) the rules prescribe the eventual outcomes in a relatively determinate way, and (b) the rules are credible. In view of Sjöberg's substantive arguments, either the first or the second of these assumptions cannot hold in a system of the type that he defends.

Sjöberg points out that one of the major problems with banks which are deemed to be systemically important, is that their debt holders operate on the assumption that the state will not permit them to suffer losses in the event of a crisis. This dampens market discipline and results in debt financing which does not take into consideration the underlying risks faced by the bank and is, accordingly, too plentiful and too cheap.

Indeed, the support that the state can extend to failed banks is not confined to direct forms of subsidised financing (say, in the form by way of lending of last resort, asset guarantees or capital injections), whose aim is to keep the banks afloat and to pre-empt the commencement of administrative or insolvency proceedings. State support can be more discrete and involve the provision of explicit or implicit protection, not to the banks' themselves, but to their debt holders. In the case of retail depositors, such protection is offered openly and officially in advance, by means of industry-wide deposit insurance schemes. These are not merely tolerated, but actually celebrated and promoted on a mandatory basis as necessary tools for the avoidance of contagious depositor runs on banks. Insofar as other classes of claimants (interbank creditors, senior bondholders, and even junior or subordinated bondholders) are concerned, the state's protection is less certain and may offered with reluctance. Ex ante, its very existence may be left in doubt, so as to discourage reliance on an eventual intervention by the state (or the central bank); this is the policy of so called 'constructive ambiguity'.[44] Nonetheless,

---

[44] Sjöberg expressly, but oddly, rejects constructive ambiguity, on the basis that it impedes an accurate valuation by existing bank stakeholders and potential new investors of the risk of losing money in the context of a subsequent rescue operation by the state, thus discouraging their participation in the bank's refinancing efforts. However, this argument would only hold in the case of a bank which is already weak and seeks recapitalisation; before the bank reaches this point, the policy will not be counterproductive –

regardless of any official protestations in favour of market discipline, potential bank debt holders will contemplate the possibility that the state will intervene in their favour in the event of bank failure. Indeed, the probability of intervention will appear to them especially high, when the bank is question is large or appears to be of systemic importance ('too big to fail'). This will influence their decision on whether to extend credit of the particular order of priority to the bank and at what price.

In each and every case, the existence of an implicit state guarantee (actual, perceived or probabilistic) entails for the various claimants a reduction of their expected losses and a transferral of the bank's underlying risk of default from them to the taxpayers. What should be absolutely clear, is that the benefit does not accrue only to the debt holders, but also to the debtor banks (whose funding costs fall as a result) and indirectly to their shareholders and managers. The precise distribution of benefits is uncertain and may change over time, with banks and their shareholders benefiting in normal times, while debt holders gain primarily through the eventual satisfaction of their claims during the crisis.

It is exceptionally difficult to pinpoint the subsidy that banks derive from the implicit guarantees offered by the state in relation to the claims of their debt holders, to put a realistic price on the subsidy or to compare costs and benefits from the state intervention. Thus, widely divergent measurement approaches have been used to calculate the implicit funding subsidy to large banks (SIFIs), primarily by comparing the observed cost of funds for such institutions to counterfactual estimates of funding costs in the absence of the state intervention,[45] but also by making deductions from various financial market prices (such as banks' bond prices, equity prices, prices of options on equity).[46] For the UK, the implicit funding subsidy provided by the government to the financial sector during the global financial crisis by way of expected protection of the claims of failed bank debt holders (but not of their shareholders, who suffered a brutal dilution of their stakes) has been variably estimated to be worth anything between £6 billion and £130 billion![47] In any event, the overall effect of state guarantees is undoubtedly very substantial and

although it may well be ineffectual, if the bank's stakeholders discount the possibility of expropriation for the reasons discussed presently.

[45] D Baker and T McArthur, 'The Value of the "Too Big to Fail" Big Bank Subsidy', CEPR Issue Brief, September 2009; Z Li, S Qu and J Zhang, 'Quantifying the Value of Implicit Government Guarantees for Large Financial Institutions' (Moody's Analytics Quantitative Research Group, January 2011); K Ueda and B Weder di Mauro, 'Quantifying Structural Subsidy Values for Systemically Important Financial Institutions', IMF Working Paper No WP/12/128 (May 2012) available at www.imf.org/external/pubs/ft/wp/2012/wp12128.pdf.

[46] AJ Warburton, D Anginer and V Acharya, 'The End of Market Discipline? Investor Expectations of Implicit State Guarantees' (January 2013) available at www.ssrn.com/abstract=1961656; Oxera Consulting, 'Assessing State Support to the UK Banking Sector' (11 March 2011) available at www.oxera.com/Publications/Reports/2011/Assessing-state-support-to-the-UK-banking-sector.aspx; J Noss and R Sowerbutts, 'The Implicit Subsidy of Banks', Bank of England Financial Stability Paper No 15 (May 2012) available at www.bankofengland.co.uk/publications/Documents/fsr/fs_paper15.pdf.

[47] See Bank of England, *Financial Stability Report* No 28 (December 2010) 51; Oxera Consulting, 'Assessing State Support to the UK Banking Sector' (n 46); Noss and Sowerbutts, 'The Implicit Subsidy of Banks' (n 46).

operates in totally predictable ways: by subsidising risk taking and operating as a free form of insurance against losses (defaults, unavailability of funds, haircuts on claims, etc), the guarantees reduce the banks' cost of funds, change their financing structure (in favour of debt as against equity financing), lead to an increase in the overall size of their activities and, simultaneously, undermine market discipline. In short, as every form of unpaid-for insurance cover (or, to be more precise, insurance cover paid by a third party), they create moral hazard.

To counteract the moral hazard generated ex ante by the expectation of state-organised rescue operations, Sjöberg proposes that the SRR should promise to inflict ex post pain on debt holders, by depriving them of value through debt write downs. Sjöberg goes one step further than the more familiar – as well as trivial – proposed remedy for the problem of moral hazard, namely, the infliction of losses on shareholders, including through their outright expropriation. In Sjöberg's view, such losses on shareholders are an integral part of the SRR: the authorities cannot proceed to write down debt without first writing down equity, since this would be contrary to fundamental priority rights. In reality, however, his proposals are not totally respectful of priority rights, insofar as they allow for junior debt holders' forcible participation to the cost of bank recapitalisation through write downs and/or debt-to-equity conversions in conjunction with a partial (rather than complete, as the order of priorities would require) expropriation of the old shareholders.

This aspect of the SRR could be fixed, but there is a more general issue of internal contradictions. It is questionable, whether the law establishing the SRR can, or should, insist on strict enforcement of the solvency constraint. Sjöberg himself insists that the infliction of losses on debt holders (say, by activating debt-to-equity conversion, so called 'bail-in', mechanisms) can be a major source of contagion. He considers that this renders bank resolution very complicated. This, however, is not a matter of technical complexity, as much as one of conflicting (or time-inconsistent) objectives. Ex ante, to contain moral hazard, the law may mandate strict enforcement, including through full expropriation of shareholders and the allocation of their fair share of losses on debt holders, always following the established order of priorities, if a bank has negative net worth. Ex post, this policy may be found to be at loggerheads with the authorities' desire to ensure a soft landing. In other words, the probable negative second-round consequences of inflicting losses on debt holders create a cleavage between the two postulated objectives of resolution policy, since the first objective (preservation of systemic stability) now appears to be better served by rescuing the debt holders – a policy openly contrary to the second objective (market discipline).

Assuming (and this is a very bold assumption) that the conflict should be resolved ex ante in favour of market discipline, one still wonders whether a policy requiring the unforgiving treatment of bank stakeholders can be credibly entrenched through the enactment of an appropriately designed SRR.

Sjöberg rightly insists that a mostly discretionary regime of bank insolvency, insufficiently defined in the law and relying instead on ad hoc solutions, can hardly be justified on the basis that banking crises require 'flexible' and practical responses. Absent clear legislative signposts and mandatory intervention tools, government officials and regulators may be tempted to grant support to distressed banks on unduly favourable terms. At the same time, the lack of a procedure whereby bank managers and shareholders can be forcibly removed from their governance role, may encourage them to hold out for better terms in negotiations with the Government. From this perspective, the legal certainty achieved through the enactment of an SRR is commendable, not only because it provides reassurance against the risk of unfair treatment, but also because it changes the dynamics of such negotiations and prevents unwarranted wealth transfers to bank stakeholders acting de facto as veto players. In particular, the legislation can strengthen the hand of the resolution authority by vesting it with wide powers of intervention, thus discouraging hold outs by stakeholders. It is less evident that the SRR can bind the resolution authority itself to a policy of strict enforcement.

Even when the law arms them with wide powers, thus enabling them to eschew negotiation with banks' stakeholders, the officials in charge of bank resolution may display a penchant for delay and forbearance. Banking regulators are known frequently to err on the side of forbearance. Their subjective incentives may predispose them to underestimate the scale of banking problems – especially if these have simmered under their watch – and to prefer crisis-management tools that maintain in life failed banks and/or cause the least disruption to their operations over more aggressive and conflictual forms of resolution. From their viewpoint, the need to minimise the expenditure of public funds will not necessarily be the determining consideration. The law may prescribe that the resolution authority selects the resolution method by applying a 'least-cost' criterion; however, the cost-benefit analysis necessary for this purpose will almost always be ambiguous and amenable to manipulation. Systemic concerns and societal costs may be invoked, as well as the potential upside of forms of rescue where the state recapitalises directly the distressed bank. Even the crossing of the threshold that the law sets for the operation of the SRR (eg balance-sheet insolvency or critical undercapitalisation) may not be crystal clear, since in times of crisis the valuation of distressed assets will give rise to controversies, with many people claiming that current market values cannot determine a bank's viability, because they are driven by the prevailing liquidity problems and significantly overstate the true extent of losses.

Moreover, SRRs do not exhaust, either conceptually or in practice, the legal options relating to distressed bank resolution. Other forms of state intervention are always possible. Implicitly or even explicitly, the SRRs leave room for the provision to failed banks of public financial assistance in non-predetermined forms, for instance, in the form of exceptional financing packages, sanctioned, if necessary, by special legislation or budgetary appropriations. In fact, Sjöberg himself considers wider schemes of public financial assistance unavoidable in the case of fully-blown systemic crises. Thus, even if, within its four corners, the standing legal framework of the SRR excludes negotiation between bankers and the state, the possibility of negotiated solutions *outside* the SRR is left open. This weakens the law's apparent commitment to the expropriation of existing stakeholders in the event of failure.

In practice, market participants will have good reasons to suspect that bank bail-outs can still occur – indeed, that they are quite likely to take place, especially in relation to larger institutions or more profound disturbances. They will anticipate the ex post relaxation of the strict-compliance postulate of the SRR – and this is bound to dent its supposed ex ante effectiveness as a 'governance tool'. Moreover, one should remember that, through its deposit insurance component, the SRR involves protection from losses for at least one class of debt holders, namely, depositors. This further reduces the scope of market discipline. Taken in its entirety, the bank resolution system is inherently bound to operate as a source of moral hazard. The precise extent of this effect will depend on the coverage ratio of the formal deposit insurance system and the credibility of the SRR's threat to allocate losses to other stakeholders. The latter will depend in part on the automatic or discretionary character of the resolution options; but it will also be in an inverse relationship to the severity of future bank crises.

In short, the SRR cannot be a truly effective 'governance tool' or a sufficient method for imposing discipline in the banking market. At most, it can provide a procedural framework for orderly resolution coupled with a set of substantive pointers, whose effect is to confine and structure the exercise of discretion by the resolution authorities and to increase the risk of expropriation for stakeholders in the event of failure (but not to turn it into anything like a certainty). By losing their veto power over the outcome of negotiations aimed at avoiding liquidation, the latter may be in a weaker position than in the past. But they can still attempt to influence developments in the direction of a broad bail-out policy. Perversely, a strict SRR may give them incentives to *increase* the dimensions of a systemic crisis (so as to discourage the appearance of willing bank buyers and make more attractive politically the provision of blanket guarantees, which also cover junior debt holders and even shareholders).

Part IV

The Limits of Legal Regulation

14

The Limits of Legal Regulation: Will the Treaty on Stability, Coordination and Governance in the Economic and Monetary Union Have A Real Legal Effect?

RUDOLF STREINZ

After the text of the Treaty had been finalised on 30 January 2012, the 17 Member States of the Eurozone and eight further Member States of the European Union signed the Treaty on Stability, Coordination and Governance in the Economic and Monetary Union (the Treaty – all Article references in this chapter are to this Treaty, unless otherwise stated) on 2 March 2012.[1] Pursuant to the Treaty, the 25 contracting parties explicitly agree 'as Member States of the European Union' first, to strengthen the economic pillar of the Economic and Monetary Union (EMU) by adopting a set of rules intended to foster budgetary discipline through a Fiscal Compact. Secondly, the Member States agree to strengthen the co-ordination of economic policies and to improve the governance of the Euro area, thereby supporting the achievement of the European Union's objectives for sustainable growth, employment, competitiveness and social cohesion.[2] Only the United Kingdom and the Czech Republic refused to participate in the Treaty and remain 'bystanders'. While both countries have adopted their positions with different motives, one shared motive is the fear to losing too much of their national sovereignty. However, even 'bystanders' are involved in the general problems of the European crisis.[3]

Budgetary discipline is at the core of the Treaty. Therefore, a commonly used abbreviation of the Treaty is 'Fiscal Treaty' or, as Title III of the Treaty stipulates, 'Fiscal Compact'.[4] It provides rules on an at least balanced budget which shall take effect in the national law of the contracting parties through provisions that have binding force and that are of permanent character – preferably constitutionally

---

[1] The Treaty is available at www.european-council.europa.eu/media/639235/st00tscg26_en12.pdf.
[2] Article 1.
[3] See, for a UK perspective, J McEldowney, 'Debt Limits in German Constitutional Law – A UK Perspective', ch 5 in this volume.
[4] Articles 3–8.

entrenched. Germany set the pace on this issue by introducing the so called 'debt brake' ('Schuldenbremse')[5] in Article 109(3) of the German constitution (Grundgesetz – Basic Law) in 2009.

Budgetary discipline is an essential but not exclusive instrument necessary in solving the crisis of the European Union and especially that of the Eurozone – be this budgetary, financial, or economic in nature. Therefore, on 30 January 2012, the Members of the European Council adopted a Statement 'towards growth – friendly consolidation and job-friendly growth'.[6] And the so called Fiscal Compact of the 25 contracting parties deals not only with stability but also with economic policy co-ordination (Title IV, Articles 9 to 11) and with governance of the Euro area (Title V, Articles 12 to 16).

Reactions to the Fiscal Compact were different: German Chancellor Angela Merkel called it a 'masterpiece', a 'huge step towards the creation of a European Stability Union', even though conscious that the crisis was far from over. European Council President Herman van Rompuy said that its effects would be deep and long-lasting to prevent a repetition of the debt crisis. Italian Prime Minister Mario Monti, however, doubted the real legal effects of the Treaty. This leads me to my core question: what are the limits of legal regulation in economic and highly political matters?

This core question remains unanswered even though the Treaty has entered into force.[7] There were a number of initial obstacles: the Treaty needed the ratification of at least 12 members of the Euro area.[8] This diverges from the amendment procedure of the EU Treaties which requires the ratification by all Member States.[9] Therefore, even a 'no' in the Irish referendum on the Fiscal Compact would not have prevented the Treaty from entering into force. Nevertheless, if the Compact does not include all members of the Eurozone – at the very least, it will be detrimental to its effectiveness. This would intensify the problem of scope as the Treaty falls under the ambit of European Union law[10] but not within the Treaties on the European Union. Regardless, the Treaty must be applied and interpreted in conformity with the Treaties on which the European Union is founded (Article 2). The new socialist French President, François Hollande, urged for modifications of the Treaty during his election campaign. In general, the governments of the Member States will have the task of convincing their parliaments and their voters that the

---

[5] cf the critical commentary on this terminus by H Siekmann, Article 109 in M Sachs (ed) *Grundgesetz-Kommentar*, 6th edn (Munich, CH Beck, 2011) para 50.

[6] Available at www.consilium.europa.eu/uedocs/cms_data/docs/pressdata/en/ec/127599.pdf.

[7] The Fiscal Compact entered into force on 1 January 2013; see European Union, Press Release of 21 December 2012, available at www.consilium.europa.eu/uedocs/cms_data/docs/pressdata/en/ecofin/ 134543.pdf.

[8] Article 14(2).

[9] Article 48 of the Treaty on European Union (TEU).

[10] This is important concerning the ratification by Germany, because the Treaty had to be ratified in accordance with Article 23 of the Basic Law. Therefore two-thirds of the votes of the Members of the Bundestag and of the votes of the Bundesrat were required. The coalition of CDU/CSU and FDP needed the consent of the opposition (SPD, Bündnis 90/Grüne). The 'Linke' was definitely against the Treaty.

Treaty was the ideal instrument to solve the European crisis (as van Rompuy pointed out).

Limits to legal regulation in politically charged matters are reflected in the Treaty itself; the 'golden rule' that balances the national budgets[11] is subject to some exceptions[12] which, while they make sense from an economic perspective, may give rise to escape clauses. For example, historically the rules of the Maastricht Treaty of 1992 and the Stability and Growth Pact of 1997[13] were weakened when France and Germany failed to reach the deficit criteria[14] in 2005. The rules were reinforced by the amendments of November 2011[15] but the written rules are not decisive. They must be enforced in practice.

In comparison to the existing law, the new Treaty will have the special effect of imposing sanctions on contracting parties if they fail to meet the requirements. These sanctions shall apply in addition and without prejudice to the obligations derived from European Union law. The Treaty prescribes programmes which will be monitored by the Commission and by the Council when implemented. Numerous politicians, especially those in Germany, believed the Court of Justice of the European Union (CJEU) should play an important role in ensuring that countries meet their obligations. Therefore, they asked for a right to file an action before the CJEU (ie the Court of Justice and not the General Court because this involves an action against Member States). The Treaty provides such an action (Article 8). But this action is available only where a contracting party has failed to comply with Article 3(2) of the Treaty, that is, the obligation to introduce the rules which are laid down in Article 3 paragraph 1 into their legal order. If interpreted in a restrictive way, the European Court will deal only with procedural law ('formelles Recht'), not with substantive law. The restrictive interpretation opens the European Commission report, required by Article 8(1) of the Fiscal Compact 'on the provisions adopted' by the contracting parties 'in compliance with Article 3(2)'; the European Court would only review whether the rules were formally introduced into the national legal orders – not if they work in practice. Consequently, the sanctions, which according to Article 8(2) could be imposed if a state has not taken the necessary measures to comply with a judgment of the European Court, are meant to push for the introduction of the rules but do not affect their actual effectiveness.[16] The case law of both the German Federal Constitutional Court and the

---

[11] Article 3(1)(a).

[12] Article 3(1)(b) and (c).

[13] Regulation (EC) No 1466/97 of the Council of 7 July 1997 on the strengthening of the surveillance of budgetary positions and the surveillance and coordination of budgetary policies; Regulation (EC) No 1467/97 of 7 July 1997 on speeding up and clarifying the implementation of the excessive deficit procedure [1997] OJ L209/6.

[14] Regulation (EC) No 1055/2005 of the Council of 27 June 2005 [2005] OJ L174/1.

[15] Regulation (EU) No 1175/2011 of the European Parliament and of the Council of 16 November 2011; Regulation (EU) No 1177/2011 of the Council of 8 November 2011 [2011] OJ L306/33.

[16] See C Antpöhler, 'Emergenz der europäischen Wirtschaftsregierung – Das Six Pack als Zeichen supranationaler Leistungsfähigkeit' (2012) 72 *Heidelberg Journal of International Law/ Zeitschrift für ausländisches öffentliches Recht und Völkerrecht* 353, 384. Otherwise this would not be in conformity with Article 126(10) TFEU.

European Court of Justice on politically contentious economic matters indicates that judicial restraint will be followed. On 13 July 2004, the European Court of Justice held that there was an infringement of deficit procedure but stressed the discretion of the Council in the deficit procedure.[17] In its decisions concerning the financial aid for Greece and the European Financial Stability Facility (EFSF), the German Federal Constitutional Court emphasised Parliament's core competence to decide on the national budget[18] and considered the special committee of nine Members of Parliament unconstitutional (except for cases when state loans shall be bought). But the Court recognised the existence of political discretion and the responsibility of the Government including Parliament, to assess economic situations and to choose the solutions they deem necessary to solve the problems.

But there are doubts as to whether the competence of the European Court according to Article 3(2) will be interpreted so restrictively. On the other hand, a less restrictive interpretation begins by considering the type of sanctions which can be imposed by the European Court if the contracting party concerned has not complied with its judgment concerning the implementation of the duties of Article 3(2). The European Court may impose on the contracting party a lump sum or a penalty payment appropriate in the circumstances and which shall not exceed 0.1 per cent of its GDP.[19] The wording 'appropriate in the circumstances' indicates that the penalty is dependent on the degree of the offence – and this indicates the real meaning of compliance with the rules of the 'debt brake', as stipulated in Article 3(1). But even then, the general approach of the European Court on politically contentious economic matters has been one of judicial restraint. It remains to be seen whether the European Court will follow a restrictive or a less restrictive interpretation.

In order to reach an answer concerning the approach of the European Court, the matter must be first brought to the Court. According to the Fiscal Compact, differently than initially planned, the European Commission cannot file an action against Member States (Articles 258 and 260 of the Treaty on the Functioning of the European Union (TFEU)). These actions can only be filed by other Member States which are contracting parties,[20] either on the basis of a report of the European Commission or based on their own considerations. Perhaps there would be greater doubts if Article 273 TFEU[21] was selected as a correct basis to involve the Commission in actions against Member States. However, keeping in mind that until recently, there have been very few actions brought by Member

---

[17] Case C-27/04 *Commission v Council* [2004] ECR I-6649.

[18] It should be noted that this is not unique to Germany ('Sonderweg'): the prerogatives of national parliaments shall be fully respected according to Article 3(2) of the Treaty too.

[19] Fiscal Compact, Article 8(2).

[20] cf Articles 259 and 260 TFEU.

[21] 'The Court of Justice shall have jurisdiction in any dispute between Member States which relates to the subject matter of the Treaties if the dispute is submitted to it under a special agreement between the parties.' Concerning the scope of application of this provision see U Karpenstein Article 273 TFEU in E Grabitz, M Hilf and M Nettesheim (eds), *Das Recht der Europäischen Union* (Munich, CH Beck, Looseleaf, 2011) para 11.

States against each other,[22] it is improbable that this mechanism will become 'law in action' and will rather end up as a 'law in the books' and an element to show that political demands were heard. But also, in this case, it remains to be seen if the Member States will change their behaviour when acting as contracting parties of this special Treaty.

However, there is another instrument available to enforce the substance of the Treaty. While the Treaty does not alter in any way the economic policy conditions under which financial assistance has so far been granted to a contracting party as part of a stabilisation programme involving the European Union, its Member States and the International Monetary Fund (IMF),[23] in March 2013, changes were introduced. The granting of financial assistance in the framework of new programmes under the European Stability Mechanism (ESM), which was signed on 2 February 2012 by the Member States of the Eurozone, is since 1 March 2013 conditional on: first, the ratification of the Treaty by the ESM Member concerned and, secondly, as soon as the transposition period noted in Article 3(2) of the Treaty has expired, in compliance with the requirements of that Article.[24] It begs the question whether it will make a difference in control compared to the role of the European Court of Justice. The answer is yes – but only if the political institutions, which are competent to decide matters of granting assistance, interpret 'compliance' in a both formal and informal substantive sense; only then can the Treaty on stability be effective.

But will they do so? Why should the Treaty on Stability, Coordination and Governance in the Economic and Monetary Union, as an instrument of international law, work well when the existing rules of the Maastricht Treaty and of the Stability and Growth Pact have failed? Will new rules solve old problems? Without the necessary political will, the Treaty on Stability, Coordination and Governance in the Economic and Monetary Union will be nothing more than an unnecessary piece of symbolism.

Our roundtable discussion in Oxford will debate whether this political will can be enforced, or at least, enhanced by the Treaty. Are the provisions of the Treaty only 'soft law' like the Statement 'Towards Growth – Friendly Consolidation and Job-Friendly Growth'?[25] Are economic and social regulations of a limited binding force – highly political, and debated in terms of a theory of different degrees of 'hardness' of law? And finally, are there limits to legal regulation and efficiency of especially economic matters? But the crucial question is whether there is a real political will to introduce legal regulations unrestricted to the Treaty on Stability,

---

[22] There have been only three decisions of the European Court: Case 141/78 *France v United Kingdom (Cap Caval)* [1979] ECR 2923; Case C-388/98 *Belgium v Spain* [2000] ECR I-323; Case C-145/04 *Spain v UK* [2006] ECR I-7917. In the 20 or so other cases brought, a compromise was reached during the proceedings, see eg Case 58/77 *Ireland v France* (sheep's meat) [1977] OJ C142/8. See Karpenstein (n 21) Article 259 TFEU paras 6ff.

[23] The assistance granted to Greece, Ireland and Portugal.

[24] cf Recital 5 ESM Treaty.

[25] See above n 6.

Coordination and Governance in the Economic and Monetary Union and – if introduced at all – to enforce such regulations. Such a question is relevant to a multitude of subjects of the current crisis, notably, the regulation of the banking system.

15

The European Public Debt Crisis and the Institutional Framework of the Monetary Union: Experience and Adjustments

FRANZ-CHRISTOPH ZEITLER

In times of financial difficulty, public discourse has often favoured policy decisions that prioritise economic and political considerations, thereby treating the legal foundations of regulation as secondary. It might be useful to recall the literal meaning of the term 'economy'. The Greek noun 'Oikonomía' means 'rules for the house', which refers to rules designed to sustain the political and economic lifeblood of a democracy. So there has never been a demarcation between the sphere of economics on the one hand and law on the other. In order for monetary union to be successful, policymakers are required to reconcile the economic and legal aspects of regulation.

The current government debt crisis has revealed several weaknesses in the institutional setup of the European Monetary Union (EMU). It has also showed that there are drawbacks to the way some governments have dealt with the institutional requirements of the EMU. There are three 'pillars' or principles on which the foundations of monetary union rest. Indeed, the Maastricht concept of a 'monetary union without a political union' has been either damaged, weakened or strained. For example, this applies to the so called no bail-out principle of Article 125 of the Treaty on the Functioning of the European Union (TFEU) – the first 'pillar', whereby no Member State is liable for other members' debt. Since May 2012, this principle has been seen to be in tension with the 'rescue umbrellas'. Another principle under strain is embodied by Article 123 TFEU, which prohibits the monetary financing of public debt. The provision is in tension with the practice of the European Central Bank (ECB) which has up till now bought €212 billion of government bonds. While these transactions were on the secondary market, the obvious goal seems to be to influence the prices on the primary market, in the direct acquisition of government bonds. Finally, the principles of monetary union are also jeopardised in view of Article 126 TFEU and the Stability and Growth Pact according to which 'excessive public deficits' must be avoided. In the extreme case, this provision has been undermined by the Greek deficit figure of 2009. The former Government first communicated this figure as 3.6 per cent of GDP, however the figure was finally reported at 15.4 per cent of GDP.[1]

Each 'basic pillar' of the EMU cannot be understood in isolation of the remaining two pillars because they are critical to the architecture of the EMU. The overarching idea of this architecture is that each Member State still has the responsibility of running its own financial affairs; in legal terms, this is understood as 'fiscal self-responsibility' or in economic terms, 'no moral hazard'. The latter refers to the absence of any temptation to shift the financial burden onto the shoulders of one's neighbours. As long as 'fiscal self-responsibility' is followed, 'market discipline' can be expected to work well; thus, efforts to avoid moral hazard and the furthering of market discipline are two different sides of the same coin.

There are theoretically three ways to solve the European public debt crisis. The first involves abandoning the Maastricht architecture of fiscal self-responsibility and establishing a 'transfer union'. However, this option would lead to dramatic effects of moral hazard, also risking a weakening of the Euro itself. Market participants know that there are limits to the financial capacity of even the stronger Member States (among them Germany). A transfer union would weaken market confidence and lead to a circuitry of events; the Euro would be exchanged at a lower rate, inflation would rise, and consequently, there would be an increase in market interest rates. Ultimately, the outcome would lead to a lower market growth. All in all this option would place the EMU itself in a position of risk.

The second way to approach the European public debt crisis is to force non-complying members out of the currency union; or to put it another way, 'cutting off the weak branches of the tree'. Not only would adopting such an approach have serious legal implications, but the economic and financial costs to the European tax payer would be very high. Further, the political consequences would be equally serious and dramatic (*respice finem* – look at the end – warned the Romans in situations like this).

Finally, the third way to respond to the crisis is to retain and adjust the current framework. This option would aim to make the framework more credible and allow for a harmonisation of legal and economic policy considerations. For example, this would target an improvement in the incentive structure of the current setup. During the last 10 years, it has become obvious that rules intended to limit deficits and debts will only be followed if supplemented by political and economic incentives; mere dependence on self-discipline or weak procedural provisions is inadequate. Therefore, to assure the long-term stability of the EMU, there should be an effort to establish a working incentive structure.

Given the European public debt crisis, there are three areas in need of reform. I shall discuss the first two areas briefly because they are frequently mentioned in public discourse.

---

[1] I will not discuss the fourth pillar – the independence of the ECB/ Euro as captured by Article 130 TFEU – as this is beyond the scope of this chapter.

The first strategy would be to sharpen the 'first line of defence', that is the Stability and Growth Pact.

From the incentive angle, the most vulnerable point of the Stability Pact – to use this term as a headline for Article 126 TFEU and the three implementing regulations – was that 'potential sinners' had to decide on a 'current sinner', so it was very difficult to bring together a positive qualified majority in order to start an excessive deficit procedure (EDP). After a series of smaller steps ahead (the 'six pack' from September 2011) and a bigger step back (the Deauville agreement between France and Germany), the 'Fiscal Compact' (ie the Treaty on Stability, Coordination and Governance (TSCG)) gives us some hope:

- The 'reverse majority rule' will be applied not only when it comes to the different sanctions *within* an EDP (as had been agreed by the 'six pack'), but also when it comes to the launch of an EDP (Article 7 TSCG); and
- National debt limits ('debt brakes') up to 0.5 per cent of GDP will be established and introduced preferably into constitutional law (Article 3 TSCG) in order to underpin the effectiveness and seriousness of the European deficit and debt limits.[2]

Admittedly, there are drawbacks that still remain in the revised Stability Pact (from 2005). There are country-specific midterm objectives (MTOs) for the deficit, instead of a clear, transparent and unambiguous 'one size fits all' rule; there are broad exceptions to deficit limits set in place; and finally, there are inefficient procedural steps and 'procedural loops'[3] set by the revised Stability Pact.

The second strategy would be necessary if the ex ante defence line of the Stability Pact has not been successful or – which cannot be excluded – did not exceptionally cover the root causes of the financial crisis of a state (see, eg, the Irish case of a burst financial sector and real estate bubble). This would involve activating the European Stability Mechanism (ESM) as an 'ex post' or 'second line of defence' with an impressive firepower of €500 billion not included the additional IMF-line of $456 billion. An incentive-based system presupposes the 'strict conditionality' of any credit and guarantee support[4] in addition to full cooperation with an IMF/EU-led macroeconomic adjustment programme (MoU: memorandum of understanding). The objective of conditionality is two-fold: (1) re-establishing market confidence by reducing public deficits and (2) restoring the economic competitiveness of the country. In other words, both necessarily entail managing the internal depreciation (the adjustment of the level of wages and prices).[5] In this context it should be noted that pursuant to Article 20 of the Treaty Establishing the European Stability Mechanism (TESM), the granting of low interest rates (just covering financing and operative costs of the creditor

---

[2] I will not touch here on the questions of legal consistency of the TSCG with European primary law.

[3] Albeit somewhat tightened by the 'six pack' rules.

[4] See the newly agreed Article 136(3) TFEU.

[5] An external depreciation of the exchange rate by definition does not exist in a currency union.

without an appropriate margin) contradicts both IMF standards and practice. Further, it does not comply with the intended logic of an incentive-oriented procedure.

The third and pivotal element would be the creation of an appropriate state insolvency law in the EMU.

The no bail out-principle is weakened by the option of gaining support in financial stability (EFSF; ESM) pursuant to the revised Article 136 TFEU. However, in order to assure the long-term stability of the EMU, it is essential that the principle of fiscal self-responsibility remains in its core intact. Indeed, it will remain intact if the so called 'missing link' of the Maastricht architecture is added to the European treaties; a state insolvency law, or – in more politically correct terms – a state restructuring law, for the members of the EMU.

The best worded Stability Pact, the best designed assistance and adjustment-MoU will not work if the relevant Member State is (eg for lack of democratic support) either not willing or not able to implement the difficult conditions of an adjustment programme. Up to now, in the case of definitive and conclusive non-compliance of a Member State, the tool kit of other governments is very restricted. The only option remaining is the 'nuclear option', which refers to an insolvent Member State leaving the EMU. Such an option is a high risk *ultima ratio* with unforeseeable consequences for the market and serious political risks. In order to avoid this situation, a restructuring regime must be introduced in an effort to create a credible incentive for Member States to undergo the pain of (internal) depreciation. The key features of such a regime should include: the introduction of collective action clauses (CACs) in all sovereign bonds and loans (as in principle envisaged in recital 11 TESM) and cross-border banking restructuring rules. In addition, a working 'state restructuring law' requires a system of valuable and valid collateral (beyond the failed government bonds) – this might include (public) property, holdings of companies or future tax revenues ('tax farming'). All pledged values should be placed in a national trust or should be used as underlying assets of 'restructuring bonds' (a new form of covered bonds which can raise confidence on the market place). The recently discussed 'escrow-account' (a special account where tax revenues are legally separated from the normal budget and earmarked for creditors) set up for Greece is a step in the right direction because it is valid and unencumbered collateral. Such a system of valid collateral seems to be a prerequisite for an insolvent state to get further access to ECB monetary refinancing and the Euro area target-2-system.

The introduction of a 'restructuring law pillar' into the Maastricht architecture is likely to have a significant impact. It will strengthen market discipline and sharpen the awareness of risk before any potential crisis. This is in stark contrast to the circumstances arising from 1998 to 2007 as there was an ill considered interest rate convergence. Thus, there is hope in the introduction of a revised legal framework of the EMU financial markets; it may pre-empt a crisis and a 'state restructuring law' can work to assure 'existence and deterrence' rather than reaction.

INDEX